JOHN GROW

of

IPSWICH, MASSACHUSETTS
AND SOME OF HIS DESCENDANTS

JOHN GROW
of
IPSWICH, MASSACHUSETTS
AND SOME OF HIS DESCENDANTS

A Middle-Class Family
in Social and Economic Context
from the 17th Century to the Present

Michael Grow

Genealogy House
Amherst, Massachusetts

First published 2020 by Genealogy House,
a division of White River Press, Amherst, Massahusetts 01004
www.genealogyhouse.net

Book and cover design by Douglas Lufkin
Lufkin Graphic Designs, Norwich, Vermont, 05055
www.lufkingraphics.com

ISBN: 978-1-887043-56-4

Library of Congress Cataloging-in-Publication Data

Names: Grow, Michael Robert, 1944- author.
Title: John Grow of Ipswich, Massachusetts and some of his descendants : a
    middle-class family in social and economic context from the 17th century
    to the present / Michael Grow.
Description: Amherst, Massachusetts : Genealogy House, [2020] | Includes
    bibliographical references and index. | Summary: "John Grow of Ipswich,
    Massachusetts and Some of His Descendants: A Middle-Class Family in
    Social and Economic Context From the 17th Century to the Present places
    ten generations of a representative middle-class family - John and
    Hannah Grow of Ipswich, Mass., and one line of their descendants through
    nine generations - in the socioeconomic context of American history over
    a period of three and a half centuries. It provides a model for
    incorporating genealogical data into a more interpretive and
    contextualized form of narrative family history"-- Provided by
    publisher.
Identifiers: LCCN 2019041552 | ISBN 9781887043564 ; (hardcover)
Subjects: LCSH: Grow family. | Grow, Michael Robert, 1944---Family. | Grow,
    John, approximately 1642-1727--Family. | Middle class families--United
    States--Biography. | Middle class families--United States--Case studies.
    | New England--Biography. | Middle West--Biography.
Classification: LCC CT274.G79 G77 2020 | DDC 929.20973--dc23
LC record available at https://lccn.loc.gov/2019041552

CONTENTS

PREFACE AND METHODOLOGY

Where do I come from? Who were my ancestors? What are my family roots? For generations, these elemental questions have been drawing more and more of us into the field of genealogy in a search for answers.[1] We typically begin by gathering information from our parents and older relatives about earlier members of the family. We immerse ourselves in the standard source materials of genealogical research: vital records, probate records, censuses, newspaper obituaries, land records. If we persevere, we eventually construct a detailed family tree and perhaps post it on the internet to share with other genealogists. With the aid of findagrave.com or other online resources, we locate and visit some of our ancestors' graves. And in the end, after years of investigation and effort, after countless hours spent compiling genealogical data and tracing our family lineages, we find ourselves frustrated by how little we actually know about the people we're descended from, and craving a fuller, more detailed picture of their lives—how they lived, what they thought, where they ranked in the social and economic hierarchies of their communities, how their individual lives intersected with the larger currents of American history. After years of research, we're left with a nagging desire to fit our genealogical data into a broader framework, one that helps us to know our ancestors better by situating them more fully within the specific historical context of their particular time and place. We're left, in short, with an urge to move beyond basic genealogy to a deeper, more interpretive and contextualized level of family history.

But how do we do that? Where do we start? What resources do we utilize to flesh out our ancestors' lives? The challenges can initially seem daunting. Most of our families left us with little written evidence to draw on, few if any of the letters, journals, diaries, memoirs, account books, or other paper records that historians traditionally use to reconstruct the lives of their subjects. How do we take the cold and colorless genealogical information we've accumulated about our forebears—the dates and locations of their births and marriages and deaths, the lines of descent that connect them to one another and to us—and turn those dry, bare-bones facts into full-bodied, flesh-and-blood family histories? How do we identify from the millions of published books and articles on American history those titles that are most relevant to understanding the history of our individual families? Where do we begin?

John Grow of Ipswich, Massachusetts and Some of His Descendants provides a model, a template, for crafting a fully developed narrative family history from a core foundation of names-and-dates genealogical data. It follows ten generations of a representative middle-class family[2]—John and Hannah Grow of colonial Ipswich, Massachusetts, and one line of their descendants—through three and a half centuries of American history from the Puritans to the internet age. Like most families, these successive generations of Grows left a sparse paper trail of written records from which to recover the details of their lives. We have basic genealogical data on the family (obtained primarily from vital records and census information found on the New England Historic Genealogical Society's website AmericanAncestors.org) dating back to John and Hannah's marriage in 1669. There is also a century-old, semi-reliable Grow family genealogy that was published in 1913, one of the hundreds of volumes published by amateur genealogists during the late nineteenth and early twentieth centuries (many of which can be found on the HeritageQuest.org website, accessible through most public libraries). But to reconstruct with any degree of historical accuracy the lives of people who lived decades or centuries ago requires extensive research in a wide variety of additional sources, several categories of which proved indispensable in researching these ten generations of Grows:

Published works of modern historical scholarship. Virtually every aspect of American history has generated a voluminous literature of published scholarship by professional academic historians. *John Grow of Ipswich, Massachusetts and Some of His Descendants* draws heavily from the fields of social, economic, and family history in tracing the Grow family's history. The following general works were particularly instrumental in shaping its chronological and thematic contours, and together they provide a useful starting point for any interpretive project in American family history:

- Walter Nugent, *Structures of American Social History* (1981). A classic overview of American social and demographic history. Nugent's periodization of American history into three distinct phases—a "frontier-rural" period from initial colonization to the 1870s, a transitional period of rural-urban "conjuncture" from the 1870s to the 1920s, and a "metropolitan" period from the 1920s to the present—proved to be especially helpful in describing the historical evolution of the Grow family over time.

- Steven Mintz and Susan Kellogg, *Domestic Revolutions: A Social History of American Family Life* (1988). A comprehensive history of the American family from the 1620s to the 1980s, emphasizing the dramatic changes that have taken place in marital roles and in the economic and psychological functions of families.

- John Demos, *Past, Present, and Personal: The Family and the Life Course in American History* (1986). A series of insightful essays on the structures of family life and the evolving meaning of childhood, adolescence, middle age, and old age in American culture over the centuries.

- Robert L. Heilbroner, *The Economic Transformation of America: 1600 to the Present* (1999). An accessible general survey of the fundamental economic forces that have shaped Americans' lives, focusing on the development of capitalism and its impact on ordinary families.

- Robert J. Gordon, *The Rise and Fall of American Growth: The U.S. Standard of Living since the Civil War* (2016). An important detailed analysis of technological progress and its impact on the living conditions of American families during the last century and a half.

- John D'Emilio and Estelle B. Freedman, *Intimate Matters: A History of Sexuality in America* (1988). An overview of reproductive patterns and attitudes toward sex in American society from the colonial period to the late twentieth century.

In addition, the five-volume "Everyday Life in America" series published by Harper/Perennial provided a wealth of detailed information about the daily lives of ordinary Americans like the Grows—their patterns of work and leisure, their living conditions and consumption habits, their manners and customs— across the generations:

- David Freeman Hawke, *Everyday Life in Early America* (1988)
- Jack Larkin, *The Reshaping of Everyday Life, 1790–1840* (1988)
- Daniel E. Sutherland, *The Expansion of Everyday Life, 1860–1876* (1989)
- Thomas J. Schlereth, *Victorian America: Transformations in Everyday Life, 1876–1915* (1991)
- Harvey Green, *The Uncertainty of Everyday Life, 1915–1945* (1992).

Together, these eleven titles constitute a basic introductory reading list for family history research projects. Their bibliographies, in turn, list additional sources of information on specific topics, leading researchers into a deeper exploration of the scholarly literature and the discovery of more details about the historical context of their ancestors' lives. As additional information was learned about the history of the Grow family generation by generation, a keyword search of WorldCat.org identified the titles of specialized works on topics of particular significance in the lives of individual family members: witchcraft, the "Great Awakening," the Connecticut militia in the American Revolution, the Erie Canal, the temperance movement, freemasonry, and more. The extensive secondary literature cited in the "Endnotes" section of this volume is merely suggestive of the wealth of modern published scholarship that such a search can identify.

Older, out-of-print published sources. In addition, a variety of obscure, long-out-of-print books published in the nineteenth or early twentieth centuries proved to be invaluable in placing the lives of several generations of the Grow family in historical context. A forty-volume collection of travel accounts and reminiscences by nineteenth-century Michigan pioneers provided firsthand descriptions of frontier life during the 1830s and 1840s when the Grows were establishing farms in that state. An 1891 "portrait and biographical album" containing biographical sketches of prominent residents of Oakland County, Michigan—one of many such local collections published in the United States in the latter decades of the nineteenth century—revealed previously unknown information about the backgrounds and living conditions of a subsequent generation of the family. Old local histories of the cities and counties where several generations of Grows resided in the nineteenth and twentieth centuries described the physical, economic, and demographic features of those communities during the time periods when family members were living there. Full-text versions of these long-out-of-print books—and millions of others—are accessible online, without charge, on the HathiTrust Digital Library website (hathitrust.org), where a keyword search by the name of an ancestor's city or county of residence quickly connects the researcher to obscure but potentially valuable sources of information.

Doctoral dissertations. The Grow family history project also benefited significantly from a category of historical scholarship seldom utilized in genealogical and family history research: unpublished doctoral dissertations. Since the late 1960s, PhD candidates at US universities have written a surprisingly large number of dissertations focused on the histories of individual American towns, ranging from the early settlements of colonial New England and other regions to nineteenth-century midwestern farming communities. Invariably based on exhaustive research in primary historical documents, these in-depth "community studies" usually include large quantities of detailed statistical and descriptive data about the local inhabitants—their economic activities, landholding patterns, social structures, religious and ethnic compositions, etc. In interpreting the lives of the first two generations of the Grow family in America, *John Grow of Ipswich, Massachusetts and Some of His Descendants* drew heavily from unpublished dissertations about the early Massachusetts Bay Colony towns of Ipswich and Andover. A keyword search of the "ProQuest Dissertations & Theses" database (proquest.com)—the most comprehensive online catalog of US doctoral dissertations—may prove equally worthwhile for other family history projects. (Full-text electronic copies of most dissertations can be obtained directly from ProQuest or through a nearby university research library.)

Tax lists. Local tax lists are another underutilized but valuable resource for family history research. From an early date, American towns large and small annually assessed the value of their residents' property holdings for tax purposes. Each year, a detailed tax list—commonly known in the eighteenth and nineteenth centuries as an "assessment list," "assessment roll," "rate list," or "rate book," depending on the time and place—was compiled by town authorities listing the name of every local property owner and the amount of taxes that he or she owed. During the nineteenth century, these lists often included detailed information about the property on which each taxpayer's tax assessment was based, including the amount of land owned, its appraised value, the appraised value of the taxpayer's house and other material possessions, and more. While family history researchers regularly use local land records to identify the location and size of an ancestor's landholdings, tax lists go further. They enable the researcher to *compare* the size and value of an ancestor's property holdings with those of the town's other residents. By carefully rank-ordering the taxable wealth of every local property owner identified on the eighteenth- and nineteenth-century tax lists of specific Massachusetts, Connecticut, and Michigan towns for the years in which a generation of the Grow family lived in them, *John Grow of Ipswich, Massachusetts and Some of His Descendants* was able to measure each generation's economic status *relative* to that of other property owners in the community. And because wealth and property largely determined social status in pre-twentieth-century America, the lists were also helpful in identifying the Grows' position in local society generation by generation.

The vast majority of pre-twentieth-century Americans farmed for a livelihood, and many nineteenth-century tax lists delineated the specific amounts of "plow-land," pasture, meadow, and woodland that each local taxpayer owned, along with numbers and varieties of livestock owned. Such data proved extremely useful in identifying the types of agriculture that Grow farm families practiced—by indicating whether they were primarily crop farmers or livestock and dairy farmers, and whether their agricultural operations were commercial or semi-subsistence in nature.

Unfortunately, eighteenth- and nineteenth-century tax lists are not always easy to locate. Some are still stored in their local town hall, while others have been transferred to the local or county historical society. And some may have found their way into the collections of the state library, state archive, or state historical society. No matter how scattered they may prove to be, however, a search for them is well worthwhile—and perhaps essential for determining where an ancestor's family ranked within the social and economic hierarchies of its local community. (Note: after 1900, as US society became increasingly urban and the populations of US cities swelled in size, local tax lists grew so large and unwieldy that they became impracticable for research on twentieth-century generations of families.)

City directories. Published annually in most American cities from the mid-1800s through the middle of the twentieth century, city directories list the names, residential street addresses, occupations, and employers of local heads of households. That information made it possible to track the employment histories and geographic relocations of three generations of city-dwelling Grows from the 1870s through the 1940s, including a generation that was forced by economic circumstances to move from one house and job to another almost every year during the Great Depression. Data from city directories in turn opened up other fruitful avenues of research. A search on google.com of the names of companies for which the family's male breadwinners worked produced links to detailed sources of information on the histories, organizational structures, and business operations of those companies. A maps.google.com search of various Grow street addresses pinpointed the locations of the family's residences, while that website's "street view" feature provided ground-level photographic views of each house and the surrounding neighborhood. Follow-up research in old local histories then helped to ascertain the general socioeconomic level of residents in that section of the city.

In most US cities, the main public library possesses a collection of local city directories, while the HeritageQuest website provides full-text access to a large online database of directories from cities nationwide.

Human resources. Last but not least, direct personal communication with a wide range of experts across the United States contributed significantly to the Grow family history project. By contacting relevant specialists and asking them specific research questions—by reaching out to knowledgeable individuals and "tapping their brains"—the project obtained valuable inputs of historical information and interpretive perspective. Emailed inquiries and requests for assistance invariably received helpful, informative replies. A Johns Hopkins University history professor drew from her extensive knowledge of colonial inheritance patterns to answer an email question about an unusual land transfer by a Grow father to one of his sons in 1740s Connecticut. A textile curator at Historic New England enthusiastically analyzed the cloth purchases of an eighteenth-century Grow housewife (as recorded in a local general store account book) and offered valuable interpretive insights into what the purchased fabrics revealed about the family's standard of living and socioeconomic status. The town historian of Homer, New York, forwarded old local history newspaper articles containing previously unknown details about the economic and religious activities of a generation of Grows living on the New York frontier in the 1820s. The author of a book on Gilded Age interior decorating analyzed an 1890s photograph of a Grow family living room to explain in detail how the furniture and other household objects pictured in the photograph reflected the family's social standing. A reference librarian at the Bay County Historical Society in Michigan found new information about late nineteenth-century family members in her library's obituary and newspaper-clipping files. A deputy clerk in the Carson City, Nevada, Office of Records solved a decades-old mystery surrounding the divorce and remarriage of a twentieth-century male family member. In-person inquiries during on-site research visits yielded equally productive results. When a Pomfret, Connecticut, town clerk was asked in passing whether any of the town's early tax lists had survived, she disappeared into the town hall's records vault and emerged with a large cardboard box filled with original copies of eighteenth-century local tax lists. During an initial exploratory visit to the North Andover Historical Society in Massachusetts, a resourceful staff archivist unearthed hand-drawn maps by an early local historian showing the location and physical layout of a Grow family farm in the 1720s. Additional examples could be cited, but the lesson for family history research is clear: to paraphrase an old biblical adage, "Ask questions, and ye shall receive useful information."

In a fundamental sense, every family history research project is doomed to inevitable frustration. No matter how diligently we pursue our research, we will simply never know all that we would like to know about the men and women we're descended from. Their personal attributes and individual human qualities—their personalities and temperaments, their psychological strengths and flaws, their inner feelings and hidden desires, the intimate details of their private lives and family relationships—have been irretrievably lost to history. The most that we can realistically hope to achieve is a partial, imperfect profile of who they were and how they lived their lives. Nevertheless, as the following history of the Grow family suggests, a well-structured and carefully planned research agenda can produce a fuller, richer, more detailed understanding of them, and ultimately leave us with a better sense of where we come from.

JOHN GROW (c. 1642–1727)

His earliest known appearance in the historical record occurs in 1669. On October 2 of that year, John[1] Grow, a 27-year-old seaman from the town of Ipswich in Massachusetts Bay Colony, testified before the Essex County Quarterly Court in Salem on behalf of his employer, Ipswich shipmaster Robert Pearce. Captain Pearce had recently acquired "an old hulk of a sloop" from a former Ipswich mariner, Hackaliah Bridges, but after finding some of the vessel's fittings in unusable condition and others missing, Pearce apparently refused to give Bridges the amount of payment initially agreed upon—at which point Bridges took Pearce to court. Testifying in Pearce's defense, Grow told the court that he and his fellow crewman John Berry had unrigged "the greatest part" of the sloop, that its "mayne saill" was "so rotten that he could hardly tell how to venture with it to sea," and that none of the ship's "cable" had been transferred to "my Master Pearce's custody." He also testified that Bridges' boatswain had told him "that the rigging and sail in question were worth about forty or fifty shillings and whoever gave more would buy it too dear." In a subsequent court appearance the following month, Grow and Berry stated that Bridges had agreed to let Pearce's cousin Stephen Pearce determine what the sloop's riggings and sail were "Realye worth." That appraisal, however, produced a valuation of 50 shillings—a figure significantly lower than Bridges presumably expected. In the end, Grow's testimonies were to no avail, because the court ruled against Pearce and attached his "house and lands to the value of forty pounds" to satisfy Bridges' claim.[1]

John Grow is traditionally regarded as the progenitor of the Grow family in America.[2] And yet we know frustratingly little about him, having only a few sparse fragments of ancient information with which to reconstruct the contours of his life. He was probably born about 1642. The records from the 1669 "Hackaliah Bridges v. Robert Peerce [*sic*]" court case—undoubtedly reflecting information personally provided by Grow himself—identify him as "Aged twentye seven yeares or thare abouts,"[3] and records from a 1671 court case in which he also gave testimony describe him—again almost certainly based on his own statement to the court—as "aged about twenty-nine years."[4] (A statement in the Ipswich town records that he was "aged upwards of 90 years" when he died in 1727,[5] suggesting a birth date of 1636 or earlier, lacks any supporting evidence and appears merely to reflect the customary Puritan penchant for inflating the ages of elderly citizens as a mark of respect, and/or erroneous information supplied by a grief-stricken and unknowledgeable family member.)

His birthplace and parentage, however, remain unknown. Statistical probability would suggest that he might have been born in America. It is estimated that a vast majority of the English emigrants who came to New England in the seventeenth century arrived during the initial "Great Migration" of 1630–1642, and that over 90 percent of English surnames in the present-day United States can be traced to that first generation of colonists. According to historian David Hackett Fischer, the pre-1642 immigrants were "the breeding stock" for New England's "Yankee population," the ancestors from whom "most families of Yankee descent trace their American beginnings." With the outbreak of the English Civil War in 1642, migration flows then "virtually ceased" until the late 1650s and remained at "scarcely above a trickle" for the rest of the seventeenth century.[6] The fact that John Grow's birth date precisely coincides with the end of large-scale immigration to New England would seem to strengthen the possibility that he was born there, to parents who arrived during the Great Migration.

The search for his origins is complicated by uncertainty surrounding his surname. The name "Grow" was subject to a variety of alternate spellings in seventeenth-century records, with "Growe" and "Grove" being the most frequently encountered variants. The "Hackaliah Bridges v. Robert Peerce" court documents, for example, refer to John Grow as both "John Growe" and "John Grove." No Grows or Growes appear in the English emigration lists of the 1630–1642 period, however, and John Grow of Ipswich is the earliest colonist with either of those surnames mentioned in the seventeenth-century records. On the other hand, several Groves appear in the emigration lists and the early Massachusetts Bay records, leading two pioneering genealogists to conclude that in America the name "Grow" was probably a mutation, both phonetically and in written form, from the original name "Grove."[7] Nevertheless, the only Grove known to have been in Massachusetts Bay early enough to have been John Grow's father—Edward Grove, a soldier serving at Boston's fort in 1636 and later a "sail-maker" in Salem—made no mention of a son, John (or any offspring other than a daughter, Mary), in his will.[8]

An alternative hypothesis concerning John Grow's origins is that he was born in England and came to Massachusetts in his youth. The surnames "Grow," "Growe," "Groue," and "Grove" appear frequently in sixteenth- and seventeenth-century English parish records, particularly those of Norfolk, Somerset, and London, while no fewer than four John Groues and three John Groves were born or christened in England between 1641 and 1643.[9] If one of them was the John Grow mentioned in the Massachusetts court records of 1669, any number of paths could have brought him to America.

By the 1650s and 1660s, a trickle of renewed English emigration to New England was underway. In addition, crewmen on English ships visiting the colonies occasionally remained in New England rather than returning home. The owners of English fishing boats that worked the banks off Newfoundland and Maine were notorious for leaving a portion of their crews behind at the end of the fishing season in order to reduce expenses on the return voyage back to England, and many of the laid-off fishermen found new employment in the maritime economy of Massachusetts Bay. Meanwhile, Boston, Salem, Gloucester, and the colony's other port towns were absorbing a steady stream of sailors from English merchant ships, most of them unmarried young men in their teens and twenties who were eager to take advantage of Massachusetts Bay's chronic labor shortage and abundant land resources.[10] It was also the case that many of the immigrants who came to New England after the Great Migration had personal ties to English colonists already established there, ties based on kinship networks, interfamily connections, and a broad range of economic and social relationships, raising the possibility that John Grow crossed the Atlantic as a consequence of some form of personal association with the Pearce family, several of whom were mariners in New England.[11] One or another of these channels of trans-Atlantic population transfer in the mid-seventeenth century may account for John Grow's presence in America. Nevertheless, pending the discovery of new information, all that can be said with any degree of certainty at present is that he was working in Ipswich, Massachusetts, in 1669.

Ipswich was a prosperous coastal community 30 miles north of Boston. First settled in 1633, it soon developed a thriving economy based on commercial agriculture, sending large quantities of surplus cattle, beef, corn, and other food products to outside markets in Boston and beyond. From an early date, Ipswich's leaders also tried to develop the town into a maritime trading center and fishing port. Geography seemed to support their ambitions. Situated midway between Boston and the Gulf of Maine, Ipswich was well-positioned to profit from fishing and coastal shipping, while the town's location on the Ipswich River, 3 miles inland from the Atlantic coast, left its riverfront harbor and wharves relatively protected from ocean storms. Steps to exploit these advantages commenced in 1641, when a newly appointed "committee for furthering Trade" was assigned the task of installing buoys and beacons on the river as aids to navigation; that same year the town granted fishing crews the use of land at the river's mouth for processing their catches, cutting firewood, and planting crops. By the late 1640s, an Ipswich fishing industry was operating, with locally based boats and crews ranging out into the Atlantic

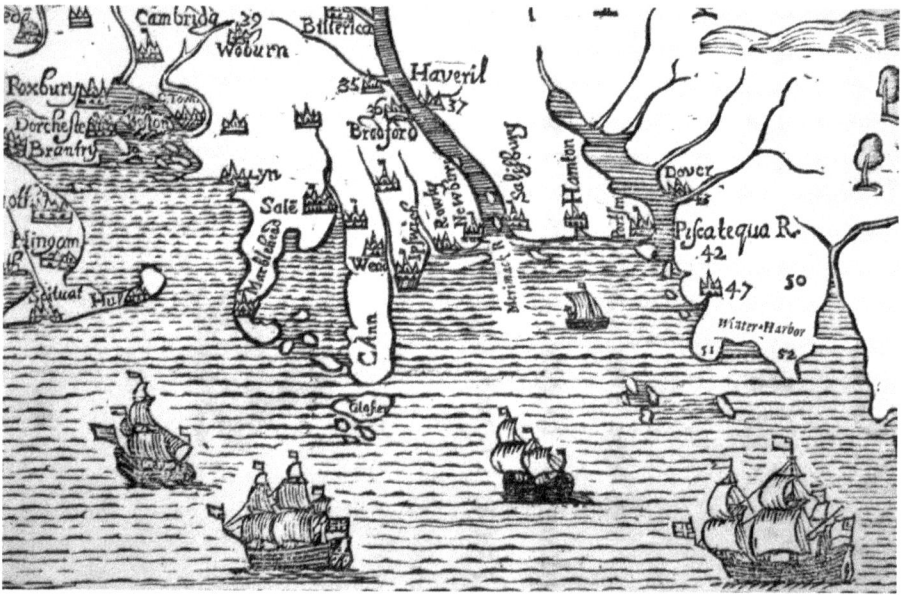

The maritime world of John Grow, from a 1677 "Map of New England" published in Ipswich minister William Hubbard's *Narrative of the Troubles with the Indians in New-England* (Boston, 1677). Ipswich is located to the immediate right (*i.e.*, north) of "C[ape] Ann." The Isles of Shoals are the cluster of small islands several miles out into the Atlantic from the mouth of the "Piscatequa [*sic*] R[iver]." The small ship depicted near the mouth of the Piscataqua may be a coastal trading ketch.

as far as Monhegan Island in Maine and bringing back catches of cod and mackerel to salt and dry.[12] In 1647, the town's leading merchants launched a private business venture, the "Ipswich Company," with grandiose plans to develop a far-reaching maritime trading network that would export the fish and forest products of northern New England in exchange for Virginia tobacco, West Indian sugar, and commodities from Europe. The Ipswich Company quickly attracted an influx of mariners, seamen, and fishermen to the town; and although many of them subsequently moved on when the company dissolved in 1652, several, including shipmaster Robert Pearce, remained in Ipswich, filling niches in the local maritime economy.[13]

By the 1660s, Ipswich was growing rapidly in both population and wealth, ranking second only to Boston in the amount of taxes paid to the colonial government. At the center of its economic prosperity was a small group of merchants—Jonathan Wade, Robert Paine, and Francis Wainwright the most notable among them—who purchased agricultural surpluses, fish, and wood products from suppliers in Ipswich and the surrounding region, sold them in Boston and Salem, and used the proceeds to acquire imported English goods that they then sold or bartered in the retail markets of Ipswich and neighboring communities farther inland. Because of the rudimentary condition

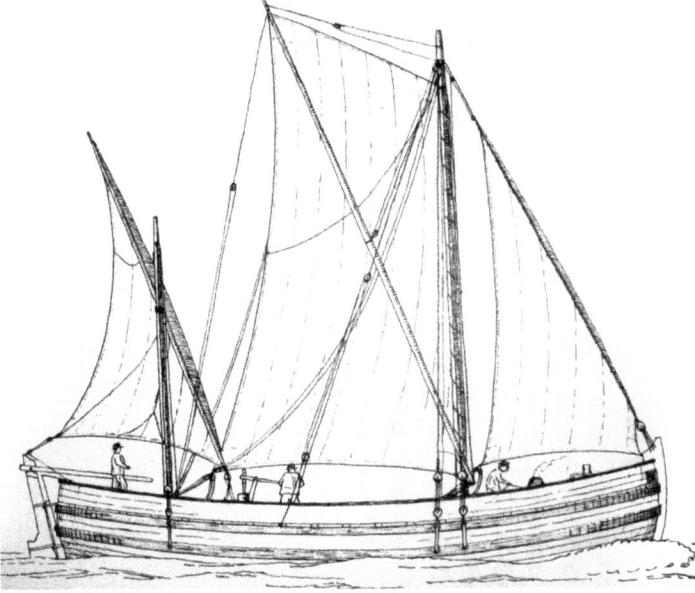

A colonial ketch (as illustrated in William A. Baker, *Colonial Vessels: Some Seventeenth-Century Sailing Craft* [Barre, MA: Barre Publishing Company, 1962], figure 33). Ketches like Robert Pearce's "The Willing Mind" were the most common coastal trading vessels in seventeenth-century Massachusetts Bay. Small (35 to 65 tons) but very seaworthy, with belowdecks' holds to carry cargo, they were usually manned by crews of three or four seamen. A ketch constructed for Ipswich mariner Robert Dutch in 1677 was made of "white oake planke" and measured "in length by ye keele thirty fower foot[,] in breadth twelve foot by ye beame[,] & six foot deep in ye hold." (Ibid., 129, 146; Vickers, *Farmers and Fishermen*, 145–146)

of Massachusetts Bay's early roads, the town's merchants relied primarily on commercial shipping to transport their trade goods, hiring locally based vessels and crews to move their merchandise up and down the coast.[14] By the time John Grow appeared on the scene, a few Ipswich shipmasters—his employer Pearce, Robert Dutch, Nathaniel Piper, Robert Cross and his sons—were handling the bulk of the merchants' carrying trade.

Docking their small, two-masted "ketches" at wharves on the town's river harbor, they loaded meat, grain, fish, pipe-staves, and other local products from the merchants' warehouses into their ships' holds, navigated the curves and shoals of the Ipswich River out into the Atlantic Ocean, and sailed southward to Salem and Boston to deliver their cargoes, returning to Ipswich with loads of English imports—metal goods, finished textiles, glassware and ceramics, liquors, and books—that the town's merchants retailed in local markets.

Pearce's ketch "The Willing Mind" and Ipswich's other commercial vessels also frequently traveled north to the Isles of Shoals, the center of the Gulf of Maine's bustling fishery, to pick up cargoes of dried cod and fish-liver oil and freight them south to Boston for one or another of the Ipswich merchants.

There were occasionally longer voyages as well. In the mid-1670s, a party of four colonists chartered Pearce's vessel "to transport their goods to the Conetico [Connecticut] river," while other Ipswich merchant ships are known to have sailed as far as Barbados on trading voyages.[15]

The details of John Grow's early life as an Ipswich seaman are lost to history, but the geographic boundaries of his maritime world were apparently far from narrow.

From its inception, Ipswich was a predominantly middle-class community. Like Massachusetts Bay's other early settlements, the town had been founded by people from the middle ranks of English society: lesser gentry, merchants, yeoman farmers, and artisans. The society they established in Ipswich was different in several respects from the one they had left behind in England. It included no wealthy aristocrats and few destitute laborers, for example, and developed into what was essentially a middle-class society almost by default. It was also a frontier society, and like other frontier societies it provided opportunities for upward mobility that were unavailable back in England—opportunities, that is, for individuals with useful skills to advance and elevate themselves in society above the level of their birth. At the same time, however, the town's early settlers were also the products of England's rigidly class-stratified society, and they brought to their new community deeply ingrained traditions of social hierarchy. As a result, sharp differences in social status soon began to divide the town's residents, and their nascent middle-class society quickly stratified into a hierarchy of unequal subgroups.[16]

In 1669—the first year that John Grow can be documented as a resident of the town—Ipswich had a total population of perhaps 1,700,[17] with a social structure divided into three general levels. The top tier of local society was a small elite that comprised no more than 6 or 7 percent of the population. Occasionally referred to at the time as "principal inhabitants" or "the better sort," this group included the town's largest landowners, a few well-to-do merchants, and the resident Puritan minister, along with their wives and children. Immediately below them on the social scale were the "middling people," sometimes described in contemporary documents as people of "ordinary rank." This group comprised the vast majority of the population—some 60 to 65 percent. It included the town's farmers ("yeomen" or "husbandmen") and the wide array of artisans essential to a seventeenth-century residential community with a predominantly agricultural economy: millers, blacksmiths, carpenters, masons, butchers, tanners, coopers, wheelwrights, weavers, rope makers, "cordwainers," "soap boilers," "biskett bakers," "maltsters," etc. The bottom tier of local society consisted of "the poorer sort," or as members of the elite sometimes labeled them, "the inferior sort." Comprising roughly 30 percent of Ipswich's population, this group included the town's hired workers and apprentices, tenant farmers and their families, and indentured servants (both male and female), along with a handful of African and Indian slaves owned by elite families.[18]

The town's social hierarchy reflected underlying inequalities of economic wealth and political power. In the 1660s, according to historian David Grayson Allen, the eight richest men in Ipswich "controlled almost half of the total wealth in the community," while the top 25 percent of local society (the elite and the upper echelon of the "middling people") owned nearly 70 percent; by contrast, "the bottom 50 percent" of the town's residents ("the poorer sort," together with the less affluent echelons of the "middling people") "shared only 12 percent of the total wealth." Allen also calculates that prior to 1670 the bottom 50 percent of the town's adult males owned less than 6 percent of its land.[19] Wealth and power went hand in hand. From an early date, government offices and leadership positions in Ipswich were dominated by a small, self-perpetuating oligarchy consisting of members of the elite and their political allies among the upper "middling" elements in society, while as late as the 1670s fewer than 30 percent of the town's adult males were allowed to vote on civic issues.[20]

A variety of status distinctions identified each resident's place in society. For example, members of the three social ranks were addressed by different titles. Men and women in the elite stratum were referred to as "Mister" and "Mistress," respectively; "middling" men and their wives were called "Goodman" and "Goodwife" (or "Goody" for short); while "the poorer sort" lacked titles altogether and were simply addressed by their common names.[21] There were also laws governing the clothing considered appropriate to people of different social strata. On at least four separate occasions between 1653 and 1676, groups of Ipswich townspeople from the middling and lower ranks were brought before the Essex County Quarterly Court on charges of "excess in apparel"—accused, in effect, of overstepping the social boundaries by dressing above their station. The most common offense was wearing silk scarves or silk hoods, a privilege reserved exclusively for members of elite society. (To avoid conviction and a fine, defendants had to prove that their family's net worth was at least £200.)[22] And in the Ipswich meetinghouse, where the community gathered every Sunday for church services, seating arrangements were determined by social rank. Members of the elite sat in "the most dignified portions" of the meetinghouse near the minister and the communion table; "those of middle rank" sat behind them; and "poorer families" were relegated to the rear galleries, farthest from God. These arrangements evidently caused resentment among the lower ranks and occasionally provoked disturbances during services, as when Rachel Clinton, an impoverished Ipswich divorcée, deliberately "hunched" (thrust) her elbow into several "women of worth and quality" as they passed by her on the way to their more socially prestigious seats.

Matters hardly improved when, in the 1670s, wealthy merchant Francis Wainwright and other prominent members of the elite received permission to construct private, six-foot-square pews for themselves and their families, essentially partitioning portions of the church's floor space to their own control for purposes of personal comfort and conspicuous social display. Church deacons soon were complaining that more and more people were "not sitting where placed." As seating disputes escalated, a committee of town selectmen was appointed to oversee the seating of the congregation, and that committee eventually was forced to impose five-shilling fines on anyone who sat in "a higher seat" than the one to which he or she was assigned. Historian Alison Vannah interprets the growing tensions over meetinghouse seating in the 1660s and 1670s as an indication that social stratification was intensifying in the town during those decades.[23]

As a young man establishing himself in Ipswich during that same period, John Grow almost certainly occupied a low social position. Vannah found that most of the people who settled in the town after the Great Migration were "in the lower middle or lower ranks" of society, and she lists John Grow among the lower-ranking residents of the 1660s.[24] His income level as a member of Captain Pearce's crew strongly suggests that he was one of "the poorer sort." In 1669, he was earning 2 shillings a day, the average wage for day laborers in New England at the time.[25] His employment in the seafaring trades is another indicator of low social status. Sailors and fishermen were not held in high regard in seventeenth-century New England. Often coarse, hard drinking, rowdy, and violent, with a notorious reputation for what Puritan theologian Cotton Mather characterized as "Filthy Speaking, Bawdy Speaking, Uncleane and Obscene Ribaldry," they were generally looked upon as a disorderly element in society.[26] Ipswich's maritime subculture was certainly no exception. John Grow's coworkers and peers had numerous run-ins with the law. Several of his fellow seamen (Stephen Cross, Obadiah Bridges, Samuel Dutch) were in court at one time or another for physically assaulting other townsmen— Cross for punching a man in the mouth during Sunday church services in the meetinghouse. Another of Grow's colleagues (fisherman John Knowlton) apparently drank so excessively that town authorities banned him from the local taverns "upon penalty of Law." Ipswich officials also monitored the house of Grow's shipmate John Berry as a place of drunkenness and "rudeness."[27]

The town's seafaring families also had a reputation for loose morals and promiscuity. Berry and his wife were fined £3 for "fornication before marriage," and Sarah Roe, the wife of an Ipswich fisherman, was sentenced to a month in the house of correction for committing adultery while her husband was away at sea. (After her release, Roe was forced to stand outside the meetinghouse during religious services wearing a sign reading "FOR MY BAUDISH CARRIAGE.")[28] Local gossips insinuated that libertine behavior was commonplace among females in Ipswich's maritime families, and even the wives of "middling"-rank shipmasters Nathaniel Piper and Robert Dutch were targets of malicious innuendo. According to a libelous piece of doggerel that circulated fairly widely throughout the town in 1671:

Sea mens wives have gallant lives
  when their husbands are gone to sea[.]
Mrs. Piper and Mrs. Dutch ... take a touch
  when their husbands are out of the way. ...[29]

By that point in time, some residents were openly expressing doubts about the wisdom of adding any more "ugly fishermen" to the town's population.[30] No hint of impropriety or scandal is associated with John Grow's name in the surviving documentary record, but as a seaman he was almost by definition a member of one of the less-respectable sectors of Ipswich society.

A final indicator of John Grow's low-ranking status is the likelihood that he was illiterate. During his life in Ipswich, he signed his name on seven property deeds and one town petition. In each instance he signed with a simple mark rather than a full signature—a strong indication that he could not write his own name (the basic test of literacy). Literate colonists occasionally signed deeds and wills with marks for the sake of convenience. Petitions, however, customarily required full signatures, and marks were used only when an individual petitioner was illiterate and incapable of writing his name.[31] And on a 1686 petition to the Ipswich selectmen, Grow was one of four petitioners

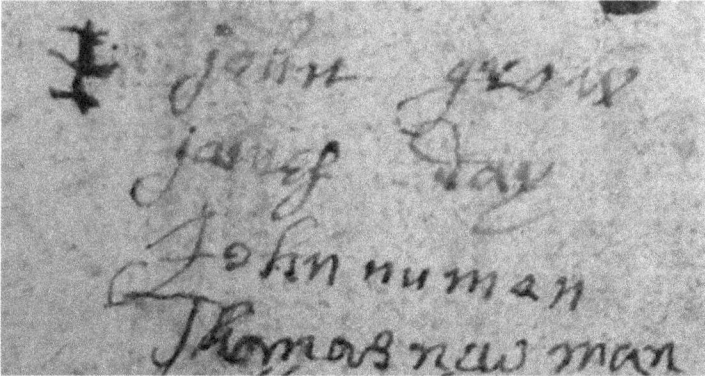

John Grow's mark, made by his own hand on a 1686 Ipswich petition. In seventeenth-century English writing, a capital "I" with or without a horizontal bar across the middle of the upright was the standard form for the letter "J" (in this case, short for "John"). The name "john grow" in cursive immediately to the right of the mark was likely written by another petitioner (possibly James Day) on Grow's behalf. The original petition is in the collection of the Peabody Essex Museum's Phillips Library, Salem, MA, and is reproduced in Appendix B. (Photograph by author.)

(out of forty) who signed with his mark rather than a signature,[32] seemingly confirming his illiteracy. In the 1660s, an estimated 40 percent of adult men in Essex County, Massachusetts, were unable to write their names, and the overwhelming majority of them were in the lower and lower-middle ranks of society.[33] Seen in that context, John Grow's consistent use of a mark provides another piece of evidence locating him in the bottom half of Ipswich society.

His social position presumably improved on 15 December 1669, when he married Hannah Lord, the daughter of a prominent local official. The Lords were one of the founding families of Ipswich. Hannah's maternal great uncle, Nathaniel Ward, was the town's first minister and the author of Massachusetts Bay's first legal code, the 1641 *Body of Liberties*.[34] Her father, Robert Lord, arrived from England in 1635 and went on to hold many of Ipswich's most important governmental offices over the next five decades. A selectman for fourteen terms and town marshal in the 1640s and 1650s, he helped make local laws and also enforced them. As town clerk from the mid-1640s to 1683, he collected the information that determined each resident's tax rate and kept official records of all decisions made at town meetings and other governmental proceedings. He represented Ipswich in court as the town's chief legal counsel, suing individuals who failed to pay their taxes and prosecuting constables who failed to collect them on time. As one of Ipswich's "lot-layers," he determined the boundaries of land grants and helped arbitrate property disputes. He was also the town's deputy to the Massachusetts Bay General Court for a term and served at various points as the Essex County Quarterly Court's clerk of court, clerk of probate, and clerk of writs, with authority to seize property and carry out "all executions in civil and criminal cases." In short, Hannah Lord's father was one of the town's most important and trusted civil servants.[35]

The Lords belonged to the upper middle stratum of society. Economically, they appear to have been comfortable but not wealthy. During his half-century of residence in Ipswich, Robert Lord accumulated 150 acres of land, which was among the smaller amounts owned by any of the town's substantial landholders. When he died in 1683 at age 80, his £645 personal estate was larger than the £261 median for participants in the Great Migration but modest in comparison with the estates left by elite patriarchs Jonathan Wade (£7,859), Thomas Bishop (£5,000+), and William Paine (£4,239). Lord's sons, Thomas, Robert Jr., and Nathaniel, were all "middling"-rank artisans (a cordwainer, blacksmith, and carpenter, respectively).[36] And yet, at the same time, in carrying out his multifaceted civic duties, Lord worked closely with the highest-ranking members of the local elite, including Daniel Denison and Samuel Symonds, two of the town's richest and most powerful leaders, with whom he arbitrated the final dissolution of the Ipswich Company in the late 1650s. He also counted among his personal friends William Paine, one of the wealthiest merchants in Ipswich. Consequently, Lord's central role in local government and his widespread connections, both political and personal, elevated him in status to one of the "leading men of Ipswich society."[37]

Marrying into the Lord family undoubtedly helped to solidify John Grow's place in the community. The Lords were established and respectable. They were relatively affluent. The family's male members were among the 30 percent of Ipswich's population that had voting rights.[38] As one of the town's principal public servants, Robert Lord was particularly well positioned to exert influence on behalf of his children and their spouses. As Lord's son-in-law, John Grow inevitably acquired some of the Lord family's cachet. He became a potential recipient of his father-in-law's material support. He gained access to Lord's influence networks. And perhaps above all, he enhanced his prospects of becoming a "commoner," the key to economic and social success for most residents of seventeenth-century Ipswich.

Land was the town's essential resource. Because everyone in the community, artisans and maritime workers included, farmed on at least a part-time basis, the need for cropland and livestock pasturage was nearly universal. Each household also needed access to enough woodland to supply the 15 cords of firewood that it burned annually for heating and cooking. To meet these basic needs, Ipswich's founders relied on a mixture of traditional English enclosed-field and open-field land use practices. Most of the early settlers were given residential house lots in the central village along with parcels of agricultural land in the surrounding countryside. The size of each land grant was based largely on the social standing and perceived "quality" of the recipient, because, as Virginia DeJohn Anderson notes, "These were, after all, seventeenth-century Englishmen thoroughly accustomed to the idea of hierarchy and hoping to use it to stabilize their New World society." So that while Richard Saltonstall Jr., a scion of the Yorkshire gentry, was awarded a 14-acre house lot and 400 acres of farmland, and Samuel Symonds, an influential "gentleman" from Essex, obtained grants totaling more than 875 acres, "ordinary" settlers received, on average, 2-acre house lots and agricultural parcels ranging from 3 to 50 acres.[39] During the first decade of settlement, approximately 11,000 of the town's 21,000 acres were distributed to private owners under this system.[40]

The remaining 10,000 acres were placed in the public domain as "common lands," or "commons" as they were known colloquially (*i.e.*, land owned "in common" by the community). Reflecting the open-field traditions of English rural villages dating back to the Middle Ages, Ipswich's commons were made available to eligible town residents for communal agriculture, and additionally served as a land trust that the local government held in reserve for future distribution as the population expanded. "Commoners"—those residents who were granted use of the commons—were entitled to plant crops in common planting fields, graze their domestic animals in communal pastures, cut hay from common meadows and salt marshes, and fell trees in the common woodlands for fuel and building material. In exchange for these "rights of commonage," each commoner was expected to make himself available for public works projects such as road building and bridge repair.[41]

Not everyone became a commoner. Initially, rights of commonage were included in the town's house-lot grants, and if a property was subsequently sold, the attached commonage rights "stayed with the house lot and belonged to the new owner." As a result, with commoner status predicated on house-lot ownership, the substantial portion of Ipswich's population that owned no land—indentured servants, day laborers, and the growing number of tenant farmers working the farms of large landowners—was excluded from access to the town's communal resource base. In 1642, when the first comprehensive list of Ipswich commoners was compiled, it included the names of only 111 of the town's 250 adult male inhabitants.[42]

The opportunity to extract free resources from the public domain was so advantageous to the material well-being of Ipswich residents that the right of commonage quickly became the town's most valuable commodity and most important entitlement. Within a quarter century, however, the commonage system was under stress. Between 1642 and 1660, the population of Ipswich more than doubled, generating a residential building boom and new demands for access to the town's public lands. Most of the original house lots were subdivided, and the owners of the new, smaller parcels invariably claimed the commonage rights attached to the original property. As more and more newcomers arrived in town, and the sons of many first-generation settlers reached maturity needing land and resources of their own, pressure on the common lands intensified. By the 1660s, there were more than 200 commoners in the town, and the escalating demand for timber and firewood was rapidly depleting its public woodlands.[43] Ipswich's government responded by tightening the qualifications for commonage rights. In March 1660, acknowledging that the commons had become "overburdened by the multiplying of dwelling houses, contrary to the interest and meaning of the first inhabitants," the town ordered that effective immediately "no house henceforth erected shall have any right to the common lands of this town" and that no "person inhabiting such a house" would be allowed to "make use of any pasture, timber, or wood growing upon said common land" without the town's express permission. One of the local officials responsible for the new policy was selectman Robert Lord.[44]

The change in land policy had significant ramifications for the community. By restricting commonage rights to those residents who lived in houses built prior to March 1660, local leaders were essentially serving the interests of the town's early settlers and their families. That Ipswich was discriminating against newcomers in favor of its established property owners became increasingly evident four years later, in 1664, when voters—themselves a privileged minority of local society—approved a measure to terminate the town's occasional practice of granting free parcels of land to new arrivals, and again in 1665 when the town's commoners, now numbering 203, were allowed to divide 800 acres of outlying common land—mostly "marsh and upland"—among themselves. The wording of the measure authorizing the 1665 land distribution, stating that the 800 acres were to "be divided to such as have the right of commonage," also implicitly established an exclusionary new precedent for the future: only those townspeople who already possessed commonage rights would share in future distributions of the town's remaining public land.[45]

By the mid-1660s, therefore, Ipswich's established families were controlling the town's common lands for their own economic benefit. Commonage provided them with free provisions and free land, assuring them an adequate subsistence and a degree of economic security. However, for those inhabitants excluded from the new arrangements—including a steady influx of unmarried, propertyless young men arriving in Ipswich in pursuit of economic opportunity—options were limited. They could try to acquire commonage rights of their own—by purchasing a pre-1660 house; by currying favor with influential local leaders to obtain a commonage grant by special "consent of the town"; or by marrying into a family of commoners and partaking of its communal privileges. Failing that, their only recourse was to purchase land, wood, hay, and other basic necessities on the open market—a prohibitively expensive proposition for low-income artisans and wage laborers hoping to sink roots in the community.[46]

John Grow initially gained access to the commons in 1672, by special consent of the town. During the early 1670s, the Ipswich government, in one of its periodic efforts to bolster the town's maritime trades, granted eight young seamen and fishermen (John Grow, Obadiah Bridges, John Knowlton, Stephen Cross, John Frinke, Giles Cowes, and brothers John and Samuel Dutch) the "liberty" to cut firewood and graze one cow apiece on the commons. In doing so, however, town leaders stated emphatically that the young maritime workers were not being granted formal rights of commonage but merely the limited *use* of the commons for the purpose of procuring necessary provisions, and that consequently they were "not to claim the right of commoners." The town also made clear that the privileges being bestowed were conditional, and that the eight young men would only have access to the commons as long as they remained employed in the town's seafaring trades "and not otherwise."[47]

Seven years later, Grow managed to obtain full commonage rights, and he had his father-in-law to thank. In March 1679, Robert Lord purchased a pre-1660 house and "the land about it" on the "streete called brooke streete" from "ye Widdow Woodham" and turned it over to John and Hannah Grow to live in, apparently under an arrangement in which John agreed to buy the property from Lord in installment payments.[48] The Brook Street house lot had a right of commonage attached to it, and Grow's name was subsequently included on a new Ipswich commoners list completed in December of that same year. He was the only maritime worker among the eight granted conditional access to the commons in the early 1670s whose name appears on the 1679 list.[49]

Attaining the status of commoner was undoubtedly a significant event in Grow's life. Full access to the commons enhanced his material well-being and that of his young and growing family. More specifically, the opportunity to utilize the town's communal pastures for sheep grazing and wool production may have been instrumental in facilitating his transition around this time from a life at sea to land-based employment as a weaver (discussed below). In addition, commonage eventually increased his landholdings. In 1709, when Ipswich distributed most of its remaining common lands to the town's commoners, Grow received allotments totaling 25 acres: an 8-acre woodlot in the Chebacco (Essex) section of the township and 17 acres in the Bush Hill/Turner's Hill area a mile west of town.[50] But perhaps equally important, commonage afforded him new status in the community. At a time when less than 50 percent of Ipswich's adult males had commonage rights, and at a time, moreover, when the town was virtually shutting its doors to any new commoners, he had managed to become a member of the exclusive "closed club" of privileged residents who owned shares of the public domain.[51] He was now a proprietary stakeholder in his community.

Statistical data on matrimony and procreation in seventeenth-century Massachusetts suggest that John and Hannah Grow were a typical married couple. At the time of their wedding, John was 27 years old, the average age of marriage for Ipswich men of that period. Hannah's birth date is not known, but if the most authoritative estimate is correct, she was probably about 20 when she married—one year younger than the usual marriage age of Ipswich women at the time.[52] The couple produced eight children over the course of their reproductive lives, the average number of offspring born to New England families in the seventeenth century.[53] Each child was conceived in late winter or early spring, peak months of conception in the Bay Colony.[54] Birth intervals (the length of time that separated one child's birth from the next) also conformed to standard New England childbearing patterns of the period: a first child born within one year of the couple's marriage, followed by an average interval of 2.2 years between each of the next six births, and then a significantly longer interval before the birth of their last child, as Hannah neared menopause.[55] Like most couples in Puritan New England, John and Hannah chose popular biblical names for their children; and like the vast majority of Massachusetts Bay parents at the time, they named their firstborn son and daughter after themselves.[56]

Children of JOHN[1] and HANNAH (LORD) GROW, all born at Ipswich, MA:

    i.   John Grow, b. 8 Dec. 1670; d. 4 June 1671 in Ipswich.

    ii.   Samuel, b. 31 Dec. 1671; prob. d. bef. 1724–1725; m. 1694 at Topsfield, MA, Ruth Foster, still in Ipswich 1712.

    iii.   John, b. 16 Dec. 1673, still in Ipswich 1697; prob. d. before 10 April 1712.

    iv.   Joseph, b. Sept. 1677; d. 1 Oct. 1748 in Ipswich; prob. unm.

    v.   Hannah, b. 3 Jan. 1679; no further record.

    vi.   Nathaniel, b. 17 Sept. 1682; prob. d. bef. 10 April 1712.

    vii.   Thomas[2], b. 20 Feb. 1684; d. 13 Jan. 1753 in Pomfret, CT; m. 1710, Rebecca Holt.

    viii.   William, b. 20 Nov. 1690; d. 9 May 1747 in York, ME; m. 1715/16 at Newbury, MA, Joanna Poor.

SOURCES: George W. Davis, comp., *John Grow of Ipswich/John Groo (Grow) of Oxford* (Washington, D.C.: privately printed by the Carnahan Press, 1913), 15–19; Michael Grow, "John Grow of Ipswich: An Update," *New England Historical and Genealogical Register*, 167 (July 2013): 202–203.

Nor was the couple spared one of the most common tragedies experienced by seventeenth-century New England families: the death of one or more of their children. At a time when childhood mortality rates in the region ran as high as 30 percent, and young couples entered marriage knowing that two or three of their children would likely die before reaching maturity, John and Hannah suffered more than their share of losses. Their firstborn child (a son, John) lived less than six months, and three of their other offspring—two sons (Nathaniel and a second John) and their only daughter (Hannah)—also probably "died early," according to Grow family genealogist George W. Davis.[57] All told, five of John and Hannah's eight children may have predeceased their parents.[58] The couple endured other family tragedies as well. Their fourth child, Joseph, lost his eyesight; and because, in John's words, he was "thereby rendered Uncapable to labour for a livelyhood, as otherwise he could have done," he lived at home with his parents for the rest of their lives.[59] In addition, Hannah's 26-year-old younger brother, Joseph Lord, was crushed to death in a 1677 tree-cutting accident.[60]

The couple's Brook Street home was located in a modest neighborhood of lower-"middling"-rank artisans. The previous owner of their residence, John Woodham, was a bricklayer. The property next door had belonged to Abraham Warr, an Ipswich swineherd whose daily duties driving the town's hogs to their common pasture may have given Brook Street its earlier name, "Hogg Lane." And Freegrace Norton, who lived across the street until 1675, was a carpenter and miller with a reputation for dishonest dealings at the local gristmill. Brook Street itself was a short, muddy, hillside road that wound up a shallow gorge to the top of Town Hill, a steep elevation on Ipswich's northeast side that helped shield the town from ocean storms. At the foot of the road, the land flattened out into a densely populated area of small house lots that extended two or three blocks to the Ipswich River.[61] (Residents there included Thomas Dennis, seventeenth-century New England's preeminent joiner and master carver, whose house John Grow is known to have visited.[62]) From Grow's residence partway up Brook Street, it was a short, easy walk to the town harbor and Captain Robert Pearce's wharf.

The Grow house lot was situated on the west side of the road, in the vicinity of present-day 20 or 22 Spring Street (Brook Street's modern name). The property totaled approximately 2.25 acres, an average-sized house lot in seventeenth-century Ipswich. There were freshwater springs to the immediate north and south—a small "upper spring" flowing out of the lane some 20 feet above the upper property line, and a large "lower great spring" (still partially visible) below the southern boundary.[63] Stone walls at least 3.5 feet high marked some of the property's borders, and wooden "fencing" was also in evidence.[64] Other than a small fruit orchard, there were probably few if any trees remaining by the time the Grows took up residence.

The house itself has long since disappeared. If the dwelling was typical (and there is no reason to believe otherwise) it was probably a one-and-a-half or two-story saltbox or cape, with an unpainted exterior of grayish-brown clapboards, a steeply pitched roof with wood shingles, and a few small windows.[65] Besides a privy, outbuildings included a barn to house the family's livestock (sheep, horses,[66] a milk cow, probably a pig or two and some poultry) during the winter months when the common pastures were not in use. Typically, there also would have been a small kitchen garden and the aforementioned orchard.

Most "first period" houses in Ipswich were small, four-room dwellings, usually less than 20 feet square, with rooms built two over two. Their most imposing interior feature was a large center chimney with a cavernous brick fireplace for cooking and central heating. The two ground-floor rooms, frequently referred to as a "hall" and a "parlor," were used for a multiplicity of purposes: cooking, eating, household work activities, sleeping, and storage. The two upstairs "chambers," which could only be reached by ladder in humbler abodes, often served as children's sleeping quarters and additional storage space. With an average of ten or more individuals residing in a single dwelling, living conditions were inevitably crowded, cramped, and lacking any modern notion of privacy (other than, perhaps, a curtained bedstead for the husband and wife).

Within this physical environment, Hannah Grow's daily life would have been devoted almost entirely to child-rearing activities and domestic household duties. During the first quarter century of her marriage, most of her energies were undoubtedly expended in a repetitious cycle of pregnancy, childbirth, nursing, and weaning, followed by a new pregnancy, and so on. Simultaneously, she also would have been multi-tasking a wide variety of specialized household functions: fire tending and meal preparation; cheese making, butter churning, brewing, and other food processing activities; candle making, wool spinning, clothes making, washing, gardening, and more.[67] By the mid-1680s, John, for his part, would have been occupied in his own specialized work space— probably either a "loom room" inside the house or an outdoor work shed— where his "weaver's loome and tackling" were housed.

At some point in his first fifteen years of marriage, John gave up maritime employment. By 1686, he was evidently working as a weaver and raising sheep to supply himself with the wool that he needed to make textiles. In a petition to the Ipswich selectmen in April of that year, he and thirty-nine other commoners complained that the town was providing inadequate security for the sheep that they were pasturing on the "Jeffrey's Neck" sheep commons. The usual practice of assigning a full-time shepherd to the common flock had apparently been abandoned, and the sheep were now being left unguarded in their fold at night, resulting in the loss of many of the animals to wolves and other predators. Complaining that their "profit" was declining as a result, Grow and his fellow commoners called on the selectmen to hire a resident shepherd so that "our sheep may be preserved," thereby ensuring "the Increasing of Wool, without which we cannot well Subsist."[68] Later documents consistently identify him as a "weaver."[69]

A confluence of factors may account for his midlife vocational transition. Captain Pearce, his shipmaster, died in 1679,[70] eliminating what may still have been his source of employment at the time. But general trends of the period almost certainly had an impact as well. By the late 1670s, Ipswich's maritime trades had entered a period of irreversible decline. Silting in the Ipswich River and the persistent formation of sandbars at the river's mouth were making it increasingly difficult for even midsized ships to reach the town harbor. Meanwhile, the fishing industry at the Isles of Shoals and Monhegan Island had begun to fall off sharply, reducing commercial freight-hauling business for coastal trading vessels.[71] Not that a seafaring career was all that appealing even in good economic times. The work was dangerous and difficult. Unpredictable ocean storms, hazardous winter voyages, and disease-infested ports resulted in high mortality rates. Ships' quarters were damp and uncomfortable. The pay was low. Little wonder, then, that before they reached middle age, Essex County seamen and fishermen usually shifted to land-based employment when they had the chance.[72] John Grow seems to fit that profile. Nearly 40 years old as the 1680s began, with a wife and a rapidly growing family to support, he presumably would have welcomed the opportunity to leave the coasting trade for the relative safety and security of life on shore as a self-employed artisan. One such opportunity presented itself in 1679 when he became a householder and a commoner. With his shipmaster dead and the local maritime economy struggling, he now gained proprietary access to the Ipswich sheep commons—a key resource in the new sheep-wool-textile complex that was emerging at the time as the foundation of the town's economy.

Wool was an essential commodity in seventeenth-century Massachusetts. Easily spun into yarn and woven into thick cloth for blankets, coats, cloaks, and other garments, wool offered Bay residents "warmth and survival" during the long, bitterly cold New England winters. In the early years of settlement, however, a scarcity of sheep left woolen cloth in critically short supply, causing considerable pain and suffering among the general population. During the 1640s and 1650s, the colony's leaders took several aggressive steps to stimulate local production, ordering towns to increase their sheep flocks, offering bounties for cloth production, and imposing mandatory yarn-spinning quotas on households. Nevertheless, it was not until the 1660s—after the towns had begun to bring wolves and other predators under more effective control and enough high-quality English hay had been planted to provide suitable fodder— that the colony's sheep population increased significantly, enabling local wool weavers to produce a sufficient amount of fabric to meet the heavy demand.[73]

Ipswich residents responded energetically to the wool shortage. Sheep raising increased dramatically in the town during the 1650s, and by 1660 some 800 sheep were being grazed on the commons, a number equal to that of the cattle being pastured there. By the 1670s, the town was operating three separate sheep commons, and by 1702 the number of common flocks had grown to nine. So enthusiastically, in fact, did Ipswich reorient its economy to sheep raising for wool production that by the end of the century the town was known primarily for its sheep flocks and pastoral agriculture.[74] Within the local sheep-raising community, the Grows were apparently well regarded. In 1698, the town government appointed John's 26-year-old son, Samuel, to inspect the sheep commons and determine if the town's "orders made concerning ye Sheep and Rams" were being properly observed. By the terms of the appointment, Samuel was empowered to "prosecute" any "breach of orders" that he discovered and to keep "half of ye fines" for himself as compensation for his "pains."[75]

Accompanying the increase in sheep ownership was a sharp rise in cloth-making activity. By the 1670s, the number of commercial weavers working in Ipswich was increasing noticeably, and ancillary enterprises were springing up to support the growing textile trade. One of the town's carpenters (Walter Roper) made looms and tackle for local weavers. Seven "fulling" mills were built to thicken (or "full") and smooth the weavers' wool cloth by moistening and heating it after it left the loom. Several dye houses began operating. And local tailors (including John's mother-in-law, Mary Lord) turned the finished fabric into clothing. All in all, of the 250–300 artisans working in Ipswich from the 1660s to the end of the century, at least 24 were employed in the cloth trades, half a dozen of them as weavers.[76]

For men like John Grow, there were strong market incentives to take up the weaver's trade. Throughout the latter decades of the seventeenth century, the ongoing high demand for warm clothing and bedding made wool weaving a potentially profitable enterprise. Between 1675 and 1682, for example, the price of wool blankets in Essex County markets more than doubled.[77] In addition, the raw material required for wool weaving was by now readily available, thanks to the multiplying sheep flocks. Typically, local sheep owners brought skeins of their homespun woolen yarn to one of the town's weavers and paid him to weave it into cloth.[78] For his services, the weaver was sometimes compensated in cash. (The going rate in 1708 was 3.5 pence for each yard of plain fabric woven.) More often, however, he bartered the textiles he produced for food and other commodities. The account book of Abraham Howe, one of John's fellow Ipswich weavers, lists a wide variety of goods—a "bushel of Rye," "2 bushells of Indian corn," 12 pounds of pork, seven pounds of butter, "a load of hay and a hors coller," etc.—that Howe received in trade for his "linsey-woolsies" and other fabrics.[79]

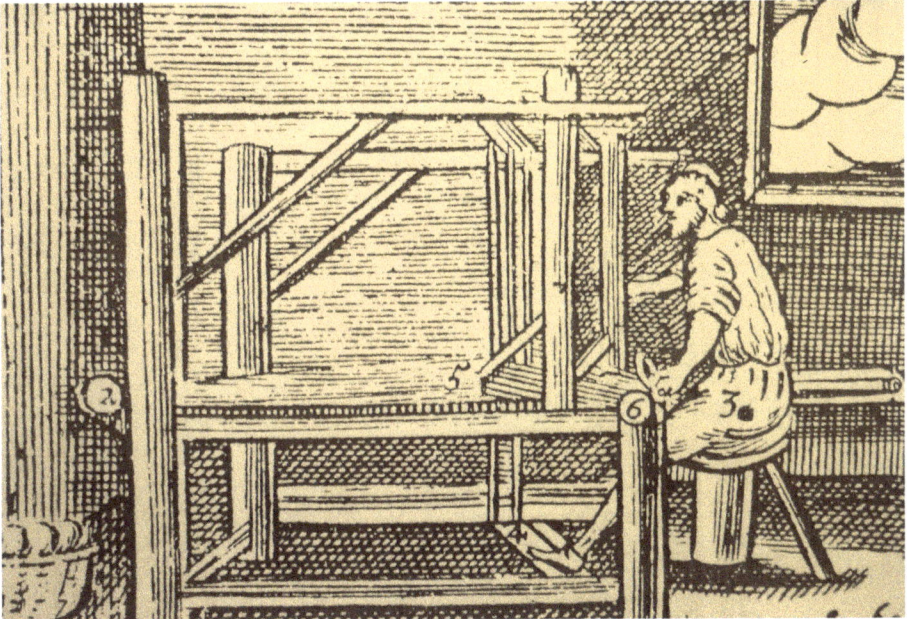

A mid-seventeenth-century weaver at his loom, as depicted in an engraving from Moravian cleric Johann Amos Comenius' *Orbis Sensualium Pictus (The Physical World in Pictures)*, published in 1657.

The weaving process itself was "wearisome and heavy work" that required considerable physical stamina. The weaver sat for long hours harnessed to a large wooden loom, laboriously operating its foot treadles, shuttles, and warp bar. On a good day, he might produce five or six yards of "merchantable" cloth. After several years the work left many weavers "round-shouldered and misshapen," according to Ipswich town historian Thomas Franklin Waters.[80] Nevertheless, for most weavers the trade's rewards apparently outweighed the toil and drudgery. Young men in seventeenth-century New England usually began their working lives "laboring in the service of others" as apprentices, indentured servants, or wage laborers; consequently, for most of them a principal goal in life was economic independence—the ability to earn an adequate living "free from outside control" as a self-employed farmer or artisan.[81] Weaving was one available means to that end. If a weaver also raised sheep, he reaped additional rewards. With wool sheared from his flock, he could weave his own textiles and sell or barter them in local markets, while his animals provided a ready source of meat, butter, and cheese for his family's larder. The economic labels attached to John Grow's name from the 1680s onward—"weaver," "sheep-owner," "commoner"—indicate that he succeeded in achieving economic independence as a self-employed artisan, presumably with sufficient skills and resources to provide at least a lower-"middling"-level standard of living for his family.

The personal beliefs of John and Hannah Grow—their philosophy of life, their spiritual worldview, their moral values and standards of behavior—are unknowable. Like most members of seventeenth-century Puritan communities, they probably interpreted the events and circumstances of their lives as the workings of an "almighty God" whose supernatural power and cosmic grand design governed every aspect of the universe. According to Puritan theology, human beings were innately depraved sinners, all but a handful of whom were predestined to an afterlife of eternal torment in the fire pits of Hell. The one thin hope of "salvation" for Puritan men and women was to live a sin-free life as a "visible saint," putting their faith in Christ and obeying the laws of God as spelled out in the Bible. Only by leading a "godly" life, resisting the temptations of Satan the antichrist, could they hope to receive God's mercy and win "eternal glory" in Heaven. To Puritans, evidence of God's power and divine judgment was everywhere. Death, disease, crop failures, storms, earthquakes and other natural calamities, Indian attacks—all were viewed as signs of "God's holy displeasure," warnings to His followers to "repent of their sins" and "mend their ways." Comets and eclipses were "portents of doom presaging the Apocalypse" and the imminent "second coming of Christ." Positive developments, such as a bountiful harvest, the birth of a healthy child, recovery from an illness, material prosperity, good weather, or a rainbow, were providential signs of "the Lord's blessing," rewards bestowed on faithful believers for their piety and godliness. Such, at least, was the ideological message disseminated by Puritan ministers in their weekly sermons to their Massachusetts Bay congregations.[82]

Cultural context and fragmentary evidence support the assumption that the Grows were practicing Puritans. First and foremost, it would have been unusual if the couple had not reflected the prevailing mores of their cultural environment, particularly in Puritan New England, where pressure to conform was intense. It is also unlikely that John would have been permitted to marry into the Lord family—whose members included Hannah's great-uncle Nathaniel Ward, the prominent Puritan theologian who founded the Ipswich church, and her father, Robert, who served as a deacon in that church[83]—unless he held conventional Puritan views and met the family's standards of religious and moral respectability. John left a hint of his spiritual worldview in a 1722 deed conveyance in which he stated that his blind son, Joseph, had been deprived of sight "by the hand of God."[84] And in old age he was granted the privilege of sitting in the "Men's Short fore seat in the front" of the meetinghouse, a bench reserved for elderly and infirm male worshippers during religious services.[85]

New England Puritans did not all share the same depth of religious conviction, however. Along with a dominant core of devout true believers, each community contained substantial numbers of superficially religious churchgoers and "indifferent Protestants" whose attendance at Sunday services was motivated as much by the need to conform to local social conventions as by devotion to Puritan religious precepts. In most Puritan communities, moreover, a majority of townspeople attended religious services without becoming fully covenanted, communion-taking members of their church.[86] Ipswich's seventeenth-century church records have not survived, but the absence of John Grow's name on a list of 222 town residents who contributed funds to pay the "elder's salary" in 1679 suggests that he may not have been a full church member.[87]

Nor did Puritans necessarily practice what their ministers preached. Throughout the second half of the seventeenth century, Ipswich authorities waged an ongoing battle against the spiritual and moral transgressions of the town's citizenry. During the 1650s, "Sabbath breaking" ordinances were enacted against the many "young people & others" who spent "the Lord's day . . . walking the streets and fields" and frequenting "houses of entertainment" "to drink, sport," and otherwise profane "the holy Sabbath" "to the dishonor of God [and] the reproach of religion."

By the time of John and Hannah's marriage, Sunday services in the meetinghouse were frequently being disrupted by "youthful disturbances," fighting, and other "disorderly carriages." In 1673, Thomas Mentor was disciplined for behaving "very irreverently and most unchristianly [during] the time of worship, by sitting with his hat upon his head . . . taking maids by the aprons as they came in to the meeting house . . . putting his hand in their bosoms . . . snatching away their posies or flowers, [and] laughing and . . . whispering with those that are like himself."[88] Not even the town minister was assured of public respect. When Reverend William Hubbard—a wealthy Ipswich clergyman with large property holdings in the town—stated in a 1678 sermon that "the good a Christian desired did not lie in lands and great farms but in the light and countenance of God's favor," Thomas Baker "laughed out loud" at the minister's apparent hypocrisy.[89]

By the late 1670s, moral and spiritual misconduct was so widespread in Ipswich that the town government established a new group of civic officials known as "tithingmen" to police inappropriate behavior in the community. In 1677, Robert Lord and 24 other "prudent and discreet inhabitants" were appointed to monitor the households of their respective neighborhoods and inform the authorities of any immoral or "disorderly" conduct, including swearing, card playing, excessive drinking, Sabbath breaking, failure to instruct children in their "Catechisms," and "whatever else tends to irreligion."[90] Lord's role as a tithingman adds weight to the supposition that the Grows were upstanding Puritans, although the town's resort to neighborhood-level morality inspectors also suggests that our modern stereotype of the Puritans as a colorless group of somber, austere zealots ignores the unruly and earthy realities of their culture.

Seventeenth-century New Englanders were also a deeply superstitious people. Most of them believed in astrology and many found fortune-telling insightful. In the lower ranks of society, folk magic and "magical healing" were widely practiced. Virtually everyone believed that the physical world was inhabited by demons, phantoms, and "evil spirits" from "the invisible world," while the existence of witches—human beings who inflicted harm on others by supernatural means—was an article of faith for colonists of every social rank.[91] Between 1638 and 1691, nearly eighty New Englanders were prosecuted for practicing witchcraft and at least fourteen were executed.[92] The famous outbreak of witchcraft hysteria that swept through Essex County in 1692 more than doubled those numbers, touching the lives of four of Hannah Grow's siblings in the process.

The basic facts of the Salem witchcraft crisis are well-known to students of American history. Early in 1692, a group of adolescent girls in Salem Village began suffering strange fits and convulsive seizures. Local authorities quickly concluded that "diabolical molestation" was to blame and charged three village women with witchcraft. When one of the accused women confessed under physical coercion that she and the other two women were supernaturally tormenting the afflicted girls as servants of Satan, the floodgates of paranoia opened. Soon, nervous townspeople throughout Essex County were identifying local misfits and neighbors with whom they had clashed as probable witches. By the end of July, at least ninety-eight people had been formally accused, and six had been convicted and publicly executed. Most of the convictions were based on "spectral evidence" and supernatural "touch tests." During courtroom interrogations of accused witches, the "afflicted" accusers frequently fell into violent fits, hysterically claiming that the defendant's "spectral apparition" was pinching, choking, or otherwise "grievously tormenting" them in an effort to take possession of their bodies on the Devil's behalf. Puritan magistrates accepted such "spectral testimony" as legitimate and damning evidence of the defendant's guilt. During the fits, court officials often forced the accused witch to physically touch one of the afflicted girls; if the fit stopped (as it usually did), the assumption was made that the witch's malignant venom and "evil spirits" had been channeled back to their supernatural source, curing the victim and providing further "proof" of the alleged witch's guilt.[93]

After Salem's jail filled to overflowing, accused witches were sent to neighboring towns to be held in confinement until their trials. Many were temporarily incarcerated in the jail at Ipswich, where Hannah's older brother, Robert Lord Jr., a town marshal and local blacksmith, forged sets of iron shackles and fastened them onto the wrists and ankles of several of the accused prisoners (including Mary Easty, who was hanged in Salem in September). Lord later billed the county court "one pound aleven Shillings" for his services.[94]

Two local Ipswich women—Elizabeth Howe and Rachel Clinton—were accused of witchcraft during the crisis. Howe had been quarreling with her neighbors for more than a decade, during which time several townspeople had spread rumors that she was a witch. Now, in the paranoid atmosphere of 1692, old and new allegations were brought forth: that Howe had bewitched and murdered a neighboring couple's child ten years earlier; that ghosts of deceased townspeople had recently appeared accusing Howe of killing them; that she had supernaturally injured her neighbors' livestock; that she "worshipped the Devil" and had been "baptized by him" at a witches' gathering in Newbury Falls, etc. Among her accusers were in-laws of Hannah's sister Abigail (Lord) Foster. A few years earlier, Abigail's brother-in-law Isaac Foster had been instrumental in blocking Howe's application for membership in the Ipswich church; and now in 1692, his son Jacob Foster (Abigail's nephew) gave testimony implying that Howe had "miserably beaten and abused" a mare that he owned as revenge for his father's actions. Abigail's sister-in-law Lydia Foster also testified against the accused woman. Howe was hanged in Salem in mid-July.[95]

By late summer, the focus of witchcraft paranoia had shifted to Andover, an agricultural community 15 miles west of Ipswich, where more than forty residents—among them Abigail Faulkner, daughter of a prominent local minister—were accused and jailed. As in Salem, the initial accusers were teenage girls who claimed to be victims of supernatural bewitchment. In early September, Hannah Grow's sister Sarah (Lord) Wilson, who was married to an Andover farmer, and "Mistress" Mary Osgood, a sister-in-law of Hannah's sister Susanna (Lord) Osgood, along with several other women from the upper strata of local society, were brought to the Andover meetinghouse and forced to confront their "afflicted" accusers, who promptly fell into the now-customary fits in their presence. After failing "touch tests," the accused women were imprisoned in Salem, where they quickly confessed their guilt. Hannah's sister Sarah Wilson told authorities that she had been "led into that dreadful sin of witchcraft" by Abigail Faulkner, and admitted that she had attended "a great Meeting of ye witches" in Andover, at which the spectral apparition of Reverend George Burroughs, the alleged "ring leader" of Massachusetts witches, had counseled the assembled witches to maintain their faith in Satan. Mary Osgood, for her part, confessed that she had "made a covenant with the devil," promising to "serve and worship" him and to "be his, soul and body, forever." Osgood also confessed that she had used an "evil eye" and other supernatural powers to torment her afflicted Andover accusers.[96]

The confessions, not surprisingly, had been coerced. In Salem, Puritan authorities violently bullied and browbeat the terrified women, warning them that they would be hanged if they did not confess, and, as the women later recounted, telling them "that we were witches, and they knew it, and we knew it," until they "made us think that it was so; and [with] our understandings, our reason, [and] our faculties almost gone, we . . . said any thing and every thing which they desired." Hannah's sister Sarah was so traumatized psychologically by the experience that—as she told Increase Mather during a prison interview in October—she began to wonder whether she might actually be a witch. Although she "knowingly . . . never had familiarity with the devil," she told Mather, witnessing her afflicted accusers "crying out [against] her . . . made her fearfull of herself," fearful that she might have supernatural powers she was unaware of, and that she might have been responsible for afflicting her accusers without realizing it.

Meanwhile, the women's families were also pressuring them to confess. It had by now become apparent that Puritan judges were not imposing the death penalty on accused witches who confessed their guilt, whereas those who persisted in maintaining their innocence usually "found themselves on the gallows." Accordingly, as the women later recalled, "our nearest and dearest relations . . . knowing our great danger, apprehended [that] there was no other way to save our lives, [and] persuaded us to confess." Consequently, "press'd & urg'd & affrighted" "even out of [their] reason," Sarah Wilson, Mary Osgood, and the others confessed to practicing witchcraft in order "to obtain favour" from the court and avoid execution.[97] The strategy worked. In late 1692, after Mather and other prominent Puritans began to question the juridical validity of spectral evidence, the courts suspended further proceedings and the wave of public hysteria gradually ebbed. Wilson and Osgood immediately retracted their confessions as "wholly false," and in late December—after fifteen weeks of imprisonment, during which they nearly perished from inadequate food and wretched conditions—the two women were released on bond. The following year, they were formally cleared of all charges.[98]

The names of John and Hannah Grow do not appear in any of the witchcraft records, but with family members involved on all sides of the crisis—as accusers, as jailors, as confessed witches—they could hardly have remained aloof from it. More importantly, the events of 1692 underscore the fact that intellectually these earliest-known Grows in America belonged to a post-medieval, pre-modern world, a world in which metaphysical beliefs, superstition, and fear of the supernatural still prevailed.

John and Hannah Grow also experienced several other historically significant events firsthand. In 1675–1676, during the Indian uprising known as King Philip's War, Native American military forces devastated much of New England, attacking more than half of the region's ninety towns, destroying twelve of them, and killing some 2,000 settlers. The interior of Massachusetts was ravaged, and although Ipswich was not assaulted, sightings of Indian raiding parties a few miles to the west kept the town in a constant state of alarm. Local authorities converted the meetinghouse into a fortified garrison to house residents in the event of an attack, and "every able-bodied man was trained" for military defense. Nearly ninety Ipswich men, including at least seven mariners and fishermen, served as soldiers in Massachusetts Bay military units during the war, the overwhelming majority of them involuntarily impressed into service by the town's elite-dominated militia committee, which targeted "troublemakers" from the lower ranks of society—law breakers, drunkards, debtors, transients, and other "undesirables"—as conscripts. Neither John Grow nor any of Hannah's brothers were called upon to fight, presumably because Robert Lord's connections to Daniel Denison and other politically influential members of the Ipswich militia committee protected the family's conscription-age males from the dangers of military service. Nevertheless, the Grows and Lords undoubtedly shared their community's collective sense of fear as enemy forces burned neighboring towns and slaughtered the inhabitants. After the war, lingering threats of Indian attack kept Ipswich residents on edge well into the eighteenth century.[99]

During the 1680s, England moved aggressively to strengthen its imperial control over Massachusetts Bay, annulling the colony's charter, levying new taxes, and threatening to revoke the land titles of colonial property owners. Ipswich quickly became a focal point of resistance to the heavy-handed new measures. In a series of politically momentous town meetings held between 1685 and 1687—meetings that John Grow likely attended—the town's eligible voters rejected the mother country's arbitrary new policies as illegal infringements of their liberties as free-born Englishmen, and royal authorities responded by arresting and imprisoning several local leaders. The political crisis ended in

1689 when the royal governor in Boston was overthrown in a bloodless coup and a new monarch more accommodating to New England Puritans came to power in England. Ipswich would later honor its early defiance of English rule by proclaiming itself the "birthplace of American independence."[100]

In the first decade of the eighteenth century, a local dispute over land policy ignited another political crisis in Ipswich, this one pitting the town's commoners against its non-commoners. Although the local population had continued to grow rapidly—doubling in the eighteen years between 1674 and 1692, and doubling again by 1713—descendants of the early settlers continued to maintain a near monopoly over the town's common lands. During the final two decades of the seventeenth century only twenty additional residents managed to acquire rights of commonage, even though Ipswich's population was multiplying exponentially at the time. Consequently, in 1699, when the town's commoners attempted to divide a portion of the common woodlands among themselves, the non-commoners rose up in opposition, claiming that as tax-paying members of the community, they too were entitled to share in any distributions of the public domain. Nearly a decade of acrimonious debate ensued, generating "much bad blood" between the two groups. Eventually, as the non-commoners steadily increased in number, their "insistent pressure" forced Ipswich's government to expand commonage rights, and in 1709 it was voted that from that date onward "all . . . Householders . . . shall be Commoners." The resentful commoners responded by challenging the legality of the proceedings, and a compromise was worked out in which the town transferred 6,000 of its remaining 7,000 acres of common land to both "ye old and new Commoners" under an unequal formula that awarded a significantly larger and more valuable proportion of the land to those residents who held "ancient" rights of commonage.[101] It was under this arrangement that John Grow, as an established commoner, received an 8-acre woodlot and another 17-acre parcel in 1709.

By the 1720s, the Grows owned several plots of land in the township, including their Brook Street house lot and a "p'cell of marsh at ye hundreds" (inherited from Robert Lord at his death in 1683); a woodlot in Chebacco and the 17-acre Bush Hill/Turkey Hill tract obtained in 1709; and two "upland" lots near the Jeffrey's Neck sheep pastures (acquired from "new commoner" John Andrews in 1712).[102] John and Hannah continued to live at the Brook Street residence for the rest of their lives. Because their children were born over a twenty-year time span, the couple was still engaged in child raising in their mid- to late-sixties. Not until about 1715, after their youngest son, William, had reached maturity and left Ipswich to begin an independent life in Maine, did the family nest become partially empty—and even then their visually impaired son, Joseph, remained at home.

Like most men at the time, John probably continued working until he was no longer physically able to do so. As he neared 80, he began to liquidate the family's real estate holdings, presumably to obtain money to live on as he reached the end of his economically productive years and to provide Hannah and Joseph with the financial resources they would need to sustain themselves after his death. In 1721, he sold the Chebacco woodlot to fellow-townsman Stephen Kinsman. Three years later, he and Hannah conveyed their 17-acre parcel to their nephews Nathaniel and Philip Lord and another local man. And in 1726, they sold one portion of their Jeffrey's Neck land to Nathaniel Hovey of Ipswich and a second parcel to local farmer Jacob Caldwell.[103]

As the couple aged, Joseph somehow managed to look after them despite his disability. In 1724–1725, in a gesture suggesting that strong bonds of affection existed within the family, the two youngest sons, William and Thomas, legally "quit-claimed" to Joseph their inheritance rights to John and Hannah's estate in order to "better . . . enable" their brother to provide for their parents' "maintenance and comfortable subsistence" in old age. Little time remained to the couple, however. John died on 9 January 1727 at approximately 85 years of age (well above the average life expectancy of nearly 70 years for New England men at the time), and Hannah followed twenty-two months later, on 16 November 1728.[104] They were probably buried in Ipswich's Old Burying Ground at the foot of Town Hill, although no grave markers or records of the burial location have survived.[105]

From a distance of three centuries, our view of John Grow is at best hazy and incomplete. He seems, in retrospect, to have been a rather ordinary individual typical in many respects of his time and place—one of thousands of obscure migrants who were sinking their roots in the formative environment of early colonial America. He first appears in the 1660s as part of an influx of young male workers who arrived in Ipswich seeking economic opportunity, married local women, and settled into the community.[106] An advantageous marriage helped him secure a respectable propertied position in the town, and he eventually carved out an economic niche for himself as a small-scale weaver and sheep owner. There is no evidence, however, that he ever rose above the lower-middle stratum of local society. His landholdings were modest in size and probably no more than average for an Ipswich artisan at the time. He was able to place at least two of his sons in apprenticeships that equipped them with the skills to become middling-rank artisans in their own right, but both William, a "cordwainer," and Thomas, a "maltster"—facing futures without any prospect of landed inheritance—left Ipswich to seek opportunity elsewhere when they reached adulthood. (Their brother Joseph was limited vocationally by his physical handicap, and was described in a 1730 document as a "laborer," presumably unskilled.)[107]

The fact that John Grow's name appears so rarely in the surviving records is undoubtedly revealing. He apparently never held public office, served on a jury, or obtained voting rights. He was neither a defendant nor a plaintiff in any known Essex County court proceedings. He left no will or probate inventory at the time of his death. All of which reinforces our image of him as a common artisan of modest means living an obscure life unmarked by distinction or notoriety in the lower half of early New England society. His sole legacy is the family that descended from him. Other early Ipswich families—the Winthrops, the Saltonstalls, the Bradstreets, the Appletons, the Symondses—were progenitors of a privileged WASP (White Anglo-Saxon Protestant) elite in America, a powerful upper class that would continue to enjoy positions of political prominence and high socioeconomic status in the generations that followed. John and Hannah Grow's descendants, by contrast—mostly farmers, businessmen, and, more recently, salaried professionals—would occupy a less visible, less privileged, but respectable position in the middle class of American society, a position that placed them in the very mainstream of American history over the next three centuries.

GENERATION TWO

THOMAS GROW (1684–1753)

By the time John and Hannah Grow's son Thomas[2] (John[1]) was born in 1684, the patterns of development that would shape the next two centuries of American history were firmly in place: agriculture was the basis of economic life, and land was the principal form of wealth for the vast majority of Americans. In New England's early coastal communities, however, population growth had already reduced the availability of affordable farmland, forcing younger sons of local families to migrate to undeveloped frontier areas farther inland in search of cheap land. As settlement expanded into the interior, those fundamental patterns of overpopulation, land hunger, and westward migration replicated themselves generation after generation, from the late seventeenth century into the second half of the nineteenth century,[1] shaping the lives of the next five generations of the Grow family in the process.

Thomas Grow was a "maltster" by occupation, a specialized agricultural artisan who grew barley and processed it into "malt," the chief ingredient in beer. Maltsters drew on their technical knowledge of temperatures and timing to convert raw barley into a coarse meal, or malt, suitable for brewing: first germinating the grain by steeping it in water at just below the boiling point, then carefully drying and roasting the sprouted kernels to lock in the maximum amount of fermentable sugar enzymes[2]—knowledge and skills that Thomas probably acquired as a teenager while serving an apprenticeship with an established Ipswich maltster. Reaching adulthood, he likely recognized that his prospects in Ipswich were limited. By the early eighteenth century, nearly all of the town's commons had been transferred to private ownership, land prices were skyrocketing, and the sons of local townsmen were departing for newer settlements elsewhere in search of economic livelihoods.[3] Accordingly, in the summer of 1710, when Thomas married Rebecca Holt of neighboring Andover, a still relatively underpopulated farming community 15 miles to the west, he made the decision to leave Ipswich and take up residence in his bride's hometown.[4]

Like his father before him, Thomas Grow married into a prominent local family. The Holts were among the largest landowners in Andover. Rebecca's grandfather Nicholas Holt was one of the town's founders, and the 500-plus acres of land that he accumulated (in an area of south Andover that came to be known as Holt Hill) provided a substantial inheritance for each of his five sons, the second youngest of whom was Rebecca's father James Holt.[5] In 1675, James married Hannah Allen, the daughter of a neighboring farmer, and over the next decade and a half the couple produced seven children, including Rebecca in 1688.[6] When Rebecca was two years old, however, tragedy struck her family's household—a tragedy that helped to precipitate Andover's 1692 witchcraft crisis.

Rebecca's mother, Hannah (Allen) Holt, was one of four daughters born to Andover farmer Andrew Allen, a Scottish immigrant. Two of the Allen daughters married well: Hannah and her older sister, Sarah, both of whom wed sons of Nicholas Holt. But the other two daughters were less fortunate in their choice of spouses. In 1665, Mary Allen married a shadowy practitioner of folk medicine and magical healing, "Doctor" Roger Toothaker, a man with little property who periodically abandoned his wife and children; a decade later Martha Allen married Thomas Carrier, "a young Welsh servant with hardly any resources," "after naming him the father of her first child." Martha and her husband spent the next fifteen years in neighboring Billerica and possibly other Massachusetts Bay towns before arriving in Andover in 1689 or 1690 "destitute and with four children." They also returned carrying smallpox, an epidemic of which broke out in the town in late 1690 claiming the lives of as many as thirteen Andover residents, including Rebecca's 40-year-old father, James Holt, and infant brother, James Jr.; her maternal grandfather; her two Allen family uncles; and at least one Holt cousin.[7]

Even before the smallpox calamity, Martha (Allen) Carrier had provoked hostility wherever she lived. By all accounts a plain, outspoken, sharp-tongued woman whose "lack of deference for her more prosperous neighbors" regularly embroiled her in acrimonious disputes, she was described by those who clashed with her as "angry, envious, and malicious." Consequently, in early 1692, when Salem's witchcraft hysteria began to spill over into Andover, she immediately fell victim to the predictable accusations: that she was "a most dreadful witch" who was using supernatural powers to "grievously torment" and torture her enemies; that she had recruited and baptized numerous fellow witches "in the devil's service" and had received Satan's assurance that she would be "a Queen in hell" as a reward; that she had already "killed 13 at Andover," etc. Jailed in Salem in May, she was tried, convicted (largely on the basis of spectral evidence), and hanged in August, defiantly maintaining her innocence to the end.[8]

Meanwhile, Rebecca's other less-fortunate aunt, Mary (Allen) Toothaker, and her family had also fallen victim to the witchcraft panic. In mid-May, Roger Toothaker was accused and jailed. He had apparently aroused suspicion by boasting of his expertise in the black arts of "counter-magic" and by claiming that under his instructions one of his daughters had used those practices to kill a witch who was tormenting a fellow colonist, telling an acquaintance that "his s[ai]d Daughter gott some of the afflicted persons Urine and put it into an Earthen pott and stopt s[ai]d pott very Close and putt s[ai]d pott [in] a hott oven and stopt up s[ai]d oven and the next morning s[ai]d [witch] was Dead." Toothaker died in jail in June before coming to trial. A month later, his widow, Mary, and a married daughter, Martha (Toothaker) Emerson, were charged with witchcraft and quickly confessed in a desperate effort to save their lives. Eventually, the two women avoided conviction when Massachusetts Bay authorities began to lose their fervor for witchcraft prosecutions in the latter months of 1692. Three years later, Mary was killed in an Indian attack on Billerica.[9]

A second tragic upheaval in Rebecca Holt's childhood occurred in 1698 when her mother died of unknown causes at age 45, leaving 10-year-old Rebecca and each of her three youngest siblings to be raised by different court-approved guardians from the surrounding community. Rebecca was placed in the care of Deacon John Abbott and his wife, Sarah, prosperous farmers with eight children of their own,[10] and presumably remained with them until she reached adulthood and married Thomas Grow in 1710.

Inexpensive farmland was still relatively abundant in Andover at the time of Thomas and Rebecca's marriage. With nearly 60 square miles (more than 38,000 acres) of territory, the town was one of the largest in Essex County, three times the size of Ipswich. As in Ipswich, the first settlers had laid out residential house lots in a central village along with planting fields in the outlying countryside. And again as in Ipswich, commonage rights, including shares in future divisions of the town's enormous public domain, were restricted to proprietors. Within two decades of the settlement's founding in 1646, those proprietors—forty to fifty in number—had voted themselves four major distributions of public land, accumulating personal estates that averaged nearly 200 acres each in the process.

During the second half of the seventeenth century, most of Andover's proprietors, Nicholas Holt among them, left their central-village house lots and took up residence on remote farms carved out of their extensive land grants. Meanwhile, the town's population was growing at a slow pace and land values remained low—in part because Andover was the target of Indian attacks well into the 1690s. As late as 1702, the population numbered only about 900 inhabitants, 102 of whom were proprietors; and land was so cheap—"generally less than £2 per acre," with large tracts of "unbroken" wilderness still selling for as little as 10 shillings an acre—that a newcomer could purchase a 20-acre parcel of the town's public domain on easy credit for a nominal payment of two or three bushels of corn or wheat a year.[11] For a young, newly married maltster seeking a promising agricultural setting in which to establish himself, Andover offered attractive possibilities.

Initially, Thomas and Rebecca lived with Holt relatives.[12] Following a brief and unexplained interlude in neighboring Lynn in 1714 and early 1715[13] (perhaps spent accumulating capital), they returned to Andover and began to acquire land. In April 1715, "Thomas Grow of Lyn" purchased 8 acres—mostly "upland and swamp" with a small, one-and-a-half story house (or "tenement")—for £62 from Rebecca's cousin Thomas Carrier Jr., Martha Carrier's youngest son (who, as a 10-year-old boy in 1692, had testified that his mother "taught him witchcraft" and forced him to sign the Devil's book).[14] A month later, "Thomas Grow of Andover" bought 4 acres from Thomas Carrier Sr., Martha's widower and Rebecca's uncle, for £32. Together with a parcel that had already come to the couple as part of Rebecca's marriage dowry, these acquisitions evidently became the nucleus of their first homestead,[15] which was located in the far south of Andover near the boundary line with Reading (the next town to the south), probably about 2 miles west-southwest of a cluster of Holt family farms on Holt Hill. (The Grow farmstead may have been located near the east side of the present-day intersection of Country Road and Old Boston Road, possibly in the vicinity of Cottage Road.)[16] Thomas subsequently purchased 2.5 acres of "meadow or mowing land" in 1719 (for £36 s10) and another 6.75-acre parcel in 1726 (for £95).[17] In addition, the properties that he had acquired from his Carrier in-laws in 1715 came with "rights in ye Share in the Common Land of Andover" attached, making him eligible for future divisions of the town's remaining public land—divisions that added another 16-plus acres to his holdings between 1716 and 1722 (including a 1.6-acre parcel on the "Reading Line," three-fourths of an acre "east of Holt Hill," and at least two woodlots).[18] By the late 1720s, Thomas' aggregate land acquisitions totaled about 40 acres—modest holdings in land-rich Andover but apparently sufficient to meet a maltster's specialized agricultural needs.

Andover was a community of family farmers. Because they could seldom afford to hire agricultural workers, who earned about 6 shillings a day in wages, most New England farmers instead relied on their own families for labor. Husbands and wives worked from dawn to dusk six days a week, year in and year out, to make their landholdings productive. They also depended heavily on the labor of their children. By age 6 or 7, sons and daughters were already participating in farm work, tending domestic animals, gardening, and helping with a variety of simple household tasks. Young boys herded livestock, mucked out barn stalls, picked fruit, helped sheave grain at harvest time, and gleaned the fields afterwards. By the time they reached puberty, boys were being incorporated into all of the farm's basic production operations (manuring, plowing, harrowing, sowing, weeding, scything, threshing, etc.) under their father's tutelage. By age 16, they were supplying much of the farm's heavy labor without supervision. Most remained at home working as members of the family labor force well into their twenties. Daughters, for their part, were also given ever-increasing responsibilities as they matured, assisting their mother with the daily and weekly tasks (fire tending, food preparation, washing, milking, churning, spinning yarn, weaving cloth, sewing and mending clothes, etc.) and seasonal activities (curing meat, drying fruit and herbs, making cheese, soap, and candles, etc.) that kept the family clothed and fed and the household running effectively. By adolescence, daughters were also actively involved in the care of their younger siblings, as their mother delivered a new child every twenty to thirty months over a twenty-year period. Large numbers of children, in short, were indispensable to the successful operation of family farms.[19]

Like their counterparts everywhere in rural New England, Andover's farm families practiced a "subsistence-plus" form of agriculture. Living in relative isolation far removed from external markets, and lacking the farm equipment, transportation facilities, and labor force necessary for large-scale commercial agriculture, most early eighteenth-century farmers were content to produce mainly for their own households. The typical farmer cultivated enough cropland (10 to 12 acres on average) and raised enough livestock (a few cows and pigs along with a dozen or so sheep) to meet his family's food needs; the flax that he grew and the wool that he sheared provided the raw material for homespun clothing; and the farm's woodlots supplied fuel and building materials.

No family farm, however, was completely self-sufficient. It invariably required goods and services that it could not provide from its own internal resources. The farmer needed plows and scythes, wagons and carts, yokes and harnesses, and a long list of other specialized agricultural equipment—while his wife could not function without kitchen and fireplace implements (pots, skillets, skimmers, trammels, trivets, peels, etc.), and cooking ingredients (salt, sugar, molasses, spices) that could only be obtained from outside sources. The household required furniture, lighting devices, and earthenware ceramics, along with muskets and pistols for protection, while the family periodically needed the services of the local doctor, shoemaker, blacksmith, miller, cooper, and wheelwright.

Nor were New England farm families immune from cravings for nonessential "luxury" goods. The husband might hanker for a dram of rum or a pipe of tobacco after a long day in the fields, while his wife likely yearned for the pewter tableware and fine imported fabrics that were becoming increasingly commonplace in "respectable" rural households. Each year, the family also had to generate enough extra resources to pay its taxes and minister's rates. And when their children reached adulthood, the parents needed to find the additional wherewithal to settle their sons on farmland of their own and provide marriage dowries for their daughters.

To pay for all of these necessities, indulgences, and obligations, New England farm families routinely produced small surpluses of agricultural goods—meat, grain, dairy products, textiles, etc.—and used them as mediums of exchange in their local economy. They bartered their surpluses for those of their neighbors. They obtained manufactured products and imported goods—metal wares, glassware, English textiles, sugar and other cooking ingredients—at the local general store, usually on credit, and paid for them at the end of the year with surplus produce, delivering previously agreed-upon quantities of corn, flaxseed, butter, or other forms of "country pay" to the storekeeper to settle their accounts. They likewise paid for doctors' visits and the services of local artisans with farm produce. And occasionally they might sell surplus commodities to a peddler or drover, or to the representative of an out-of-town merchant in exchange for trade goods or cash.

Most farm families also utilized their own labor power as a medium of exchange. They paid for goods and services, balanced their accounts, and sometimes met their tax obligations by performing work for those to whom they owed money. Husbands plowed fields, transported goods, and built stone walls for their trading partners and creditors; wives provided midwife and spinning services; parents hired out their teenage sons and daughters to work without wages in the fields and households of townspeople to whom they were in debt. In Andover, Rebecca's uncle Henry Holt sent his sons to cultivate the farmland of the local minister, Reverend Thomas Barnard, as a way of paying the family's annual minister's rate.[20] We know almost nothing about Thomas and Rebecca Grow's agricultural practices, but based on the prevailing patterns of New England family farming, it seems probable that they produced primarily for their own subsistence and relied on non-monetary transactions involving surplus goods and labor to meet their additional needs.

Thomas and Rebecca shared many characteristics in common with other Andover farm couples of their generation. At the time of their marriage, Thomas was 26 years old and Rebecca was 22—the average ages at which young men and women of that period wed.[21] They produced six children during their married life—the average number of offspring for Andover couples marrying in 1710.[22] When their final child was born in 1727, they were 42 and 38 respectively—the precise average ages at which New England couples of the early eighteenth century concluded reproduction.[23] They were also typical with regard to literacy: Thomas, like 80 percent of New England's rural males during this period, was able to write his full signature on legal documents; Rebecca, like 80 percent of New England women at the time, was unable to sign her name, employing a mark ("R") instead.[24] On the other hand, the couple was exceptional in one statistical category: infant mortality. All six of their children lived to adulthood, a remarkable achievement during a period when more than 25 percent of Andover children died before age 10.[25]

Children of Thomas[2] and Rebecca (Holt) Grow, all born in Andover, MA:

    i.   Rebecca, b. 21 April 1712; d. 30 Jan. 1762, Pomfret, CT; m. 1734 at Pomfret, Stephen Ingalls.

    ii.   Thomas[3], b. 7 Nov. 1714; d. 10 Aug. 1806, Guilford, VT; m. (1) 1738, Susanna Eaton; m. (2) 1786, Martha Winter.

    iii.   Joseph, b. 16 Oct. 1717; d. 3 May 1782, Newbury, VT; m. 1742 at Pomfret, Abigail Dana.

    iv.   Ruth, b. 2 Aug. 1720; living in Woodstock, CT, 1757, date/place death unk.; m. 1740, Joseph Williams.

    v.   Hannah, b. 8 Nov. 1723; d. 29 July 1765, Windham, CT; m. 1752 at Pomfret, Ephraim Barker.

    vi.   James, b. 25 Oct. 1727; d. 29 Oct. 1799, Norwich, VT; m. 1754 at Pomfret, Anne Adams.

SOURCES: *Vital Records of Andover, Massachusetts, to the End of the Year 1849*, 2 vols. (Topsfield, MA: Topsfield Historical Society, 1911–1912), 1:185; George W. Davis, comp., *John Grow of Ipswich/John (Groo) Grow of Oxford* (Washington, D.C.: privately printed by the Carnahan Press, 1913), 19, 29–31; Hannah Grow death data from *Connecticut Vital Records to 1870 (The Barbour Collection)*, online database at AmericanAncestors.org, citing Windham Vital Records, 2:86.

Their farmstead was perhaps 10 to 15 acres in size[26] with additional small parcels scattered throughout the surrounding countryside. Like most Andover farmers, Thomas probably grew corn, rye, and flax. But his "cash crop"—his specialized surplus crop—was undoubtedly barley, which he processed into malt in his "malt house," located directly across the road from the family's dwelling house.[27]

Converting barley into malt was a weeklong process. If Thomas was a conventional maltster, he first placed a portion of his grain in a large vat of water and heated it at carefully controlled temperatures for two or three days until it began to germinate. The sprouted grain was then poured out onto a "malting floor" where it was turned and raked for a day or two to assure uniform development. Then, when the sprouted seedlings were approximately the length of the grain husks, they were shoveled into the malt house's drying kiln and slowly roasted for one-and-a-half to two days, bringing their growth to a stop at the precise point when their sugar content was at its peak. Once dried, the sprouted grain was ground into a crunchy meal, placed in baskets or sacks, and delivered to its consumers, who cooked the ground malt into a "mash" and mixed it with water, yeast, and locally grown hops to produce beer.[28]

Several consumer markets were available for Thomas' malt. One was the neighboring population of south Andover and the adjacent border areas of Reading and Billerica. From the earliest days of colonization, beer had been a staple of the New England diet. "Small beer," a common variety low in alcoholic content and widely regarded as both "wholesome" and nutritious, was consumed daily at mealtimes by men, women, and children alike. Most families brewed a batch every week or two for household consumption, thereby creating a steady demand for malt, two pounds of which were needed to brew five gallons of beer. And because malt making was a temperature- and time-sensitive process that required "a great deal of skill and experience," most households opted to obtain their malt from a local maltster. Even "farmers who made beer from their own barley usually took their grain to a maltster" for processing, according to beer historian Sanborn Connor Brown. In addition to the individual households of the surrounding area, the taverns and inns of Andover and neighboring communities also regularly brewed beer—albeit much stronger varieties—to serve to their patrons, providing another stable market for malt. And commercial "brew houses" in the coastal towns to the east offered a third potential market for Thomas' malt. Ipswich brewers and merchants traditionally purchased large quantities of malt; and if Thomas was sufficiently ambitious or desperate, he could have transported his malt to Salem, where the local brewing houses conducted a high-volume business provisioning the hundreds of ships that arrived in the port each year.[29]

Because barley grain could be stored for an extended period of time, Thomas was able to practice his craft year round. By the mid-1720s, he was undoubtedly being assisted by his eldest son, Thomas[3].[30]

As Thomas and Rebecca's oldest children neared adulthood, farm families throughout New England were facing a fundamental crisis. Over time, the large numbers of children needed to make family farming economically viable created a population explosion that was rapidly depleting available land resources. In most families, sons willingly worked in partnership with their father and brothers to make the family's agricultural enterprise productive in the expectation that they would eventually receive a share of the property, through gift or inheritance, and become independent farmers in their own right; while most fathers, for their part, considered it a primary parental responsibility to settle their adult sons on farms of their own. Throughout the seventeenth century, liberal allotments of common land had provided most farming families with substantial reserves of "unimproved" wilderness that, when cleared, could accommodate the next generation's need for farmland. By the eighteenth century, however, nearly all of New England's common lands had been distributed and most family estates had been subdivided multiple times among two or three generations of sons. As a consequence, rural fathers were finding it increasingly difficult to provide each son with the minimum 40-acre parcel considered necessary for subsistence-level farming. To compound the problem, the growing land shortage was pushing the price of farmland beyond the reach of many families, making it all but impossible for most fathers to purchase the additional acreage that would provide independent landholdings for their sons. By the 1720s, the numerous male offspring needed for successful family farming were ironically threatening to undermine family farming as a way of life, as their sheer numbers overwhelmed the amount of affordable farmland available.[31]

The problem became particularly acute in Andover. During the late seventeenth and early eighteenth centuries, the town experienced a period of "remarkable demographic growth"—the result of robust natural increase and an influx of new settlers—that increased its population from approximately 700 in the mid-1690s to 1,425 by 1730. Accompanying the growth in population was an intensified demand for land, resulting in a sharp rise in land values. The average price of land in the town increased from £2 per acre in the first decade of the eighteenth century, to £4 per acre between 1710 and 1720, to £8 per acre in the 1720s, with an acre of prime "upland" or meadow selling for as much as £12 during the latter decade.

By 1730, Andover was overcrowded and running out of farmland.[32] Local fathers responded by adopting new strategies to meet their sons' need for land. The traditional mechanism of distributing family property—"partible inheritance," in which existing estates were divided up relatively co-equally among the family's sons at or near the time of the father's death—was no longer sustainable, because any further subdivisions would result in parcels too small to support viable farming operations. Instead, many Andover fathers turned to a system of "primogeniture," in which the family's eldest son inherited the entire estate and younger sons were aided in moving to frontier areas where inexpensive land was readily available. Other fathers followed an alternative strategy, opting to move their entire family to the frontier—selling their high-priced landholdings in Andover and using the proceeds to purchase a larger quantity of cheaper land in a newly settled region in order to provide farms for their sons.[33]

It was this latter strategy that Thomas Grow adopted. In the winter of 1731–1732, he uprooted his family from Andover and migrated 100 miles southwest to the recently opened agricultural frontier of northeastern Connecticut's Windham County.

In moving to the Connecticut frontier, the Grows were by no means plunging blindly into an unknown wilderness. They relocated as part of a well-established "chain migration" of Andover residents who had been departing for the newly incorporated farming communities of northeastern Connecticut since the late 1690s. A substantial portion of the migrants were third-generation Holts and other members of Thomas and Rebecca's extended family, while others— including Chandlers, Abbotts, Ingalls, Farnums, and Osgoods—were from neighboring families. In all, no fewer than twenty-five Andover families settled in the three Windham County towns of Pomfret, Windham, and Ashford. By the time Thomas and his family set out for the county, one of Rebecca's uncles and at least ten of her cousins already lived there. That some of those relatives played instrumental roles in facilitating Thomas and Rebecca's migration seems almost certain. Most of them continued to maintain close connections to their families back in Andover after moving to Connecticut—with several Holt males returning to Andover to obtain wives—and they undoubtedly provided Thomas with valuable information about the quality and availability of Windham County farmland, along with guidance about how to relocate there. According to historian Philip Greven, there is "no doubt" that Thomas Grow moved to the Connecticut frontier "because of his kinship ties with the Holts."[34]

But other factors were also involved in the decision to emigrate. The recent deaths of Thomas' father and mother in Ipswich in 1727–1728 had eliminated any obligations or ties to aging parents that might have kept him in Andover. In addition, if his father was born in England and came to Massachusetts Bay in his youth, frontier migration may have been an established pattern in the Grow family. But the key factor in Thomas' decision making was probably an economic one: the opportunity that migration afforded him to "sell high and buy low"—to liquidate his Andover landholdings in a highly inflated real estate market and plow the windfall profits into significantly larger amounts of property on the Connecticut frontier, where abundant wilderness land was available "for very little money."

The reverse side of opportunity was, of course, necessity. With three sons (one of whom, 17-year-old Thomas[3], was nearing maturity) and insufficient land in Andover on which to settle them, Thomas' decision to emigrate was likely driven by a growing concern that if he did not seize the opportunity and accept the risks and hardships of pioneering in Connecticut, he would not be able to fulfill his parental responsibilities to his sons.[35]

Accordingly, in early 1731, he began selling off his properties in Andover to raise capital for the move. The only transaction for which a record has been found was the March 1731 sale of a 4-acre parcel to John Carlton Jr. for £70, or more than £17 an acre.[36] It also appears that Thomas may have sold the family's house lot (for an unknown sum) to Andrew Allen, one of Rebecca's cousins on her mother's side.[37] Simultaneously, he began purchasing much larger properties in Pomfret, Connecticut: over 100 acres of unimproved land in February 1731 for £230, or a little over £2 an acre, and another 100 "improved" acres with a dwelling house for £410, or about £4 per acre, the following December.[38] All told, he apparently managed to parlay his estimated holdings of 40 acres in Andover into more than 200 acres in Connecticut.

With land and housing acquired, the family—consisting of 47-year-old Thomas, his 43-year-old wife, and six children ranging in age from 19 to 4—set out on the ten-day journey to Windham County. Most New England pioneers migrated during the winter, stocked with provisions from the previous season's harvest and prior to the start of planting time on their new frontier farms.

Despite the freezing temperatures and extreme discomfort, winter was also the easiest season to transport the family's heavy goods, which could be hauled over ice and snow on ox-drawn sleds.[39]

Like most emigrants from Andover to Connecticut, the Grows probably headed south through Reading, picking up the "Mendon Way" outside of Boston and continuing southwest through Medfield and Mendon onto the "Old Connecticut Path," which passed through Webster and Dudley before entering present-day Connecticut in what is now the Fabyan district of Grosvenor Dale, across a ford at the Quinebaug River, and continuing southwest to Woodstock, where they would have turned south on a small dirt road (present-day State Route 169) and traveled the final 4 miles to their new home in Pomfret.[40] There they, and the next two generations of the family, would prosper.

Pomfret was a 42-square-mile tract of rolling hills and fertile meadows that had been purchased from the Nipmuck Indians in the mid-1680s. Initially known as the "Mashamoquet Purchase" for the fast-flowing Mashamoquet Brook that served as the dividing line between its northern and southern portions, the tract remained largely unoccupied until the mid-1690s. Then, after the northern section's 15,100 acres had been surveyed and sold to a handful of proprietors and land speculators, settlers began moving in. Their farms were initially clustered around Prospect Hill (today's Pomfret Center), a mile-long elevation in the tract's northeastern quadrant.[41]

One early settler was Philemon Chandler, a 25-year-old Andover emigrant who in 1696 purchased for a mere £32 more than 550 acres of meadowland and woods, including nearly 200 acres along Wappaquians Brook at the southern foot of Prospect Hill on the road leading south from Woodstock. Thirty-five years later, in December 1731, Chandler sold Thomas Grow a portion of that property—the 100 acres and dwelling house that became the Grow family farm. Partially "bounded on [the] South [by] Wappaquians Brook," and with boundary markers that included a "heap of stones," an "ash tree," "a white oak tree," and "a black oak tree," it was probably located in the vicinity of present-day 87 Quaker Road (at the northwestern corner of the intersection of Quaker Road and State Route 169 [Pomfret Street]).[42]

As of 1713, when the Mashamoquet Purchase was granted township status and renamed Pomfret, only its northern portion had been settled, most of the 10,000 acres south and west of Mashamoquet Brook having been held in reserve as "undivided and uncultivated" common land. Six years later, however, in 1719, that land was also transferred, in equal shares, to the original Mashamoquet proprietors or their heirs, who immediately began selling off parcels to newly arriving settlers.[43] Among the ensuing land transactions was Thomas Grow's February 1731 purchase of 100-plus acres from Thomas Goodell Jr. (the son of an original proprietor) in the extreme southwestern corner of Pomfret on the

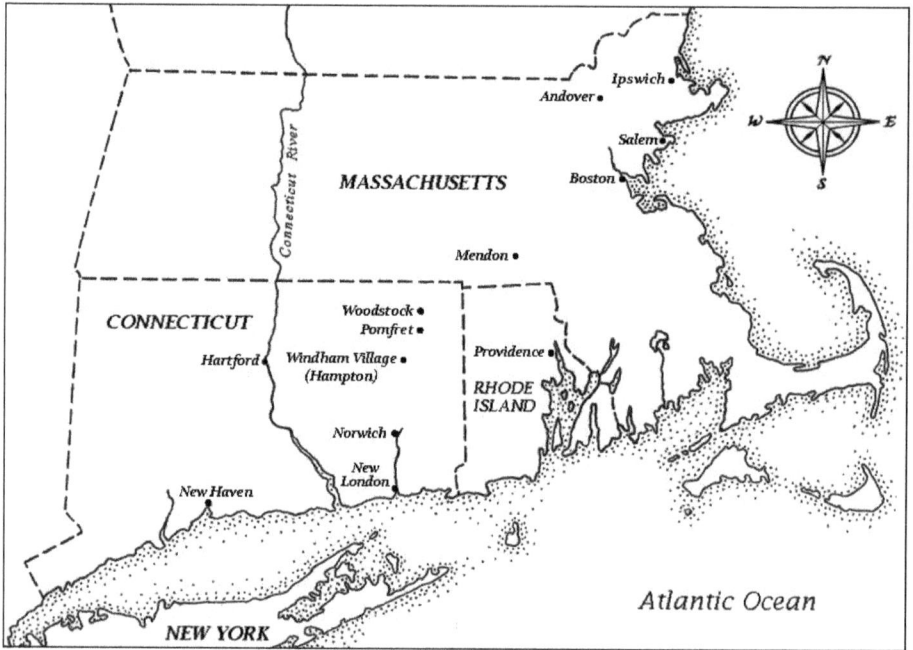

The New England world of Thomas and Rebecca Grow. Map by Margaret McWethy.

boundary line with Windham Village (present-day Hampton), a neighboring settlement to the south. A number of former Andover residents had already settled in that area, including several members of the Ingalls family, and, across the border in Windham Village, no fewer than nine of Rebecca Grow's Holt family cousins.[44]

By the time the Grows arrived, Pomfret was a "flourishing and prosperous" agricultural community of 129 landowners, with a Congregational church, a local militia unit, one or more schools, a sawmill, a gristmill, and at least four taverns.[45] The population consisted almost entirely of farm families living on large, isolated estates. Like their Andover counterparts, Pomfret farmers engaged in diversified agriculture, growing grain crops and raising livestock. Because the township's rocky soil proved better suited to grazing than to tillage, however, cattle raising and dairy production soon surpassed grain farming as the basis of the local economy.[46]

Pomfret's settlers were also subsistence-plus farmers, producing mainly for themselves but also bartering with their neighbors and trading surplus farm commodities for store goods.[47] Beginning in the 1720s, improvements in transportation increased their access to outside markets, creating new outlets for their surplus products. In 1721, a newly completed road from Pomfret to Providence, Rhode Island, 36 miles to the east, opened a profitable trading relationship with that port city's merchants, who were eager buyers of Pomfret's meat and dairy products.[48] Ten years later, the Pomfret section of the "King's Highway" was extended southward through the town's recently opened southwestern district to Windham Village, providing a direct route to Windham County's principal market town, Windham Center, whose merchants also actively purchased Pomfret's agricultural surpluses.[49] (A portion of the King's Highway extension ran through the middle of Thomas' newly acquired 100-acre parcel on the Windham line and was facilitated in part by a permanent right-of-way that he gave the town in September 1731.[50]) By the 1730s, Pomfret's expanding transportation arteries were enabling many local farmers to earn a cash income from the sale of their surplus commodities in outside markets—income that they usually invested in purchases of additional land.[51]

Thomas Grow apparently engaged in both dairy farming and malt production after settling in Pomfret. Local land records identify him variously as a "yeoman," a "husbandman," and a "maltster,"[52] while a 1760s deed to the family homestead lists "barns" and a "malt house" among the property's outbuildings.[53] Evidence from another source—a 1740s account book from a Pomfret-area general store—suggests that Thomas generated a cash income from his malting operations, and that Rebecca, like other Pomfret farmwives, contributed to the family income by making butter, cheese, and perhaps clothing for trade in the local economy. Between 1740 and 1745, according to the account book's ledgers, the Grows purchased a variety of items on credit—a farmer's almanac, three knives, a sickle, a pair of shears, nails, "wyer," imported fabrics, ribbon, thread, buttons, a "cheese tub," and a broom—and settled their account with various forms of payment, including cash, a bushel and a half of "barley malt," a "firkin [of] butter," and three cheeses.[54] Eventually, Thomas was able to accumulate enough capital to acquire a third large parcel of land: in 1747, he purchased 100 acres in the northwestern quadrant of Pomfret from Nathaniel Sessions, a town selectman and tavern keeper, for £430.[55]

For Thomas[2] Grow and his family, as for so many early American pioneers, migration to the frontier brought social as well as economic gains. Social status in rural New England was largely determined by wealth, and specifically by the amount of property an individual owned. Thomas had been born and raised in a lower-middle-class family in Ipswich, a socially stratified town with a highly unequal pattern of land distribution (in which eight men controlled nearly 50 percent of the land and the bottom half of the population owned less than 6 percent). Both Andover and Pomfret, by contrast, had relatively equalitarian social structures typical of frontier farming communities, with the top 10 percent of the inhabitants owning a mere 20 to 25 percent of the taxable wealth while the bottom half owned a third or more.[56]

The original 1731 deed in which Thomas Grow transferred to the Town of Pomfret a quarter-mile-long, 22-yard-wide strip of land through his 100-acre property in the town's southwestern corner for an extension of the King's Highway (present-day State Route 97) to Windham, signed by Thomas in his own hand. (Pomfret Town Records: Highway Documents, 1686–1893, Town Hall, Pomfret, CT, leaf 39) (Photograph by the author.)

Detail.

By the time Thomas established himself in Andover, however, population growth and rising land prices were beginning to make upward social mobility increasingly difficult. Consequently, over the course of nearly two decades in the town, he and his family consistently occupied a low position in local society, as reflected in their annual tax assessments. In 1717, Thomas' landholdings and other taxable assets placed him 176th among Andover's 235 taxpayers, situating him in the bottom quarter of the town's social structure. Twelve years later, his taxable wealth ranked 187th out of 272 taxpayers, indicating that he was still in the lower third of Andover society on the eve of his departure for Pomfret.[57]

The move to Pomfret produced rapid and dramatic improvements. Thomas' purchase of two 100-acre parcels of land in the town in 1731 immediately elevated him into the top 35 percent of Pomfret's taxpayers (46th out of 129).[58] Sixteen years later, after adding another 100 acres to his landholdings, his taxable wealth placed him in the top 12 percent of the town's tax list (27th out of 216). And by 1748, at age 64, he was ranked in the top 8 percent (19th out of 233), despite the fact that he had already begun the process of transferring land to his sons.[59] By the late 1740s, Thomas' 300 acres of land placed him in the upper fifth of all farmers in colonial Connecticut, and his estimated net worth of more than £900 ranked him in the top 11 percent of the colony's male inhabitants.[60] The Grow family's experience in moving to the Connecticut frontier was not one of the classic "rags-to-riches" success stories of frontier migration—they hardly lived in poverty in Andover, after all—but the resulting record of their immediate upward mobility in Pomfret is striking nonetheless.

A high tax-list ranking did not mean that Thomas and Rebecca were members of an upper-class Pomfret elite, however. It is difficult, in fact, to identify a distinct upper class, or class hierarchies of any sort, in the town during the first several decades of its existence. No men of conspicuously great wealth were found among the inhabitants, nor can a large lower class of landless workers or tenant farmers be discerned. Aside from a few African American and Indian slaves owned by the town minister and another affluent family or two, the overwhelming majority of Pomfret's laborers were the sons of local families working for their fathers on their home farms. Instead, the population consisted almost entirely of middling-level yeoman farmers of "roughly equal means." So equitable was the distribution of wealth in the town that the bottom tiers of the annual tax list were filled not by poor or marginalized residents but by the young adult sons of local farmers—in effect, a younger generation of middle-class farmers in the early stages of establishing viable farms of their own. Consequently, the town's social structure was largely unstratified, and although an informal status hierarchy inevitably developed, the social distance among local families remained relatively small.[61] In such a society, the Grows' relative prosperity, as measured by their landholdings and taxable wealth, would have earned them respect but not social deference.

Nor did a high tax ranking necessarily signify that the family enjoyed an affluent standard of living. Pomfret farm families of the early eighteenth century lived a plain and simple lifestyle. Their houses were small, sparsely furnished capes and saltboxes, their furniture was "rude and scanty," and their food and clothing "mainly of home production." The larger landowners, those like Thomas Grow who had accumulated more than 200 acres of land, lived "comfortably but frugally," purchasing enough to provide their families with essentially a middle-class standard of living, but indulging in neither luxury nor elegance. Their wealth was concentrated in their land, and for most families land had a two-fold value: it supplied their basic needs, and it provided their sons with an adequate start in life, thus safeguarding the family line into the next generation. Consequently, most of the profits extracted from the family's land were spent on farm improvements and additional land acquisitions rather than on material goods or the trappings of affluence.[62] In an exhaustive study of eighteenth-century Connecticut probate inventories, historian Jackson Turner Main found that although farmers with 120 or more acres of land had nearly eight times as much property as the colony's smallest landowners, the value of their consumption goods was only twice as high. The reason, Main concludes, is that the prosperous larger landowners preferred to invest their profits in land and farm equipment "rather than in comfort."[63]

Because Thomas left neither an estate inventory nor a will at the time of his death, we know almost nothing of a specific nature about the Grows' standard of living. Nevertheless, the record of their purchases at a local general store during the 1740s offers at least a minuscule glimpse into their consumption habits. Between 1741 and 1745, Rebecca and her daughters purchased some £9 worth of fabrics and other sewing materials from the storekeeper, including 41 yards of "brocaded Persian," 12 yards each of "crape" and "red wool," 7 yards of "muzlin," at least 4 yards of imported silk, and 2.5 yards of "garlick." The quality of the fabrics purchased ranged from expensive to cheap. Crape was a high-grade textured silk and muzlin was a fine cotton imported from India, while red wool was an inexpensive, scarlet-dyed English broadcloth, and garlick (or "garlet") was a cheap linen commonly imported from Silesia. The quantities purchased indicate that the fabrics were probably used to meet the family's domestic clothing needs rather than to make surplus apparel for trade in the local exchange economy. Seven yards of muzlin, for example, were enough to make a few shirts or chemises; 12 yards of crape would have made one gown; 12 yards of red wool, a great coat or a blanket or two; and 2.5 yards of garlick, a man's shirt or a woman's work smock. Laura Johnson, an authority on colonial New England textiles, suggests that, taken together, the family's fabric purchases are essentially what one would have expected to find in a prosperous rural-middle-class family that was seeking to present "a genteel face to the world." On the other hand, the Grows' overall expenditures at the general store between 1740 and 1745 totaled approximately £16, while those of Pomfret's most prominent families (Grosvenors, Sabins, and Sessions) ranged from £100 to over £180, and those of the Grows' closest peers among the town's respectable middling farmers (Ingalls, Chandlers, Paines) averaged about £64—an indication that the family's level of material consumption might have been considerably lower than that of its neighbors, perhaps owing to the Grows' relatively greater frugality.[64]

Although economic factors were the primary determinants of social status in Pomfret, they were not the only criteria by which social standing in the community was measured. Each family's level of participation in the town's religious, civic, and military affairs also helped determine its position in the local status order.

In the religious sphere, the most prestigious positions were held by the minister and deacons of the Congregational church, along with their wives; next came the church's formal members, followed by town residents who regularly attended services but had not formally joined; and at the bottom were a handful of local ne'er-do-wells—blasphemers, adulterers, drunkards, etc.—who had been expelled from the church for their sacrilegious or immoral behavior.

In civic affairs, the positions of highest status were held by the leading office-holders in the local government: the moderator of the annual town meeting, the local selectmen, the town clerk, the treasurer, and Pomfret's representative to the colonial legislature in Hartford; below them were the community's eligible voters, consisting of every adult male landowner who owned at least 50 shillings of tax-assessed property; while a few disenfranchised small landowners and slaves made up the bottom tier of the civic order.

Military affairs were headed by the officers of the local militia, while young men from "good families" filled the militia's general ranks, followed, in terms of social prestige, by a few lowly conscripts who served as common soldiers in the colonial army regiments that were assembled during New England's occasional military emergencies. Pomfret might not have had a class-stratified society, but a finely graded and multifaceted status hierarchy existed all the same—one that was based on distinctions of wealth and property, religious piety, moral virtue, and civic-military service.[65]

Within that social world, the Grows seem to have occupied a respectable position, but not a prominent one. They were among Pomfret's upper tier of landowners, and they were active in the town's Congregational church (located a few hundred yards up Prospect Hill north of the family's farm). But there is no evidence that Thomas played any significant leadership role in the church, or that he served in any capacity in the local militia. He was, however, elected to two mid-level offices in the town government when he was in his fifties and sixties—offices of moderate responsibility that were usually filled by men of mature judgment. In 1736–1737, he served one term as the town's "Grand Jury man" on the Windham County Court in Windham, during which he and eleven fellow grand jurors from around the county helped to adjudicate more than 100 cases, most of them involving debt or land disputes, along with several fornication and "lascivious carriage" prosecutions, and one "cruelty" case involving a master who had beaten his servant. A few years later, in 1744, he served as one of Pomfret's four "listers," local officials who compiled lists of each town resident's assets—real estate, livestock, household goods, etc.—in order to determine the town's tax assessments for the year.

As Thomas' sons reached maturity, they also performed their share of public service, serving in various lesser offices typically held by younger men in the community. His eldest son, Thomas[3], served multiple terms as one of the town's "surveyors of highways" (each of whom supervised road maintenance in his neighborhood, assembling work crews of able-bodied neighbors to make repairs when necessary), while Thomas' younger sons, Joseph and James, were elected to single terms as town "haywards"—low-level functionaries who caught stray livestock and herded them to the town pound. Sons Thomas[3] and Joseph also served single terms as grand jurors when they reached their late thirties. Overall, however, the family's record of office holding was neither exceptional nor indicative of high social status. Pomfret customarily spread the burden of office holding among all of its property-owning families, and most male residents were minor office holders at some point in their lives. In addition, although Thomas held two of the town's more responsible mid-level offices, he never served as a selectman, a town meeting moderator, or a leader of any other sort in the local government. Instead, his record essentially reflects the typical service activity of an ordinary Pomfret property owner fulfilling his normal share of civic obligations.[66] Nor was he among the thirty-five Pomfret-area men described as "warm friends of learning and literature" who in 1739 established the town's first library association.[67]

Because Thomas was able to accumulate an above-average amount of land in Pomfret, his fellow townsmen undoubtedly regarded him as an economically successful member of their community. On the Connecticut frontier, however, 300 acres of land did not necessarily imbue the landowner with social prominence, particularly when, as in the Grows' case, as much as two-thirds of that land was apparently left uncultivated and held in reserve for the family's sons. Nor, as Thomas' public service record shows, was he one of the town's civic leaders or "principal men." And although a trace of tentative evidence seems to indicate that his wife and daughters may have harbored aspirations of gentility in their choice of wearing apparel, there is nothing in the historical record to suggest that the family enjoyed a prominent position in local society. The most that can be said, perhaps, is that the Grows were an upper-middling-level farm family in a community of middling-level yeoman farmers.

Over the course of Thomas and Rebecca's lives, cultural values in New England gradually evolved. By the early eighteenth century, few New Englanders still adhered to the rigid moral standards of their seventeenth-century Puritan forebears. Economic growth, increased wealth, and a flood of imported English trade goods had generated a growing tension between the traditional Puritan values of self-denial and personal privation on the one hand and impulses of self-gratification on the other. And over time, the strict morality of early Puritanism inevitably gave way to more "worldly" attitudes and relatively more "permissive" and "relaxed" standards of behavior among the region's inhabitants.[68]

Evidence that eighteenth-century New Englanders were less "puritanical" than their forefathers was everywhere to be seen. Card playing, for example—a clear-cut moral transgression in the eyes of seventeenth-century Puritans—had become so widespread by the 1730s that decks of playing cards were appearing in the probate inventories of New England ministers.[69] A further indication of changing values was the complete abandonment of the old seventeenth-century "excess in apparel" laws that had prohibited lower- and middle-class colonists from wearing the fashionable finery favored by men and women of the "better sort"; by the 1740s, a new "culture of style" was spreading throughout New England—including, as Rebecca Grow's fabrics purchases attest, the frontier farming communities of Windham County, Connecticut—and silk clothing, corsets, jewelry, makeup, and parasols were widely in vogue.[70]

But perhaps no issue revealed the evolution in cultural values more emphatically than New Englanders' attitudes toward sex. In the seventeenth century, Puritan authorities severely punished couples that engaged in premarital or extramarital sexual relations, publicly whipping adulterers and imposing heavy fines on unmarried men and women found guilty of fornication. Even married couples were fined for fornication if the birth of a child too soon after their wedding provided proof that they had engaged in premarital intercourse. By the early eighteenth century, however, rates of premarital pregnancy had begun to rise sharply throughout New England, reaching a high of 30 percent of all pregnancies by mid-century (the highest of any period in American history prior to the twenty-first century); while the punishments meted out for premarital fornication were at the same time becoming milder, with average fines in Essex County, Massachusetts, decreasing from £2 early in the century to 5 shillings by the 1780s, and prosecutions of fornication cases steadily declined until they eventually disappeared completely from court dockets at the end of the century. The dramatic increase in premarital pregnancy rates, combined with an equally dramatic decline in fornication prosecutions, indicates that traditional controls on sexual behavior were breaking down in eighteenth-century New England, and that Puritan values had loosened their grip on the region's population.[71]

As New England courts gradually stopped enforcing laws against fornication, they in effect turned punishment responsibilities over to their local churches. The church continued to play a central role in the lives of most eighteenth-century New Englanders. Residents of every community were expected to attend Sunday services, and each household was taxed annually to pay the minister's salary and fund the church's operations. Ministers exercised enormous influence within their communities, essentially functioning as part of the local governing apparatus. By the early eighteenth century, they also were becoming a last bastion in the defense of New England's traditional Puritan values. Throughout the region, ministers used the power of their pulpits to rail against the increasingly lax moral standards of their parishioners, admonishing them for loving money and pleasure more than religion, rebuking them for their growing pursuit of the "gods" of land and trade, and punishing moral misconduct in their parishes by subjecting parishioners found guilty of sinful behavior to "public shaming" ceremonies in which the guilty party was forced to confess his or her sin before the entire congregation, on pain of excommunication.[72]

The minister of Thomas and Rebecca's South Parish church in Andover, Reverend Samuel Phillips, was in many respects a model of the imperious Puritan clergyman. Phillips served as south Andover's pastor from his ordination in 1711 until his death in 1771, governing the parish with the firm and heavy hand of a "benign tyrant." (When a traveler passing through Andover once asked him "Are you, sir, the parson who serves here?" he replied: "I am, sir, the parson who *rules* here!") "Stern and inflexible" in temperament, he maintained a close supervision—a "holy watchfulness"—over his flock, personally visiting each home in the parish at least once a year and seeing to it that every resident of the community was baptized. As head of his church's "examining committee," he was vigilant in rooting out immorality and quick to impose doses of humiliating "church discipline" that forced wayward parishioners to publicly confess their acts of sexual misconduct, drunkenness, "neglect of Publick worship," and other failings in front of the assembled congregation. Every Sunday morning, Phillips solemnly walked from his parsonage to the meetinghouse, "his Negro servant on his left and his wife, with her maid, on his right," in "a slow and stately procession[,] which the congregation rose to greet as it entered the church door." Regal and austere, "rigid and demanding," he was universally deferred to in the town and much feared, "especially [by] the young."[73]

Phillips' theology was as authoritarian as his leadership style. His spiritual role in the community, as he saw it, was to subordinate his parishioners' egos to the will of God in order to save their souls, and his sermons were regularly based on themes of obedience and submission. "True liberty," he declared in 1727, consists "in having the mind truly enlightened; and the power of sin and lust broken in the soul; and the appetites and passions under the government of right reason . . . and every thought brought into captivity, to the obedience of

The Reverend Samuel Phillips (1689–1771). A 1708 graduate of Harvard College, Phillips was ordained as the first minister of Andover's South Parish church in 1711 and held that post until his death. (Source: George Mooar, *Historical Manual of the South Church in Andover, Mass.* [Andover, 1859], frontispiece)

Christ." "Such truly walk in liberty . . . who have no will of their own, but resign themselves to the commanding and disposing will of the only wise God."[74]

Like most Puritan clergymen of his day, Phillips made a sharp distinction between parishioners who were full members of his church and those who regularly attended services without becoming formal members. To gain admission as full, communion-taking members of the church, parish residents were required to publicly describe a "personal conversion experience"—a transformative moment or episode in their lives when they consciously took Jesus Christ into their hearts and were "born again," thereby receiving God's "sanctifying Grace" and becoming eligible for eternal salvation.

The second tier of Phillips' congregation consisted of parishioners who had been granted "half-way status" in the church. Those individuals who had not experienced the "New Birth" required for full membership were still accepted into the church (albeit without voting rights or the privilege of taking the sacraments) when they "owned the Baptismal covenant"—publicly acknowledging the "One True and Living God to be our God"—and agreed to submit themselves to "the watch and care [*i.e.*, discipline] of the church . . . in anticipation of eventually receiving the grace they hoped for and sought."

Phillips exhorted his parishioners to seek New Birth and the "gift of grace" essential for salvation, but he grudgingly accepted those who merely "owned the covenant," while nevertheless warning them that God "'abhors half-way Christians' and will damn all but full Christians" to Hell.[75]

Thomas and Rebecca were evidently among the "half-way" parishioners in Phillips' congregation. Their names do not appear on any lists of the church's "members in full communion,"[76] but Phillips baptized at least five of the couple's six children, which, in view of his customary unwillingness to baptize the children of unbaptized parents, would seem to indicate that Thomas and Rebecca had themselves "owned the covenant" at some previous point.[77] Thomas regularly paid taxes in support of the church, contributing several shillings each year in ministers' rates and deacons' assessments.[78] Rebecca, on the other hand, is largely missing from the church records. Phillips' parish record book, for example, in which the minister meticulously recorded every baptism that he performed, routinely identified both the father and mother of each child baptized. The entries recording his baptisms of the five Grow children, however, identify each child as the son or daughter of "Thomas and _____ Grow" (with the mother's name left blank) or simply "Thomas Grow," suggesting that Rebecca may not have been part of Phillips' congregation or, more likely, that the minister was so little acquainted with her that he did not recall her name.[79] Either explanation would imply that the Grows were less than zealous participants in the religious life of their community.

An episode of sexual misconduct in Andover in the early 1720s may well have placed the Grow family in an awkward position within the parish. In September 1721, Elizabeth Nichols, an unmarried servant girl in the household of Nathaniel Frie [Frye], gave birth to an illegitimate son. Several days later, the unwed mother apparently died of complications from childbirth. Her newborn son was given the name "John Grow" and "bound out" to the Frie family to be raised. The identity of the boy's father is not revealed in the surviving records, but it is likely—given the naming patterns prevalent in New England at the time, with a firstborn son commonly receiving his father's Christian name—that the child was named after his father. A John Grow is known to have resided in Andover during this period, and a man with the surname "Grow" was "warned out" of the town by local authorities at the time of the illegitimate child's birth.[80]

Both George W. Davis, the Grow family genealogist, and Charlotte Helen Abbott, an indefatigable Andover genealogist, concluded that the father was probably Thomas' 20-year-old nephew, John Grow (1701–?), his brother Samuel's second son, and the grandson of John and Hannah Grow of Ipswich.[81] Many itinerant laborers were passing through Andover on their way to the Connecticut and New Hampshire frontiers during this period, and if the John Grow who fathered Elizabeth Nichols' illegitimate child was one of them, it would have been natural for local authorities to warn him out of town as soon as it became apparent that he was unable to financially support his bastard son.[82] Why Thomas and Rebecca did not assume guardianship of the child—who was, after all, a blood relative, no matter how unsavory his origins—will probably never be known. They may have chosen to remain aloof from the scandalous affair for moral reasons, or they may simply have lacked the resources at the time to provide the child with adequate care. Whatever the reason, the unfortunate episode was presumably the source of ongoing embarrassment and discomfort for the family as the child grew up in a neighboring household, was baptized by Samuel Phillips in the South Parish church in 1728, and remained in the town into the 1740s.[83]

After moving to Connecticut, the Grows joined Reverend Ebenezer Williams' Congregational church in Pomfret. Williams, like his Andover counterpart Phillips, distinguished between full church members and parishioners who merely "owned the covenant," but because a fire in the 1920s destroyed the church's early records, Thomas and Rebecca's official membership status remains unknown. Nevertheless, within four years of his arrival in Pomfret, Thomas was chosen to collect the church's annual minister's rates for 1736, while his son Joseph performed similar duties in 1756, 1759, and 1761, which would seem to indicate that the Grows might have been full members of the congregation. In addition, Joseph's election in 1754 as one of Pomfret's "tithingmen"—local officials charged with monitoring immoral behavior and reporting instances of Sabbath breaking, blasphemous swearing, violations of tavern licensing laws, etc.—suggests that the family enjoyed solid moral standing in the community.[84]

Windham County churches mirrored their Massachusetts counterparts in many of their procedures, including the use of public shaming as a preferred form of church discipline. The lack of early records for the Pomfret church leaves us without any examples from Thomas and Rebecca's congregation, but the public punishments inflicted in a neighboring church in Windham Village (Hampton) undoubtedly reflect methods of discipline commonly in use throughout Windham County during this period. In 1729, when a member of Reverend William Billings' Windham Village congregation confessed to saying that he would "rather hear my dog bark than Mr. Billings preach," the minister forced him to publicly acknowledge that the remark "was a vile and scandalous expression, tending to ye dishonor of our Lord Jesus Christ and his ambassadors, as also of religion in general," and that "I do hereby declare before God and ye church my sorrow and repentance for it, humbly asking your forgiveness, and resolve to have greater watch and guard over my tongue."[85] Two years later, Billings forced a young male parishioner who was frequently "over-taken with inebriating drink" to publicly confess that he "drank too much strong drink, and ha[d] sinned before ye Great Lord . . ., for all of which I desire to be deeply humbled, and take shame to myself, and to pray a pardon from the

Great Lord the Christ, and ask forgiveness of the Church, hoping and resolving, in the strength of Christ, to walk more watchfully for time to come."[86]

In dealing with cases of serious sexual misconduct, Connecticut authorities continued to rely on harsh Puritan punishments well into the eighteenth century. As late as 1719, for example, a large crowd in New London, 40 miles south of Pomfret, witnessed the public punishment of Dr. William Blogget, who "being Convicted of Adultery with the wife of Lt. Timothy Pierce, was whipt 25 Stripes & Branded on ye forehead with [the letter] A & a halter put on his neck there to Remain forever."[87]

Two decades later, however, the punishment of sexual immorality in the colony had grown considerably more lenient, as a sensational and ultimately tragic case in Pomfret makes clear. In 1742, 19-year-old Sarah Grosvenor became pregnant by 27-year-old Amasa Sessions. Both participants in the affair came from prominent Pomfret families and were undoubtedly well-known in the Grow household. (Thomas and Rebecca's daughter Hannah was the same age as the Grosvenor girl, while their son Thomas[3] was only nine months older than Sessions.) Rather than marry his pregnant lover or offer to support the illegitimate child once it was born, Amasa instead persuaded Sarah to obtain a secret abortion. He procured the services of a quack doctor, John Hallowell, from neighboring Killingly, who first provided the girl with an abortion-inducing medicinal "powder," and then, several weeks later—after the powder proved ineffective—attempted to "Remove her Conseption" manually with an iron "instrument." The latter procedure succeeded in producing the desired miscarriage, but shortly thereafter Sarah began to experience feverish convulsions and died a month later. Sessions and Hallowell were subsequently brought to trial in the Windham County Superior Court, and the outcome of the court case says much about the shifting moral standards of eighteenth-century New England. Hallowell was convicted of a "highhanded misdemeanor" and sentenced to twenty-nine lashes "on the naked back" but escaped to Rhode Island before the sentence could be carried out, avoiding punishment altogether. Sessions, who in the seventeenth century would have been whipped and severely fined for his role in the affair, was acquitted of all charges related to Sarah's death and not even prosecuted for fornication. He went on to live a long, prosperous, and eminently respectable life in Pomfret, and died of old age in 1799.[88]

For Thomas Grow, as for other colonial Connecticut farmers, advancing age brought a pressing need to finalize the property arrangements that would secure his sons' futures. In most New England farm families, the father continued to increase his landholdings into his sixties, at which point he began transferring portions of the property to his sons. The process of transferring land was usually completed within a comparatively short period of time, with the family's male offspring—by then typically ranging from a married eldest son in his thirties or early forties to an unmarried youngest son in his twenties—receiving their portions within a few years of one another. According to historian David Hackett Fischer, the land transfers "marked a kind of 'retirement' by the father from the business of farming; not a complete disengagement, but a passing on of the major responsibility for managing the family's lands." Most "retired" fathers retained a core portion of their home farm for their own use, holding it in reserve for a younger son who customarily remained at home looking after his parents as they aged, and who eventually inherited the property at the time of his father's death, at which point he became his widowed mother's caretaker and unofficial guardian during her remaining years.[89]

The concluding phase of Thomas' life fit the above pattern fairly closely. He purchased his final large parcel of land in 1747, when he was 63 years of age, and began transferring property to his sons the following year. In the Grow family, as in "a substantial minority" of Connecticut cases, the land transfers took the form of purchases rather than gifts.[90] Each of Thomas and Rebecca's sons was allowed to reside on, and work, the parcel of land that he would eventually own, improving the property and gradually accumulating the capital needed to acquire it by purchase from Thomas. To modern sensibilities, the phenomenon of a father selling land to his children rather than bestowing it as gifts and bequeathments suggests a rather crass and unaffectionate family dynamic. But to historian Toby Ditz, a leading authority on colonial Connecticut inheritance patterns, it simply reflects the way in which early New England's "cultural cosmos combined into one seamless package emotional attachments and pragmatic considerations." By purchasing his inheritance while his father was still alive, a son gained early ownership of his own farm and the father obtained the "savings" needed to remain independent in old age. "Otherwise," Ditz concludes, "the son would remain an economic dependent" and be "responsible for the direct care of an aging parent."[91]

That reasoning may explain the Grow family's method of transferring property. In 1748, Thomas' 34-year-old eldest son, Thomas[3], bought the northern half of his father's 100-acre parcel on the Windham line in southwestern Pomfret for £300,[92] and 31-year-old Joseph, the family's middle son, purchased approximately half (45 acres) of the family homestead at the foot of Prospect Hill for £400.[93] Four years later, in 1752, Thomas' 25-year-old youngest son, James, purchased his father's recently acquired 100-acre parcel in northwestern Pomfret for the original 1747 purchase price of £430,[94] and Thomas Jr. bought the remaining 50-acre southern half of the 100-acre property on the Windham line for £300.[95] The proceeds presumably went into the family's estate as a reserve of capital that would support Thomas and Rebecca in their approaching old age, with any residual balance to be returned to the children after their father's death.

The latter eventuality came sooner than expected. In January 1753, one month after transferring most of his remaining land to his sons and moving into partial "retirement," Thomas died suddenly, at age 68, in the midst of a large-scale epidemic of "pleuratic distemper," or pleurisy, that two months later claimed the life of Pomfret's minister, Ebenezer Williams.[96]

Epidemics of pleurisy and other respiratory diseases (influenza, pneumonia) were widespread in New England during the late 1740s and early 1750s, commonly occurring during the winter months when the combination of cold temperatures, drafty and poorly insulated houses, crowded living conditions, and unheated churches provided ideal conditions for the spread of respiratory infections. Pleurisy was a particularly gruesome disease; an inflammation of the lungs that caused fluid to collect in the chest cavity, making breathing difficult and causing severe chest pain and painful coughing, its victims essentially strangled to death.[97]

In accordance with colonial law, Rebecca inherited none of her husband's estate at the time of his death. Instead, all of Thomas' remaining land and personal possessions went to the couple's children, with Rebecca receiving "use rights" to the estate during her lifetime as well as the legal assurance that her children would provide her with "a comfortable maintenance" for the rest of her life.[98] Accordingly, in settling Thomas' estate, his sons Thomas[3] and James, and their sisters, quitclaimed their rights to the remaining 55 acres of the family homestead to their brother Joseph in exchange for a token payment of £5 each.[99] The three brothers also quitclaimed to their "Loving Sisters" all rights to the "Indoer moveables" (furniture and other household objects) "Now in the Custody and Possession of our Hon[orable] Mother Rebeckah Grow."[100] Rebecca subsequently continued to reside in the home farm's dwelling house, cared for by Joseph and his wife, Abigail, until her death in November 1762 at age 75. She and Thomas were buried beside one another in the Old Pomfret Burying Ground next to Wappaquians Brook, "a few rods" south of their homestead.[101]

The couple's gravestones reflect some of the cultural changes that took place during their lives. The inscription on Thomas' headstone, for example, identifies him as "Mr. Thomas Grow," but the title "Mister" had long since lost its seventeenth-century connotation as a mark of elite social status and by the mid-eighteenth century was routinely attached to the name of any respectable male colonist.[102] The principal design elements on Rebecca's headstone—a human-faced "soul effigy" crowned by a laurel victory wreath over the inscription, with climbing vines blossoming into celebratory "whirl rosettes" on the two vertical border panels—were Puritan symbols of the soul's successful ascension to Heaven, emphasizing victory over death and eternal life in Christ. The stone-carver's incorporation of animated eyes (with pupils) on Rebecca's soul effigy nevertheless represents a stylistic transition from traditional Puritan gravestone art of the seventeenth and early eighteenth centuries, which commonly featured grim, blank-eyed death's-heads and winged skulls with "dead," empty eye-sockets—terrifying imagery designed to warn the living to be ever-mindful of death's imminence and the need to avoid sin if they hoped to be spared an afterlife of eternal torment in Hell. The effigy on Rebecca's stone, by contrast, reflects a relatively more optimistic mid-eighteenth-century view, in which death was perceived less as an object of dread than as an opportunity for salvation and eternal life. The iconographic message of her headstone is clear: Rebecca's living soul has "departed this life"—*i.e.*, her mortal life—and successfully completed its celestial journey to an afterlife of everlasting bliss in Heaven. As such, its imagery is another reflection of the gradual "softening" of New England's traditional Puritan beliefs as the eighteenth century progressed.[103]

In most respects, Thomas Grow appears to have been a typical New England colonist. Like countless thousands of other men of his generation, he took advantage of the opportunities available in the region's expanding interior frontiers to become an independent, and eventually, in his case, prosperous farmer. At two key points in his life, he uprooted himself from the confines of a demographically and socioeconomically constricted environment and migrated westward in order to obtain inexpensive farmland. As a young newlywed, he left his overcrowded hometown of Ipswich and moved to underpopulated Andover, where he acquired enough land to establish himself as a maltster and small-scale farmer. Two decades later, as a middle-aged father of six, he exchanged his relatively modest properties in by-then-overcrowded Andover for significantly larger landholdings on the Connecticut frontier, achieving prosperity and higher social standing in the process. In both instances, his decision making appears to have been prudent, cautious, and relatively conservative—characteristics distinctly at odds with our modern stereotype of the frontier pioneer. By the time he took up residence, for example, neither Andover nor Pomfret was any longer regarded as untamed wilderness or a potential target of Indian attack. Instead, both towns were rapidly growing agricultural settlements equipped with basic infrastructure and amenities. Andover, moreover, was only 15 miles west of Ipswich, and a substantial number of Thomas' in-laws and other kin were already living there by the time he arrived in 1710; while Pomfret and neighboring towns had been attracting a steady flow of Andover residents, including many of Thomas and Rebecca's Holt family relatives, for more than three decades by the time the Grows joined that well-established chain migration in 1731. In addition, Thomas was able to purchase an already constructed dwelling house in each town prior to his arrival. Pioneer migration was an arduous and risk-filled undertaking, to be sure, but for Thomas and his family the experience did not entail the stereotypical building of a log cabin in a howling wilderness filled with hostile Indians.

Here
Lies the Body
of Mr. Thomas Grow
Who Died January
the 13th 1753
In the 68th Year
of His Age

Thomas Grow headstone, Old Pomfret Burying Ground (South Cemetery), Route 169, Pomfret, CT. (Photograph by the author.)

Novembr ye 9th
1762 Departed
this Life Mrs.
Rebekah Grow
In ye 75th Year
of Her Age

Rebecca Grow headstone, Old Pomfret Burying Ground (South Cemetery), Route 169, Pomfret, CT. (Photograph by the author.)

The dangers, instead, were mainly economic and environmental. Frontier farming was a precarious enterprise that was vulnerable to a host of potentially ruinous forces beyond the farmer's control: uncertain markets, unpredictable weather (spring floods, summer droughts, late and early freezes, and the damaging "nor'easters" common in New England), and other calamities, including plant and animal diseases and plagues of insects. With hard work and luck, however, the rewards could be ample. In Pomfret, Thomas was able to purchase enough land to eventually settle all three of his sons on 100-acre farms of their own—farms considerably larger than average for men their age in eighteenth-century Connecticut. That achievement, which would have been virtually impossible back in Andover, secured the family's future for the next generation. But it also had important ramifications for subsequent generations of their descendants, because as a result of the labors of Thomas and Rebecca Grow, the family was now firmly rooted in the agricultural mainstream of the American economy and the upper echelons of America's rural middle class.

THOMAS GROW (1714–1806)

Like his father, Thomas[3] Grow (*Thomas[2], John[1]*) was a maltster and farmer. Born in 1714 in Andover, Massachusetts, he migrated with his family to Pomfret, Connecticut, as a teenager. In 1738, at age 24, he married 22-year-old Susanna Eaton of neighboring Woodstock,[1] at which time his father gave the couple the use of the 100-acre parcel of undeveloped land that he had purchased in the southwest corner of Pomfret at the time of the family's move to Connecticut. There Thomas and Susanna Grow built a house, established a farm, and raised a family of nine children, at least two of whom died young.

Circa 1740, Grow Hill farmhouse of Thomas and Susanna Grow on the Pomfret-Hampton line (present-day 1102 State Route 97, Hampton, CT), as pictured in a 1930s photograph. Source: WPA Architectural Survey—Census of Old Buildings in Connecticut: Hampton Historical Building #031a (Connecticut State Library Digital Collections, online at ctstatelibrary.org), accessed August 2013. The partially visible service ell extending from the right side (or east end) of the rear lean-to provided additional workshop or woodshed space, and was a common addition to Pomfret-area houses during the late eighteenth and early nineteenth centuries. (*Historic and Architectural Survey of Abington in the Town of Pomfret, Connecticut* [Pomfret Historical Society and Connecticut Historical Commission, May 1998], 81)

Children of THOMAS³ and SUSANNA (EATON) GROW, all born in Pomfret, CT:

i   Rebecca, b. 16 Oct. 1738; d. date and place unk; m. in 1773 in Pomfret, Baptist elder Whitman Jacobs, living in Guilford, VT in 1790s.

ii.   Susanna, b. 14 Nov. 1740; d. 6 Oct. 1749 in Pomfret.

iii. Thomas⁴, b. 14 April 1743; d. 5 June 1824 in Hampton, CT; m. (1) 1767, Experience Goodell; m. (2) 1811, Sarah Hyde; m. (3) 1821, Experience Abbott.

iv.   Lydia, b. 25 March 1745; d. date and place unk.; m. Baptist preacher Elisha Ransom, living in Bridgewater, VT in 1780s, prob. accompanied husband to Indiana in 1818.

v.   Hannah, b. 14 April 1747; no further record.

vi.   William, b. 8 April 1749; d. 7 May 1830 in Bridgewater, VT; m. 1776, Priscilla Morse.

vii. Timothy, b. 20 April 1751; d. 19 Aug. 1754 in Pomfret.

viii. Nathaniel, b. 29 May 1753; d. 9 July 1838 in Henderson, NY; m. 1775 at Pomfret, Susannah Dow.

ix.   Ebenezer, b. 10 Nov. 1755; d. 31 Oct. 1827 in Hampton, CT; m. Catherine
_____.

SOURCES: George W. Davis, *John Grow of Ipswich/John Groo (Grow) of Oxford* (Washington, D.C.: privately printed by the Carnahan Press, 1913), 29–30, 35, 36, 39, 40; Clarence Winthrop Bowen, *The History of Woodstock, Connecticut: Genealogies of Woodstock Families*, 8 vols. (Norwood, MA: privately printed by the Plimpton Press, 1926–1943), 6:381. For Rebecca (Grow) Jacobs' residence in Vermont, see *Official History of Guilford, Vermont, 1678–1961* (Guilford, VT: Town of Guilford and Broad Brook Grange No. 151, 1961), 247–248; for Lydia (Grow) Ransom's marriage: Michael G. Kenny, *The Perfect Law of Liberty: Elias Smith and the Providential History of America* (Washington, D.C.: Smithsonian Institution Press, 1994), 46, 56–57.

The property was situated on a large hill straddling the Pomfret-Windham line, 6 miles southwest of the home farm of Thomas' parents and 3.8 miles north of the Windham Village green. "Grow Hill," as it came to be known locally, was part of Pomfret until 1786, when Windham Village became the independent township of Hampton, at which point adjustments in the Pomfret-Hampton boundary shifted the property into Hampton's jurisdiction.

Thomas and Susanna's farmhouse sat at the summit of Grow Hill some 150 feet south of the King's Highway, which bisected the property. Thanks to a Connecticut historic-buildings survey conducted by the Works Progress Administration in the 1930s, we have a detailed description of the house's architecture. A typical Connecticut farmhouse of the first half of the eighteenth century, it was a two-story, center-chimney dwelling, one room deep with two rooms below and two above, and with a lean-to kitchen added across the rear at an early date, resulting in a standard saltbox profile. The original

house block (there were later additions) measured approximately 41' wide ×
19' deep, and the lean-to addition at the rear measured 41' wide × 13' deep. The
house's exterior was covered in "thin clapboards with white birch bark lining
underneath." Framed with thick timbers that would withstand the heavy snow
accumulations of winter, the drenching rains of spring, and the nor'easters and
hurricanes that periodically pound New England from September to April, it
was a house built to last.[2]

The front façade of the dwelling faced southward and featured nine
symmetrically placed windows that provided the interior with significantly
more sunlight than would have been available in the house of Thomas'
grandparents in Ipswich two generations earlier. Like many Connecticut
houses of this period, the front entrance consisted of a plain door topped with
a horizontal row of four small transom lights below a simple cornice. Directly
inside the front door was a small entry area with two sets of stairs, one leading
to the second floor and the other to the cellar. The cellar stairs were constructed
of solid square logs, a common feature of early Connecticut homes. The steep,
narrow second-floor staircase fronted the center chimney and was sheathed
in beaded boards. On the left and right sides of the entry area were doorways
opening into the two first-floor rooms, each of which had a 6' 6" ceiling
with exposed, heavily chamfered summer beams and girts. The front left (or
southwest) room, which contained a raised-panel fireplace wall and a built-in
raised-panel corner cupboard, was probably a multi-use parlor in which the
family would have received neighbors and other guests. Directly behind the
two first-floor rooms was the lean-to kitchen, a long room extending the full
width of the house, with a 6' 2" ceiling, splayed rear posts, and a large stone
fireplace containing a brick oven with a separate flue. At one end of the kitchen
was a small corner pantry also sheathed in beaded boards. Upstairs, the two
second-floor sleeping chambers featured exposed, unchamfered beams and
heavily splayed corner posts, with horizontal feather-edge sheathing on the
walls. A batten door with wood hinges provided access to the lean-to's attic.[3] As
Thomas and Susanna's family grew, ten or more people at a time lived within
the confines of the house's roughly 2,090 square feet of space.

Testifying to the quality of its construction, the house was still standing and
still functioning as a residence in the second decade of the 21st century. Time,
however, has not been kind to the ancient dwelling. At the time of this writing,
Grow Hill was owned by a large commercial dairy, and the Grow farmhouse
was being used to house the dairy's migrant farm laborers—its interior carved
up into small apartments, its fireplaces boarded over, and its sills deteriorating
badly. The dwelling is currently hemmed in by two modern houses, four
agricultural storage buildings, and numerous large pieces of farm equipment.
Nevertheless, looking beyond the clutter and physical deterioration, the visitor
is struck by the extraordinary pastoral beauty of the surrounding countryside,

a landscape that appears to have changed little since the eighteenth century. Situated atop one of the highest elevations in Windham County, with vast expanses of open sky above and a stunning 360-degree panorama of rolling hills, verdant woodlands, and neatly fenced fields as far as the eye can see, the setting would almost certainly have imbued a family as deeply religious as this generation of Grows with a profound sense that they were living close to God amidst the splendor of His creation.

Like eldest sons in most colonial farm families, Thomas[3] remained economically dependent on his father well into adulthood. Although farmers' sons in New England customarily relied on their fathers to provide them with the land they needed to establish farms of their own when they came of age, rural fathers usually retained ownership of their farmland until they retired or died—thus delaying the economic independence of their older sons until they were mature men, often "well into middle age" with families of their own. Thomas[3] for example, was a 34-year-old father of five before he gained legal title to a portion of his father's land and became a fully independent farmer in his own right. In 1748—with Thomas[2] nearing retirement and beginning the process of transferring property to his sons—Thomas[3] purchased the northern half of his father's 100-acre parcel in southwestern Pomfret for £300, thereby acquiring formal ownership of land that he and Susanna had been farming since their marriage ten years earlier. Four years later, at age 38, he completed the acquisition by buying the southern half of the parcel from his father for another £300.

For elder sons in some families, the long wait for their share of the family estate was undoubtedly a frustrating experience, but for those like Thomas[3] who managed to purchase their inheritance from their father while he was still alive, there were compensatory benefits: they achieved autonomy from their father earlier than would otherwise have been the case had they been forced to wait until his death to inherit land, and at the same time they fulfilled a basic filial obligation to their aging parents by providing them with a substantial sum of money for retirement in lieu of years of service and care.[4] In Thomas' case, that sum of money totaled £600, and the burdens of parental care were assumed by his younger brother Joseph.[5]

The deed to Thomas[3]' 1748 land purchase identified him as a "Pomfrett malster" [sic], whereas subsequent land records consistently describe him as a "husbandman."[6] The shift in his occupational designation from maltster to farmer might be a reflection of the changing consumption habits of eighteenth-century New Englanders, because by mid-century, apple cider was rapidly replacing malt-based beer as the fermented beverage of choice among the region's inhabitants. Historian Sarah McMahon writes that although "considerations of taste" could have influenced the transition from beer to cider, "agricultural incentives offer a more probable explanation." Apple orchards, which thrived in New England's climate and soil, could be planted on hillsides and other marginal land not suitable for grain production. Apple-growing also required significantly less labor than the sowing and harvesting of barley. And apple cider stored longer than beer, so an entire year's supply could be processed during the autumn months, whereas barley had to be malted and brewed throughout the year to supply the demand for beer. By the second half of the eighteenth century, as a result, virtually every New England homestead was maintaining its own apple orchard, cider mills were operating seasonally in nearly every town in the region, and in many communities malt and beer had "ceased to be made" altogether.[7] Consequently, as the consumer market for beer declined, Thomas seems likely to have reduced or abandoned barley growing and malt production in favor of more profitable agricultural pursuits.

For Windham County's farmers, the third quarter of the eighteenth century was a period of economic growth. Several factors—a strong market for military provisions during the French and Indian wars, the food needs of New England's rapidly growing urban population, and a steadily expanding export trade with the West Indies—fueled an accelerating demand for the county's agricultural commodities. Local farmers, most of whom still adhered to "subsistence-plus" farming practices, responded by placing greater emphasis on the "plus" element in that equation, producing larger surpluses of beef and pork, cheese and butter, poultry and eggs, apples, and other food products to trade at their towns' general stores, which now functioned increasingly as local collection centers for the farm commodities that merchants in Providence, Norwich, New London, Newport, and Boston eagerly bought up.[8] That Thomas Grow prospered financially during this quarter-century of economic growth seems evident from a major land purchase that he made at the very end of the period. In March 1776, he was able to add another 176.5 acres of land to his Grow Hill farm for the substantial sum of £700.[9]

Measured by the standard determinants of status in colonial New England, Thomas[3] and his family attained a relatively higher position in local society than his parents had achieved. Economically, they ranked in the upper quarter of the community, one that continued to consist almost entirely of middle-class farmers. In 1771, at age 57, Thomas ranked 27th out of 123 taxpayers on the annual tax list of Pomfret's southwestern district, placing him in the top 22 percent of local property owners as measured by taxable wealth.[10] Six years later, his 1777 tax assessment—tabulated after he had nearly tripled his landholdings with the purchase of 176.5 additional acres—would have rated him the fourth wealthiest taxpayer in the district if he had not recently transferred substantial amounts of his property to his sons.[11]

Based on historian Jackson Turner Main's detailed analysis of the wealth patterns of eighteenth-century Connecticut farmers, Thomas' tax assessments (and the landownership on which they were primarily based) suggest that the Grow family enjoyed a "comfortable" or perhaps even a "well-to-do" standard of living.[12] Increased prosperity generated by the economic growth of the 1750s and 1760s led to a sharp rise in household consumption in Windham County, as middle-class farm families took advantage of their newfound disposable income to purchase more of the "foreign luxuries" that were increasingly available in their local general stores: fine textiles and fashionable wearing apparel; tea, coffee, molasses, and other "exotic" foods and beverages; imported china and silver for their tables (and for display in the open cupboards of their parlors, such as the one in the Grow farmhouse); clocks, "looking glasses," etc.[13] Evidence of the Grow family's participation in the growing consumerism of the period can be found in a 1772–1773 account book from Abel Clark's general store in Pomfret. Among the items purchased by the family, according to Clark's records, were "lymons," a "cake of chocolate," "2 pair [of] kneebuckles," and "8 yards of bone lace."[14]

Thomas[3'] public-service record—another revealing indicator of social status—surpassed that of his father. Like virtually every other male property-owner in Pomfret, Thomas fulfilled his civic responsibilities by periodically serving in one of the town's low- or mid-level offices: "Grand Jury man" in 1752; surveyor of highways in 1751, 1761, and 1766; and "lister" (or tax assessor) in 1785.[15] But in addition, he was elected to a term as "Constable and Collector of the State Tax" in Hampton in 1786 (the year Hampton became an independent entity and Grow Hill shifted into its jurisdiction).[16] Constables were responsible for tax collection and the maintenance of public order in their towns, and the men chosen for the office usually had reputations for vigor, toughness, and integrity—suggesting that, at age 72, Thomas was regarded by his fellow citizens as a man of vitality and strong character. Although not a position of political leadership or high status, the constable's office was nonetheless a higher-ranking post than any his father had held.[17]

It was as a religious leader, however, that Thomas made his most notable mark in local society. In his mid-fifties, he played an instrumental role in founding the first Baptist church in Pomfret and subsequently assumed a senior leadership position in the church's organizational hierarchy as its deacon.

Thomas[3] and Susanna Grow lived during a period of intense religious turmoil in New England, a period known as the "Great Awakening" or the "Protestant Evangelical Awakening." At the time of the couple's marriage in 1738, a few young fundamentalist ministers were beginning to criticize the region's Puritan churches for failing to meet the spiritual needs of their congregations. According to these critics, the churches had grown soft in doctrine and lax in standards. Most Puritan ministers had by now abandoned the strict Calvinist doctrine of predestination (the belief that men and women were innately depraved sinners doomed to damnation, whose only hope of salvation was to throw themselves on Christ's mercy) in favor of the more optimistic belief that an eternal afterlife in heaven could be won by living a sin-free Christian life and doing "good works"—a "dangerous heresy," the critics argued, that was imperiling parishioners' souls. They also complained that the churches were admitting too many "half-way" members—people who obtained church membership merely by affirming their baptismal covenant, without publicly testifying to a personal conversion experience or giving evidence that they had been "born again"—resulting in congregations increasingly filled with what the young critics regarded as "people of lesser faith," "pretended Christians," and hypocrites, and ultimately leading to "a great and visible decay in Godliness" within the churches (a situation that was becoming even more intolerable to fundamentalists as more and more ministers allowed their half-way members to take communion and participate in the Lord's Supper). A third criticism centered on the "dull and lifeless" style of preaching that had become prevalent in Puritan churches. All too often in the early eighteenth century, ministers' sermons consisted of tedious moralizing homilies, long-winded exegeses of biblical texts, and scholastic lectures on arcane theological doctrines such as antinomianism, Arminianism, sanctification, and justification—sermons that ministers invariably read to their congregations from carefully composed manuscripts in a dry, formalistic manner directed to the intellect and "the head" rather than "the heart" and the emotions. To young fundamentalists, such an uninspiring style of "cold and sapless" preaching, devoid of spiritual passion and "the spirit of God," was contributing significantly to a widespread decline in piety and religious fervor in New England.[18]

In 1734–1735, a 31-year-old minister in Northampton, Massachusetts, Reverend Jonathan Edwards, took it upon himself to bring an end to what he regarded as a "time of extraordinary dullness in religion" in New England. In a series of fire-and-brimstone sermons, Edwards terrified his congregation with stark and vivid depictions of the agonies of hellfire that awaited those who failed to repent their sinful wickedness and give themselves unconditionally to Christ. "Consider what it is," he warned his listeners,

> to suffer extreme torment forever and ever; to suffer it day and night, from one day to another, from one year to another, from one age to another, from one thousand ages to another, and so, adding age to age, and thousands to thousands, in pain, in wailing and lamenting, groaning and shrieking and gnashing your teeth, with your souls full of dreadful grief and amazement, with your bodies and every member full of wracking torture, without any possibility of getting ease; without any possibility of moving God

to pity by your cries . . . ; without any possibility of obtaining any manner of mitigation, or help, or change for the better [in] any way. . . .[C]onsider how dreadful [your] despair will be in such torment. To have no hope; when you shall wish that you might be turned into nothing, but shall have no hope of it . . . ; when you would rejoice if you might but have any relief, after you shall have endured these torments millions of ages, but shall have no hope of it; when, after you shall have worn out the age of the sun, moon, and stars in your dolorous groans and lamentations, without any rest day or night, or one minute's ease, yet you shall have no hope of ever being delivered, but shall know that you are not one whit nearer the end of your torments; but that still there are the same groans, the same shrieks, the same doleful cries incessantly made by you, and the smoke of your torment shall still ascend up, forever and ever; and that your soul . . . will still exist to bear more wrath; your bodies, which shall have been burning all this while in these glowing flames, yet shall not have been consumed, but will remain to roast through eternity.

Nor would "good works" and "humanitarian do-goodism" save them, Edwards cautioned; only an "ecstatic mystical union with Christ" offered any hope of salvation. Edwards' bracing message struck a responsive chord, and the influence of his sermons quickly spread throughout the Connecticut River Valley south to the Connecticut coast and eastward into Windham County, resulting in the conversion of several hundred frightened souls to Christ within six months' time.[19]

Edwards' sermons were a prelude to one of the most sensational events in the history of New England religion. In 1740, a charismatic 36-year-old English evangelist, Reverend George Whitefield, traveled through Massachusetts, Connecticut, and Rhode Island on a whirlwind, six-week speaking tour. Whitefield's message to his audiences was similar to that of Edwards: they were doomed sinners dangling by a slender thread over the abyss of hell, and only those who acknowledged their sins, repudiated their covetousness and lusts, and experienced a heartfelt spiritual "new birth" in Christ would be eligible to receive God's forgiveness and saving grace. A brilliant orator by all accounts, Whitefield introduced New Englanders to a new style of preaching, one that was lively, passionate, and highly theatrical. His sermons—or "sermon performances," as historian Douglas Winiarski has characterized them—were delivered extemporaneously without notes, in everyday language that lower- and middling-rank colonists could relate to, and they were punctuated with dramatic gestures and heart-wrenching illustrations that unleashed powerful emotions in his listeners. The overwhelming sense of guilt and despair that he elicited in his audiences as he forced them to confront their iniquities and the horrific fate that awaited their souls caused many to weep hysterically and groan in agony, after which his mellifluous assurances that their sins might yet be forgiven and their souls saved from damnation inevitably produced surging cries of joy accompanied by waves of clapping and singing. As word of Whitefield's oratorical powers spread, New Englanders began traveling from miles away to hear him preach, and by the midway point of his speaking tour vast, enthusiastic, emotionally charged crowds of 8,000 or more were attending his open-air sermons.[20]

Whitefield's visit ignited a firestorm of fundamentalist revivalism in New England. Soon dozens of native-born itinerant evangelists—many of whom had been spiritually "awakened" and "reborn" as a direct consequence of Whitefield's preaching—were traveling the New England countryside, exhorting their listeners to come to Christ before it was too late. Everywhere they went, these unordained, frequently uneducated and semiliterate lay preachers encountered large crowds eager to hear their impassioned accounts of an omnipotent, wrathful God possessing the power to bestow eternal life on repentant sinners. As a result, within three years of Whitefield's tour, "hundreds of thousands" of men and women had been swept up in an emotional popular movement to revive the "spirit of God" in the hearts of New Englanders.[21]

Many of the evangelists followed Whitefield's lead by publicly berating the established ministers in parishes where they preached for being "lukewarm" pastors and spiritually "dead men"—ministers, they charged, who had not undergone a spiritual "new birth" or personal conversion experience of their own, and who consequently were preaching about "an unknown, unfelt Christ" in their sermons, preaching "mere words" rather than "The Word" at a time when their congregations of "perishing sinners" desperately needed "spirit-filled" preaching and sermons filled with "the power of the Holy Spirit."[22] These direct attacks on New England's entrenched Congregational ministers—who almost invariably were privileged Harvard- or Yale-educated members of the colonial elite—injected a populist tone into the burgeoning evangelical movement. According to historian William McLoughlin, the evangelists "preached a folk form of Calvinism [and] brought the rarified intellectualism of Puritanism down to the level of the common man," infusing Congregationalism in the region with a "fervent, anti-intellectual, popular, egalitarian . . . and flamboyant" quality that gave ordinary colonists the confidence to trust their emotions and spiritual experiences more than the erudition of their more highly educated "betters" in the colonial religious establishment.[23]

It was not long before the maligned ministers of the established order began to take action in defense of their interests. Unaccustomed to competition or to having their credibility challenged, they tended to look upon the evangelists as misguided rabble-rousers, men whose "illiterate ravings" were steering the "thoughtless multitude" in dangerously erroneous directions and posing a "pernicious threat to orthodoxy and to order" in their parishes in the process. Accordingly, they turned to the civil authorities of their colonies for support. In Connecticut, where the Puritan Congregational establishment and the colonial government were closely interconnected, the result was a new law—the "Act for Regulating Abuses and Correcting Disorders in Ecclesiastical Affairs" passed by the colony's legislative assembly in 1742—which made it illegal for any unordained layman to preach in a parish without the permission of the local minister. The act also prohibited ordained ministers (including, by definition, Edwards and Whitefield) from preaching in another minister's parish without a prior invitation; while under another of its provisions, any non-Connecticut resident found preaching in Connecticut could be legally expelled from the colony by force. Almost immediately, Connecticut authorities began jailing itinerant evangelists and deporting the non-Connecticut residents among them.[24]

From the standpoint of the evangelists and their growing legions of followers, such acts of official repression left them no alternative but to separate from the established churches and form new religious bodies of their own. The first of the so-called "Separatist" or "Separate" churches in Connecticut was founded in 1744, at Canterbury in Windham County, approximately 12 miles southeast of Grow Hill; and by the mid-1750s nearly 100 such churches were functioning throughout New England.[25] In their structures and practices, these new churches reflected the fervent desire of their members to return to the purer, "more scriptural ways" of their seventeenth-century Puritan forefathers. Their ministers were predominantly untrained, poorly educated laymen, common farmers and artisans for the most part, chosen for their "spiritual ardor" and "holy zeal," and who served without salaries, supported instead by voluntary donations from their congregations. Separatist churches also institutionalized the popular new evangelical style of preaching, stipulating in their ordinances that their ministers were to preach extemporaneously and not read their sermons. In addition, they invariably adopted restrictive admission standards that rejected "half-way" membership and required all applicants seeking admission to stand before the congregation and describe a transformative personal conversion experience in which they took Christ into their hearts and acquired "saving faith." The new churches also rigorously enforced a stern, disciplinary "watch and care" over their members, expelling those whose conduct failed to live up to their strict moral standards.[26]

Faced with the prospect of mass defections from the established churches, colonial authorities moved aggressively to crush the Separatist movement. Itinerant evangelists who defied the prohibition on unsanctioned preaching were arrested; all marriages and baptisms performed by Separate preachers were declared illegal; and members of Separate churches were banned from holding public office.

The most effective weapon in the authorities' arsenal, however, was taxation. By law, residents of New England towns were required to pay annual religious taxes to fund the operations of the local church and provide money for its minister's salary. In parishes where spiritually "awakened" evangelical converts left the established church and formed their own Separate church, the local authorities invariably required them to continue to pay taxes in support of the established church and its minister. When the Separatists refused to pay, arguing that compulsory taxation to support a "corrupt" church that they no longer attended and a "dead" minister they no longer respected was "extortion," the authorities threw them in jail and confiscated their livestock and household possessions, auctioning them off to pay the Separatists' delinquent tax obligations and fines, thereby leaving many families in a state of acute deprivation.

From the mid-1740s into the 1770s and beyond, New England's Puritan churches were embroiled in a bitterly divisive internal conflict in which the Congregational establishment ruthlessly strove to enforce order and obedience to its traditional authority while Separatists struggled to practice their preferred form of fundamentalist Christianity free from official persecution and compulsory religious taxation.[27] Eventually, a majority of the Separate churches gravitated to the Baptist denomination. At the time of the Great Awakening, New England's Baptists were a small, socially ostracized group that had been harshly persecuted by the Puritans for opposing infant baptism (in the belief that baptizing children not yet capable of reason or conscious religious belief was a violation of the Scriptures), and who instead practiced "believer's baptism," which restricted the rites of baptism to men and women who had reached the age of reason and had made a conscious decision to accept Christ as their savior.

After the Separatists also became targets of persecution, they discovered that they had much in common with the Baptists. Like the Separatists, Baptists were committed to forming "pure" churches comprised exclusively of "born-again" Christians. Separatists also found the Baptist practice of "believer's baptism" to be a logical extension of their own "new birth" doctrine (which restricted church membership to "true believers" who had committed to Christ as reasoning adults), and they soon came to accept the Baptist view that the admission of members whose baptism had occurred in childhood was as damaging to a church's purity as the admission of half-way members. And finally, both Separatists and Baptists vehemently resisted compulsory religious taxation and all other measures that discriminated against their freedom of worship. Consequently, from the 1750s onward, Separatist congregations throughout New England were actively reconstituting themselves into new "Separate Baptist" churches and formally affiliating with the Baptist denomination, dramatically increasing the number of Baptist churches in the region (from ten to sixty in Massachusetts and from three to thirty-three in Connecticut between 1740 and 1780), and infusing the Baptist movement with a powerful new strain of evangelical Calvinism in the process.[28] It was a Separate Baptist church that Thomas[3] Grow helped to establish in Pomfret in the 1770s.

Thomas' first exposure to religious conflict came during a local dispute over geography rather than theology. During his early years in Pomfret, he had attended the town's first Congregational church, located on Prospect Hill within easy walking distance of his parents' farm. After taking up residence on his father's property in southwestern Pomfret and starting a family of his own, however, the arduous 6-mile trip to the meetinghouse over poor and "ill kept" roads made regular attendance at the Pomfret church problematical, especially during winter months.

By the mid-1740s, the church was periodically freeing Thomas from his obligation to pay the annual "minister's rate"—an indication, perhaps, that he and Susanna were among the several residents of southwestern Pomfret who, for the sake of convenience, were attending church services in Windham Village less than 4 miles south of Grow Hill. The situation worsened as Pomfret's "abundantly too small" meetinghouse became increasingly overcrowded, to the point where outlying residents who made the long journey to attend Sunday services often discovered upon arrival that all of the church's pews were full.

When members from the town's southwestern district proposed a variety of solutions—including an expansion of the existing meetinghouse, the construction of a new and larger meetinghouse, or the division of the town into smaller parishes—their proposals were consistently voted down by a majority of the congregation that was unwilling to either fund new construction or accept any loss of the church's tax base. Consequently, in 1749, Thomas and twenty-eight of his neighbors successfully petitioned the Connecticut General Assembly in Hartford for permission to form their own separate parish, one that was assigned the name "Abington." Pomfret angrily appealed the division and two years of legal wrangling ensued. Nevertheless, by 1753, a church meetinghouse had been constructed, a minister had been ordained, and a congregation of sixty-three founding members—thirty-four men and twenty-nine women, including Thomas and Susanna Grow—had begun formal worship at the new Abington Congregational Church, located approximately 2.5 miles northeast of Grow Hill.[29]

Although several Windham County towns became hotbeds of Separatism during the Great Awakening, the Pomfret, Abington, and Windham Village churches managed to avoid serious internal discord and remained firmly within the establishment camp.[30] Periodically, however, small, localized religious revivals sprang up in the area, and one of them in particular seems to have had a significant impact on the Grow family. In December 1763, a Separate Baptist evangelist traveling through West Woodstock, a few miles north of Pomfret, preached a sermon that caused 20-year-old Abiel ("Biel") Ledoyt, the

Abington Congregational Church, State Route 97, Abington, CT. Constructed in 1751 (and extensively remodeled in 1840), it is the oldest church building in continuous use in Connecticut. Thomas and Susanna Grow were founding members. (Photograph by the author.)

leader of a group of "frivolous" young Woodstock "merrymakers" and a self-acknowledged sinner, to fear for the fate of his soul. After feeling God "take hold of [his] heart" in a classic epiphany of religious awakening and rebirth, Ledoyt began talking with his friends "about death and the need of being prepared for it." In doing so, he spoke "with such earnestness and power" and "with such convincing force that some forty young people were converted." Soon Ledoyt and his companions were meeting together two or three times a week to pray, sing hymns, and discuss their prospects for salvation.[31] He later recalled:

> Parents were surprised to see their giddy children distressed for their souls. Some old professors [earlier converts], who had thought themselves Christians, now began to see that their building was upon the sand, and cried "God be merciful to us sinners!" . . . Frolicking [and dancing], which had been much practiced, came to a stop. The Bible, and other good books, that had never been regarded, were now much in use. Our groves rang with the bitter outcries of the distressed youth. God was soon merciful to some of them, and delivered them from their distresses, and their sorrow was turned to joy, and their mouths filled with praise to their

Redeemer, and they . . . then call[ed] upon all to praise the Lord
with them . . . and [began] recommending him to others . . .[32]

As the spontaneous revival gained momentum, it provoked strong hostility
from the leaders of West Woodstock's Congregational Church—with Ledoyt
barely managing to avoid physical assault on at least three occasions—and in late
1764, the young converts withdrew from their "unsympathetic local church"
and formed their own loosely organized Separate religious society. Less than
two years later, they transformed that body into a formally constituted Separate
Baptist church which they named the Woodstock Baptist Church, with Ledoyt
as their principal preacher and a rapidly growing congregation that soon
included nearly one-third of the residents of their parish. As the church grew
in membership and influence, Ledoyt worked energetically to facilitate the
founding of sister churches in neighboring towns. In 1770, after preaching "in
the south part of Pomfret" and converting "a happy number" of people in that
area—members of the Grow family almost certainly among them—he led the
effort to organize the new converts into a Pomfret branch of his Woodstock
church, one that eventually became known as the Grow Hill Baptist Church.[33]

By the time Ledoyt began proselytizing in the area, dissatisfaction with the
Congregational ministers of both Abington and neighboring Windham Village
was already generating potential Separatist impulses among discontented
members of both congregations. For several years, ill health had prevented the
pastor of the Abington church, Reverend David Ripley, from preaching on a
regular basis, to the point where some of his parish's "rate-payers" had come
to feel that they were getting an insufficient return on their ministerial taxes.
(The congregation eventually began withholding Ripley's salary in 1776 and
dismissed him from his post two years later.) Simultaneously, 6 miles to the south
in Windham Village, the authoritarian proclivities of Congregational minister
Samuel Mosely were provoking strong opposition within his congregation;
and when Mosely's declining health and "Bodily infirmities" began to interfere
with his ability to consistently "perform Publick Preaching," the local residents
who paid the ecclesiastical taxes that supported him began to feel that, like their
Abington counterparts, they, too, were being short-changed.[34]

A further source of discontent in both Abington and Windham Village
was the ubiquitous issue of travel distance. Residents of the borderland
where the two parishes abutted—including the Grows and neighboring
farm families on both sides of the Pomfret-Windham line—lived on the far
geographic peripheries of their respective parishes and had to travel 2 or 3
miles or more through hilly terrain riddled with swamps and streams in order
to attend Sabbath services. For them, the prospect of "gathering" a new church
closer to home would have had a strong appeal from the standpoint of sheer
convenience.[35] Consequently, when the charismatic young evangelist Biel

Ledoyt extended his West Woodstock revival into the southern portion of Pomfret, he found a fertile and receptive environment in which to sway minds, attract new followers, and plant the seeds for a local Separate Baptist church.[36]

On 22 December 1770, Ledoyt and Whitman Jacobs (the Baptist minister in neighboring Thompson, Connecticut) met in Abington with a group of seven local men—including two of Thomas[3] and Susanna's sons (27-year-old Thomas[4] and 21-year-old William)—who agreed to form a new "Baptist Society Unitedly to Cary on the Publick Worship of God among our Selves in this place."[37] Seven weeks later, Thomas[3]' name was added to the membership list (an indication, perhaps, that the initial impetus for the Grows' conversion to the Baptist faith came from the family's two eldest sons, both of whom were close in age to Ledoyt, and presumably the most receptive to his style of revivalism).

Before long, the Grows had assumed a leadership role among the Abington Baptists. By 1772, Thomas[3] and Susanna were hosting virtually all of the group's activities at their Grow Hill farm, with Thomas serving as "moderator" of its business meetings and likely providing a venue for its Sunday worship services in his farmhouse or barn.[38] In 1776, when the society established a full-fledged, twenty-five-member Baptist church,[39] their son William was selected as its first preacher (officially its "elder," the title that Baptists of this period preferred instead of "minister" or "reverend"[40]), while Thomas[3] became its deacon—an office of "high status" and "considerable prestige" in Abington's small social world,[41] and one that he continued to fill for nearly two decades. A few years later, his son Thomas[4] was chosen to serve as the Baptist society's clerk, in which capacity he recorded the minutes of its business meetings for the next twenty years. Eventually, in 1791, after the congregation had grown to include more than fifty Abington-area families, Thomas[3] gave the church a tract of land in the southern portion of his Grow Hill farm for the construction of a "public meeting house," a 42' × 30' building that was completed the following year.[42]

As leaders of the Grow Hill Baptist Church, the Grows were personally acquainted with many of the top Baptist officials in New England. In October 1773, Isaac Backus, the Separate Baptist movement's preeminent evangelist and its most forceful crusader for religious freedom, made a two-day visit to the Grow farm, where he delivered three sermons and administered the Lord's Supper to "a lovely number of christians" before departing for Biel Ledoyt's house in West Woodstock accompanied by Thomas and daughter Hannah Grow.[43] The following year, Thomas and Susanna's son William Grow prepared himself for the ministry by studying with the prominent Baptist theologian James Manning, the president of Rhode Island College in Providence, America's first Baptist college. Founded by Manning in 1764, the school later became Brown University.[44]

In June 1776, both Manning and Isaac Backus traveled to Grow Hill, where they personally presided over William Grow's ordination as a Baptist preacher

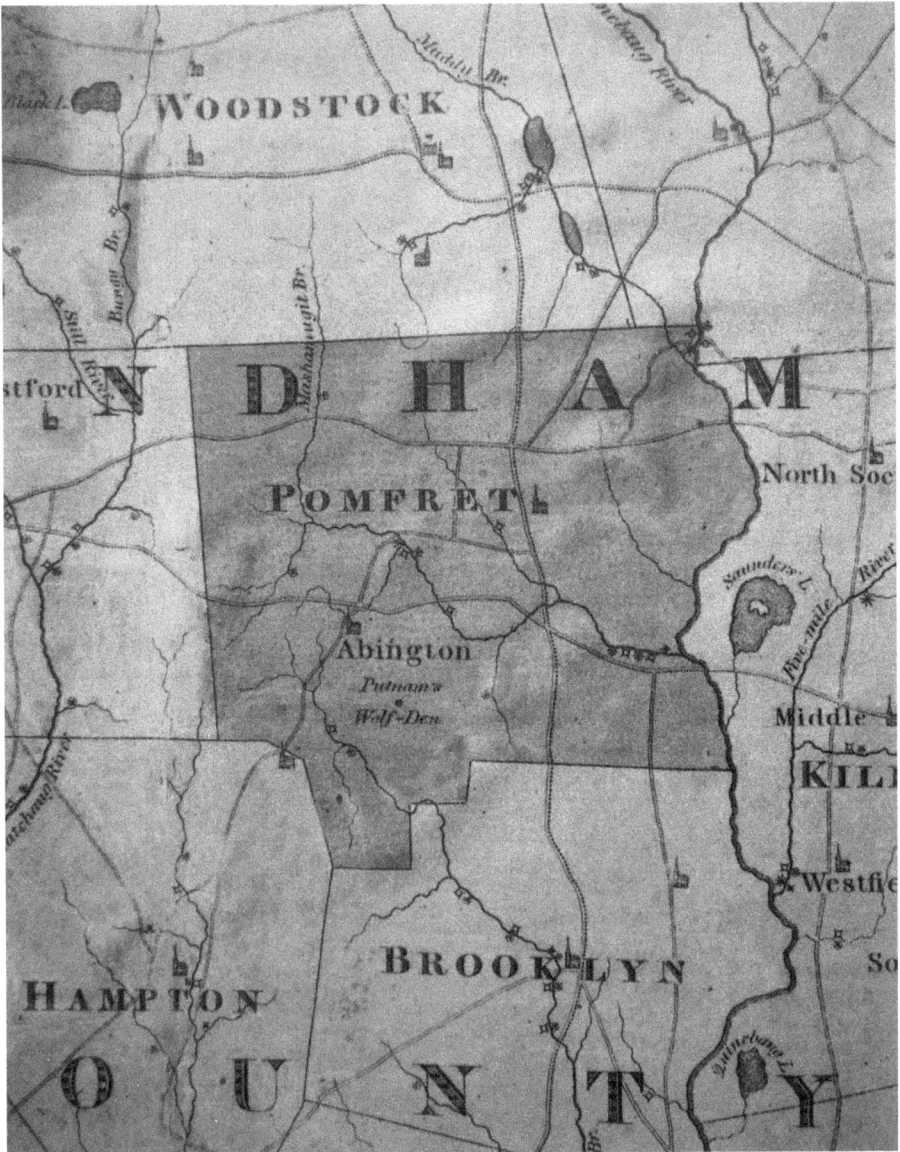

Detail from an 1812 map of Connecticut by Moses Warren and George Gillet, Connecticut State Library, Hartford. Church symbols indicate the locations of "Houses of Public Worship," including (from northeast to southwest) the Congregational Church of Pomfret, the Abington Congregational Church, the Grow Hill Baptist Church (on the Abington-Hampton border), and the Hampton (Windham Village) Congregational Church. (Photograph by the author.)

Isaac Backus (1724–1806). (Source: Isaac Backus, *Church History of New England from 1620 to 1804* [Philadelphia: Baptist Tract Depository, 1839], frontispiece)

James Manning (1738–1791). (Source: Reuben Aldridge Guild, *Life, Times, and Correspondence of James Manning, and the Early History of Brown University* [Boston: Gould and Lincoln, 1864], frontispiece)

in a solemn and well-attended daylong ceremony that featured sermons by Backus and Manning before concluding with a "laying on of hands."[45] Three years earlier, Thomas and Susanna's 34-year-old daughter, Rebecca, had married the Thompson Baptist elder Whitman Jacobs, and their third daughter, Lydia, later became the wife of Baptist preacher Elisha Ransom, a "staunch partisan of... religious liberty" in Vermont.[46] Together, these personal relationships and connections helped integrate the Grows into a wide-ranging Baptist influence network that would continue to shape the contours of family members' lives for the next three generations.

The Grow Hill Baptist Church's formal written covenant, entitled "Articles of Belief," provides a useful window into the Grows' religious views and practices.[47] The document makes clear, first and foremost, that the church practiced a strict, fundamentalist form of Christianity based on a literal reading of the Bible. William McLoughlin has described Separate Baptists as "the strictest biblical literalists of their age," a sect whose "doctrines and practices come closest to those of New England's 17th-century Puritan founders," and whose popular appeal with the masses came from their insistence on "complete adherence to the plainest sense of the Word of God."[48] The Grow Hill Baptists clearly fit that description. According to their "Articles of Belief":

> We believe that there is one living and true God, who is a spirit of himself, from eternity to eternity, unchangeably the same, infinitely holy, just, merciful and gracious, longsuffering, and abundant in goodness and truth . . ., forgiving [of] sins, [but who] will by no means clear the guilty . . . We believe that this God is revealed in the Scriptures . . . [and that] the holy Scriptures of the old and new Testament are the Words of God wherein he hath given us a perfect rule of faith and practice.[49]

Prior to their admission to church membership, every member of the Grow Hill Baptist Church was required to give "a personal verbal account to the church of what God has done for their souls, to the satisfaction of the church." As the "Articles of Belief" stated: "the door of the Church is to be carefully kept at all times against such as cannot give scriptural evidence of their union with Christ by faith."[50]

Like other Baptists, the Grows and their fellow church members also practiced "believer's baptism by full immersion." For them, the ritual of plunging new converts underwater and then raising them to the surface was a richly symbolic act that celebrated the core element of their faith: the death and resurrection of Jesus Christ. According to McLoughlin, the visual "imagery of burial and resurrection" represented by full-immersion baptism "recalled vividly the redemptive work of Christ, who died for sin, was buried, and rose triumphant over death." By depicting the newly reborn Christian as washed clean of sin and "risen to walk in the newness of life with Christ," the water-baptism ceremony "portrayed the hope and belief of the Christian in bodily resurrection and life beyond the grave." The Grow Hill Baptists' "Articles of Belief" explained the practice as follows: "We believe [that] to be baptized with water is to go down in the water, and be overwhelmed or buried with water, to witness and hold forth our faith in the death, burial, and resurrection of our Lord Christ."[51]

In their personal lives, members of the Grow Hill church were expected to wage "continual war" "against every temptation and lust," and to "watch over" the moral conduct of their fellow members as well. As a consequence, church business meetings were largely devoted to examining complaints about moral misconduct on the part of individual members, resolving internal quarrels within the congregation, and other matters of discipline. In 1784, for example, "Sister Sarah Rogers" was "admonished" for her "immodest Lascivious Deceitful Conduct." Two years later, the church expelled Elizabeth Cleveland after she "confessed herself guilty of the Sin of fornication." Several members (Elizabeth Hale, John Gramman, and others) were excommunicated for committing adultery, while the church was forced to "withdraw the hand of fellowship" from Abraham Ford "for Lascivious Carriage in attempting the chastity of a young woman in the Night Season." Jacob Wilson was expelled for "drinking to excess." Church leaders also intervened repeatedly to mediate "Brother" Nehemiah Dodge's disputes with fellow members over the purchase of farm animals and other business transactions, and in 1792, they found it necessary to admonish Dodge "for his abuse of his Apprentice Noah Lyon and Denying of it."[52]

And finally, like Separate Baptists everywhere in New England, the Grow Hill Baptists were ardently democratic in matters of church governance. To prevent the kind of autocratic rule that had become commonplace in the region's Congregational churches, they wrote into their covenant provisions that limited the power of the elder and placed the church's members on an equal footing with its leaders. As the "Articles of Belief" put it: "We believe that Elders by virtue of their office have no more power to decide any case in controversy in the Church than any private brother." Instead, church decision making was based on "the consent of the brethren," with the elder's role restricted to "administer[ing] the ordinances and . . . devot[ing] himself to the work of preaching the gospel, warning and exhorting publicly and from house to house, [and] visiting the sick," while the church's deacon "[took] care of the poor of the church, and . . . serve[d] at the Lord's table" during communion.[53]

Reflecting the eighteenth-century "age of enlightenment" in which they lived, New Englanders of Thomas and Susanna's generation had largely freed themselves from the fear of witchcraft and evil spirits that held their grandparents' generation in its grip. Nevertheless, Separate Baptists and other evangelicals still interpreted major events in the world around them in supernatural terms, as signs from God. In his diary, Isaac Backus recorded numerous stories in which "the hand of God" had reportedly acted "to awaken men to the necessity of their salvation": "scoffers at religion . . . struck dead," "earthquakes sent to warn men that the day of judgment" would soon be upon them, etc. To Backus, sudden deaths, natural catastrophes, and accidents of any sort were all to be regarded as "solemn warnings from God."[54]

In addition, the Separate Baptist worldview contained a strong element of apocalyptic millennialism—a fervent belief in the imminent "Second Coming of Christ," a cataclysmic "end of days" event in which all non-believers would perish and the Messiah would return to establish his thousand-year (millennial) Christian kingdom on earth as the Bible had prophesied.[55] Uncertainty as to when this cosmic apocalypse would take place led many Separate Baptists (allegedly including Thomas[3] Grow or his son Thomas[4]) to engage in intensive Bible study in search of prophesies and other clues that would enable them to calculate the precise date of the "Glorious Day."[56] Extreme weather events invariably sparked widespread speculation that the millennium might be at hand. On the morning of 19 May 1780, for example, when the skies over southeastern New England suddenly "filled with dense black clouds" that blotted out the sun and cast the region into a darkness so black "that a candle in the window gave no light outside," James Manning interpreted the mysterious phenomenon as "a prelude to that great and important day when the final consummation of all things is to take place." (The blackout was actually caused by smog—a combination of heavy fog mixed with the soot and ashes from extensive fires in Vermont, where frontier settlers were burning forests to clear land for farming.)[57] Traces of millennialism can also be found in the Grow Hill Baptist Church's "Articles of Belief," according to which the church dedicated itself to devoutly following "the Word and Spirit of God Almighty" while eagerly "watching for the coming of our Lord and Saviour Jesus Christ."[58]

Over time, Connecticut authorities reached an accommodation with the colony's Baptists over the volatile issue of compulsory religious taxation. Under the arrangement, a Baptist was exempted from paying taxes in support of his parish's Congregational church if he provided local officials with a written certificate signed by the minister or another officer of his Baptist church verifying that he was a member in good standing of that church.[59] The members of the Grow Hill Baptist Church participated in this certificate system, and Thomas and Susanna's son Thomas[4] signed large numbers of certificates on behalf of the church in his official capacity as its clerk.[60]

During the 1770s, however, many Separate Baptists began to oppose the certificate system. Those who filed the signed certificates with their town officials often found that they became objects of scorn and social harassment in their local Congregational community for being "tax dodgers" who had hypocritically submitted the certificate in order to evade their ecclesiastical tax obligation and "save a few shillings of their money." Isaac Backus and other Separate Baptist leaders eventually came to regard the certificate system as an unacceptable violation of their denomination's religious liberty. In their view, church funding was an exclusively religious matter, one in which the civil government had no legal right to interfere. By participating in the certificate system, they argued, Baptists were in effect subordinating their religious affairs to the control of "secular authorities"—who, by regulating the collection of religious taxes, were usurping a power that rightfully belonged "to God alone to rule over His church." Rather than gratefully accept the "crumbs of toleration," Backus urged Baptists to "cease turning in certificates . . ., refuse to pay religious taxes," and demand full religious equality with Congregationalists.

Accordingly, from the 1770s into the nineteenth century, Backus and other Separate Baptists carried out a campaign of nonviolent civil disobedience against the certificate system as a discriminatory infringement of their freedom of worship—their "liberty of conscience" or "soul liberty," as they often referred to it.[61] As local Backus protégés, Thomas Grow and his sons may have opposed the certificate system in Abington and/or Windham Village, because nearly two centuries later they were still remembered as "pioneers in defense of the doctrine of religious freedom" in the area.[62]

Although Separate Baptists were conservative fundamentalists in matters of theology,[63] their contentious relations with the civil and ecclesiastical authorities of their parishes had subconsciously prepared them for a new role as political revolutionaries by the time of the war for American independence. Years of struggle to sustain their religious liberty in the face of what they regarded as tyranny and oppression on the part of their local leaders in effect predisposed them to respond sympathetically to the call for political liberty from British tyranny and oppression. In breaking away from New England's Congregational establishment and forming their own independent churches, they had already succeeded in carrying out localized rebellions against constituted authority at the parish level, while their long and ongoing resistance to compulsory religious taxes had turned them into bitter enemies of "taxation without representation." Consequently, when the British Parliament, in an effort to increase revenues, imposed a series of unpopular new taxes on the American colonies—the Sugar Act of 1764, the Stamp Act of 1765, the Tea Act of 1773—Separate Baptists joined their fellow colonists in a revolutionary struggle to free themselves from British despotism and the "unrepresentative" British Parliament's imperial tax policies.[64]

On 20 April 1775, "messengers on horseback" raced through Windham County informing town officials that British troops had fired on Massachusetts colonists the previous day at Lexington. In response, the local militias of

Pomfret, Windham Village, and other Windham County towns immediately mobilized for a march to Boston to confront the main body of British forces in Massachusetts. Seven weeks later, thirty Pomfret militiamen led by Colonel Israel Putnam and Captain Thomas Grosvenor fought in the battle of Bunker Hill, and members of their unit subsequently helped to pressure the British into abandoning Boston in 1776.[65]

The fragmentary nature of Connecticut's revolutionary war militia records makes it difficult to determine whether members of the Grow family participated in any of the initial military engagements of the war, but by the second half of 1776, as British forces sailed south from Boston in a campaign to seize New York City, three of Thomas and Susanna's four sons were serving in Connecticut militia units that had been deployed to New York to prevent the city from falling under British control. The couple's two youngest sons—23-year-old Nathaniel and 21-year-old Ebenezer—were privates in Captain Zebediah Ingalls' "Militia of Abington in Pomfrett," a company in the state's 11th Militia Regiment,[66] while their eldest son, 33-year-old Thomas[4], was a private in Captain Walter Hyde's company of a Connecticut militia regiment commanded by Colonel Erastus Wolcott.[67] As a Baptist preacher, William, the family's other son, presumably received a clergyman's exemption from military service.[68]

Of the three sons who fought in the American Revolution, it was Ebenezer Grow who compiled the most extensive military record. Ebenezer apparently suffered from a form of mental impairment. One of his commanding officers during the war—Thomas Grosvenor of Pomfret, who knew him well—described him as "a person somewhat deranged in Mind by turns."[69] The nature and extent of his mental illness are not known, but his condition might have been related to the fact that his mother was 40 years of age when she gave birth to him. Landless and probably illiterate[70] at the time of the revolution, with few prospects beyond those of a low-wage agricultural laborer, he was a young man who, like the vast majority of revolutionary war soldiers, had "little or nothing to lose," and for whom military service in the revolutionary army presented opportunities in the form of enlistment bounties, monthly wages, and adventure. Patriotism might or might not have been a motivating factor in his decision to fight.[71]

During the war Ebenezer compiled what George W. Davis described as "a notable record" of nearly continuous military service.[72] In 1775, according to Davis, he "marched from Killingly to Boston on the occasion of the Lexington Alarm."[73] In 1776, as a private in Connecticut's 11th Militia Regiment, he was evidently in combat during the disastrous military defeats of August and September, when American forces were driven out of New York City, and he was "commended for gallantry at the battle of Long Island" in late August, if Davis' unverified statement is to be believed.[74] In May 1777, Ebenezer enlisted for an additional three years as a private in "Sherburne's Regiment," a newly formed infantry regiment in George Washington's Continental Army comprised of troops from Rhode Island and eastern Connecticut under the command of Colonel Henry Sherburne of Rhode Island.[75] Almost immediately, he and his new regiment were ordered to Peekskill, New York, to secure the Hudson Highlands, the strategically important heights on both sides of the Hudson River 50 miles north of New York City and 25 miles west of Connecticut. To prevent the British from gaining control of the Hudson River and cutting New England off from the rest of the American colonies—with potentially "fatal consequences" for the revolution—Washington stationed a large American military force at the Highlands throughout the war, employing the soldiers in the construction of fortifications on the 150-foot bluffs overlooking a key bend in the river at West Point.[76] The following year, Sherburne's Regiment was briefly deployed in Rhode Island, where it fought in the inconclusive Battle of Rhode Island in August—an operation in which American forces attempted to push the British out of Newport.[77]

The regiment spent the winter of 1778–1779 encamped at Redding, Connecticut, where their division commander, Israel Putnam, by then a major-general, employed raiding parties to attack enemy forces in towns along the New York-Connecticut border. In a famous incident in February 1779, Putnam and 150 of his soldiers were surprised by 1,500 British troops outside an Episcopal church at Horseneck (West Greenwich, Connecticut). The church was situated on the crest of a hill that descended steeply to the valley floor below, and "to avoid the tedious walk [up] the circling road [that led] to the summit," the congregation "had placed 70 broad stepping-stones" on the hillside leading directly up to the church. Nearly surrounded, and with British dragoons "but a sword's length" behind, Putnam and some of his men made a spectacular escape by "plung[ing] down the steep precipice" on horseback under heavy British gunfire. According to "family tradition"—a notoriously unreliable historical source—Ebenezer was one of the soldiers who "rode with his chief down the stone steps at Greenwich."[78]

By May of 1779, Sherburne's Regiment was back in the Hudson Highlands building fortifications. After enduring the "hard winter" of 1779–1780 at Morristown, New Jersey, alongside Washington's main forces, the regiment returned to the Highlands, where it remained until May 1780, when it was disbanded and its men were discharged.[79] Ebenezer quickly joined the Continental Army's 4th Connecticut Regiment on a short-term enlistment for the remainder of the year,[80] and in January 1781 he reenlisted in that same regiment for an additional three-year tour of duty.[81] In late January, while serving as a private in Major Benjamin Throop's Company, he may have been part of a detachment of Connecticut soldiers that George Washington sent 30 miles south into New Jersey to put down a mutiny in one of that state's Continental Army regiments.[82]

As part of a 1781 reorganization of forces, the 4th Regiment was subsequently incorporated into the Continental Army's 1st Connecticut Infantry Regiment, and Ebenezer served in that regiment for the duration of the war, stationed primarily at the Hudson Highlands.[83] In June 1783, following the climactic American-French military victory at Yorktown and with a peace agreement about to be signed granting the United States of America their formal independence, the 1st Connecticut Infantry Regiment was disbanded and he was honorably discharged.[84]

Ebenezer was amply compensated for his military service throughout the war. Recruits in Sherburne's Regiment received an enlistment bonus, or "bounty," of $20 from the Continental Congress along with an equal amount from the state of Connecticut.[85] By the time he reenlisted in 1781, service in the Continental Army had become so physically onerous that Connecticut regiments were offering "bounty money" of $200 or more as an inducement to enlist.[86] In addition, Ebenezer was paid a standard infantryman's wages of $6.60 a month throughout the war.[87] Unfortunately, most of the money that he received was virtually worthless. Paper currency issued by the Continental Congress was not backed by gold or silver (or taxes, for that matter), and consequently it immediately depreciated to a small fraction of its face value as soon as it was put into circulation. By 1780, for example, a $100 Continental bill was worth "a mere fifty cents in hard money." As a result, "galloping depreciation" combined with rampant wartime inflation meant that most enlisted men were "virtually 'soldiering' for free" during much of the war.[88]

Common soldiers like Ebenezer also endured nearly subhuman living conditions in their army camps. Tents, blankets, bedding, uniforms, shoes, and other basic provisions were in woefully short supply throughout the revolution, while the Continental Army's commissary system functioned so poorly that food rations were seldom available in sufficient quantity, leaving the enlisted men perpetually hungry and occasionally starving. Sanitation and hygiene were almost nonexistent in the camps, and diseases such as smallpox, typhus, yellow fever, dysentery, and a maddening malady that the men referred to as "the Itch" posed a far greater threat to soldiers' lives than British gunfire.[89] By the time Ebenezer joined Sherburne's Regiment in 1777, the wretched conditions of service in the Continental Army had already become so well known among the general populace that only men "from the fringes of society" were enlisting.[90]

Conditions in Sherburne's Regiment mirrored those in the army in general. The regiment's recruits were receiving inoculations to eradicate smallpox at the time of Ebenezer's 1777 enlistment.[91] The following year, the regiment was reported to be utterly "destitute" of provisions, with "discontent" widespread among its men.[92] In December 1778, Sherburne's second-in-command warned the governor of Connecticut that the regiment's soldiers had yet to receive the provisions promised them, and that if something was not done, "it is my

Private's uniform, Sherburne's Continental Regiment, 1778–1780, consisting of a black felt hat laced with white wool braid, white leather cross-belts worn over a brown coat with yellow trim, a dark green waistcoat and breeches, white wool stockings, and black half gaiters of painted canvas, together with a canvas knapsack and haversack for supplies. (Source: Lt. Charles M. Lefferts, *Uniforms of the American, British, French and German Armies in the War of the American Revolution* [New York: New-York Historical Society, 1926], 16–17, plate II)

opinion that mutiny or desertion will reduce our battalions to nothing before Spring."[93] However, the worst was yet to come.

During the winter of 1779–1780, Ebenezer and his fellow soldiers had barely settled into the regiment's winter quarters at Morristown, New Jersey, when they were hammered relentlessly by week after week of unusually heavy snowstorms—twenty-eight between December and April—accompanied by temperatures "cold enough to cut a man in two."[94] Clothing and food supplies soon ran out, and by December a Connecticut officer on the scene was reporting that "the men have suffer'd much without shoes and stockings, and working half leg deep in snow." The following month a fellow officer informed Connecticut's governor that "the distress of the army . . . hardly admits of a description. It is a melancholy fact that the troops, both officers and men, have almost perished for want of provisions." In February, another Connecticut officer reported that "not more than Fifty men in the Regiment [are] fit for duty—many a good Lad with nothing to cover him from his hips to his toes save his Blanket."[95] Food became so scarce that the soldiers "existed for months on one-eighth of their meat ration," until May when "the supply gave out entirely."[96] Joseph Plumb Martin, like Ebenezer Grow, a private in a Connecticut regiment at Morristown during the excruciating winter, recalled in his memoirs:

> We were absolutely, literally starved. I do solemnly declare that I did not put a single morsel of victuals into my mouth for four days and as many nights, except a little black birch bark which I gnawed off a stick of wood, if that can be called victuals. I saw several of the men roast their old shoes and eat them, and I was afterwards informed by one of the officers' waiters that some of the officers killed and ate a favorite little dog that belonged to one of them.[97]

By all accounts, the Continental Army soldiers who wintered at Morristown in 1779–1780 suffered more than the soldiers at Valley Forge the previous winter.[98] By April of 1780, sickness and desertions had reduced Sherburne's Regiment to only 86 men (down from 272 the previous August), leading to the unit's disbandment in May.[99]

Although conditions were not as grim at Ebenezer's subsequent encampments in the Hudson Highlands, the enlisted men stationed there experienced a severe shortage of food rations in late 1781 and subsisted "for half the winter" of 1782–1783 "on tripe and cowheels." In addition, epidemics of smallpox and measles broke out at West Point during 1782–1783, and at one point the soldiers encamped there went so many months without pay that some of them began to organize a mutiny. One of Ebenezer's fellow soldiers in the 1st Connecticut Regiment, Lud Gaylord, was hanged for his role in the plot.[100]

Meanwhile, as Ebenezer endured the wretched realities of Continental Army life, his parents were experiencing privations of their own back on Grow Hill. No British invasions or military battles took place in Windham County, but its economy was nonetheless severely dislocated by the war. British naval control of Long Island Sound and the presence of powerful British military forces in Newport, Rhode Island, cut local farmers off from access to their regular outside markets and trading networks. As a result, the county's inhabitants soon began to suffer acute shortages of flour, grain, salt, sugar, and other basic commodities. In addition, a series of devastating summer droughts and brutally harsh winters between 1777 and 1780 made an already difficult situation worse, leading to "great hardship and suffering" among the general population.[101]

At the same time, however, the revolution was also an economic boon to many Windham County farmers, especially for meat and dairy producers like Thomas Grow. From the start, there was money to be made from selling provisions—beef, pork, butter, cheese, root crops, leather, and other farm products—to the army; and thanks to wartime inflation, prices for those commodities rose steadily. By 1781, the overall price of food products in Connecticut was at least 20 percent higher than pre-war levels, while a barrel of pork had increased in value from 60 shillings to 100, and the price of oxen had risen from £10 a head to £13. Meanwhile, in 1780, the arrival in Rhode Island of General Rochambeau's 6,000-man French expeditionary force had opened another lucrative military-provisions market for the county's agricultural producers. Consequently, for many Windham County farmers the revolution proved to be an economic windfall.[102] Lacking detailed records of Thomas' agricultural operations, it is impossible to assess the net impact of the war on his personal wealth or his family's standard of living. Nevertheless, several voluntary contributions that he made to the war effort in Pomfret— including a £28 cash advance to the town "for hiring Soldiers," £2-5-0 for a blanket for a Continental soldier, and extensive assistance to the Lyon family while its men served in the army—suggest that his pre-war level of economic prosperity remained reasonably intact.[103]

After the revolution, Thomas continued to enjoy a respected position in local society as a large landowner, church deacon, and town officeholder. Like other leading citizens, he also supported less fortunate members of the community out of his own pocket. In the late eighteenth century, modern concepts of public welfare were still unknown in New England; instead, poor, disabled, or elderly residents unable to support themselves were routinely "bid off" to those more affluent townspeople who would agree to look after them. Thomas seems to have taken such social-welfare responsibilities to heart as one of his Christian duties, because in one two-year period alone (1790–1791) he provided financial or material assistance to no less than ten of his Abington and Hampton neighbors who had fallen on hard times—including, among others, the "Widow Fuller," a local Indian woman named Hannah Johns, and the Abraham Snow family that had been ravaged by illness.[104]

Nevertheless, the Grow family's postwar moral standing in the community was not entirely exemplary. Instead, it had been tarnished rather badly by a scandal that erupted at the very end of the revolution. In June 1783, Thomas and Susanna's 34-year-old son William, the pastor of the Grow Hill Baptist Church, fathered an out-of-wedlock child with Eunice Abbott, an unmarried young woman from his congregation. William, who was said to have "a pleasing address, persuasive manner, and a melodious and commanding voice," was a married man with three daughters ranging in age from 4 years to 10 months at the time of the illegitimate child's birth. A few days after the delivery, the church expelled Eunice for "the Sin of fornication"—despite what the church records refer to without explanation as her "repeated" attempts to "deny" the charge and her "astonishing" efforts to "cover" the act "with a mask of religion." Two weeks later, in a meeting held "at Deacon Thomas Grow's house," church members "put to a vote whether this Church is satisfied that Elder William Grow is gilty [sic] of whoredom or fornication." The measure "past [sic] in the affirmative." A second vote was then taken to determine "if it be the minds of this Church to reject Elder William Grow as Being Either our Elder or a brother with us on account of his Being gilty of the Sin of whoredom or fornication." That measure, too, "past in the affirmative."[105] Recording the sordid affair in his diary, Isaac Backus described it in a single word: "terrible!"[106]

In late August, six weeks after his expulsion, William appeared before the church to publicly confess his "Iniquity" and request "to Be Received again as [a] member." By this point, the young pastor's adulterous act with a female parishioner had created acrimonious divisions within the congregation, giving rise—as the church records put it—to many verbal "imprudences," acts of "ungodlyness" by various members against one another, and charges of a lack of Christian "fellowship" on the part of some members. By early 1784, a faction consisting of the Grows and their supporters had managed to secure William's readmission to church membership along with the restoration of his preaching privileges. Those decisions, however, seem to have morally outraged a second faction that included members of the Dodge, Adams, Paine, Dean, and Peck families, among others, fueling a bitter quarrel within the church that lasted for a generation and at one point led Thomas and Susanna's son Thomas[4] to physically strike one of William's Paine-family critics. During 1784, as "contention" and "great Difficulties" continued, several members of the congregation "withdrew from the church." Then, in April 1785, the second faction succeeded in rescinding the restoration of William's preaching privileges, and the following December, the church voted to "admonish" him for having brought a "Charge Against Brother Nehe[miah] Dodge in Publick meeting."[107]

A short time later, William and his wife, Priscilla, and their four children (a fourth daughter having been born some seventeen months after the scandal first broke—suggesting, perhaps, that Priscilla forgave her husband for his transgression) left Connecticut for the Vermont frontier town of Bridgewater, where William obtained a position as pastor of the United Baptist Society of Woodstock and Bridgewater, a pastorate previously held by his brother-in-law Elisha Ransom (the husband of William's sister Lydia). Within a few years, however, word of William's immoral conduct in Connecticut reached his new congregation in Vermont, and after another long interlude of "contention and bitter strife," that church also expelled him, citing what it characterized as his "misbehavior and chicanery." He and Priscilla apparently remained in Bridgewater until they died—William in 1830 at age 81, Priscilla in 1841 at age 89.[108]

Meanwhile, back on Grow Hill, things had quickly gone from bad to worse. In May 1786, a few months after William and his family departed for Vermont, Susanna Grow died at age 71. Although the cause of her death is unknown, it is tempting to speculate that a contributing factor was the emotional stress and public embarrassment caused by her son's scandalous affair. Curiously, she was buried in the Old Abington Burying Grounds nearly 2 miles northeast of her home, rather than in the cemetery on the family farm at the northeastern foot of Grow Hill where two of her children who predeceased her were interred.

In Memory of
Mrs. Susanna
Wife of Mr. Thomas
Grow Who Died
May ye 17, 1786
In ye 72 Year of
Her Age

Susanna (Eaton) Grow headstone, Old Abington Burying Grounds, Route 97, Abington, CT. (Photograph by the author.)

Her gravestone reflects the continued evolution of New England funerary art away from the grim Puritan iconography of the seventeenth and early eighteenth centuries toward more uplifting symbolic representations of death as an opportunity for eternal salvation and celestial reunion with one's deceased loved ones. The central feature on Susanna's headstone—an almost pleasant-looking "winged-cherub" soul effigy wearing a "crown of righteousness"—symbolizes her victorious transcendence of death, while a scalloped border at the top of the stone, representing clouds, symbolically reinforces the theme of her soul's successful ascension to Heaven.[109]

Less than six months after Susanna's death, Thomas—now 72 years old—married a local Hampton woman, Martha Winter.[110] He had by this time nearly completed the process of distributing land to his sons in preparation for retirement. After adding 176-plus acres to his farm in 1776, he apparently transferred the original 100-acre Grow Hill parcel and farmhouse to his eldest son Thomas[4] and moved onto his newly acquired parcel, building a new house on the opposite side of the King's Highway several hundred feet northwest of the original farmhouse.[111] Two years later, he transferred 12 acres of land to William.[112] Then, in 1785, adhering to the standard practice of eighteenth-century Connecticut farmers as they made arrangements to be cared for in old age, he gave his second-youngest son, Nathaniel, "one half of the farm I now live upon . . . together with one half of the Dwelling House and Barn thereon standing."[113] Normally, the youngest son of the family became the designated caretaker of his aging parents. In this case, however, Ebenezer apparently lacked

Grow Hill farmhouse, probably constructed during or shortly after the American Revolution. Destroyed by fire in the 1960s, the dwelling was located on the site of present-day 1135 State Route 97, Hampton, CT. (Undated photograph from Susan Jewett Griggs, *Folklore and Firesides of Pomfret, Hampton and Vicinity,* Hampton section: p. 24d, photograph 1)

the capacity to fulfill that role; instead Nathaniel and his wife Susannah assumed the responsibility in exchange for land and housing.[114] Five years later, according to the new United States government's first federal census, Thomas was serving as the head of a twelve-person household that included his son Nathaniel, three males under the age of 16 (including Nathaniel's 2-year-old son and two unidentified boys), and seven females (Thomas' wife, Martha; Nathaniel's wife, Susannah; four young daughters; and an unidentified woman or girl).[115]

A major late-life change was still to come, however. In 1794, 80-year-old Thomas and his wife, Martha, accompanied by Nathaniel and his family, pulled up their deep roots on Grow Hill and moved 120 miles north to the frontier town of Guilford in the far southeast corner of Vermont. Windham County residents had been migrating to Vermont since the third quarter of the eighteenth century, propelled by New England's familiar patterns of population growth, rising land prices, and soil exhaustion, and lured by prospects of cheap, fertile farmland in the sparsely populated territory to the north.[116] In Thomas' case, the move to the frontier might have been prompted by a sense of patrimonial responsibility to his family at a time when Grow Hill was being impacted by increased ecological pressures. By 1794, Thomas and his sons had apparently come to the conclusion that the family farm could no longer remain economically viable as a subdivided agricultural estate; consequently, the entire property was placed in the hands of the family's eldest son Thomas[4], and Thomas[3] accompanied his other farming son, Nathaniel—with whom he evidently shared special bonds of affection—in moving to Vermont (William being employed in the ministry rather than agriculture, and Ebenezer apparently incapable of operating an independent farm of his own).[117]

Religious considerations might also have played a role in Thomas' decision to relocate. From the start, Baptists and other evangelicals were heavily represented in the northward migration, many apparently having concluded that the Vermont frontier's climate of religious freedom was preferable to life under Congregational hegemony in Connecticut. Evangelical Christians had dominated the drafting of Vermont's constitution, which granted citizens "complete liberty of conscience in religion . . . with the right to worship as they pleased" (while at the same time excluding Catholics, Jews, and anyone else who did not embrace "the protestant religion" from holding public office). In addition, during the 1790s local courts in many Vermont towns were still enforcing "morals laws" against swearing, drunkenness, and neglect of religious worship on the Sabbath, making the state doubly attractive to pious Baptists.

From the 1770s onward, West Woodstock's Biel Ledoyt and other evangelists had been actively at work establishing Baptist churches in pioneer communities in the Vermont portion of the upper Connecticut River Valley; and those organizing efforts had produced notable results in Guilford, where four Baptist churches were formed between 1770 and 1791.[118] In 1792, Thomas' daughter Rebecca and her husband, the Baptist elder Whitman Jacobs—who had preached for a year at the Grow Hill Baptist Church in the wake of the William Grow scandal—took up residence in Guilford, with Jacobs becoming pastor of the town's Second Baptist Church.[119] Two years later, perhaps driven in part by the toxic factionalization present in the Grow Hill Baptist Church following William's removal as pastor, Thomas and his household joined them. In that sense, his relocation to Vermont bore some of the characteristics of a Baptist chain migration.

In February 1794, Thomas[3] and Nathaniel purchased joint ownership of 94 acres of land abutting Whitman and Rebecca Jacobs' farm 1.2 miles south of Guilford's village center. The fact that the property had already changed hands at least four times since the 1760s suggests that it may have been partially cleared and "improved" when the Grows acquired it. Purchased for £355, the parcel was located on the south side of what would later be called the Jacksonville Stage Road (currently Stage Road), in rugged, hilly terrain sloping upward to a high plateau of fields and pastures.[120]

By 1800, according to that year's federal census, Thomas had ceded "head of household" status—and undoubtedly the day-to-day management of the farm—to Nathaniel.[121] Thomas continued to reside in Guilford until his death on 10 August 1806 at age 92.[122] His grave in the bucolic Guilford Center Cemetery a mile north of his farm is marked with a transitional headstone that combines traditional Puritan motifs with newer, more secular elements that were coming into fashion in the early nineteenth century. The headstone's dominant feature—a neoclassical covered urn, a common mourning symbol in ancient Greece and Rome—reflects the national mood of the early republic, as Americans celebrated the country's new institutions of self-government by highlighting their antecedents in classical Greek democracy and Roman republicanism. At the same time, however, the urn on Thomas' stone is encircled with two vestigial features of eighteenth-century Puritan iconography: a laurel wreath symbolizing the soul's triumph over death, and a ring of clouds symbolizing the successful enshrinement of Thomas' soul in Heaven.[123]

Of Thomas[3] Grow, the man—his personality, his temperament, his behavioral characteristics—we of course know nothing. Modern academic scholarship suggests that like other Separate Baptist farmers in eighteenth-century New England, he was probably a hardworking, plainspoken, rustic individual and a pious, dogmatic religious fundamentalist who believed with unquestioning certainty that "all truth resided in the Bible."[124] The extent to which he personally conformed to that general stereotype, however, is unknowable. Nor is it possible to recapture the internal dynamics of Thomas and Susanna's family life. Historians describe the family structure of eighteenth-century New England

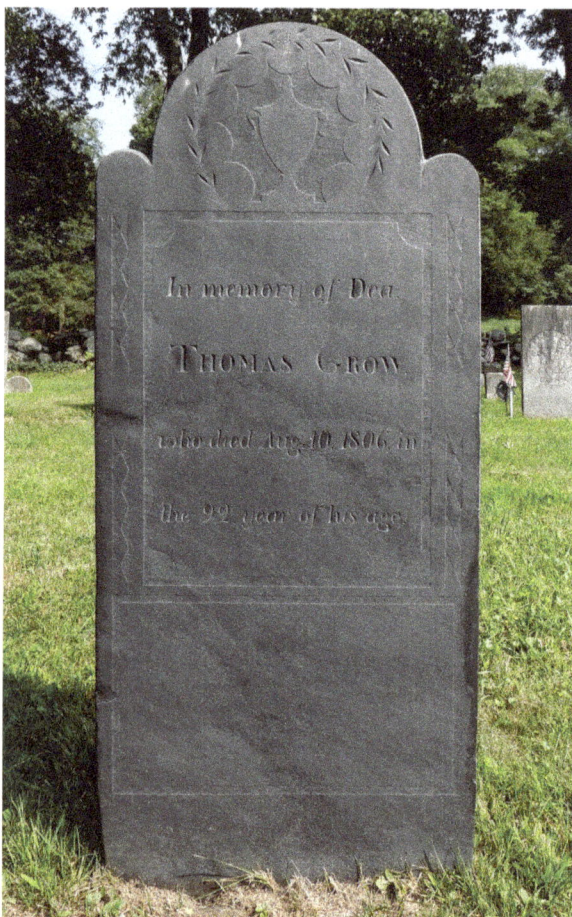

In Memory of Dea.
Thomas Grow
who died Aug. 10, 1806 in
the 92 year of his age.

Thomas Grow headstone, Guilford Center Cemetery, Cemetery Hill Road, Guilford Center, VT. (Photograph by the author.)

farmers as a legally and biblically sanctioned patriarchal hierarchy in which the male head of household had sole legal ownership of the family's assets, made all important economic decisions, and ruled as an authoritarian patriarch over his wife and children, organizing their labor to assure a productive and successful agricultural enterprise.[125] But again, the extent to which that stereotypical profile is specifically applicable to the Grow family is impossible to determine.

What can be said with certainty is that the couple lived during one of the most eventful periods in American history, and that they actively participated in two of the eighteenth century's most transformative events: the Great Awakening and the American Revolution. As lay leaders of a breakaway Separate Baptist community in Abington in the aftermath of the Great Awakening, they played a direct role in the grassroots spiritual upheaval that brought a greater degree of pluralism to American religion; while as the parents of three revolutionary war soldiers and as contributors to the war effort at home, they were fully invested in their country's struggle for independence. The couple's impact on the class status of their Grow family line was less dramatic but by no means inconsequential. Building on his father's record of social and economic achievement, Thomas[3] became a respected, perhaps even a prominent, figure in local society along the Abington-Windham border. A prosperous farmer, religious leader, and civic official, he helped consolidate the family's position in the upper middle class of rural American society.

THOMAS GROW (1743–1824)

The next Thomas Grow in the family line, Thomas[3] and Susanna's eldest son, took advantage of widening opportunities available in the early republic to become a wealthy farmer and successful businessman, as well as a respected civic and religious leader in his community. In doing so, he elevated the family to new heights of local prominence in the Pomfret-Hampton area.

Thomas[4] (*Thomas*[3], *Thomas*[2], *John*[1]) was a lifelong resident of Grow Hill. Born in his parents' farmhouse in 1743, he married 20-year-old Experience Goodell, the daughter of a local Abington farmer, in 1767, when he was 24.[1] After their wedding, the young couple resided on Grow Hill, assisting Thomas' parents in running the family farm. Within a decade, following custom, they were rewarded for the "sweat equity" that they had invested in the family enterprise when Thomas' father transferred 100 acres of the property to him.[2]

Thomas and Experience Grow apparently took to heart the biblical injunction "Be fruitful and multiply," because at a time when the average New England farm family included seven to ten offspring,[3] they produced a family of fourteen children—nine daughters and five sons—all but one of whom lived to adulthood. Over the course of her first twenty-five years of marriage, Experience gave birth to a child every twenty-one months on average, with intervals of barely thirteen months separating three of her first four deliveries. By the time she was 35, she was already a mother of ten—and the fact that eight of those first ten children were daughters was undoubtedly a source of considerable comfort to her, because as the older girls neared adolescence they provided their mother with much-needed child care for the new babies she continued to deliver at regular intervals until her childbearing years came to a close at menopause.

Thomas was a 32-year-old father of five when the American Revolution broke out. Like many other mature "middling"-level farmers with family responsibilities, he served only briefly as a member of a militia unit during the early stages of the war, and chose not to reenlist, leaving the fighting instead to poor, landless, unmarried younger men like his mentally challenged brother, Ebenezer. For the most part, men of Thomas' background preferred to serve in

Children of THOMAS[4] and EXPERIENCE (GOODELL) GROW (all born at Grow Hill on the Pomfret-Windham (Hampton), CT border; births were recorded in one or both jurisdictions):

i.   Dillie (Dilla?), b. 14 Sept. 1768; d. after 1824, date & place unk.; m. _____ Bacon.

ii.   Olive, b. 27 Jan. 1770; d. 20 Aug. 1858 at Hampton, CT; m. Dr. Jacob Hovey.

iii.   Lois, b. 6 March 1771; d. 22 Nov. 1843 at Scotland, CT; m. 1790, Deacon William Burnham.

iv.   Phoebe, b. 2 April 1772; d. 6 June 1853 at Homer, NY; m. 1795, Israel Hicks.

v.   Chloe, b. 13 Oct. 1773; d. 21 Oct. 1862 at Homer; m. 1803, Deacon Asa Bennett.

vi.   Hannah, b. 31 Aug. 1775; d. 16 Nov. 1853 at Homer; m. at Hampton, Isaac Rindge.

vii.   Anna, b. 15 Feb. 1777; d. 30 June 1806 at Homer; m. 1796 at Hampton, Joseph Darby.

xiii.   Elisha[5], b. 9 Feb. 1779; d. 22 Aug. 1850 at Waterford, MI; m. 25 Dec. 1801, Lois Palmer.

ix.   Rhoda, b. 6 Sept. 1780; d. 24 Dec. 1874 at Homer; m. 1802, Rev. Alfred Bennett.

x.   Thomas, b. 19 Aug. 1782; d. 25 Dec. 1852 at Hampton; m. (1) 1811, Polly Bennett; m. (2) 1831, Jerusha Wales.

xi.   Experience, b. 19 July 1784, d. 19 Feb. 1810, place unk.; m. _____ Clark.

xii.   Joseph, b. 11 Sept. 1787; d. 17 March 1827 at Ashford, CT; m. 8 Dec. 1808, Elizabeth Robbins.

xiii.   David, b. 2 Oct. 1791; d. 13 Dec. 1846 at Pomfret, CT; unm.

xiv.   John, b. 28 Dec. 1793; d. 4 Jan. 1810 at Pomfret; unm.

SOURCES: George W. Davis, *John Grow of Ipswich/John (Groo) Grow of Oxford* (Washington, D.C.: privately printed by the Carnahan Press, 1913), 36, 51–56; Clarence Winthrop Bowen, *The History of Woodstock, Connecticut: Genealogies of Woodstock Families,* 8 vols. (Norwood, MA: The Plimpton Press, 1926–1943), 6:384–385; *Connecticut Vital Records to 1870, The Barbour Collection,* online database, AmericanAncestors. org, citing Pomfret Vital Records, 2:122 (Phoebe Grow), Hampton Vital Records 1:240 (Thomas Grow first marriage); online at findagrave.com, memorial 54950381 (Lois Grow Burnham), memorial 80746280 (Olive Grow Hovey); Dillie Grow Bacon may have been the "Dilla Bacon," wife of Daniel Bacon, who died 16 February 1829 at age 61 in Charlton, Worcester County, MA. (Online at findagrave. com memorial 20498098)

the militia, which offered shorter enlistment terms than the Continental Army and usually deployed its members closer to home, enabling them to obtain food, clothing, medicine, and other support from their families.[4] In Thomas' case, his military service was apparently limited to a single six-month period as a private in a Connecticut militia company that marched 150 miles from Lebanon (the state's wartime military headquarters) to New York City in September 1776 to reinforce George Washington's Continental Army in the aftermath of the British rout of American forces on Long Island in late August.[5] It is possible that his combat record was less than heroic, given the woeful performance of Connecticut militia units in the fighting around New York City. According to observers on the scene, Connecticut's "raw militiamen" "were so little disposed to stand in the way of Grape Shot" that they "almost instantly retreated nay fled" and "skulked home."[6]

Returning to his family and farm after his term of enlistment ended, Thomas went on to perform valuable administrative service as a member of various wartime committees in Pomfret. In 1778, he served on a committee that provided economic assistance to the wives and children of local soldiers.[7] From 1780 to 1782, he was a member of several recruitment committees that procured men to fill the town's enlistment quotas for the state militia and the Continental Army,[8] at one point contributing £54 of his own money to pay his brother Ebenezer's military wages for six months.[9] And in 1781, he was one of three men assigned to collect a special war tax of "one penny on ye Pound in Hard Money" to fund the recruitment of additional local soldiers.[10]

His wartime committee work was the prelude to a long period of increasingly high-level local office holding after the revolution, commencing with his election to consecutive terms as a Pomfret lister (tax assessor) in 1784 and 1785.[11] Beginning in 1786, when adjustments to the Pomfret-Windham boundary shifted Thomas' Grow Hill property into the jurisdiction of the newly incorporated town of Hampton, that town became the focal point of his government service. In 1786–1787, he was a member of one committee that fixed the permanent location of the Pomfret-Hampton border and another that settled a dispute over Hampton's public-debt obligations to Pomfret for the financial support of "poor Persons" in the shifting border area.[12] He also served on committees that determined the administrative boundaries of Hampton's road and school districts.[13] In 1788, he was appointed town "Constable and Collector of the State Taxes" (a position his father had held two years earlier), followed by a term as the town's "First Constable" in 1789.[14] His public-service career then culminated in 1790 when, at age 47, he was elected simultaneously to three of Hampton's most important government offices: moderator of the annual town meeting, town selectman, and town constable.[15]

The post of town meeting moderator (i.e., presiding officer of the annual meeting) was perhaps the most prestigious of Hampton's major offices, requiring a man of "commanding presence and universal respect within the community who could not only maintain order in the meeting, but also keep . . . attention" focused "directly on the business at hand." The office of selectman was an equally high-status position; Hampton's three selectmen functioned as the "chief executive authorities" of the town, with primary responsibility for managing all of its administrative, financial, and regulatory affairs. The office of constable, by contrast, was not considered a leadership position *per se*, but its arduous and time-consuming duties—maintenance of public order, tax collection, etc.—were vital to the town's well-being; and accordingly, the position was usually filled by men with a reputation for honesty and strength of character. By 1790, Thomas had clearly established himself as a Hampton civic leader and one of the town's most "prominent and respected men."[16]

In the years that followed, he continued to accept more than his share of office-holding responsibilities, including another term as "Constable and Collector of the State Taxes" in 1792 and three additional terms as a town constable between 1794 and 1796.[17] In addition, he was elected to two terms as a Hampton grand juror on the Windham County Court (1800–1801),[18] and served in 1793 and 1797 as one of the town's "tithingmen"—local watchdogs who monitored moral behavior in the community and prosecuted incidents of Sabbath-breaking, public profanity, and other offenses not policed by the local churches.[19] All in all, during a quarter century of public service in Pomfret and Hampton, Thomas held at least eight different town offices, serving multiple terms in most of them, including seven terms as a Hampton constable.

As a local leader, he also continued his father's tradition of giving personal aid to destitute and infirm members of the community. During 1785, he provided corn to "Dolph," an impoverished former slave residing in Pomfret.[20] And from the early 1790s onward, he supplied a variety of material provisions (food, clothing, tallow for candles, etc.) to "the Poor of the Town of Hampton," including the "Widow Ormsby," Edward Coburn's family, Jethro Rogers, Sarah Smith, and Eunice Abbott, the woman with whom his brother William had fathered an illegitimate child at the end of the revolution.[21]

Simultaneously, Thomas was also assuming ever-greater leadership responsibilities in the Grow Hill Baptist Church, which he had helped found in 1770 as a young man in his late twenties. He served for two decades (from 1784 onward) as clerk of the local Baptist society, recording decisions made at its meetings, certifying memberships, and handling other paperwork.[22] In 1791, he contributed the single largest monetary donation of any church member (£22, nearly 25 per cent of the total) to a building fund for the construction of a church meetinghouse at the foot of Grow Hill.[23] Thereafter, he was consistently the church's most generous source of individual financial support, usually providing a quarter to a third of its annual preaching expenses out of his own pocket.[24] In 1804, at age 61, he was appointed deacon of the church, a position of considerable local prestige. (According to historian Jackson Turner Main, church deacons and ministers, together with the principal town officers and the militia captain, comprised the local elite in most Connecticut communities.)[25]

As deacon, he gradually assumed a somewhat patriarchal role within the Grow Hill Baptist Church. According to nineteenth-century local historian Ellen Larned, writing barely a half century after his death, Deacon Thomas Grow "was a man of strong faith and large heart whose fatherly care embraced the whole church. . . . It is said that he was accustomed to furnish dinner at intermission hour to all who came to worship."[26] Another source reported: "His custom was to send out his conveyances on Sunday and fetch members and their families to the meetings if they lived at a distance, to dine them at his home table, and to send them to their homes after the p.m. services."[27] George W. Davis, the Grow family genealogist, describes Thomas as a man of "kindly disposition" who "was greatly respected by all."[28]

Thomas' local prominence was also based to a significant extent on his economic accomplishments. Like other American farmers of the revolutionary war generation, he found himself in a rapidly changing economic environment after the war, one filled with new opportunities and challenges. The elimination of British imperial controls unleashed the productive energies of America's population, triggering an explosion of innovation, entrepreneurial enterprise, and economic growth. Throughout the new nation, ambitious artisans and craftsmen started up small-scale manufacturing establishments to supply their domestic markets with a long list of products—textiles, metal goods, ceramics and glassware, books, paper, etc.—that had previously come from England. The rapid growth of state-chartered banks after 1790 (from 3 to more than 300 by 1820) provided lending capital for additional manufacturing enterprises and for large-scale transportation and infrastructure projects (turnpikes, canals, bridges) that facilitated a massive expansion of internal commerce in the early republic by enabling farmers, manufacturers, and merchants to market their goods more widely. During the first four decades of national independence—a period that encompassed the second half of Thomas' life—agriculture remained the foundation of the US economy, but the seeds of commercial capitalism and industrial diversification—the dynamic engines of the country's future economic development—were successfully being sown.[29]

Windham County's economy mirrored the general trends. County farmers had prospered during the revolution from the sale of agricultural provisions to American military forces and their French allies. Wartime prosperity was then followed by a long period of economic growth extending into the early nineteenth century, as farmers increased their surpluses of meat, grain, and dairy products to supply New England's steadily growing urban consumer markets and Connecticut's flourishing export trade with the southern states and West Indies. Early in the nineteenth century, the construction of new turnpikes through the county—one from Hartford to Boston, another linking Hartford and Providence, a third running north-south from Worcester,

Massachusetts, to the Connecticut port of Norwich—stimulated a new burst of commercial growth and agricultural prosperity by improving farmers' access to outside markets, enabling them to transport their goods greater distances, more rapidly, and in larger volumes. Simultaneously, new manufacturing enterprises were bringing the industrial revolution to the county. A water-powered textile factory was established in Pomfret in 1806, and within little more than a decade a wide variety of mechanized industrial enterprises—including twenty-two cotton mills, ten woolen mills, thirty-seven fulling mills, and two paper mills—were in operation along the banks of Windham County's rivers and streams.[30]

Economic progress was only part of the picture, however. By the late eighteenth century, the county's towns were experiencing the same population and land pressures that other New England frontier settlements had faced as they evolved into mature farming communities. County residents, a large number of them younger sons of local farm families, responded in the typical New England manner: by moving to the frontier—in this case undeveloped areas of Vermont, New Hampshire, western Massachusetts, and northeastern New York—in search of affordable farmland. The outward flow of migrants, which was already getting underway in the 1760s, became a torrent after the revolution, and included Thomas' father and two of his brothers among its participants. So massive did the exodus eventually become that during the final decade of the eighteenth century, Windham County experienced a net loss of population—nearly 700 inhabitants—despite the prolific rates of natural increase still prevalent among its farm families. For those farmers who stayed behind—men like Thomas Grow—their fundamental challenge was to find economic strategies that would enable them to maintain prosperous farms and provide independent futures for their children in a complex new economic landscape of expanded commercial markets and reduced land availability.[31]

Thomas met that challenge by diversifying his sources of income. He continued to rely primarily on traditional subsistence-plus agriculture to support his large family.[32] In 1809, 20 acres of the Grow Hill farm were being utilized as "plowland" for the cultivation of grain crops—mainly corn and rye,[33] along with smaller amounts of oats and flax—while another 140 acres consisted of pastures and hay fields for the family's livestock, which included two oxen, thirteen cows, four steers, six horses, and thirty sheep. (Interestingly, two generations of Grows in the Pomfret-Hampton area, including Thomas and his uncles Joseph and James, branded their livestock on the ear with the figure "7"—the significance of which is not known but might have reflected the family's belief in the biblical prophecy that the "Second Coming of Christ" would occur after the Lamb of God broke "the seventh seal" and sent "the seven angels who had the seven trumpets" to destroy all non-believers, preparing the way for Christ's return and the establishment of his millennial kingdom on earth.[34])

The family also raised swine and poultry, and produced cider from apple orchards planted on the south slope of Grow Hill. Like most Windham County farmers, Thomas generated income from the sale of beef and pork, salted and packed in barrels, to local merchants, while his wife and daughters made a significant contribution to the family income by producing cheese, butter, lard, bayberry candles, and homespun woolen and linen fabrics woven with yarn obtained from the farm's supply of sheep's wool and flax—commodities that were also sold to area merchants.[35]

But Thomas also found new ways to make money in New England's increasingly commercialized economy. By the late 1790s, he was operating his own general store on Grow Hill, selling "West India goods" that he and his son Joseph obtained in Providence.[36] He also took advantage of Connecticut's improved roads to expand the geographic range of his trading activities, selling horses in Norwich[37] and oxen in New London,[38] and becoming an "early dealer" in coal dug from "the pit" in Abington.[39] As the boundaries of his commercial world widened, he relied increasingly on a new financial instrument for his commercial transactions: promissory notes. Prior to the revolution, New England farmers conducted their trading activities almost entirely within their own local communities, exchanging goods and services with people they knew personally, and usually on the basis of informal credit arrangements in which each transaction was simply recorded in the seller's account book as an incurred debt obligation on the part of the buyer. Based as they were on personal familiarity and trust, such debts often remained "on the books" for months or even years, interest-free, until the "debtor" eventually "settled his account" with a payment of commodities, labor, or cash. This highly personalized form of local exchange continued to be an essential component of economic life in rural New England after the revolution. But as the region's economy expanded, and more and more commercial activity took place between men from different towns—men who neither knew one another well nor shared a relationship based on mutual trust—traders turned increasingly to an impersonal new credit instrument for their commercial transactions: promissory notes—formal, legally binding, signed documents in which individuals who obtained goods or services on credit promised in writing to pay the creditor an agreed-upon sum, with interest, by a specified date.[40] Occasionally such arrangements ended up in litigation when the debtor failed to meet his stipulated payment deadline. Between 1793 and 1821, for example, Thomas filed lawsuits in the Windham County Court against five different trading partners—two men from Norwich (Cushing Elles and Adonijah Perkins), two from Ashford (Aaron Tufts and Jacob Wilson), and one from Pomfret (Christopher Green)—demanding payments ranging from $20 to $1,050.[41] Nevertheless, by the early nineteenth century, promissory notes had become the standard currency for trading on credit in New England; and at the time of his death in 1824, Thomas held twenty-two notes totaling nearly $4,400 in value.[42]

He also speculated aggressively in the Pomfret and Hampton real estate markets. Between 1777 and 1822, he completed no fewer than fifty-nine land transactions in the two towns, buying and selling parcels ranging in size from 1.25 acres to 200 acres.[43] In the process, he developed a collateral income stream as a lender of capital by personally financing mortgages for the buyers of several of his properties.[44] Following the departure of his father and brother to Guilford, Vermont, in 1794 and his father's death there in 1806, he speculated in Guilford real estate as well, acquiring in 1810 the 94-acre farm that his father and brother had owned, along with another 50-acre Guilford property that he purchased from in-laws of his brother Nathaniel in 1813. (He suffered a net loss of $343 on his father's farm when he sold it in 1813 but turned a quick $800 profit on the 50-acre parcel when he sold it 18 months after acquiring it—and added to his profit by financing the purchaser's mortgage at 6 percent interest.)[45] And finally, like other enterprising men of his generation, he shifted a portion of his assets out of land and agriculture and into newer, more liquid forms of wealth.[46] He was a major investor in the Pomfret Woolen Manufacturing Company, a small textile mill on Mashamoquet Brook in Abington that was destroyed in an 1817 flood.[47] He was also a stockholder in Norwich's chartered bank, owning ten shares valued at $850 at the time of his death.[48]

Ultimately, then, Thomas successfully adapted to the new economic conditions of the early national period by expanding the scope of his income-generating activities—as a trader, a merchant, a land speculator, a capital lender, and an investor as well as a farmer. In doing so, he accumulated significant wealth and earned a local reputation for shrewd dealing. At his death in 1824, although he had already transferred more than half of his land and property to his sons, he left an estate worth approximately $10,500[49] (more than $265,000 in twenty-first-century dollars[50]), prompting his granddaughter Diantha's husband Chauncey Cleveland, a Hampton attorney (and future governor of Connecticut) who helped settle his estate, to remark that "Deacon Grow . . . was the best business man he ever knew."[51]

All of which raises a question that has recently been the focus of a vigorous debate among academic historians: were post-revolutionary war farmers like Thomas Grow modern market-oriented capitalists motivated to pursue commercial profits and financial gain by their "love of money" and the higher standard of living that wealth could provide? Or were they traditionalists using the emerging market economy to obtain the capital that they needed to sustain their family farms and preserve a traditional agrarian way of life?[52] In Thomas' case, evidence can be found to support each of those interpretations.

On one hand, his financial-investing and mortgage-lending activities indicate that he was a man motivated to some extent by capitalist incentives, whatever the intended purpose. There is evidence as well that commercial market forces had an influential impact on his farming operations. By the early nineteenth century, he was enclosing his various Grow Hill pastures and planting fields with stone walls in order to separate them more effectively from one another, a "sure sign" that he was farming his land more intensively to produce higher yields for commercial purposes.[53] In addition, the quantities of farm produce that he had on hand at his death—300 pounds of pork, 50 pounds of beef, 22 pounds of butter, 20 pounds of lard—far exceeded his family's immediate food needs, a clear indication that he was selling substantial surpluses in Windham County markets and perhaps beyond.[54] And finally, his occasional use of hired men to help him work his farm reflected the county's gradual transition during this period from an agricultural economy based on traditional family labor toward a more modern, capitalist wage-labor system. In 1806 and 1807, for example, he was employing a Hampton revolutionary war veteran, Jonathan Holt, to carry out a variety of farm tasks, including "laying wall," "hoeing corn," and "haying," for 5 to 6 shillings a day.[55]

On the other hand, Thomas always remained first and foremost a traditional subsistence-plus farmer like his father and grandfather before him. He may have produced larger surpluses than they did, and he may have traded more actively in outside markets, but the quantities of produce that he and other Windham County farmers sent to market were usually relatively small. At no point did he expand his farming operations into full-scale commercial agriculture by specializing in the production of one or two commodities for wider markets. Instead, he continued to practice the diversified agriculture traditionally favored by New England farmers—in his case, a combination of livestock, dairy, and mixed-crop farming. According to historian James Henretta, subsistence-plus farmers like Thomas were primarily concerned with satisfying the subsistence needs of their families and only secondarily with selling surplus commodities for profit. The variety of foodstuffs and fibers obtained from diversified farming strengthened a farmer's odds of being able to feed and clothe his family adequately, providing him with a degree of economic security as well as partial protection from unstable markets and fluctuating commodity prices. As a practitioner of diversified farming, therefore, Thomas was basing his livelihood on a relatively conservative form of agriculture, one that was in some respects averse to the risks of market capitalism.[56] The fact that he had only $1.43 in cash in his estate at the time of his death is a further indication that his involvement in the market economy was not particularly deep.[57] And his aggressive real estate dealings appear to have been motivated largely by a determination to accumulate as much land as possible to leave to his children.[58]

Deacon Thomas Grow Estate Inventory (1824)

Real Estate

1/2* of Home Farm	
(176.5 acres @ $23/acre)	$2,029.75
Stephens Farm	
(91.5 acres @ $12/acre)	1,098.00
½* of Fuller Pasture	
(20 acres @ $16/acre)	160.00
Kinne's Wood	
(10 acres @ $16/acre)	160.00
Pasture Adjoining Joseph Farm	
(8 acres @ $18/acre)	144.00
½* Old (Stoddard) Swamp	
(10 acres @ $6/acre)	60.00
Paine Meadow	
(2.5 acres @ $20/acre)	50.00

Capital Assets

Promissory Notes (22)	4,383.68
10 Shares in Norwich Bank	850.00
Cash	1.43

Household Goods

Furniture, cloth & yarn	$181.72
Wearing Apparel	33.07
Silk Stockings	1.00
Knee buckles and sleeve [?]	.50
Books	11.92
Guns (2)	4.50
Pistols (2)	.25
Watch	1.00
Spectacles and case	1.00
Umbrella	.17

Farm Equipment

Farming Tools	77.34
Chaise and Harness	15.00
Cutter	3.00
Neck Chains (3)	.74
Hog Chains (2)	.68

Livestock

½* of 6 Oxen	50.00
6 Cows	98.00
4 Calves	12.00
½* of Two-Year-Old Bull	4.00
26 Sheep and Lambs	20.54
625 lb. of Swine [3–4 hogs]	25.00
1 Bay Horse	35.00
1 Brown Mare	25.00
3 Two-Year-Olds	34.00
4 Yearlings	28.00

Farm Produce

300 lb. Pork	20.00
50 lb. Beef	2.00
¼ Quintal of Fish	1.00
30 Bushels of Rye	17.40
23 Bushels of Corn	11.50
6 Bushels of Oats	1.50
½* of 3 Stacks of Hay	6.00
38 lb. of Wool	14.45
1 lb. of Pulled Wool	.38
6 Barrels of Cider	7.50
22 lb. of Butter	2.75
20 lb. of Lard	1.50
2.75 Bushels of Salt	2.29
2 Barrels of Soap	4.00
20 lb. of Candles	2.00
1990 Feet of Board, Planks, & Scanthing	10.45
2/3rds* of 800 Feet of Square Timber	16.84
Leather	4.20
Deer Skin (1)	1.50

Other Assets

6.5 Pews in Baptist Meeting House	64.00

Liabilities

Debts	2,469.75
Probate Expenses	50.93

TOTAL ESTATE: **$10,548.38**

* Remainder owned by son Thomas Grow Jr. (1782–1852), with whom Thomas shared the Grow Hill farm from 1811 onward.

SOURCE: Compiled from Thomas Grow Estate Papers (Hampton 1824), Windham Probate District file no. 1706, in Probate Estate Papers, Records of the Windham District Probate Court, Connecticut State Library, Hartford. (See below p. 303n32.)

At first glance, the numerous material possessions itemized in Thomas' probate inventory seem to indicate that he and his family had modern materialistic values and perhaps even a taste for conspicuous consumption. Among the household furnishings identified in his estate were one "desk & book case" (also known as a secretary), a "high case of drawers" (or highboy), a "large maple table," three looking glasses, a "great chair," seven Windsor chairs, a silver tea kettle and five silver tea spoons, three large silver spoons, four pewter platters, a large pewter basin, three brass kettles, and two brass candlesticks.[59] In addition, Thomas counted among his personal possessions a brass clock, a silver watch, and a small two-wheel carriage known as a "chaise."[60] In the context of the 1820s, however, the various objects that he owned were nothing more than the typical consumer goods found in the estates of prosperous upper-middle-class Connecticut farmers of the period. If Thomas and his family were more materialistic than his parents and grandparents, their materialism was essentially a reflection of the rising standard of living that accompanied economic growth in New England in the decades following the revolution, as middle-class farm families acquired more and more of the sophisticated and increasingly affordable furnishings being produced by local and regional craftsmen—the fashionable new furniture, tableware, and other consumer goods that they valued as symbols of gentility and refinement, as symbols of social and economic status. Conversely, his probate records contain no mention of tea tables, dressing tables, upholstered chairs, imported delftware, fine china, painted portraits, or other luxury goods commonly found in the households of New England's upper-class elites.[61]

Another clue as to Thomas' economic values can be found in the books he owned. Book ownership was becoming increasingly widespread among New England's farmers in the years after the revolution—the result of a proliferation of book printers and booksellers combined with the ever-higher levels of male and (especially) female literacy being achieved through the growth of rural schools. The books accumulated by those farmers provide a useful glimpse into their owners' mentalities. In Thomas' case, it is revealing that of the thirty-three volumes identified in his estate inventory, twenty-nine were religious in nature, while only four were secular works—and of the latter, one (Jedidiah Morse's *American Geography*) was written by a Congregational minister, and another (a Noah Webster grammar) was authored by a devout Calvinist. (See Appendix C for a full listing of Thomas' book collection.) Conspicuous by their absence were works by the influential Enlightenment liberals John Locke and Adam Smith or the widely read anti-Calvinists Thomas Paine and Edward Gibbon; popular novels of the day such as Oliver Goldsmith's *The Vicar of Wakefield* and Daniel Defoe's *Robinson Crusoe*; or any of the instructional books on etiquette and proper social conduct being read by ambitious middle-class Americans seeking to "get ahead" in the world. Instead, nearly 90 percent of Thomas' collection consisted of bibles (five copies), published sermons, collections of psalms and hymns, Baptist histories, devotional treatises, and other works of theology, including a bound volume of *The Christian Herald*, a biweekly journal popular with evangelical Protestants. Among the titles that stand out are John Bunyan's *Pilgrim's Progress*, the classic seventeenth-century Christian allegory and perennial favorite of evangelicals; the collected sermons of the Rev. George Whitefield, the leading instigator of the Great Awakening; Richard Baxter's *Call to the Unconverted* by a seventeenth-century English evangelist who exhorted middle-class farmers to maintain their religious piety as they accumulated wealth; and one of English clergyman Richard Watson's *Apologies*, direct rebuttals of the anti-Calvinist writings of Paine and Gibbon. In short, Thomas' reading matter consisted almost entirely of material that reinforced traditional spiritual values and "old ways of thinking and living." As a window into his intellectual universe, his book collection, if anything, reveals a conservative, traditionalistic, and devoutly religious mind rather than an intellect focused on progress and change.[62]

Consequently, Thomas can perhaps best be seen as a transitional figure, a man who remained firmly rooted in traditional practices and beliefs but who was equally at home in the "modern" world of nineteenth-century commerce and consumerism. Part traditional farmer, part capitalist businessman, he exemplified the period of economic transition in which he lived.

At age 66, Thomas was one of the richest men in Hampton, ranking among the wealthiest 5 percent of its taxpayers (13th out of 254) on the 1809 tax list. With 210 acres of land, he was the town's sixteenth largest landowner, a ranking that would have been considerably higher if he had not already transferred 123 acres to his sons Elisha and Joseph. He also owned the fifth-largest number of horses (six), the sixth-largest flock of sheep (thirty), the eleventh-largest cattle herd (nineteen), and one of only seventeen horse-drawn "chaises" in the town.[63]

Among other benefits, his affluence enabled him to carry out a much-needed expansion of his Grow Hill farmhouse. At some point in the late eighteenth or early nineteenth century, a new one-room-deep, two-story, center-chimney ell was attached perpendicularly to the west end of the original house (with a separate front entrance facing west), producing the asymmetrical, partially hipped-roof dwelling that is still inhabited in the twenty-first century. Measuring approximately 39' wide × 16' deep, the new addition increased the farmhouse's living space from less than 2,100 square feet to more than 3,300— surely a welcome development for the fifteen or so men, women, and children, including members of the Grows' extended family, who lived crammed together within its confines. According to the Federal Census of 1790, for example, Thomas' household consisted of nine "females" (Experience and eight of the couple's daughters—a ninth, Lois, having recently left the nest for marriage), three "males under 16 years" (their first three sons, Elisha[5], Thomas, and Joseph), and three "males above 16 years" (Thomas, his 21-year-old cousin, James Grow [a young school teacher and farmer who lived with the couple for three years until his marriage], and possibly Thomas' mentally impaired brother, Ebenezer).[64]

Grow Hill farmhouse of Thomas and Experience Grow after its enlargement in the late eighteenth or early nineteenth century, as pictured in a 1930s photograph. (Source: WPA Architectural Survey—Census of Old Buildings in Connecticut: Hampton Historical Building #031, Connecticut State Library Digital Collections [ctstatelibrary.org], accessed August 2013)

The final two decades of Thomas' life were filled with trials and tribulations, tragedies and loss. In addition to his father, his daughter Anna also died in 1806, at age 29, leaving a husband and five small children. In 1810 his 17-year-old son John and 25-year-old daughter Experience died within six weeks of one another. The following year brought the premature deaths of Experience, his 64-year-old wife of 43 years, and an infant grandson. Then in 1819, his second wife, Sarah (Hyde) Grow—a local widow he had married six months after his first wife's death—passed away at age 66. Meanwhile, in 1812, his eldest son, Elisha, and family had permanently departed Abington to begin a new life on the New York frontier. And another of his sons, Joseph, was proving to be a failure as a businessman due to his financial improvidence and mounting indebtedness.[65]

Throughout this difficult period, Thomas was also shouldering an additional family burden as the primary source of support for his brother Ebenezer.

After completing military service as a revolutionary war soldier, Ebenezer returned home to a marginalized existence in Hampton—landless, illiterate, and increasingly dependent on Thomas for economic and other assistance. Although he eventually married a woman named Catherine, about whom almost nothing is known, he apparently never established an independent household of his own. In documents that he submitted to the US government between 1818 and 1821 in support of his application for a revolutionary war pension, Ebenezer described himself as "poor" and "in need of assistance from my Country" "by reason of my reduced circumstances." He was, he stated, "infirm & in bad health almost past any labor," with "a wife of 67 years of age [also] past labor pretty much." Supporting statements from men who served with him during the revolution described him as "destitute" and "unable to support himself," with "neither House nor Home" of his own. According to a former commanding officer, Thomas Grosvenor of Pomfret, Ebenezer "is & ever was poor, and is now beholden to his brother for support." An inventory of his possessions, which he submitted to the War Department in 1821 (at age 65) to document his pension eligibility, reveals the extent of his poverty:

1 cow	$16.00	1 old chest with drawers	0.75
1 small Brass kettle	2.50	2 old tables	0.75
1 Iron pot	1.00	2 pewter basons [sic]	0.50
1 dish kettle [sic]	0.67	3 pewter plates	0.40
2 old wheels	1.00	1 pewter qt. cup	0.25
2 old tubs	0.50	1 pewter Platter	0.50
2 old pails	0.25	some old poor crockery	1.00
½ doz. old chairs	1.50	**[Total value of] all he owns:**	**$27.57**

In the end, only "the Care and providence of his Brother," augmented by a $100 annual pension compensating him for seven years of indescribable sacrifice during the revolution, kept Ebenezer and his wife from becoming publicly supported wards of the town of Hampton.[66]

Adding to Thomas' travails during this trying period was a renewed outbreak of factional strife in the Grow Hill Baptist Church. As the church's records make clear, the internal divisions and animosities created by the William Grow adultery scandal of 1783–1785 (see preceding chapter) never completely healed. During that crisis, a hard-line group of parishioners, proceeding from the conviction that a Baptist preacher must be an unimpeachable model of morality and piety for his congregation, contended that William had become too morally compromised by his adulterous behavior to continue as elder of the church. The Grows and their supporters countered that the hard-liners' unwillingness to forgive William for his transgression was a fundamental violation of Jesus' teachings. Harsh words were apparently exchanged on both sides, with Thomas angrily accusing William's critics of a lack of Christian charity and at one point physically striking one of them, a brother of former revolutionary war Captain Nathan Paine, during a verbal confrontation.

Nearly twenty years later in 1804, following Thomas' elevation to the office of church deacon, it quickly became evident that a strong residue of ill will still existed. The first indication of lingering animosity came in June of that year, when a female member of the congregation, "Sister Daine," quit the church in protest over its "Chusing Thomas Grow for a Deacon." A few months later, Nathan Paine brought a series of charges against Thomas and demanded that the church formally censure him. The charges were a diverse mix of grievances, mostly relating to the rancorous dispute of two decades earlier: that Thomas had publicly stated that Paine "opposed the gospel" and was no friend of religion; that he had struck Paine's brother "unreasonably"; that he had impeded the recruitment of a new preacher to replace William; that in his capacity as church clerk he had "Cut . . . Leaves out of the Church records without the knowledge of the Church"; and that he had acted unethically in a transaction involving the sale of a horse. After due deliberation, a majority of the church concluded that Paine had failed to prove any of his accusations and that there was nothing in them that was "Sufficient to Censur [sic] a brother." The church acknowledged that it would have been "better" if Thomas had not accused Paine of opposing the gospel but felt that "in as much as it was 18 years ago . . . it ought not to have been brought up Now." As for Thomas' physical assault on Paine's brother, the church concluded that it was "not a Censurable Evel [sic] Every thing Considered."[67]

In May of the following year, Thomas brought charges of his own against Moses Edmonds, one of Paine's in-laws, "for Saying Several Things that ware [sic] not true" concerning disputes over a property deed and the ownership of a fence. The church, "after long and serious consultation," concluded that Edmonds was "gilty" [sic] of speaking falsehoods "and that he ought to take them Back." When Edmonds filed counter-charges against Thomas a month later for allegedly preventing him from receiving communion or participating in church meetings, the church found Thomas "not guilty of [a] breach of any divine rule in what he did."[68]

Twelve years later, Thomas was still serving as deacon, but power in the church had shifted into the hands of the Paines and their allies, including Moses Edmonds and members of the Elliot family. In February 1817, in the midst of an unspecified dispute that probably centered on a struggle for church leadership, James Elliot brought new charges against Thomas "for saying that the Church [was now] united in opposing the work of God and [that] Brother John Paine was the ring leader of it." A month later, after listening to statements from "Brother John Paine and Sister [Lois or Louisa] Paine," a majority of the church decided that Thomas had indeed made the "railing accusation against the Church" that had been attributed to him, and a delegation was dispatched to admonish him, at which time he apparently "refused to recant or withdraw his criticism."

The following September, in a meeting "at the house of Brother Nathan Paine," the church "took the case of Dea. Thomas Grow into consideration and after some conversation voted to exclude him from our fellowship." His forced expulsion provoked angry recriminations from two of his married daughters, Olive (Grow) Hovey and Lois (Grow) Burnham, both of whom were also expelled in 1818. The Paines and Moses Edmonds now assumed leadership of the church, with a member of the Elliot family replacing Thomas as deacon. In 1819, newly ordained Elder John Paine took over the church's preaching duties.[69] The Grows had now been completely removed as leaders (and in the case of Thomas and two of his daughters, members) of the church that they had played an instrumental role in founding, building, and funding for half a century—with the six-and-a-half pews that Thomas continued to own until his death[70] presumably sitting conspicuously empty during Sunday services in mute testimony to the family's lost power struggle.

More than two centuries later, it is difficult to know what interpretation to place on Thomas' troubles in the Grow Hill Baptist Church. Was he the victim of unjust and "high-handed" treatment by a band of usurpers seeking control of the church, as family genealogist George W. Davis seems to imply?[71] Or had he instead brought his misfortunes on himself by making unnecessary enemies with his overly aggressive and hotheaded defense of his brother William, perhaps combined with a somewhat uncompromising and imperious demeanor as deacon—as a Paine family historian might contend? Was the bitter outcome the product of some combination of those factors or the result of other, unknown issues and circumstances? On such questions of causation, the church records, and the historical record in general, remain silent.

Thomas remained vigorous and active to his dying day. Having already outlived two wives and three of his children, he married again in 1821 at age 78. His new wife was Experience Abbott, a 66-year-old "maiden lady" from Providence, Rhode Island, who apparently insisted on receiving legal guarantees of economic security for herself before marrying a man of his advanced age, as indicated by a prenuptial agreement that she and Thomas signed prior to their wedding. According to that document, which Thomas appears to have personally hand-written:

> Thomas Grow ... agrees with ... Experiens [sic] Abbott ... that if [he] Should die first ... Experians [sic] Shall have all the things She brought [with her into the marriage] & all the west Square room [in the recent addition to the Grow Hill farmhouse] & half the citchen [sic] & all the beadroom [sic] & half the wood house and

a cow kept somer [*sic*] & winter for hur [*sic*] use[,] and Priveledg [*sic*] in the Sellar [*sic*] as long as She remains my widow[,] and if She Should [re-]marry She Shall have all the things She brought hear [*sic*] and a Cow to carry away whare [*sic*] She pleases[,] and She Shall have seventy dollars a year in provisions[,] & wood found for hur [*sic*] at the door to support one fire . . . and if She dies first I and my ares [*sic*] Shall have all the things She brought hear [*sic*].[72]

It was not uncommon for rural husbands to provide their heirs with instructions that spelled out in minute detail the provisions and privileges that their wives were to receive as widows. Such instructions, however, were usually included in wills rather than in prenuptial agreements.[73]

In his late seventies and early eighties, at an age when most men had slowed down and settled into full retirement, Thomas remained economically active and directly involved in his farm's operations. During the final years of his life, after conveying half of the Grow Hill farm to his son Thomas Jr. and an additional 12 acres to another son, David, he still managed to increase his total landholdings from 210 acres to more than 230. During that same period, he also increased the number of horses he owned by 50 percent, from six to nine.[74] In the end, one of those horses proved to be the cause of his death. On 5 June 1824, at the "advanced age of eighty-one, he undertook to drive a colt the first time it was harnessed, and when but a half-mile from the barn he was thrown from the wagon, and, falling upon a pile of stones at the roadside, he was instantly killed."[75]

As part of the distribution of his large estate, Thomas' daughters (or their heirs, in the case of the deceased Anna and Experience) and his unmarried 33-year-old son, David, received parcels of real estate ranging from 4 to 17 acres, together with a cash distribution of nearly $1,000 each from the liquidation of property and promissory notes, along with an apportionment of furniture, textiles, farm implements, books, and other personal possessions from his estate. His three other surviving sons, Elisha[5], Thomas Jr., and Joseph, received no distributions, having already "received by advancement more than their Shares in Said Estate."[76] In 1825, his children quit-claimed to their brother Thomas Jr. all rights to the remaining half of the Grow Hill farm that their father had continued to own until his death.[77] Thirty years later, after Thomas Jr. had struggled unsuccessfully to keep the farm financially solvent, mortgaging it repeatedly, his son and heir, Thomas Wales Grow, sold it to a member of the Elliot family for $3,800.[78]

Thomas was buried at the eastern foot of Grow Hill in "Burying Hill" (later known as the "Grow Hill Burying Ground" or "Grow Cemetery"), a beautiful small graveyard situated "on a steep hillside above a fine marsh."[79] At the crest

Prenuptial agreement between Thomas Grow and Experience Abbott, 11 March 1820, in Thomas Grow Estate Papers, Connecticut State Library, Hartford. The manuscript's erratic penmanship and phonetically based spelling probably reflect the rudimentary education that Thomas received in his youth. Farm boys in eighteenth-century Windham County attended school for only a few short years (usually until they were about 12 years of age) and only during summer and winter months when their fathers could spare them from the fields. Instruction consisted of little more than the fundamentals of reading, writing, and "ciphering." Dictionaries were unknown and lessons in grammar and punctuation nonexistent. (Opal, *Beyond the Farm*, 27–29; Appleby, *Inheriting the Revolution*, 104; Anne S. Lombard, *Making Manhood: Growing Up Male in Colonial New England* [Cambridge, MA: Harvard University Press, 2003], 37; Elias Smith, *The Life, Conversion, Preaching, Travels, and Sufferings of Elias Smith* [Boston: 1840], 21, 29) (Photograph by the author.)

of the cemetery, enclosed within its surrounding stone wall and border of evenly spaced ancient oak trees, lie the graves of Thomas, his three wives, his brothers Ebenezer and Timothy, his sister Susanna, three of his sons (Thomas Jr., Joseph, and David), and at least four other members of the family (see Appendix D). The crown (or tympanum) of Thomas' headstone is decorated with the classic weeping-willow mourning symbol commonly found on New England gravestones of the early nineteenth century, as funerary art in the region, increasingly reflecting "the secular sentiments of the Enlightenment," evolved from a focus on the soul of the deceased to the grief of those left behind.[80] The religious verse inscribed on the headstone's lower portion—partially (and intentionally) buried in the early twenty-first century when the stone, which had fallen, was re-set more deeply to protect its structural integrity—is a passage from Hymn 49 of eighteenth-century English minister Joseph Hart's *Hymns Composed on Various Subjects*, a work much loved by evangelical Christians.

According to Thomas' probate records, his funeral expenses consisted of:

Coffin	$5.50
Digging Grave	0.25
Tolling Bell	0.50
Grave Stones	11.00
	$17.25

Judged by standard measurements of wealth, status, and local prestige, the family line reached its zenith in New England with Thomas[4] Grow. None of Thomas' four sons was ever able to equal his financial success or match his record of civic and religious leadership. Instead, each son found his prospects in life handicapped by the deteriorating health of New England's farming economy between the War of 1812 and the Civil War, as the region lapsed into a long period of agricultural decline brought on by ongoing land pressure, soil exhaustion, and, beginning in the 1830s, commercial competition from other commodities-producing areas of the nation.[81] As the rural economy turned stagnant, Joseph, Thomas Jr., and David, the three sons who remained in Windham County, experienced financial difficulties, a declining standard of living, and, in the cases of Joseph and David, premature deaths (at ages 39 and 55 respectively). Only Thomas' eldest son, Elisha[5], managed to achieve a semblance of his father's success, and he did so only after joining the mass outflow of emigrants who abandoned New England in search of better opportunities in new frontier regions lying far to the west.[82]

Dea. Thomas Grow
Died
June 5, 1824
Aged 81 Years

Every sea and lake and river
Shall restore their dead to view
Shout for gladness O believer
Christ is risen so shall you

Thomas Grow headstone, Grow Hill Burying Ground, Carter Road, Hampton, CT. (Photograph by the author.)

Top of Grow Hill Burying Ground, Hampton, CT. Headstones (*left to right*) of Experience Grow (1747–1811), Sarah Grow (1753–1819), Deacon Thomas Grow (1743–1824), Experience Grow (1755–1835). (Photograph by the author.)

ELISHA GROW (1779–1850)

As a young man, Elisha[5] Grow (*Thomas[4], Thomas[3], Thomas[2], John[1]*) seemed destined to follow in his father's footsteps as a prosperous farmer and community leader in the Pomfret-Hampton border area. The eldest of Thomas[4] and Experience Grow's five sons, he was born on the family farm in February 1779, during the middle of the American Revolution. In 1801, at age 22, he followed family tradition by marrying a young woman from a respectable local family: Lois Palmer, the 17-year-old daughter of Rev. Abel Palmer, a "brilliant young Baptist" minister who was serving at the time as the preaching elder of the Grow Hill Baptist Church and who owned a farm bordering Grow Hill on the south.[1]

An "advancement" from his father soon provided Elisha and Lois with a farm of their own. Nine months after their wedding, Thomas gave Elisha 110 acres of land located "about three-quarters of a mile" north of Grow Hill in Pomfret's Abington district. According to the deed, the generous land transfer was an indication of Thomas' "Parental Affection" for his son as well as compensation for unspecified "obligations" that Elisha had fulfilled to his father's satisfaction.[2] By age 23, as a result, Elisha owned more land than many Windham County men twice his age.[3] In his farming operations, he almost certainly practiced the diversified form of agriculture (a combination of livestock, dairy, and mixed-crop production) favored by his father and other local farmers. An account book kept by an Abington merchant lists him as one of the area's large-scale "butter makers."[4]

Meanwhile, Elisha was beginning to acquire the requisite credentials for a future leadership role in local civic affairs. In 1803, at age 24, he was elected by his peers to the rank of corporal in Hampton's prestigious Grenadiers Company, a unit of the town militia that included numerous revolutionary war veterans among its members. Every year on the first of May, the Grenadiers conducted a public training exercise or "muster," a lively and colorful event that was invariably attended by large crowds from throughout the area. The Grenadiers Company was a source of great civic pride in Hampton, and to be selected as an officer in the unit—even at the low rank of corporal—was considered a mark of status in the community and a stepping-stone to higher public office.[5]

Elisha and Lois also followed prevailing family custom by producing a large number of offspring. In the first nine years of their marriage, Lois gave birth to seven children—four girls and three boys, including a set of male twins (Elisha Jr. and Elijah), born in 1810. Consequently, by his early thirties, Elisha appeared to have settled firmly into the lifestyle patterns of the preceding generations of Windham County Grows—as an established middle-class farmer, a prolific father, and a respected member of his community.

Children of ELISHA[5] and LOIS (PALMER) GROW, born in Pomfret, CT:

i. Lois, b. 23 April 1803; d. 21 March 1863 at Milford, MI; m. (1) 1822, Homer, NY, Waterman Phillips; m. (2) 1826, Homer, Dea. Albert Robinson.

ii. Julia, b. 13 Nov. 1804; d. 3 Feb. 1877 at Plymouth, MI; m. 1826, Homer, Wanton Godfrey.

iii. Dilla, b. 25 Dec. 1805; d. 17 March 1866 at Highland, MI; m. 1828, Homer, Usial Phillips.

iv. Stillman Thompson, b. 15 April 1807; d. 25 April 1888 at Atlas, MI; m. (1) 1828, Homer, Derenda Graham; m. (2) 1843, Atlas, MI, Mary Britton.

v. Anne, b. 17 Aug. 1808; d. 9 Sept. 1896, prob. in Pontiac, MI; m. (1) 1826, Homer, Jacob Bishop; m. (2) 1866 in MI, Usial Phillips.

vi. Elijah, b. 24 Aug. 1810; d. 24 April 1887, Pontiac, MI; m. 1833, Pittstown, NY, Charity Baker.

vii. Elisha, b. 24 Aug. 1810; d. 4 March 1887, Highland, MI; m. 1832, Homer, Malvina Hakes.

SOURCE: George W. Davis, *John Grow of Ipswich/John (Groo) Grow of Oxford*, 54–55, 85–91; online at findagrave.com memorial 155336827 (wife of Stillman Thompson Grow); online at findagrave.com memorial 55162768 (wife of Elisha Grow Jr.).

In 1812, however, Elisha and Lois Grow suddenly uprooted themselves from their traditional way of life and became pioneers, moving their family 300 miles west to the frontier settlement of Homer in the wilderness of north-central New York.

New Englanders had been pouring across the Hudson River into New York State since the end of the American Revolution, when the region's original inhabitants, the Iroquois Indians, were pushed out. The influx of settlers into New York was propelled by the same "push-pull" factors that had been driving population movements in New England for more than a century and a half—namely, demographic pressures and rising land prices in older, settled communities combined with the availability of cheap, fertile, empty land beyond the existing boundaries of settlement. In all, "more than 800,000 people" moved into upstate New York between 1790 and 1820, quadrupling the state's population in the process. Most of the migrants came from Massachusetts and Connecticut, but large numbers of Vermont settlers, disappointed by the poor quality of the agricultural land in their state, also participated in the mass migration (including Elisha's uncle Nathaniel and family, who left Guilford, Vermont, in 1808, for Henderson, New York, on the eastern shore of Lake Ontario).[6]

A large proportion of the Connecticut migrants came from Windham County. In the first three decades after the revolution, the county experienced a "constant outflow" of inhabitants, as population growth and economic development made farmland increasingly scarce and expensive. By the early nineteenth century, there was no more unoccupied land left in the county, land values were soaring, and young male residents found that they had few employment options available—they could attempt to make do with substantially smaller farms and lower standards of living than those of their parents; they could abandon agriculture and work for wages in one of the county's growing number of mills and factories, or they could pull up stakes and move to the frontier. Many of them chose the latter option, in such large numbers that by 1820 the populations of several Windham County towns, including Hampton and Brooklyn, were noticeably smaller than they had been thirty years earlier.[7] In the words of county historian Ellen Larned, "The Nineteenth Century had come," bringing with it new conditions that led "hundreds of valuable families and scores of enterprising young men to seek more favoring chances in wider fields." It had become "increasingly evident," Larned noted,

> that a large population could not be supported by agriculture alone, that six or eight hearty boys and girls could hardly find sustenance, much less a life settlement upon a Windham County homestead. . . .The farmer who owned land free from encumbrance . . . might . . . secure a competence, but it is doubtful if a majority of the population could do more than make a scanty livelihood. Children were numerous, trades few, wages low. Three shillings a day, paid in produce, was the common price for farm laborers, and a working woman would drudge through the week for two and six-pence. . . . Young men roved about . . . swingling flax and tow on shares, and picking up any odd jobs they could find. The few ways for earning money made it very difficult for a young man to make his way in the world, and after years of hard labor he would scarcely have enough to stock a farm without the closest economy.[8]

It was in this environment of constricted opportunity that Elisha Grow made his decision to leave for the New York frontier. In his case, two fundamental factors shaped that decision: his large, rapidly growing family (Lois was pregnant with the couple's eighth child at the time), and high local land prices. With three sons already born and a strong likelihood of more to come, and with farmland in the Abington area increasingly unaffordable, it was apparent that Elisha would be unable to acquire enough land to place all of his male offspring on farms of their own when they reached adulthood—and, in addition, that there would almost certainly be a shortage of prosperous, landowning young men available in local society for his numerous daughters to marry when they came of age. Years later, an Abington neighbor, describing the family's departure for New York, recalled: "Elisha said he had so many children he must get where land was cheaper."[9]

Accordingly, in late 1811, Elisha began selling off his Abington landholdings—which by then totaled 113 acres—to neighboring farmers (including, ironically, Nathan Paine, whose ongoing quarrels with Elisha's father eventually culminated in the latter's expulsion from the Grow Hill Baptist Church, as described in the preceding chapter).[10] Then, in February 1812, he loaded his pregnant wife and seven children, along with his household possessions and farm equipment, onto large ox-drawn sleighs for the three-week winter journey to Homer, New York,[11] where he immediately purchased 271 acres of land.[12] The price differential of land in eastern Connecticut and central New York at the time graphically illustrates the economic appeal of frontier migration. In Abington, Elisha was able to sell his 113 acres for more than $32 an acre and a total return of $3,656. He then used that money to purchase more than twice as much land in Homer for only $9.60 an acre, or a total outlay of $2,600. By moving to the frontier, he increased his landholdings by 240 percent and generated a cash surplus of more than $1,000 to help settle his family in their new surroundings.[13]

Homer was located in a fertile river valley 150 miles west of Albany and a short distance east of New York's Finger Lakes region. Pioneers began arriving in the area in the early 1790s, and in the land rush that followed, the settlement's population multiplied rapidly, from six families in 1793 to nearly 3,000 inhabitants by 1810.[14] Among the early settlers were no fewer than five of Elisha's married sisters—Lois (Grow) Burnham, Anna (Grow) Darby, Hannah (Grow) Rindge, Chloe (Grow) Bennett, and Rhoda (Grow) Bennett—all of whom had migrated to Homer with their husbands prior to 1807. Another sister, Phoebe (Grow) Hicks, and her husband, were also residing there from an early but indeterminate date.[15] In addition, Lois' parents, Abel and Lois Palmer, had moved from Hampton to Exeter, New York, 75 miles east of Homer, shortly after 1800.[16] In that sense, Elisha's migration to the New York frontier perpetuated another family tradition. Like his great-grandfather's migration from Andover, Massachusetts, to northeastern Connecticut in 1731, and his grandfather's relocation from Connecticut to Vermont in 1794, Elisha's move to

Homer took place as part of a kinship-based chain migration—one that, like the migratory experiences of the two earlier generations, was undoubtedly aided and abetted by other family members who had already established themselves in the new frontier environment.

Homer pioneers endured the primitive living conditions typical of frontier communities. In its early years, the settlement was an "unbroken wilderness" of dense primordial forests. On arrival, pioneer families erected "rude, unadorned," two-room log cabins—usually about 20' square, with one or two windows—and immediately began to wage war on the surrounding forest, clearing land, planting crops, and hunting food.[17] Carnivorous predators posed a "constant threat" to settlers' livestock pens, prompting local authorities to offer $10 bounties on wolves and panthers.[18] In one incident, a "huge bear" carried off a hog from the barnyard of Elisha's brother-in-law Alfred Bennett. Grabbing his gun, Bennett gave chase, and when the bear suddenly turned on its pursuer, Bennett—discovering that he had neglected to bring any musket balls with him—killed the beast by firing the gun's ramrod into it.[19]

By the time Elisha and Lois arrived in 1812, Homer had acquired a few accoutrements of civilization, including a school, a general store, a sawmill, a gristmill, a tavern, two churches, and a newspaper.[20] Several small distilleries had also sprung up, however, supplying copious quantities of cheap, 25-cents-a-gallon whiskey that helped fuel the local culture's reputation for crude, boisterous frontier behavior. For years, in fact, travelers passing through the area were struck by the "heavy drinking" and "tobacco-spitting" that they observed among the inhabitants.[21] Like other frontier communities, Homer also struggled with conditions of lawlessness—as indicated by the presence of a local vigilante organization, the Society to Suppress Horse Stealing, in the 1820s.[22]

The land that Elisha purchased was located on Homer's northern border at the south end of Upper Little York Lake and directly east of a millpond that an earlier-arriving settler from Pomfret, Jabez Cushman, had created by damming a stream that flowed out of the lake. (The Grow property stretched along the north side of present-day Little York Crossing Road, between State Routes 281 and 11 near the Interstate 81 overpass.) There the family built a rudimentary dwelling and "cleared a farm."[23] The work was undoubtedly backbreaking, but the financial resources that Elisha brought with him helped to partially mitigate the family's hardships. As historian Allan Kulikoff notes, pioneering was an expensive proposition. "Only families with assets . . . could afford to move long distances. Frontier migration required money for lodging, a wagon, livestock, and farm tools as well as food to feed the family until the first crop came in."[24] In Homer, "a yoke of oxen cost $60, a cow from $16 to $25, and the necessary farming tools, including the oxcart, could be purchased for $50. A well-to-do settler was one who had $150 in capital after his land was purchased."[25] Even with Elisha's financial cushion of more than $1,000 to finance the development of his frontier farm, however, it still took nine years of toil before he was prosperous enough to be able to replace the family's initial primitive dwelling with a larger, more substantial timber-framed farmhouse.[26]

Homer rapidly developed into a prosperous agricultural community. By 1820, the local economy had made a successful transition from subsistence farming to market-oriented commercial agriculture, and local farmers were selling large surpluses of wheat, corn, pork, butter, and apples to the town's three merchants, who in turn transported the commodities in "four-horse wagons" to Albany, where they were shipped down the Hudson River to New York City.[27]

Almost nothing is known of Elisha's farming practices, but the fact that in 1826 he had 25 acres planted in corn—which would have produced a yield far greater than his family could consume—suggests that he was producing for external markets.[28] Some Homer farmers also generated income by investing in local enterprises. The millpond that bordered Elisha's property seems to have become something of an early "industrial center," with two sawmills, a gristmill, and a small textile mill or "woolen factory." Many of the neighboring farmers owned shares in these enterprises, and those who raised sheep sold their wool to the textile mill—the Homer Woolen Manufacturing Company—which, according to its advertisements, produced "casimeres, satinets and flannels [in] all colors except indigo blue," as well as "country cloth" and "Superfine Broad Cloths . . . in a stile [sic] far superior to any in this country."[29] One local source claims that Elisha owned one of the millpond's sawmills for a brief period of time.[30]

During their years in Homer, Elisha and Lois had ten more children—three daughters and seven sons (including a second set of male twins, Edward and Edwin, in 1822)—giving the couple a staggering total of seventeen offspring in the first twenty-six years of their marriage. Lois gave birth, on average, every twenty-one months from age 19 to 44, when menopause finally—some would say mercifully—brought the reproductive phase of her life to an end. She bore children for so many years, in fact, that she was still producing babies after she had become a grandmother four times over; by the time her youngest child, Rhoda Bennett, was born in 1828, three of her oldest daughters—Lois, Julia, and Anne—had already given birth to one or more children of their own.[31]

Nevertheless, although Lois' record of fecundity seems astonishing to modern sensibilities, it was not unusual at the time. Birth rates in the United States were extraordinarily high from the 1780s through the 1850s, with the national population doubling every twenty-two years (from 3.9 million people in 1790 to 31.4 million in 1860). Several factors contributed to the explosive demographic growth. For one, birth control was little known and seldom practiced by Americans of this period. In addition, with agriculture still largely unmechanized, rural Americans continued to regard large numbers of children as essential for successful farming operations. And as hundreds of thousands of pioneer families like the Grows migrated westward into the country's undeveloped interior, the daunting task of bringing millions of acres of virgin land into cultivation intensified the need for families to produce as many children as possible to provide labor for their farms. Consequently, the enormous size of Elisha and Lois' family simply reflected a prevailing trend of the times—particularly on the frontier, where families with twelve or more children were not uncommon.[32]

Children of ELISHA[5] and LOIS (PALMER) GROW, born in Homer, NY:

viii.   John Alonzo, b. 9 July 1812; d. 3 Oct. 1892 at Milford, MI; m. (1) 1836, Stattira H. Shattuck of Commerce, MI; m. (2) 1876, Mrs. Henry Delano.

ix.   Abel Palmer, b. 7 Aug. 1814; d. 29 June 1896 at Milford, MI; m. 1837, Sally Wilder.

x.   William Breed, b. 9 Oct. 1816; d. 1 Jan. 1913 at Carbondale, PA; m. 1838, Auburn, NY, Mary Ann Hackett.

xi.   Thomas[6], b. 22 March 1818; d. 25 Oct. 1902 at Pontiac, MI; m. 1841, White Lake, MI, Margaret Morris.

xii.   Sarah Matilda, b. 29 Sept. 1819; d. 9 Aug. 1865 at Oakland County, MI; m. 1842, Simeon Andrews of Homer, NY.

xiii.   Edward, b. 8 March 1822; d. 19 Dec. 1908 at Saginaw, MI; m. 1848, Clarkston, MI, Susan Landon.

xiv.   Edwin, b. 8 March 1822; d. 8 Feb. 1898 at Vernon, MI; m. (1) 1843, Percis L. Hoit of Independence, MI; m. (2) 1864, Mrs. Anna Dunn; m. (3) 1872, Mrs. Ophelia Crawford.

xv.   Waterman Phillips, b. 20 Dec. 1824; d. 9 March 1897 at Waterford, MI; m. (1) 1850, Elizabeth Hackett; m. (2) 1893, Mrs. Sarah J. Kempston of Detroit, MI.

xvi.   Olive, b. 7 Aug. 1826; d. 9 Aug. 1827 at Homer.

xvii.   Rhoda Bennett, b. 4 Oct. 1828; d. 12 March 1889 at Waterford, MI; m. (1) 1845, Joseph A. Rowley of Orion, MI; m. (2) 1874, Barnwell Olmstead.

SOURCE: George W. Davis, *John Grow of Ipswich/John (Groo) Grow of Oxford*, 55, 91–97; online at findagrave.com, memorial 47646421 (Thomas Grow date of death); online at findagrave.com, memorial 105801793 (Edward Grow date and place of death).

Everyday life for the family's members was much the same as it had been for earlier generations over the preceding 200 years. Elisha managed the farm's agricultural operations to assure a productive enterprise, working in his fields, pastures, and barns, supervising the labor activities of his sons, and presumably exercising his patriarchal authority as head of the family to maintain domestic peace in an overcrowded household of sixteen or more individuals living together under one roof. Lois, like her female ancestors for countless generations, spent her days in an endless routine of household tasks—fireplace tending and food preparation, unrelenting child care, washing, cleaning, dairying, food preserving, gardening, clothes-making, etc.—assisted by her daughters as soon as they reached adolescence.[33] The children received a rudimentary education at a nearby district school built on a parcel of land that Elisha had donated to the town for that purpose.[34] At one point, thirteen Grow children attended the school at the same time, carrying their lunches from home "in three buckets, strung to a pole," as one of them later recalled.[35] Beginning at an early age, the boys in the family were utilized for farmwork during the spring planting and fall harvest seasons, limiting their school attendance to the summer and winter months. By the age of 10, they were old enough to help with summer plowing and hoeing as well, at which point their schooling was reduced to a single three-month term in the winter. Their formal education ended in their mid-teens when they began working full-time on the farm or in a local trade.[36]

Although family members' roles generally adhered to traditional patterns, some aspects of their daily lives were impacted by the technological advances of the early nineteenth century. By the 1830s, innovations emanating from the industrial revolution had begun to ease some of Lois' household burdens. The new cast-iron stoves that Homer's merchants were offering for sale in their general stores—"Cooking, Franklin and Box Stoves," "Six-Plate Stoves," "Oven Door and Parlor Franklins"—significantly reduced the amount of time and energy that local farmwomen spent tending fires for cooking and heating. In addition, the growing commercial availability of inexpensive factory-made soaps, candles, and medicines was freeing rural women from the tedious labor involved in making those household staples by hand. And the ever-increasing quantities of machine-made wearing apparel and other manufactured fabrics pouring out of northeastern textile mills like the Homer Woolen Manufacturing Company were rapidly liberating farmwomen from the laborious tasks of household textile production, thus eliminating any further need for them to spend countless hours processing wool and flax, spinning yarn and thread, weaving cloth, and hand-stitching clothes for their families. So enthusiastically did rural American women respond to the growing availability of factory-made textiles, in fact, that by the end of the 1830s, many farm families had relegated their spinning wheels, looms, and other textile-making equipment to their attics, effectively bringing "the age of homespun" to a close. In various ways, early nineteenth-century technological progress was making household labor less arduous for farmwomen like Lois Grow.[37]

The Grow family's internal dynamics might also have been undergoing subtle changes during this period. Rather than pursue the traditional livelihood of farming, three of Elisha's sons—William, John Alonzo, and Abel— instead "learned the carpenter's trade and took up the business of building construction."[38] In doing so, they—like thousands of other young men in American society who were abandoning agriculture for wage-based occupations in the commercial trades and manufacturing sector of the US economy— gained a measure of economic independence from their father, weakening his patriarchal authority over them in the process. In most rural families, sons who aspired to become farmers remained heavily dependent on their father for the farmland they needed to initially establish themselves, giving him enormous economic power over their lives. For those sons who chose to pursue a non-agricultural vocation, however, their prospects in life depended not on what their father could pass on to them but on what they could "go out and get" for themselves, significantly reducing their father's leverage over them.[39] While there is no direct evidence that traditional hierarchies were breaking down in the Grow family during its quarter-century in Homer, there are indirect indications that Elisha's patriarchal power might have been softening to some extent. In 1831, when the family's 15-year-old son, William, was apprenticed to Homer carpenter Samuel Wallace for three years, it was Lois, not Elisha, who negotiated the terms of the apprenticeship contract with Wallace—an indication, perhaps, that Elisha had ceded some degree of patriarchal authority to his wife. William's later complaint that "our father failed to give us [sons] the encouragement which boys should have had in the way of tools and material" also raises questions about the extent to which Elisha's relationship with his sons reflected traditional patriarchal behavior.[40]

William Grow's firsthand account of his apprenticeship experience provides a glimpse into the realities of employment for young men endeavoring to learn a trade during this period:

> For the first year I was to receive thirty dollars, three months' schooling, and my board and wash. The [work] day was from sunrise to sunset, and in addition to the labors of this painfully long day, as the youngest apprentice, I was obliged to do the chores before sunrise and after sunset. For the second year I was to receive the increased wages of thirty-five dollars, no chores, and no schooling. I was glad of the liberal (?!) increase in my wages, and also the release from the chores, but regretted the loss of the school privileges. The new apprentice was Wallace's nephew, who came from Boston, and it was upon him that the choring fell. Fortunately for him, he knew so little about milking that the cow was rapidly drying up under his manipulations, and so I was again asked to do the milking, being given the promise of a suitable present. I saw the cow and milked her twice a day, but I

haven't seen the present yet. . . . For the third year another large (?!) increase in my salary of five dollars was made, and again no schooling, and no chores. This brought me to my nineteenth year, when my trade [training] was completed. Here my life may [be] said to have begun in earnest. I bought my outfit of tools, built my own chest, and began work at one dollar a day and board, my work being in and around Homer.[41]

The family knew both joys and sorrows during its years in Homer. Eight of the children (four sons and four daughters) were married there, leading to the births of seventeen grandchildren while Elisha and Lois resided in the town.[42] In addition, the couple's eldest son, Stillman, became the first member of the family line to receive a secondary education when he attended Homer's prestigious Cortland Academy, a coeducational prep school that attracted students from throughout central New York.[43] But the period was also marred by tragedy. The couple's second youngest daughter, Olive, died in 1827, two days after her first birthday. (She was buried in Little York Crossing Cemetery, on land that Elisha had donated to the town for use as a community burying ground.)[44] One of their grandchildren, Dilla's daughter Margaret, died in 1835 at the age of three. And their son Edward was "badly burned" in childhood, resulting in "great suffering" and serious impairment to one of his limbs, which eventually had to be amputated. Moreover, the fact that their son William was working in a local tannery at age 11 while another, John Alonzo, was sent to live with a maternal uncle in Exeter, New York, for three years at about the age of 10, would seem to suggest that the years in Homer were not altogether prosperous ones for the family.[45]

Although Elisha's donations of land to the town for a school and a cemetery indicate a strong sense of civic-mindedness on his part, he does not appear to have been actively involved in local government. His office holding in Homer seems to have been limited to three terms (in 1813, 1815, and 1817) as a "pathmaster," the New York equivalent of a "surveyor of highways" in Connecticut (*i.e.*, an individual appointed annually to supervise road maintenance in his neighborhood).[46]

Not surprisingly, given the Grow and Palmer families' religious backgrounds, Elisha and Lois were devout Baptists. They named their firstborn son Stillman after a prominent Baptist minister of the revolutionary war era, Samuel Stillman of Boston.[47] They also raised their children in an environment pervaded by Baptist religious influences.[48] The focal point of those influences was the Homer Baptist Church, to which the family had extremely close ties, personally as well as spiritually. The church's pastor, Rev. Alfred Bennett, and his brother Asa Bennett, its deacon, were Elisha and Lois' brothers-in-law.

Alfred and Asa Bennett came from a pious and godly Mansfield, Connecticut, family. In the late 1790s, while still in their teens, the two boys responded to a wave of local evangelical revivalism by joining the nearest Baptist church, the Grow Hill Baptist Church in Hampton, 15 miles to the east. In their early twenties, both brothers married into the Grow family, with Alfred marrying Elisha's sister, Rhoda Grow, in November 1802, and Asa marrying her sister Chloe four months later. Soon thereafter, the two young Bennett couples departed Connecticut for the Homer frontier as pioneer farmers. Arriving in Homer they discovered a small, "feeble" Baptist community with no meetinghouse or pastor. To remedy the latter situation, Alfred began training himself to become a Baptist preacher. Although he was, by his own admission, "devoid of scholastic accomplishments and mental discipline," and with "no elder ministers to counsel" him and no books other than "a Bible, a volume of hymns, and a spelling book," he threw himself into an intense study of the Bible. "I would carry it about my person to my labor," he later recalled, "While chopping down the forest I would work a while, then sit down upon a log and read for a while, and pray a while, and weep a while; then to my labor again." After two years of effort and wracked with self-doubt, he began preaching the Gospel to the local Baptists, with enough success that in 1807 he was formally ordained as a Baptist minister in a ceremony conducted in a neighbor's barn. Soon he and Asa were traveling the surrounding region, sometimes for weeks at a time, visiting isolated pioneer families in their log houses, "exhorting and praying," and promoting Baptist interpretations of the scriptures. Although they were "[o]ften held in deep distrust by Christians of other [denominations] and menaced by petty persecution," their efforts helped to increase the church's membership in Homer from sixteen individuals in 1804 to seventy-eight in 1810, providing sufficient resources for the construction of a Baptist meetinghouse in the town two years later. By 1827, after a series of successful revivals, the church's membership had increased to "nearly 500."[49]

As members of Alfred Bennett's congregation, the Grow family practiced a conservative, traditionalistic version of the Baptist faith. By the early nineteenth century, a majority of American Protestants had moved away from the strict Calvinist belief that God predetermined the fate of each person's soul at birth and that eternal salvation was solely the "gift of God, over which human action could have no influence." Many Protestant denominations, including several branches of the Baptist church, had come to believe instead that an individual's moral behavior and personal character determined his or her prospects for salvation—"that each sinner, not God, was responsible for his or her eternal fate" and that human beings "could choose to be saved" by their own "free will" and the way in which they chose to live their lives. In this view, "sin was no longer conceived as something inherent in the depravity of human beings but as a kind of failure of a person's will and thus fully capable of being eliminated by individual exertion."[50] To Bennett, however, the belief that sinners could achieve salvation through their own "good works" was "lax theology" that reflected a "lowering [of] the standard of godliness." He continued to adhere instead to the traditional Calvinist belief in "predestination"—that each person's salvation was "solely dependent on the will of God." In his view, men and women were innately vile sinners whose only possibility of salvation rested in placing their "hope in Christ." He considered it his duty as a Baptist preacher to "show . . . the sinner that, while his misery was the result of his own choice" of personal behavior, "his salvation and ultimate happiness depended entirely on God's choice" and that "there was no hope but in the mercy of God."[51] As members of Bennett's church, the Grows presumably shared these spiritual convictions.[52]

Alfred Bennett (1780–1851), pioneer preacher, first ordained pastor of the Homer, New York, Baptist Church, and brother-in-law of Elisha and Lois Grow. (Source: Hezekiah Harvey, *Memoir of Alfred Bennett* [New York, 1852], frontispiece)

From the start, Bennett was appalled by the licentiousness that he observed in Homer's frontier culture. "Iniquity abounds" here, he complained to a relative in 1804. The specific iniquities that he found disturbing included many of the town's most popular recreational pastimes: horse racing and gambling, raucous public dances and theatrical performances, and above all, heavy drinking fueled by the town's growing number of whiskey distilleries and taverns. "By 1830," historian Curtis D. Johnson writes, "those [Homer residents] who wanted to find God went to church" and "those who simply wanted social interaction and amusement went elsewhere." Consequently, to prevent his congregation from being engulfed in what he saw as a rising tide of immorality and "worldliness," Bennett's Homer Baptist Church imposed strict church discipline on members who succumbed to any of the "worldly temptations" around them—and it did so, according to Johnson, "with the most vigor" of any church in the area. Male and female members found guilty of intoxication were made to appear before the full congregation and publicly confess that they "had drunk too much," with several members eventually being expelled from the church for their "excessive use of Ardent Spirits." Younger members of the congregation were sternly admonished for "joining in vain amusements such as plays and dancing," and one young woman, Charlotte Collins, was expelled from the church for engaging in such morally unacceptable "worldly" behavior.[53]

Bennett also felt that Homer's residents were too much motivated by the pursuit of money and material affluence. Like most evangelical Protestants of the period, he believed that the successful accumulation of wealth was a gift from God—"a sign of divine approval" and a reward for an individual's devotion to the Christian faith. But he was concerned that his fellow townspeople had become obsessed with "the prospect of gain" to the detriment of their spiritual welfare, and that their "acquisitive instincts" had "overwhelmed their commitment to Christian piety." "Money" was their "great object," he later recalled. So "engrossed" had they become in their materialistic ambitions and "lust [for] things" that he feared they would "lose their souls" unless someone "warn[ed] them of the danger and direct[ed] them to Jesus." Consequently, he frequently focused on themes of "self-denial" in his sermons; while under his leadership the Homer Baptist Church regularly disciplined members who engaged in "commercial wrongdoing" or unethical behavior of any sort in their pursuit of wealth. Charges, for example, were brought against John Cleveland for his "deception" involving a bond and a mortgage, against James Monrose for "defrauding his creditors," and against Sylvanus Hopkins for "forfeiting his word in a matter of material consequence," while sister Miriam Foster was reprimanded for "cheating in counting yams."[54]

Like many evangelical ministers, Bennett preached about the terrifying realities of "Judgment Day" with a "fire and energy" that frequently left his listeners weeping in fear and despair.[55] There was more to his ministry than Puritanical gloom and doom, however. Sunday services were occasionally lightened by levity. On one occasion, "some mischievous boys" in the congregation tied a live sheep to Bennett's church pulpit, with the animal's front legs "resting on the desk." The congregation then "assembled and [was] quietly enjoy[ing] the joke" when Bennett entered the pulpit, turned to the smiling assemblage, and said, "I see you [already] have someone to instruct you, so I will leave you in his hands."[56] The church's members also took seriously their Christian obligation to look after those in need. Elisha, for example, helped to support a neighboring widow by plowing her fields for her.[57] He also provided "horse-drawn wagons every Sabbath for those needing transportation to attend church services,"[58] emulating one of his father's practices as deacon of the Grow Hill Baptist Church back in Connecticut.

Homer experienced remarkably rapid growth during the Grows' years of residence there. The heavy influx of settlers that was already underway when the family arrived in 1812 continued unabated through the 1820s, with the population increasing by some 235 percent, from 2,975 to 6,980, between 1810 and 1830.[59] By the latter year, Homer was the most prosperous township in Cortland County, with a flourishing agricultural economy, eleven sawmills, seven gristmills, two textile factories, an iron furnace, and a nail factory. At the same time, its central village was developing into a bustling commercial and cultural hub, with a cluster of architecturally imposing buildings—the Cortland Academy, four stately churches, Jedediah Barber's Great Western mercantile emporium, and a growing number of "elaborate brick houses in the Greek Revival style"—surrounding its picturesque village green. In less than a quarter-century, the town had transformed itself from an "empty frontier" into "a rich and prosperous farming community."[60]

But its dynamic growth phase was already coming to an end. By the early 1830s, thanks largely to two decades of intense population growth, Homer had completed its transition from an underpopulated frontier settlement to an economically mature farm town—in effect replicating in one generation a process that had typically taken at least two or three generations to complete in frontier areas of New England. The steady stream of new settlers pouring into the town dramatically increased its population density from three persons per square mile in 1800, to thirty per square mile in 1814, to sixty by 1820 (the only years for which data are available),[61] producing the inevitable problems of land scarcity and inflated land prices that had been fueling migratory impulses in New England—and in the Grow family—for generations.

As in New England, mounting land pressures meant reduced economic opportunity for younger residents. Soon signs of growing poverty and inequality were everywhere to be seen. By the mid-1830s, 23 percent of the town's male heads of household were landless, while only 18 percent owned more than 50 acres, barely above the minimum required for subsistence. Average per capita wealth had fallen by 11 percent in the preceding decade and a half, and, as if to symbolize the growing lack of opportunity, a publicly funded "house for keeping paupers" had begun operating. The response was predictable: again following the long-established New England pattern, younger residents began leaving for the western frontier, which the expanding boundaries of settlement had by now pushed deep into the upper Great Lakes region of the Northwest Territory. Between 1830 and 1835, for the first time in Homer's brief history "out-migration exceeded in-migration," as more and more sons came to realize that they could no longer count on their fathers to provide them with land, and that, as Curtis Johnson puts it, "their chances of ever owning their own farm were slim unless they moved west."[62]

In 1836–1837, the Grows liquidated their landholdings in Homer and migrated 465 miles west to the Michigan frontier. Although the 252 acres of land that Elisha owned in the town on the eve of the family's departure[63] ranked him in the top 2 percent of local landowners,[64] 252 acres were but a tiny fraction of the land he would have needed to place his ten sons—who ranged in age from 29 to 12 at the time—on farms of their own. That two of those sons, 29-year-old Stillman and 26-year-old Elisha Jr., had recently married and were sharing a small, mortgaged, 60-acre farm[65] was a harbinger of the unpromising future that awaited the next generation of the family if it remained in Homer. The fact that another newlywed son's total household possessions consisted of "a bed constructed of [his] own labor, a cook-stove, a three-foot cherry table, six chairs, a rocker and dishes for two" also suggests that Elisha's resources were largely concentrated in land rather than in liquid wealth that could have been used to improve his children's economic circumstances.[66] Accordingly, the decision was reached to migrate once again to a frontier environment of greater opportunity and greener (or at least cheaper) pastures—even though that decision meant that Elisha, now 58 years old, and Lois, 53, would be subjecting themselves to the enervating hardships of pioneer homesteading for a second time in twenty-five years.

Elisha Grow (1779–1850) and Lois (Palmer) Grow (1784–1850), from photographs taken in the 1840s shortly after photography was invented. (Photograph collection, Oakland County Pioneer and Historical Society, Pontiac, MI) (Both photographs were published in William B. Grow's *Eighty-Five Years of Life and Labor* [Carbondale, PA, 1902], following page 12.)

Michigan's geographic remoteness and relative inaccessibility left it sparsely populated long after other areas of the "Old Northwest"—notably Ohio and Indiana—had been settled. As late as 1820, there were fewer than 9,000 white inhabitants in the entire territory.[67] The pace of settlement began to quicken during the ensuing decade, however, in response to developments taking place back in the East. In 1820, the United States Congress passed a piece of legislation popularly known as the "Ten Shilling Act" which set the purchase price of public land in Michigan Territory at $1.25 per acre.[68] Five years later, the completion of New York's Erie Canal—a 363-mile "artificial river" connecting Albany on the Hudson River with Buffalo at the eastern end of Lake Erie—opened a "water highway" between the northeastern states and the Great Lakes, providing settlers heading west with a "relatively easy and affordable" transportation "pipeline" to Michigan.[69] Soon, East Coast speculators were buying up enormous quantities of Michigan's public land and, in collaboration with the territory's political leaders, actively promoting immigration. A series of Michigan maps and gazetteers published by John Farmer beginning in 1826 described the territory's resources in laudatory terms. Promotional circulars distributed throughout New York and New England lured northeastern farmers with seductive descriptions of the territory's rich, fertile, "stoneless soil" and flat ("level as a barn floor") terrain.[70] A "Michigan song" purportedly written by one of the territory's land promoters became "immensely popular" in the Northeast, its lyrics reflecting the unabashed boosterism of the period:

> *Come, all ye Yankee farmers who'd like to change your lot,*
> *Who've spunk enough to travel beyond your native spot,*
> *And leave behind the village where Pa and Ma do stay,*
> *Come follow me and settle in Michigan-i-ay.*
> *Yea, yea, yea, in Michigan-i-ay.*
>
> *What country ever growed up so great in little time,*
> *Just popping from the nurs'ry right into like its prime;*
> *When Uncle Sam did wean her 'twas but the other day,*
> *And now she's quite a lady, this Michigan-i-ay.*
>
> *Then come ye Yankee farmers who've mettle hearts like me,*
> *And elbow grease in plenty to bow the forest tree;*
> *Come take a "Quarter Section," and I'll be bound you'll say,*
> *This country takes the rag off, this Michigan-i-ay.*[71]

By the 1830s, a full-blown land rush was underway. Pioneers "smitten with the Michigan fever" began flooding in from the Northeast, most of them via the Erie Canal, to buy up large parcels of cheap "ten shilling" land while it was still available—resulting in a spectacular increase in the territory's population from 8,800 in 1820 to 32,000 in 1830, to 87,000 in 1834, to 175,000 in 1837, and 212,000 in 1840, making Michigan the fastest-growing territory in the United States during the period.[72] By 1831, an estimated 2,000 settlers a week were arriving in Detroit, the territory's main entry point and only city.[73] Sales of public land at Michigan's government land offices increased from less than 150,000 acres in 1830, to 2 million acres in 1835, to more than 4 million in 1836, the peak year of the land boom.[74] The territory's land offices did such a "land office business," in fact, that at one point the Detroit office was forced to temporarily lock its doors and receive payments "through a window, because too many people were trying to squeeze into the building."[75] By 1837, Michigan had met the population requirements for statehood, which was granted in January, a few weeks before Elisha and Lois arrived.

The Erie Canal influenced the Grow family's migration to Michigan in at least two important respects. Economically, the new waterway had an immediate "negative impact" on agriculture in Homer, placing additional strains on local farmers. From the start, New York farm towns directly adjacent to the canal enjoyed comparative advantages in transportation and market access over communities such as Homer that were geographically farther removed from the waterway. (As one historian puts it, "proximity to the Canal brought boom and distance brought bust.") In addition, by cutting travel time between Buffalo and Albany "nearly in half," the canal brought major reductions in freight rates on goods shipped between Lake Erie and New York City (from 19 cents a ton per mile before the canal opened in 1825 to less than 2 cents a ton by 1830). As a result, it soon cost less for farmers in western New York and the Midwest to ship their wheat, flour, and other commodities to New York City than for Homer's farmers to transport their surpluses 30 miles overland from their isolated township to the canal. Consequently, left at a competitive disadvantage with other agricultural producers because of geographic distance and transportation costs, a Homer farmer, in Curtis Johnson's words, "had already lost the price war before he and his wagon full of grain rolled into the streets of either Syracuse or Ithaca, the two nearest towns in the canal system." By the 1830s, as a result, Homer was rapidly becoming "an agricultural backwater," intensifying the pressure on local farm families like the Grows to leave.[76]

At the same time, the canal also offered those farm families a convenient way out by providing them with a state-of-the-art waterway ready and waiting to transport them to the frontier.[77] The Grows were among the many Homer residents who took advantage of that opportunity. Unsurprisingly, it was the family's three oldest sons, Stillman, Elisha Jr., and Elijah—all recently married and struggling economically—who provided the initial impetus for the move. In 1836, the three brothers and their wives and children migrated from Homer to the new farming settlement of Independence in Michigan's Oakland County,

26 miles northwest of Detroit. The journey—which included 150 miles of westward passage on the Erie Canal followed by 250 miles overland across Lower Canada (present-day Ontario) in horse-drawn covered wagons—took three weeks.[78] Arriving in Michigan, a sibling later recalled, the group initially "intended to go to the Grand River district [an area between Jackson and Battle Creek that was a focal point of land speculation and pioneering activity in the mid-1830s] but stopped at the first ten shilling land they met, and it was in Oakland County."[79] After purchasing land, the group erected a 24' wide × 16' deep, one-room log house, in which the three families—eleven people in all, including five small children between the ages of 2 and 7—spent the ensuing winter crammed together. The following spring of 1837, most of the other members of the family joined them from Homer.[80]

The family's move to Michigan once again displayed the characteristic features of a kinship-based chain migration. Prior to 1836, two of Lois' brothers and one of her sisters had left Exeter, New York, to found a settlement in Monroe County, Michigan, while in-laws of Elisha and Lois' son John Alonzo had recently settled in Oakland County, a short distance west of Independence Township.[81] After Stillman and his two brothers arrived, they wrote letters to family members back in Homer extolling the virtues of the Michigan frontier, and based on their reports one of their married sisters—Elisha and Lois' eldest daughter Lois (Grow) Robinson—and her husband, Albert, decided to migrate. That decision in turn prompted Elisha and Lois to accompany them because, as a younger son later recalled, their daughter Lois "was very dear to their hearts" and they were reluctant to be separated from her. Eventually, all but one of Elisha and Lois' children joined the exodus.[82]

In March 1837, a small caravan of covered wagons carrying twenty-nine members of the Grow family departed Homer for the Erie Canal town of Syracuse 30 miles to the north. The traveling party consisted of Elisha and Lois; their two other newly married sons (John Alonzo and Abel) and their brides; three married daughters (Lois, Julia, and Anne) accompanied by their husbands and ten children aged 1 to 10; and seven of Elisha and Lois' unmarried younger children (William, 20; Thomas, 19; Sarah Matilda, 18; twins Edward and Edwin, 15; Waterman, 12; and Rhoda Bennett, 8).[83] The participants left few descriptive accounts of their journey to Michigan, but after reaching Syracuse they almost certainly boarded an Erie Canal "line boat," a long, narrow freight barge with a cabin at each end for sleeping and dining and a middle section piled high with migrating farmers' household possessions and supplies. Pulled by teams of horses walking the canal's towpath, the boats traveled at a slow, steady speed of two-to-three miles per hour. On-board accommodations were spartan, with passengers providing their own food and bedding and women often complaining about the lack of privacy. Travelers with any refinement found the canal's cultural environment appalling. According to historian Carol

Sheriff, the boatmen were "vulgar and violent" for the most part, and the teenage boys (mostly Irish immigrants) who drove the towpath horse teams were notorious for their profanity and lewd behavior. (As one female passenger put it, "the depravity of the drivers is dreadful.") In addition, "alcohol was plentiful on the Canal," with "more than fifteen hundred grog shops" situated along its banks and an average of "one tavern or [alcohol-selling] grocery store . . . every quarter mile." In the larger canal towns, houses of prostitution had also sprung up alongside the waterway. As a result, the typical "sights, sounds, and smells" of the canal included filthy, foul-smelling canal workers "stumbling out of grog shops," drunken "boatmen shouting obscenities, in a variety of accents, at 'respectable' passengers on other boats," and disreputable young women entering and leaving tawdry "houses of 'ill fame.'"[84] For pious Baptists like the Grows, their three-day voyage on the canal would have been an uncomfortable experience, both physically and morally.

Disembarking in Buffalo, the family immediately crossed into Canada and headed west by land. One of the sons, John Alonzo, later recalled that the family endured "many trials in traveling through Canada," but he unfortunately provided no details. Other American pioneers who traveled across Lower Canada during the same period, however, complained about the "extremely bad roads and worse lodgings and fare." They described long, arduous days trudging through miles of dark, towering pine forests "thick with mosquitoes," along roads clogged with snow or riddled with mudholes or washed away by "gullies fifty or sixty feet deep." To reach Michigan from Buffalo, travelers had to cross at least three rivers, either by fording them on foot or inching fearfully over rickety "corduroy" bridges. The few inns that existed were little more than crude, one-room log huts inhabited by "uncouth and scoundrelly looking men," with a "sleeping-place . . . divided off at one end by a few planks." By choice or necessity, pioneers usually camped out along the road at night, their sleep interrupted by "the occasional howl of wolf or scream of panther." After two weeks or so, the lucky ones managed to reach Windsor, the Canadian town on the east bank of the Detroit River opposite Detroit.[85]

To re-enter the United States, the Grows would have boarded one of the river ferries that regularly crossed between Windsor and Detroit. An English novelist who took passage on one such ferry shortly after the Grows passed through the area left a firsthand description: The "ferry-boat," she wrote, was "a pretty little steamer, gaily painted, with streamers flying, and shaded by an awning." Crossing "continuously" back and forth "from shore to shore," the vessel carried a colorful assortment of passengers, including "English emigrants and French Canadians; brisk Americans; dark, sad-looking Indians folded in their blankets; farmers, storekeepers, speculators in wheat, artisans, [and] trim girls with black eyes and short petticoats, speaking a Norman patois, and bringing baskets of fruit to the Detroit market."[86] Approaching the Detroit waterfront, the ferry passengers were greeted by a skyline of "queer low French buildings," vestiges of the town's early years as a French settlement prior to 1760. After disembarking, they were immediately swarmed by a "motley crowd" of "people with things to sell"—"hotel hawkers, stage-coach owners and land agents." To many arriving settlers, Detroit was "a foreign port" where "Indians and fur trappers were commonly seen and French was [still] the predominant language."

By the time the Grows arrived, the city was teeming with transient pioneer families moving through on their way to frontier districts farther inland. A local journalist writing in the mid-1830s reported that the streets were "alive with covered wagons by the hundreds, laden with women and children, articles of household furniture packed all around and sheep following . . .; away to the interior they form a long line to Oakland, Washtenaw, St. Clair, and Monroe."[87] At the peak of the land rush in 1836, another local observer estimated that "one wagon left Detroit for the interior every five minutes, dawn to dusk, from early spring to late autumn."[88]

After resting briefly and re-provisioning themselves, Elisha's traveling party set out for his sons' log house in Independence Township a few miles outside of Pontiac, a frontier village that was developing into a market center for the pioneer farming settlements springing up in the surrounding countryside. The road leading from Detroit to Pontiac was notoriously bad, an often nearly impassable "mud-clogged quagmire" strewn with wreckage from broken wagons and abandoned stagecoaches that lay scattered along its roadsides as stark "reminders of the trials of those emigrants who had gone before."[89] Nevertheless, by early April, Elisha and the rest of his family had managed to reach Independence, and he and the other household heads were actively scouting the area for land to buy.

Meanwhile, the family's farm equipment and other heavy belongings were being transported to Michigan by a separate route, under the supervision of Elisha's unmarried 20-year-old son William. William's later account of his adventures suggests, among other things, that his father might have underestimated some of the expenses involved in migrating to Michigan:

> ...it fell to my lot to load the goods on an Erie canal-boat and accompany them to Buffalo. There the goods were transferred to a lake-boat, and the journey was continued to Detroit. So limited were my cash resources that, after paying the freight, I was left to make a four-hundred-mile trip without one cent of money, but through the kindness of the captain I was given every privilege and comfort. Arriving in Detroit, I attended to the storing of the goods, and then found that twenty-six miles lay between me and the home of my brother Stillman. There was no way but to walk,

and this I started to do, with a satchel weighing about seventy pounds. The roads had been recently ditched, and were, without exception, the worst roads that I have ever seen. About three miles out of Detroit, I overtook two men driving cattle, who asked me to put my satchel in the wagon and drive the team. I felt greatly elated at this seeming smile of fortune, but when I found myself going through a mud hole, where the front of the wagon dipped a box full of mud[,] which flowed out the back of the wagon as I came out of a sink hole, I at once surrendered the lines, preferring to help drive the cattle. We made twelve miles the first day, staying at Birmingham over night, where the cattle-men paid all bills. Before nightfall of the following day I reached my brother's house, a tired but happy youth, the several families having previously arrived.[90]

In June, Elisha purchased 160 acres of land in Waterford Township, 7 miles northwest of Pontiac. The township, which took its name from the thirty or more pristine lakes found within its borders, had a terrain that consisted largely of "oak openings," grassy prairies scattered with enormous oak trees "nine to fifteen feet in circumference." Because they were relatively easy to clear and plow, and their "exceedingly rich soil" was considered "first rate for grain," oak openings were highly prized by settlers.[91] They also attracted intense interest from speculators, many of whom were making "quick fortunes" by buying Oakland County land at low prices and immediately re-selling it to newly arriving pioneer families or other speculators at a hefty price increase.[92] Elisha bought his Waterford property at the height of a speculative buying frenzy that had sent the township's land values soaring. In the six years prior to his purchase, for example, his 160-acre tract had already changed hands three times and increased in value by more than 1,000 percent. The property's first private owner, Daniel Huntoon, had acquired it from the US government in 1831 for only $200, or $1.25 (*i.e.*, 10 shillings) an acre. Three years later, in 1834, Huntoon sold the property to Charles Harbach of Waterford for $475, or just under $3.00 an acre. Harbach in turn sold it to Julius Peck in October 1836 for $1,850, or more than $11.50 an acre; and Elisha bought it from Peck eight months later, in June of 1837, for $2,250, or $14.06 an acre.[93]

Having recently sold his farm in Homer for $6,140 ($35.50 an acre),[94] Elisha had more than enough capital available to purchase his new Waterford property with cash. Nevertheless, because the cost of establishing a 160-acre farm on the Michigan frontier in the mid-1830s ranged from $2,000 to $3,000, he instead chose to finance more than half of the purchase with a two-year mortgage of $1,250 in order to preserve a sufficient amount of money for "farm-making" expenses. Many Michigan pioneers of this period financed their land acquisitions with similar mortgages, willingly accepting the 10 percent interest rate that came with them in the optimistic belief that they would be able to pay the mortgage off with profits from their first two years of agricultural production.[95] In Elisha's case, that optimism apparently proved to be warranted, because he paid off his mortgage in full in June 1839.[96]

The land that Elisha purchased was located in the northwest quadrant of Waterford, overlapping the then-marshy western end of Huntoon Lake. A later reference to the property's "oak and hickory" groves[97] suggests that it was situated in one of Waterford's oak openings, which would help to account for the rapid rise in its land value. (The 160-acre tract stretched southwestward from the intersection of present-day Williams Lake Road and Airport Road to Lansdowne Road on the west and Wilson Drive on the south. In the 1920s, it was converted into a residential subdivision known as Maceday Gardens consisting of some 400 small house lots.[98] In the early twenty-first century, it was a nondescript blue-collar neighborhood of modest homes bordered by small commercial establishments.)

When Elisha acquired the property in 1837, it was almost completely undeveloped. As his son Thomas later recalled, only "very slight improvements had been made" by its three previous owners, and "much work was to be done in clearing land and erecting good buildings."[99] As a result, for the second time in a quarter century, Elisha and Lois directed their energies to carving out a wilderness homestead virtually from scratch, suffering the discomforts and primitive living conditions of frontier life once again despite the fact that they were now well into their fifties. Addressing their most urgent priority, they immediately constructed a "roomy log house" to live in. One of the couple's

A log house on the Michigan frontier, 1836. (Source: William Nowlin, *The Bark Covered House* [Detroit, 1876], illustration following page 90)

granddaughters, Julia (Bishop) Taft, who spent a winter with them in 1838–1839 at the age of 11, vividly remembered "the huge fireplace in the main room downstairs" and "the pony which, from time to time, dragged a huge four-foot backlog right into the room to be rolled into the fireplace and burn there for weeks before being replaced by another."[100]

As in Homer twenty-five years earlier, the family faced many "privations and difficulties" on the Michigan frontier. Wolves and bears were still common in Oakland County at the time of their arrival, and there were snakes, especially Massasauga rattlesnakes and six-foot blue racers, everywhere. Wooded areas were "alive" with "clouds of mosquitoes," while "various types of enormous biting flies" tormented settlers and livestock alike.[101] In addition, virtually every Michigan pioneer came down with "ague," also known as "wood fever"—a non-fatal mosquito-borne form of malaria that left its victims "wan and debilitated" for days or weeks at a time. A typical case of ague began with chills and violent shaking, followed by a raging fever accompanied by severe headaches and back pain, followed by more chills, and finally ending in "profuse sweats." Because the illness usually struck in the spring or early summer immediately after the plowing season, the pioneers believed that it was caused by "miasma"—poisonous vapors rising up out of the freshly plowed soil—when in fact the sickness was actually caused by the swarms of mosquitoes that appeared after the final frost of the spring.[102]

Supplies were scarce and expensive in Waterford during its frontier phase, and newly arrived pioneer families usually relied on hunting and fishing to supply themselves with food until their first crops of corn, wheat, potatoes, and oats came in. They also made occasional pilgrimages to Pontiac to purchase provisions, but were often appalled by the high prices charged by village merchants. With sugar unobtainable at any price, most settlers produced maple syrup or collected wild honey as substitutes. And for several years, until their newly planted orchards began to produce, apples were regarded as "luxuries."[103]

A major downturn in the national economy added to the pioneers' woes. Although the Grows could not have known it beforehand, they had chosen a particularly bad time to migrate. In 1836, in an effort to curb runaway inflation in the United States, the Andrew Jackson administration tightened credit and imposed strict new rules on banking practices. The measures triggered a financial panic in May 1837—two months after Elisha and Lois arrived in Michigan—and caused an economic depression that lasted into the mid-1840s. The economic turbulence had a devastating impact on Michigan's settlers. Land prices in the state plummeted by as much as 90 percent, bursting the speculative bubble once and for all, while prices for farm products "dropped drastically," and all but three of Michigan's forty-some "woefully undercapitalized" banks failed. Thousands of pioneer families were ruined and left the state. Those who survived—including the Grows—did so by farming at a subsistence level and bartering with their neighbors in what the settlers referred to as "swap and dicker" transactions. For many, the worst phase of the economic crisis was the exceptionally severe "Long Winter of 1842–1843," when many pioneers nearly ran out of food and large numbers of their livestock starved to death for lack of fodder.[104]

While Elisha and Lois were struggling to survive the hard times in Waterford, their adult children were dispersing out into the agricultural settlements of the surrounding region—Milford, Highland, White Lake, and elsewhere—seeking niches in the depressed frontier economy and enduring "hardships and privations" of their own. One of the sons, Abel, lived "in a sort of shanty house" during his first year in Michigan, while Elijah's wife, Charity, kept their household afloat financially by making home-sewn woolen pants that she sold "at six shillings per pair" and sometimes bartered for food. Abel and his brother William initially worked as day laborers for "a daily wage of one dollar and a half," and out of their "slender earnings" eventually managed to buy "two lots, side by side" in Milford "for fifty dollars apiece" on which they "erected a suitable double dwelling house" to live in. In addition, Stillman's 34-year-old wife, Derenda, died within a few years of their arrival in Michigan, leaving him with four young children between the ages of 3 and 13.[105]

The economic depression eventually ran its course, and by 1845 Michigan's settlers were beginning to enjoy a welcome period of growth. For the next few years, however, farmers in Waterford and neighboring communities continued to operate at a near-subsistence level. Lacking adequate roads or the market infrastructure needed to support larger-scale commercial farming, they instead continued to produce "small agricultural surpluses for local exchange," bartering with their neighbors and maintaining "an essentially subsistence lifestyle."[106]

Although the standard of living in Oakland County's frontier settlements remained uniformly low for several years, local status hierarchies inevitably developed based on the quantity and quality of each farmer's landholdings. In Elisha's case, the surplus capital that he brought with him from Homer appears to have served him well in that regard, because according to Waterford tax lists from the first half of the 1840s he consistently ranked in the top 20 percent of local landowners. In 1840, at a time when nearly 60 percent of the township's farmers (73 of 130) owned 80 acres or less and a quarter (32) owned no more than 40, the 200 acres that Elisha had by now accumulated made him the 18th largest landowner in Waterford and ranked him in the top 14 percent of its property-owning residents. (His landholdings were still relatively modest, however, when compared with those of the top six local landowners—the upper 5 percent of the community—who owned between 400 and 840 acres each.) The tax records also indicate that Elisha's taxable wealth was increasing more rapidly than that of his neighbors, an apparent indication that he was better equipped financially to improve his farm than most local farmers. Between 1840 and 1845—a period that saw the average value of landholdings in the township decline by nearly 14 percent (from $546 in 1840 to $471 in 1845) as a direct result of the depression—Elisha's landholdings increased in value by 35 percent, even though he sold off 18 of his acres during that time span. In 1840, the tax-assessed value of his 200 acres was $800, the 23rd highest among the town's 130 landowners, ranking him in the upper 18 percent of its property owners. By 1845, the assessed value of his remaining 182 acres had risen to $1,076, elevating him into the top 10 percent of local landowners (15th out of 151). His annual taxes increased correspondingly, and again at a relatively faster rate than those of the average Waterford resident. His 1840 tax bill of $7.51 was the 23rd highest among the township's 138 taxpayers, ranking him in the top 17 percent of the community; the following year, his $10.13 tax bill was 15th highest out of 150 taxpayers, positioning him in the top 10 percent of the tax list; while by 1845 his $12.17 tax payment was the 13th highest in the township out of 159 taxpayers, ranking him in the top 8 percent of Waterford's residents as measured by total taxable wealth.[107] All in all, Elisha's Waterford tax records indicate that his economic position in the community was consistent with the upper middle-class status of the preceding three generations of the family line.

By 1846, the rigors of pioneer life had taken a sufficiently heavy physical toll on Elisha and Lois that they began making arrangements for a live-in caretaker to look after them—even though they were still only in their sixties at the time. In March of that year, adopting the method that aging New Englanders traditionally relied upon to secure home care in their declining years, they transferred ownership of their Waterford farm to their youngest son, 21-year-old Waterman, for $1; in return Waterman leased the property back to his parents under a "life lease," in which he legally committed himself to support them and provide them with "all necessaries during their natural lives."[108] Four years later when Waterman married, he and his bride immediately took up residence with Elisha and Lois and began providing them with support. Those caregiving responsibilities had barely begun, however, when, on the morning of 22 August 1850, Elisha died at age 71, followed a mere fourteen days later by Lois, who was only 66 at the time. The cause of their deaths is unknown, but nearly four decades of backbreaking frontier labor might well have been a contributing factor. The couple was buried 3 miles north of their farm, in the village of Clarkston where they had been members of the local Baptist church.[109] The inscription on the upper portion of Elisha's gravestone offers a fitting epitaph for their lives of pioneering toil: "There is rest in Heaven."

"*There is rest
in Heaven*"

ELISHA GROW
DIED
AUGUST 22,
1850
AGED 70 YEARS

"*I am the resurrection & the life
He that believeth in me though
he were dead yet shall he live.*"

Elisha Grow gravestone, Lakeview Cemetery, Clarkston, MI, with an incorrect age of death (70 rather than 71). The religious inscription at the bottom is from John 11:25, King James Bible. The stone was irreparably damaged by vandalism at some point in the twentieth century, and was replaced by a modern replica in 2005. See memorial 69036564, www.findagrave.com. (Photographs by the author.)

LOIS
WIFE OF
ELISHA GROW
DIED
SEPT. 5, 1850
AGED 66 YEARS

"*They were lovely & pleasant in
their lives and in their death
were not (long) divided*"

Lois Grow gravestone, Lakeview Cemetery, Clarkston, MI. Fallen and broken as a result of twentieth-century vandalism; top quarter missing. Religious inscription at base paraphrases a biblical description of Saul and Jonathan in the Second Book of Samuel, 1:23, King James Bible. The stone is also pictured in memorial 69036567, findagrave.com. (Photograph by the author.)

Elisha and Lois Grow belonged to the post-revolutionary war generation of Americans who extended the new nation's settlement boundaries deep into the interior of North America, occupying more territory in a single generation, historian Gordon Wood notes, "than [Americans] had occupied during the entire 150 years of the colonial period." The hundreds of thousands of pioneer families who carried out that epic mass migration were, like the Grows, land hungry, geographically mobile, and fully prepared to uproot themselves more than once in pursuit of a better life for themselves and their children—with many of them migrating "at least three or four times" over the course of their lives, "selling their land . . . at a profit each time" before moving on to a more promising new frontier region farther west.[110]

At a large family reunion held on Elisha and Lois' Waterford farm thirty-five years after their deaths, their children proudly memorialized them as "sturdy pioneers" who "braved hardships and danger" and "labored unceasingly" to construct successive homesteads on the New York and Michigan frontiers. The couple's eldest son, Stillman, took the occasion to add that they were also "good parents" who always tried to see to it that their children grew up "respectable and honest."[111] In remembering their parents as "sturdy pioneers" and "good parents," the couple's sons and daughters were in essence describing core characteristics of the American farm families who settled the nation's vast interior, characteristics that in most pioneer families were inextricably interconnected. Intrinsic to the pioneering experience was the willingness of parents in frontier households to endure a low standard of living in anticipation of future prosperity for the next generation(s) of the family line.[112] Traveling through the Pontiac-Waterford area shortly before the Grows settled there, the perceptive French observer of early American life Alexis de Toqueville described the Yankee pioneers he encountered as people who were "willing to undergo the privation of a life in the wilds in order to afford their children a better start in life."[113] That characterization of pioneer motives clearly explains Elisha's 1812 decision to leave his established life in Connecticut for the New York frontier (a decision prompted by his recognition that, in his words, he "had so many children he must get where land was cheaper"),[114] and it also probably underlay the 1836–1837 decisions of his older offspring to migrate west from New York to Michigan.

At the same time, frontier migration provided many pioneer parents with a way of keeping their family together at a time when land pressures were driving its young adult members westward. As one pioneer father put it while preparing to move his family to the Ohio frontier: "My wishes . . . and my exertions have in view . . . a place where my whole family, for a generation or two to come, may sit down, in *one* neighborhood, in peace, competence, and humble virtue."[115] That factor—the desire to maintain the family's physical cohesion—accounts in large part for Elisha and Lois' 1837 decision to accompany their departing eldest daughter and other adult children to Michigan.

Above all, however, pioneer parents regarded the frontier as an environment of future opportunity for their family line, an environment in which their children, through hard work and self-denial, could carve out "respectable" middle-class lives for themselves as economically independent landowners— and in the process perpetuate the traditional agrarian way of life that, from the perspective of devoutly religious farmers like Elisha and Lois Grow, gave their children and their children's children the best chance of growing up to be morally upstanding adults living virtuous and "honest" Christian lives.

In Elisha and Lois' case, the years of personal sacrifice and toil paid off. Most of their children went on to prosper in Michigan in the decades after 1850 as the state's rapidly expanding economy provided widespread opportunities for personal advancement and financial gain. Of the couple's ten sons, six became farmers (at least three of them rather affluent ones), two (Stillman and William) became well-regarded Baptist ministers, and two were carpenters, one of whom (Abel) amassed a "comfortable fortune" in the building trade. Of the six daughters who survived to adulthood, five were the wives of Oakland County farmers or businessmen, while Lois' husband became superintendent of the State Reform School for Boys in Lansing.[116] For a fourth time in five generations,[117] the Grows had exploited the opportunities available on America's expanding geographic frontiers to improve their economic prospects and achieve respectable positions in the middle ranks of rural society.

Major changes loomed on the horizon, however. By the late nineteenth century, the last remaining frontier land in the United States had been settled, bringing the "frontier-rural" phase of American history to an end.[118] With the elimination of a readily available farming frontier, future generations of the family would instead pursue economic well-being and social respectability in the new commercial and professional frontiers opening up in the nation's rapidly growing cities.

The ten sons of Elisha and Lois Grow. (Source: William B. Grow, *Eighty-Five Years of Life and Labor*, undated photograph following page 18)

Elisha and Lois Grow and their daughters. (Source: William B. Grow, *Eighty-Five Years of Life and Labor*, undated photograph following page 12) Rhoda's facial expression reflects her grief from the recent death of her husband of seventeen years, Joseph A. Rowley, which had left her with five young children to raise alone. (Davis, *John Grow of Ipswich*, 96)

GENERATION SIX

THOMAS GROW (1818–1902)

Over the course of his life of 84 years, Elisha and Lois Grow's son Thomas[6] (*Elisha[5], Thomas[4], Thomas[3], Thomas[2], John[1]*) saw greater changes take place in the world around him—economically and technologically, socially and culturally— than perhaps any other generation of the family line. Born on a frontier farm in upstate New York in 1818, at a time when the United States was still an agrarian society of yeoman farmers relying on horses for transportation and fireplaces for heating and cooking, he was living in a modern urban-industrial America by the time of his death in Pontiac, Michigan, in 1902, part of a new urban middle class whose living conditions were being radically transformed by the industrial revolution's dazzling array of technological advances: including electricity, the telephone, gas heat, indoor plumbing, and a revolutionary new mode of transportation known as a "horseless carriage."

Thomas Grow was the seventh of ten sons in a family of seventeen children. During his childhood in Homer, New York, he suffered from "poor health," and as a result "his schooling was very much interrupted." In 1837, at age 19, he accompanied his family on its migration to the Michigan frontier, where he took up residence on his parents' new 160-acre farm in Waterford.[1] Shortly after his arrival, a severe economic depression undermined his chances of earning enough money to purchase farmland of his own, and consequently the following year he headed west to Chicago, "on foot . . . alone and . . . without money," to seek employment on a canal construction project that had recently broken ground and was actively recruiting workers.[2]

At the time, Chicago was a small frontier settlement of 4,000 people, many of whom still "dressed in deerskin," with a physical landscape consisting of a few hundred wooden buildings on a handful of unpaved streets pocked with knee-deep mudholes. A single hotel was available to accommodate travelers at the time of Thomas' arrival. Chicago's leaders—mostly young businessmen and speculators from New York and New England—nevertheless had ambitious plans to develop the "raw and slovenly looking" little settlement into the leading commercial metropolis of the West. Their plans hinged initially on the construction of a canal linking Chicago, on the western shore of Lake Michigan, with a tributary of the Mississippi River 97 miles to the southwest. By connecting "the two great water systems of North America"—the Great Lakes and the Mississippi River—the canal would position Chicago as the central "terminus of an all-water route between New York and the Gulf of Mexico," virtually assuring the settlement a dynamic future as the leading commercial-trading hub of the North American interior. Excavation work on the Illinois & Michigan Canal, as it was officially known, commenced in 1836, but the canal company's directors immediately encountered a serious labor shortage and began advertising for workers in newspapers as far afield as New York.[3] Word that the company was hiring apparently reached Thomas in Michigan, and after walking the 125 miles from Waterford to Chicago, he succeeded in obtaining a job on the project.

Work on the canal brought Thomas into contact with a world radically different from the one he had known growing up on his family's farm. The initial phase of the project, which involved the excavation of a channel 60' wide and 6' deep alongside the Chicago and Des Plaines Rivers, was carried out primarily by newly arrived Irish immigrants that the company recruited in New York City. The Irish "shovel crews" worked ten to twelve hours a day, digging through muddy, foul-smelling swamps infested with mosquitoes and leeches, before returning to the filthy, overcrowded log huts that the company provided them, where they spent their evenings drinking and fighting.[4] Sickness was endemic in the canal's work camps. During 1838, the year that Thomas began working on the construction project, a malaria epidemic felled "between 700 and 1,000 men," prompting a Catholic priest who ministered to the Irish workers to report that "The diseases in this area are horrible and so many die that there is hardly any time to give Extreme Unction to everybody. We run night and day to assist the sick." (The priest was not entirely sympathetic to the Irishmen's plight, however, believing that the epidemic was God's punishment to the workers for "getting drunk all the time, their riots, their fights and homicides.")[5] There were also sporadic outbreaks of labor violence in the camps. A few months before Thomas was hired, the canal company had responded to the economic downturn of 1837 by reducing workers' monthly wages from $26 to $22, triggering a work stoppage and attacks on company property during which one worker was fatally shot. A subsequent dispute over the firing of rebellious workers led to another eruption of violence in March 1838 during which ten people were reportedly killed.[6]

Thomas was not one of the canal project's ditch diggers. Instead, he drove a horse-drawn wagon that hauled explosives from Chicago's lakeshore to blasting sites a few miles inland along the Des Plaines River, where canal engineers were cutting a channel through a series of rocky cliffs and narrow gorges. The work was dangerous—blasting powder in the 1830s was notoriously fragile, and workers were frequently killed or injured by flying rocks—but the job apparently paid a higher wage than that of a common laborer, because "after a few months thus employed" he was able to return to Michigan with earnings of $120 "clear"[7]—and, undoubtedly, enough personal adventure stories to last a lifetime.

He spent the next two years living and working on his parents' farm in Waterford. Then, in 1841, at age 23, he married 20-year-old Margaret Morris of neighboring White Lake, in a ceremony conducted by his eldest brother, Stillman Grow, a newly ordained Baptist preacher.[8] Following the wedding, the young couple lived for a year or so in a house that Thomas built on his parents' farm. By 1843, however, they had taken up residence on the 160-acre homestead of Margaret's recently widowed mother in White Lake, presumably in order to assist her in operating her farm.[9] Within four years, Thomas had acquired ownership of the property.[10]

Most farmers in White Lake and other outlying townships in Oakland County were still farming at a semi-subsistence level in the first half of the 1840s, largely because poor roads and a lack of adequate transportation facilities left them isolated from outside consumer markets, with little incentive to produce commercial surpluses. That situation began to change in 1843, however, with the completion of a railroad link between Detroit, Michigan's principal Great Lakes port, and Pontiac, the Oakland County seat. The 26-mile Detroit & Pontiac Railroad was a quaint, rickety little line with wooden rails and a wood-powered locomotive. It was also notoriously slow, taking some two and a half hours to complete a one-way trip between its two terminuses—in part because the train's engineer carried a rifle with him to shoot deer and other game along the route, and "if he hit his target the train stopped while the fireman retrieved the prize."[11] Nevertheless, by providing county farmers with transportation access to outside markets, the railroad made commercial agriculture economically feasible in Oakland County for the first time. The county's farm products could now be conveniently shipped to the consumer markets of Detroit, or transshipped from there via Great Lakes steamships and Erie Canal barges to New York for sale in the rapidly growing and "increasingly food-deficient" cities of the East Coast, or even shipped overseas to supply the United States' burgeoning export markets in England and continental Europe.[12]

Soon county farmers were abandoning semi-subsistence agriculture and increasing their production of surplus crops "for market consumption"— aggressively expanding their cultivation of wheat in particular, the cash crop with the greatest commercial value at the time and increasingly "the market grain of choice" for Michigan farmers.[13] By 1850, so many farmers were hauling wagonloads of surplus wheat into Pontiac to sell to local merchants and the agents of eastern grain brokers that long lines of farm wagons and horse teams regularly clogged the town's streets during harvest season.[14] By 1853, the Detroit & Pontiac Railroad was shipping an average of 19,000 bushels of wheat per week to Detroit,[15] and Oakland County's previously isolated, subsistence-level farmers found that they were now "prosperous . . . and making money."[16]

In White Lake, Thomas Grow prospered more than most. By 1850, at age 32, he was the township's 18th largest landowner and ranked in the top 12 percent of its 150 property-owning residents.[17] He was also apparently producing more commodities than most other White Lake farmers. According to Michigan's 1850 agricultural census, 100 of his farm's 160 acres consisted of "improved"—i.e., cultivated and productive—farmland, the sixth highest total among the township's 137 farmers, ranking him in the top 4 percent of local farmers in the amount of improved acreage owned—and, presumably, in the quantity of agricultural commodities produced.[18] (By comparison, his 100 improved acres were nearly twice the 55.5 acres of improved land owned by the average Michigan farmer at the time.)[19] That he was also paying higher taxes than all but 11 of White Lake's 239 taxpayers in 1850, placing him in the top 5 percent of the township in taxable wealth, and ranked in the top 2 percent of the community in the assessed value of his "personal estate" or household possessions,[20] further suggests that his farming operations were yielding a relatively higher return than those of other local farmers, and that he was taking advantage of the county's rapidly expanding commercial-agricultural economy more successfully than most of his neighbors.

Pioneer farmers on the Michigan frontier harvesting grain by hand in a field not yet completely cleared of tree stumps. (Undated photograph from the Grand Rapids Public Museum, Grand Rapids, MI, published in George S. May, *Pictorial History of Michigan: The Early Years* [Grand Rapids, MI: William B. Eerdmans Publishing Company, 1967], 156. Reproduced courtesy of Eerdmans Publishing Company)

Farmers assembled for a wheat market auction in a Michigan farm town, c. 1870s. (George S. May, *Pictorial History of Michigan: The Early Years* [Grand Rapids, MI: Eerdmans Publishing Company, 1967], 156. Reproduced courtesy of Eerdmans Publishing Company)

By the early 1850s, most Oakland County farmers were fully integrated into the national market economy and earning cash incomes from commercial agriculture. With market prices, production costs, transportation expenses, and profit margins now central to their farming operations, the distance and time involved in shipping their commodities to market became increasingly significant factors in their "cost-price calculus."[21] Such considerations seem to have had an influential impact on Thomas' economic decision making, because in 1851, he sold his White Lake farm and moved 20 miles east to rural Pontiac Township, where he purchased a 134-acre farm located less than 3 miles north of the Detroit & Pontiac Railroad's Pontiac railhead. The real estate transactions involved in the relocation netted him a tidy profit—he sold the White Lake farm, which he had acquired for $200 only five years earlier, for $2,000 (a quick 1,000 percent profit), and purchased his new Pontiac farm for $1,500, leaving him with $500 in cash for improvements.[22] But closer proximity to the railroad, and the opportunity to reduce the time and expense involved in transporting his agricultural surpluses to outside markets, seem likely to have been key factors in his decision making.

The move to Pontiac coincided with a period of explosive growth in Oakland County agriculture, one that was driven largely by the continued expansion of the region's transportation infrastructure together with major advances in agricultural technology. The county's rail links to outside markets improved significantly during the 1850s. Installation of steel rails on the Detroit & Pontiac Railroad in 1852 helped reduce the trip from Pontiac to Detroit to "about one hour,"[23] while the construction of a railroad between Detroit and Toledo four years later gave Oakland County farmers their first direct rail access to New York City, "the commercial mecca of the nation," via lines running east from Toledo through northern Ohio and Pennsylvania.[24] (The new long-distance rail network linking Pontiac with New York City had the added advantage of operating year round, eliminating any further reliance on water transportation, a slow and seasonal means of transporting goods that invariably brought the county's export trade to a complete standstill in the winter when the Great Lakes and Erie Canal froze over.[25]) And the construction of steam-powered grain elevators in Detroit in 1851, and in Pontiac a year later, effectively converted the shipment of Oakland County wheat and corn "from a slow, piecemeal procession of sacks" into a flowing "river of grain" by giving the merchants who purchased the grain increased storage capacity that enabled them to ship commodities more expeditiously in larger bulk quantities.[26]

Simultaneously, a technological revolution in farm machinery was helping the county's farmers produce dramatically higher yields with significantly less labor. The introduction of new horse-powered agricultural machines in the 1850s fundamentally changed the way that Oakland County farmers farmed. The new cast-iron plows that many farmers adopted during the decade "dug a deeper furrow" than their wooden predecessors, with less friction and "half the effort," making it possible to bring significantly more land into production. New mechanical seed drills soon made hand-sowing, the traditional method of planting seed, obsolete by enabling one man and a team of horses to plant nearly 10 acres of wheat or corn a day. The introduction of mechanical harvesters and reaping machines revolutionized the way in which crops were harvested, allowing farmers to "cut more grain, faster, and more cleanly" than they did when harvesting the old-fashioned way, by hand with sickles and scythes. (By comparison, an individual farm worker using hand implements could harvest no more than half an acre to 2 acres a day, whereas the popular new McCormick reapers of the 1850s "were warranted to cut at least two acres *an hour*.") The threshing of harvested grain from the stalk, traditionally "performed manually, using flails and tethered animals," could now be completed more quickly and efficiently, with less waste and considerably less work, using new mechanical threshers that became increasingly common in the county during the decade.[27] As Oakland County's farmers mechanized their agricultural operations, farm output soared, with wheat yields "skyrocketing" from some 200,000 bushels in 1840 to over 500,000 bushels by 1860.[28]

The agricultural trends of the 1850s continued to gain momentum during the decade that followed. The US Civil War (1861–1865) was a time of "unprecedented prosperity" for Michigan farmers, as the immense food requirements of the Union Army, along with widespread crop failures in England and continental Europe in the early 1860s, intensified demand for the state's farm products. To meet that demand (and at the same time alleviate the severe labor shortage that was created when 66,000 Michigan men marched off to fight for the North), the state's farmers aggressively increased their investments in new labor-saving farm machinery. So many Michigan farmers "rushed to buy mowers and reapers" during the war, in fact, that "demand sometimes outran supply." In 1863, a Pontiac farmer reported: "Over two hundred and fifty mowing machines have been sold in this town this season, and the demand was not fully met."

Over the course of the war, the overall value of farm machinery in Oakland County doubled, enabling the county's farmers to ship "banner harvests" of wheat, corn, oats, and rye eastward by rail to meet the food needs of Union soldiers, East Coast city dwellers, and the food-starved populations of Europe. Record quantities of beef and pork were also shipped out of the county during the war years, while county farmers drastically increased their production of wool to help fill the federal government's enormous wartime orders for uniforms and blankets. As wartime commodity prices surged upward—wheat from 99 cents a bushel in 1861 to $2.55 in 1866; corn from 41 cents to $1.25 a bushel between 1861 and 1865; wool from 28 cents a pound at the beginning of the conflict to $1.03 by the time it ended—Oakland County's farmers reaped windfall profits. At the same time, an inflationary spiral in wartime land values was further increasing their wealth; between 1860 and 1867 the value of farmland in the county rose by some 70 percent, while "the dollar value of farms more than doubled in the course of the decade." As one local farmer noted at the end of the war, "The farmers around here were never as well off . . . as they are at present."[29]

Once again, it appears that Thomas Grow profited more than most. In 1867, he ranked in the top 5 percent of Pontiac's taxpayers (12th out of 228) in taxable wealth, and his farm had the 10th highest land value in the township, placing him in the top 4 percent of local taxpayers as measured by value of acreage owned.[30] Not yet 50 years of age, he had taken full advantage of a quarter century of agricultural progress in Oakland County to establish himself as a successful and prosperous farmer.

Thomas Grow in middle age. (Source: William B. Grow, *Eighty-Five Years of Life and Labor,* undated photograph following page 18)

The mechanization of agriculture did more than transform farming practices in Oakland County; it also had a significant impact on the size of farmers' families. The increasingly widespread use of machines that performed the work of eight to ten men reduced the need for rural parents to produce large numbers of children to help them operate their farms. Beginning in the 1850s, as agricultural machinery rapidly replaced the manual labor of farm workers, and farming became less labor intensive, children increasingly came to be viewed not as economic assets essential to successful family farming but as "extra mouths to feed, as consumers rather than producers," who used up valuable "resources that might otherwise be sent to the marketplace." The consequence, in the second half of the nineteenth century, was "a sharp decline in birthrates" and a notable reduction in the size of farm families, as more and more rural parents chose to limit the number of children they conceived.[31]

The reproductive life of Thomas and Margaret Grow reflected the change in fertility patterns. Over the course of their marriage, the couple produced six children—in stark contrast to the seventeen and thirteen children, respectively, that the two preceding generations of the family line had conceived. But even more telling was the spacing of the six childbirths. During the first eleven years of her marriage, Margaret gave birth, on average, once every two years—a rate of reproduction typical of frontier farming areas—resulting in a total of five children. Following the birth of the fifth child in 1852, however—as the frontier phase of Oakland County agriculture came to an end, and the county's farmers turned increasingly to mechanized commercial agriculture—they conceived only one additional child.

Children of THOMAS[6] and MARGARET (MORRIS) GROW:

    i.   Andrew Simeon, b. 13 Jan. 1843 at White Lake, MI; d. 26 June 1905, Greenville, MI; m. 1865, Martha Lansing (or Lanning) of Waterford, MI.

    ii.   Mary Jane, b. 13 March 1845 at White Lake; d. 15 Aug. 1847, White Lake.

    iii.   Elisha Palmer, b. 18 Aug. 1848 at White Lake; d. 29 Nov. 1901, Philadelphia, PA; m. 1873, Nettie Bradford of Detroit, MI.

    iv.   DeWitt[7], b. 4 April 1850 at White Lake; d. 24 May 1921, Bay City, MI; m. 1874, Alice Smith of Commerce, MI.

    v.   Kitty E., b. 13 May 1852 at Pontiac, MI; d. 8 Oct. 1928, Pontiac; m. 1882, Fred M. Burch.

    vi.   Thomas, b. 13 Aug. 1862, Pontiac; d. unk. date or place; m. 1883, Jessie Craft of West Bay City, MI.

SOURCES: George W. Davis, *John Grow of Ipswich/John (Groo) Grow of Oxford*, 94, 130–131; findagrave. com memorials 5726911 (Andrew Grow date of death and wife's maiden name), 47646483 (Mary Jane Grow middle name), 47646312 (Kitty [Grow] Burch date of death).

Numerous forms of birth control were available to American couples in the mid-nineteenth century. The traditional and "most commonly used method," *coitus interruptus* (male withdrawal prior to ejaculation), does not seem to have been practiced by the previous two generations of the Grow family line, considering that in both generations the wives regularly became pregnant again a year or so after bearing a child. By the 1850s, however, a variety of new contraceptive products were emerging out of the industrial revolution, including condoms, vaginal sponges, spermicidal douches, and diaphragms (known at the time as "womb veils" or "vaginal tents"), and information about their use was circulating widely in marital advice books and pamphlets, as well as in newspaper advertisements.[32] Nineteenth-century Americans rarely recorded the intimate details of their sex lives, but the abrupt falloff in Thomas and Margaret's childbirths after 1852—when they were still in their thirties— strongly suggests that they had begun to use some form of contraception to deliberately limit the size of their family.

Oakland County's agricultural economy continued to flourish in the post-Civil War period, with the county at one point ranking "first in the state and fifth in the counties of the United States in . . . agricultural wealth," according to a Grow family source at the time.[33] Thomas again appears to have taken full advantage of the ongoing boom by operating his Pontiac farm—which by now consisted of "one hundred and thirty-five acres of well-improved land with good buildings and farm equipment"[34]—at maximum productive capacity. In 1870, 120 of his 135 acres were classified as "improved" (with the remaining 15 acres likely consisting of wood lots). Only two of the township's 154 farmers owned farms containing a higher percentage of improved land.[35]

Reunion of Oakland County pioneers, Pontiac, MI, 10 September 1874, Thomas Grow dressed in white coat, middle row, fourth from left; photograph by W. H. Brumitt. (Reproduced courtesy of the Burton Historical Collection, Detroit Public Library)

Detail.

By 1873, Thomas had become sufficiently wealthy that he and Margaret were able to retire from active farming and take up residence in the city of Pontiac. He was only 55 years old at the time, in a period when 88 percent of American males between the ages of 65 and 74 were still in the labor force and most men "worked until they dropped." During the remaining three decades of their lives, the couple apparently lived on multiple sources of income. After moving into the city, Thomas retained ownership of his Pontiac farm and continued to generate income from it, presumably either by renting it out to tenant farmers or turning its operation over to a hired manager. Like his brother Edward, a retired Clyde, Michigan, farmer whose wealth was mostly invested "in money," Thomas and Margaret might also have lived partially off of dividends from investments in stocks, bonds, and other securities issued by the large industrial corporations—the railroads, oil and steel companies, food-processing and other consumer-goods companies, etc.—that were increasingly coming to dominate the national economy. That Thomas was regarded in Pontiac as a "well respected" "retired farmer" and "successful business man"[36] suggests that he might have enjoyed a reputation for effective money management and sound investing during his years of retirement.

In leaving their farm for a life in the city, Thomas and Margaret personified the United States' momentous late nineteenth-century transformation from a rural agricultural country to a modern urban-industrial nation. At the time of their move in 1873, American society was beginning a rapid transition from what historian Walter Nugent has characterized as a traditional "frontier-rural" mode of development to "an entirely new" urban-industrial or "metropolitan mode," a transition that was complete by about 1920. Central to that historic transformation was "the most spectacular urbanization" process the world had ever seen.

A combination of factors turned American cities into population magnets during the final three decades of the nineteenth century. The growing numbers of factories, manufacturing facilities, and commercial enterprises sprouting up in urban areas led hundreds of thousands of young rural men and women to abandon their parents' farms and migrate to a nearby city in order to pursue employment opportunities in the emerging commercial-industrial economy. At the same time, a wide range of technological advances and cultural amenities—public water works and sanitation systems, gas lines, electricity, trolley cars, retail stores, restaurants, theaters, parks, and other recreational attractions—was turning America's cities into more comfortable and attractive places to live for young and old alike (including retired farmers like Thomas and Margaret Grow), in contrast to the dull, isolated, culturally "backward" farms and country villages of rural America. The result was a massive internal migration from the countryside to the city in the late nineteenth century. In the Midwest, the exodus became so great during the 1880s that more than half the rural townships in the region recorded net losses of population. By 1890, the US population was already "one-third urban," and by the turn of the century only two-fifths of the American people were still living on farms.[37]

Pontiac's urbanization process mirrored the patterns unfolding in the nation's big cities, albeit on a smaller scale. Between 1870 and 1900, the city's population more than doubled (from 4,867 to 9,769), and by 1877, the local

Pontiac, Michigan, 1882, a parade scene on Main Street. Note the streetlamp at lower right. (Source: 1998 calendar of the Waterford Township Historical Society, Waterford, MI)

Pontiac, Michigan, c. 1897–1898—Saginaw Street scene highlighting one of the city's recent technological innovations, an electric trolley-car line, juxtaposed with older features of the downtown streetscape: an unpaved street, plank sidewalks, and remnants of hitching posts. (Source: Gottfried Brieger, *Pontiac, Michigan: A Postcard Album* [Chicago: Arcadia Publishing, 2000], 36. Reproduced courtesy of Gottfried Brieger)

economy developed a rudimentary industrial and manufacturing base, with five flour mills, four carriage and wagon factories, several iron foundries and machine shops, a textile mill, and a brewery in operation. The city also became more cosmopolitan. By the latter half of the 1870s, dozens of retail businesses had sprung up to supply the needs of Pontiac's residents, including seventeen grocery stores, eight restaurants, six dry-goods houses, six meat markets, six barbershops, five pharmacies, five hardware stores, four clothing stores, four book stores, two jewelry stores, two bakeries, and two banks. In 1877, the city also boasted five hotels and three newspapers. A decade later, it constructed its first public water works, and by the early 1890s a municipal sewage system, telephone lines, electric street lights, a gas works, and an electric trolley-car line had improved the lives of the Grows and other local residents.[38]

With their move into the city, Thomas and Margaret entered the ranks of an emerging new class in American society: an *urban* middle class distinctly different in lifestyle and values from the "middling" farmers and artisans who had comprised the core of that society during the preceding two-and-a-half-centuries-long agrarian phase of American history. The explosive growth of the US industrial economy in the late nineteenth century generated a wide range of new urban-based employment opportunities for mid-level workers, resulting in growing numbers of job openings for salaried, non-manual, "white-collar" employees: factory managers and plant foremen, accountants and bookkeepers, secretaries and other office workers, store managers, shopkeepers, clerks, salespeople, and more. As the pace of industrialization accelerated and the white-collar occupational sector continued to expand in the three decades after 1870, observers became increasingly aware that a new intermediate social class was forming in America's cities—a new "middle" class of white-collar workers and their families, positioned midway between a small, wealthy, upper-class elite of "Gilded Age" industrialists, financiers, and large proprietors at the top of the social pyramid and a burgeoning urban proletariat of lower-class factory workers and slum dwellers, many of them recently arrived foreign immigrants, at the bottom. Made up of people who "lived well but lacked great wealth," this new urban middle class had already become a major segment of American society by the end of the nineteenth century.[39]

A distinguishing characteristic of the urban middle class was its materialistic, consumption-oriented value system. Unlike the farms and small villages of rural America, where everyone knew their neighbors and their own place in society, the nation's rapidly growing cities concentrated large numbers of ethnically diverse strangers together in a limited geographic space. For white-collar city dwellers, "conspicuous consumption" and displays of material affluence quickly became an important way of acquiring social status and establishing a distinct class identity for themselves that differentiated them from their working-class neighbors. As their salaries rose in the late nineteenth century, white-collar employees earned sufficient incomes to purchase comfortable homes, attractive household furnishings, fashionable clothing, the latest appliances (telephones, phonographs, "iceboxes," etc.), and other new consumer goods that the industrial revolution was churning out. Soon, "the visible display of affluence"—in the form of a tastefully furnished home, fashionable possessions, "proper" dress, etc.—became an important measure of middle-class respectability in the social world of America's cities. By the end of the century, the traditional biblically sanctioned values of the nation's agrarian past—self-restraint, self-denial, personal privation—had given way to a materialistic new "consumer ethic" that defined success in life not by inner virtue or spiritual grace or personal salvation but by "the accumulation and display" of material possessions—by money and the things that money could buy. As historian David Blanke puts it, "by the turn of the century" America's urban middle classes had "come to define their sense of belonging"—their social status and personal self-worth—"by the goods that they consumed."[40]

That Thomas and Margaret's values reflected the growing materialism of the period was evident by 1887 when the couple built a "handsome [new] residence" for themselves in the fashionable "Queen Anne" style of architecture that was in vogue at the time among middle-class homeowners in the Midwest. Featuring ornate exterior facades adorned with multiple gables and castle-like rounded turrets, and with interiors that incorporated grand oak staircases and stained-glass windows in their designs, Queen Anne houses were prized by their owners as visible symbols of an affluent and "genteel" lifestyle. Thomas and Margaret's new house—located at 179 Perry Street in Pontiac—also incorporated one of the industrial revolution's latest technological advances: a centralized system of steam heat, with a coal-fueled boiler in the basement that delivered forced heat to each room of the house through a newly invented device known as a "radiator." According to a contemporary description, the interior of the couple's new Perry Street home was also "finished in hardwood throughout" and "fitted up" with "fine furnishings" designed to impress: elaborately carved and upholstered furniture, imported French china, expensive glassware, and more.[41]

Further evidence that status considerations were important to the couple was the money that they spent to have Thomas' biography included in the *Portrait and Biographical Album of Oakland County, Michigan*, a collection of biographical sketches of the county's "prominent and representative citizens," published in 1891. Status-conscious county residents paid as much as $70—a considerable sum in those days—to have their personal biographies included in the volume. Working closely with the publication's staff writers, individual residents—almost invariably male heads of households—drafted "flattering and . . . idealized" profiles of themselves and their families for inclusion in the *Album*. As a reflection of how Thomas wanted to be seen by others in the community (and perhaps how, at age 73, he wanted to be remembered by posterity), his sketch focused on his family's pioneer background, his status as a successful farmer and "respected . . . private citizen," and his stylish new Pontiac residence.[42]

The *Portrait and Biographical Album* also identified Thomas as "a Republican" in his political leanings. From its founding in 1854, in Jackson, Michigan, until well into the twentieth century, the Republican Party attracted strong support from Michigan's Yankee immigrants and their descendants. Initially, the party's free-soil, anti-slavery, pro-temperance platform proved popular among settlers from New York and New England, particularly those like the Grows who came from evangelical Protestant backgrounds. After the Civil War, the party's "blatantly pro-business orientation" and "boundless devotion" to "unfettered economic development" won it a loyal following among the state's prosperous commercial farmers and businessmen,[43] Thomas Grow among them. Thomas' party affiliation seems to have been shared by most of his Michigan relatives. Of the 183 Grows who attended an 1885 family reunion in Waterford, all but one were Republicans.[44] One member of the family even rose to a position of national prominence in the party. Thomas' first cousin, Galusha Grow, a Republican congressman from Pennsylvania, served as Speaker of the US House of Representatives during the first three tumultuous years of the Civil War.[45]

Other sources describe Thomas as a "sober man" and "a persistent temperance advocate."[46] Grow family attitudes toward alcohol consumption seem to have shifted over the generations. Two of Thomas' eighteenth-century Connecticut ancestors—his great-great-grandfather Thomas (1684–1753) and great-grandfather Thomas (1714–1806)—were "maltsters" who earned at least a portion of their livelihoods by supplying their communities with malt, a key ingredient in the brewing of beer. From the Great Awakening through the early republic, evangelical Baptists like the Grows may have taken a harsh view of drunkenness, but they were not necessarily averse to moderate drinking. In fact, some of their ministers were even known to imbibe. Isaac Backus, "the heart and soul of the Separate Baptist movement" in New England and an occasional house guest at the family's Grow Hill farm on the Pomfret-Hampton border, "always carried a small jug of rum in his saddle bags when he traveled."[47]

In reality, most seventeenth- and eighteenth-century Americans, men and women alike, drank beer, hard cider, or some other form of alcoholic beverage as part of their everyday lives—at home during meals and at community gatherings such as barn-raisings, where copious quantities of free liquor were customarily provided to participants as the expected reward for a hard day of voluntary labor.[48] Then, in the early decades of the nineteenth century, for reasons not fully understood, alcohol consumption "increased alarmingly" in the United States. According to historian Thomas Pegram, "Americans between 1800 and 1830 drank more alcohol, on an individual basis, than at any other time in the history of the nation." By 1830, the average US citizen was consuming more than seven gallons of distilled spirits per year (as compared to the 2.8 gallons per person being consumed annually in the United States in the late twentieth century).[49] By the mid-nineteenth century, as saloons and other drinking establishments proliferated in US cities, American society was experiencing a full-scale "epidemic of alcoholism" accompanied by a variety of ancillary social ills—with males addicted to drink beating their wives, neglecting their children, squandering their wages, losing their jobs, and reducing their families to poverty in ever-increasing numbers. In the eyes of many observers, Pegram writes, "nineteenth-century America had become a 'nation of drunkards.'"[50] To combat the growing scourge of drunkenness and ruined lives, concerned citizens everywhere began organizing local temperance societies aimed at reducing or eliminating the sale and consumption of alcohol in their communities. Occasionally such efforts achieved short-term success. In 1853, after vigorous lobbying by temperance groups, the Michigan state legislature passed a law "prohibiting the manufacture or sale of any alcoholic beverage in the state." Ultimately, however, such laws proved to be unenforceable, and Michigan's ineffectual statute was eventually repealed in 1875.[51]

Thomas and his siblings seem to have been lifelong teetotalers. Late in life, his brother Elijah proudly recalled that after arriving on the Michigan frontier in 1836, he "built a barn 30 x 40 ft. and raised it without liquor, which was an unheard of thing,"[52] while another brother, William, boasted that during his long career as a Baptist preacher, he and his wife consistently refused to partake of even a glass of wine at dinner.[53] Thomas' own commitment to temperance was undoubtedly influenced by the drunken, brawling behavior that he witnessed among his co-workers on the Illinois & Michigan Canal in 1838—most of whom were recent emigrants from Ireland, reputed at the time to be "the drunkenest nation in Christendom."[54] From that point onward, public campaigns to curtail alcohol consumption were an ever-present background feature of his environment. In White Lake, the Oakland County township where he and Margaret farmed during the early years of their marriage, an active local temperance movement quickly developed in response to the township's "flourishing" taverns and "substantial number . . . of Irish immigrants."[55] And when they subsequently moved into the city of Pontiac, the couple was exposed firsthand to the widespread tawdriness and disorder that liquor establishments were producing in Michigan's cities. Statistics are lacking for Pontiac, but in 1866, there were some 500 "saloons, bars, and grog shops" in Detroit and 300 in Grand Rapids.[56]

The principal temperance organization in Pontiac—and the one to which Thomas more than likely belonged—was the "Red Ribbon Club of Pontiac," a branch chapter of Dr. Henry A. Reynolds' nationwide Red Ribbon movement. During the 1870s, Reynolds, a Harvard-trained physician from Bangor, Maine, who had overcome a long personal addiction to alcohol, traveled throughout the Northeast and Great Lakes establishing local temperance clubs made up of men who agreed to sign a pledge reading "We, the undersigned, for our own good and the good of the world in which we live, do hereby promise and engage with the help of Almighty God, to abstain from buying, selling, or using alcoholic or malt beverages, wine and cider included." Members paid dues of 25 cents per month, attended a monthly meeting, and wore a membership insignia consisting of a red ribbon permanently fixed to their lapels. Pontiac's club was established in 1876 after a three-day public crusade in which Reynolds persuaded 438 local men to sign his movement's pledge of total abstinence. Within a few years, the group's membership had grown to 700 or more.[57]

Like most temperance societies of the period, the Red Ribbon movement drew a majority of its members from the new urban middle class. Reynolds himself stated that his clubs were "made up of middle-class men" and that "high-toned people" in "the higher circles of society" chose not to join.[58] In explaining the strong link between the middle class and temperance, historian Stuart Blumin, a leading student of middle-class identity in pre-twentieth-century America, suggests that from the start, the temperance movement transcended "the immediate issues of drink and drunkenness" and spoke to "deeper issues of [middle-class] social identity" and "status anxiety." For many middle-class city dwellers, he writes, participation in a crusade to prevent lives from being ruined by "demon rum" was not only a noble undertaking in its own right, it also embellished their self-image of "bourgeois respectability" and burnished their reputation as a morally upstanding, socially responsible element in society—differentiating them from the groups directly above and below them in the local social structure: the rich, upper-class business and professional elite that middle-class residents tended to view as aristocratic, self-indulgent, and intemperate in its use of alcohol; and the "vice-ridden" immigrant working class, which, from a middle-class perspective, spent too much of its time and money in beer halls and saloons. Membership in a temperance organization, Blumin concludes, helped the members of a "still inchoate middle class" gain social respectability and their own distinct class identity.[59]

Significantly, perhaps, neither the *Portrait and Biographical Album* nor Thomas and Margaret's obituaries made any mention of their religious affiliation or church membership. Over the course of the couple's lives, the religious landscape of America changed dramatically. Within the nation's Protestant churches, sectarianism gave rise to a multiplicity of denominations, totaling some two dozen by 1870. In addition, a number of eccentric Christian splinter groups—Shakers, Mormons, and others—sprang up during the antebellum period, while a Spiritualist movement that believed in the possibility of communication with "the spirits of the dead" attracted a large following from the 1850s through the 1880s. And in a development that would have horrified New England Puritans of the colonial period, a large influx of Irish, German, and other European immigrants made Catholicism "the nation's single largest religious community by the time of the Civil War."[60]

The new pluralism in American religious life was reflected in the Grow family. Although most of Thomas' siblings remained Baptists after migrating to Michigan, one of his brothers, Abel, joined the Methodist church, while—to the family's acute embarrassment—another brother, Elijah, and his wife, Charity, became Spiritualists, a development that mortified Thomas' brother William to such an extent that he was unable to "control [his] emotions" when talking about it in public.[61]

Inside the mainstream Protestant denominations, substantive changes were taking place as well. Traditional Calvinism, with its belief in predestination, the inherent depravity of human nature, and the total dependence of human beings on the will of "an omnipotent and incomprehensible God," gradually faded away as the doctrinal foundation of Protestant theology. By the mid-nineteenth century, most Protestant churches were practicing a more liberal, less dogmatic form of Christianity—one that viewed human beings as essentially good and capable of controlling their destinies by their own actions. Protestant ministers no longer "tried to frighten people into good behavior with threats of fire and brimstone," but instead preached the more uplifting and comforting message that anyone who adhered to God's commandments and lived a moral Christian life could be saved. For most Protestants of Thomas and Margaret's generation, the path to Heaven and life everlasting depended less on God's mercy or the hand of Providence than on their own personal behavior and good deeds.[62]

Meanwhile, as Protestant doctrines evolved, the fundamental tenets of Christianity itself were coming under challenge from the scientific community. In 1859, the British biologist Charles Darwin published his seminal theory of evolution, in which he posited that the various living species of the animal kingdom had acquired their physical characteristics through an eons-long evolutionary process of "natural selection." The broader implications of Darwin's findings were immediately evident: if he was correct, all living things on earth, including human beings, were the products not of a supernatural deity but of biological evolution and immutable laws of nature. Darwin's path-breaking work stimulated a wide range of new scientific research—in biology, geology, paleontology, archeology, and other fields—that increasingly called into question the validity of the Christian creation myth and the Bible's "cramped six-thousand-year" timeline of human history. The resulting scientific advances, based as they were on empirical research and tangible evidence, forced "many Americans to question the supernatural components of their traditional religion." For many Christians, Darwinian science raised difficult questions about the very foundations of their faith. How could rational, scientifically informed individuals be expected to believe any longer in biblical fables about Adam and Eve, Noah's ark, Jonah and the whale, Moses parting the Red Sea, or "Joshua making the sun stand still," let alone continue to accept on faith such core Christian concepts as virgin birth and the resurrection of the dead? By the end of the century, a growing science-based skepticism about the credibility of the Bible had begun to dilute the faith of many US churchgoers.[63]

At the same time, the growing consumerism in American society was also helping to weaken traditional religious values. As more and more Americans concentrated their energies on the accumulation of money and goods, secular values—and above all the desire to "get ahead" economically—became increasingly more central to their lives than qualities of inner virtue or religious piety. By the late nineteenth century, the "spirit of capitalism" seemed to be overshadowing the "Protestant ethic" in the American value system, and ministers everywhere were expressing "anxiety over the future of belief in an age of increasing materialism."[64]

They had legitimate cause for concern. Historian Daniel Sutherland estimates that by the 1870s "no more than half the nation attended church regularly," while for many of those who continued to do so, "going to church" had become more of a religious duty or a social activity than a meaningful spiritual experience. And yet at the same time, according to Sutherland, "most Americans, whether or not they attended church regularly, [still] considered themselves Christians." Religion continued to play an important role in American life, particularly for members of the new urban middle class, in part because, as Sutherland notes, "Church attendance, like being married and owning a house, conferred respectability and implied an honorable character." Consequently, if Thomas and Margaret were typical middle-class Americans of the late nineteenth century, they probably "did not abandon their religious beliefs; they simply relegated them to a more remote part of their minds while they busied themselves with the material world." They might well have attended one of Pontiac's churches every Sunday, perhaps from force of habit or for the sake of appearances, but—as the lack of any mention of their church membership in their obituaries or the *Portrait and Biographical Album* would seem to indicate—they no longer regarded their religious affiliation as a primary focus of their self-identity.[65]

For American women, the role of housewife also changed dramatically over the course of the couple's lifetime. In earlier generations, the daily lives of married women had been largely devoted to child-rearing, food production, and the making of clothing and other household necessities. The technological innovations of the industrial revolution, however, helped to liberate women—and particularly urban middle-class women like Margaret—from many of those traditional tasks. New birth-control devices enabled them to limit the number of children they conceived, drastically reducing the amount of time and energy that pregnancy, nursing, and child care consumed in their lives. In addition, when farmwives like Margaret moved to the city, they immediately gained access to an array of retail stores and specialized shops selling many of the manufactured goods that women had previously made at home by hand. By the 1870s, many American housewives were already purchasing ready-made clothing for their families from local retailers. In addition, the shelves of urban grocery stores were filled with an ever-expanding variety of conveniently packaged food products, including canned fruits and vegetables, Pillsbury flour, Campbell soup, Van Camp beans, Shredded Wheat, Quaker Oats, and Cream of Wheat cereal, Aunt Jemima pancake mix, Heinz ketchup and relishes, Borden's condensed milk, processed butter, and Chase and Sanborn coffee, to name but a few. By 1900, 90 percent of urban households in the United States were purchasing their bread at local bakeries, eliminating any further need for women "to reserve one day of the week" for home baking. And thanks to the development of industrial meatpacking plants and refrigerated railroad cars, neighborhood butcher shops were supplying their local residents with a large and growing variety of fresh meat products. By the end of the century, as a result of "a boom in commercial laundries," "two-thirds of urban families" were also sending at least some of their clothing and linens "out of the house" to be cleaned.[66]

The end result was nothing less than a domestic revolution in women's lives. For urban middle-class housewives of the late nineteenth century—especially those like Margaret who had reached menopause and completed the child-raising phase of their lives—much of the toil and drudgery of traditional women's roles had been eliminated by technological progress. Middle-class women were now "consumers, not producers" of household goods, and a new activity—"shopping"—was becoming an increasingly important part of their daily and weekly routines. They now purchased their families' essential staples in local stores—not only food and clothing but also the fashionable home furnishings and cultural accoutrements that "helped define the middle-class household." With more leisure time available to them than their maternal ancestors on the family farms of the American frontier could have fathomed, middle-class wives of the 1870–1900 period devoted significant amounts of time and effort to interior decorating, striving to furnish their homes tastefully and aesthetically in order to transform them into more beautiful and refined living environments. They also placed considerable importance on gracious entertaining and the hosting of private social gatherings where their family's material affluence and genteel tastes could be put on display for friends and acquaintances to appreciate.[67] Of the various contributions that Margaret made to her marriage in the later years of her life, it was her role as "a good hostess" that Thomas' 1891 *Portrait and Biographical Album* profile chose to highlight when it noted, "His wife dispenses the hospitality of their beautiful home with cordial grace."[68]

Margaret died unexpectedly of "apoplexy" (the pre-twentieth-century medical term for a stroke) on 20 July 1899. She was 78 years old. According to her obituary, "after retiring" to bed on the evening of Friday the 18th, "she complained of a severe headache," and with her husband's assistance "resorted to the usual remedies for relief." Later that night "the family physician was summoned," but "medical aid was without avail," and "after many hours of unconsciousness" she expired at 3 a.m. on the morning of Sunday the 20th.[69] A funeral service was held at the couple's residence the following Friday afternoon,[70] and its timing reflects another of the ways in which American culture was changing in the late 1800s. The five-day interval between Margaret's death and her funeral indicates that her body had been embalmed, a procedure rarely performed in the United States prior to the 1880s, but one that was increasingly utilized by the new "funeral industry" that emerged during the century's final two decades as a new occupational category of professional "undertakers" began to handle funeral arrangements for grieving families, temporarily preserving the deceased's corpse so that it could be carefully and unhurriedly prepared for a public visitation and funeral service, providing a suitably dignified coffin, and arranging for the transportation of the body to its burial site—all for a substantial fee. In the growing "consumer culture" of late-nineteenth-century America, historian Gary Laderman notes, even death had become "a business."[71]

Shortly after Margaret died, Thomas' health began to decline. He soon gave up his Perry Street home and took up residence with his daughter Kitty (Grow) Burch and her husband, Fred, a Pontiac architect. Then, in November 1901, sixteen months after losing his wife, he experienced another tragic loss when his 53-year-old son, Elisha Palmer Grow, who was working at the time in Philadelphia, died from "injuries received by a fall down an elevator shaft"—a victim of modern progress in the form of the new elevator-equipped, high-rise office buildings that were springing up in the commercial centers of US cities. Ten months after his son's death, Thomas suddenly grew "very sick," and after a week in which "his appetite failed him and his heart action became weak," he died at 7 a.m. on Saturday, 25 October

Thomas Grow in old age. (From the author's family photograph collection.)

The graves of Thomas and Margaret Grow, Oak Hill Cemetery, Pontiac, MI. The combination of individual headstones and a large, imposing monument denotes a prosperous, status-conscious middle-class family at the turn of the century. The secular style of the stones—with their lack of biblical inscriptions or Christian iconography of any sort—reflects a weakening of religiosity in late nineteenth-century American culture. (Photograph by the author.)

1902—of "old age," according to his obituary. He was 84. The obituary, which was published later that same day, was front-page news in Pontiac's leading newspaper, *The Daily Press.*[72]

The lives of Thomas and Margaret Grow marked a pivotal transition in the history of the family line. They were the last generation that would earn its living from agriculture. Both were the products of an early nineteenth-century agrarian society, born and raised in pioneer families that migrated west from rural upstate New York to the Michigan frontier in the late 1830s. Following their marriage in 1841, they were the beneficiaries of a quarter-century-long wave of economic growth and prosperity in Oakland County as its farmers shifted from semi-subsistence frontier farming to high-volume commercial agriculture. In the process, they became sufficiently well-to-do that they were able to retire from farming while still in their fifties. Their decision at that point to leave their farm and move into the city of Pontiac represents a fateful watershed moment in the history of the family line, because, for better or worse, the Grows had now moved off the land and into the modern new world of urban America, with its fast-paced, ruthlessly competitive, money-driven economy and its materialistic, secular, increasingly hedonistic cultural values—an environment filled with new opportunities and dangers, new risks and rewards, new temptations and stresses that would shape the lives of family members over the next several generations.

DEWITT GROW (1850–1921)

The children of Thomas and Margaret Grow completed the family's transition from its traditional agrarian way of life to a new metropolitan mode of living. All five children (a sixth having died in infancy) were born and raised on their parents' farms in rural Oakland County, Michigan. As soon as they came of age, however, three of the four sons—DeWitt[7] (*Thomas*[6], *Elisha*[5], *Thomas*[4], *Thomas*[3], *Thomas*[2], *John*[1]), Elisha Palmer, and Thomas Jr.—quickly left for city-based employment in retail commerce, while their sister Kitty married a Pontiac architect and remained in that city for the rest of her life. Only the eldest son, Andrew Simeon, continued to earn a living in agriculture—as a breeder and trainer of pureblooded horses, however, rather than as a farmer.[1]

In previous generations, most boys in rural America grew up aspiring to be farmers. They learned agricultural practices while working alongside their father on the family farm, and after reaching maturity, they awaited their opportunity to acquire farmland of their own, usually with their father's assistance in the form of a gift or bequeathment. From the perspective of many farm boys entering adulthood in the 1860s and 1870s, however, the most attractive opportunities for a satisfying life were to be found not in the rural countryside but in the nation's cities, in the form of salaried, white-collar jobs in the rapidly growing world of business and commerce. In the three decades following the Civil War, the US labor market created hundreds of thousands of new employment openings for white-collar workers—the skilled and semi-skilled employees needed to staff the offices and stores and public services of the nation's burgeoning commercial-industrial economy. During the 1870s alone, the number of office workers, store clerks, and salesmen in the US labor force increased from less than 250,000 to more than 500,000, while bookkeepers and accountants nearly doubled in number, from 36,000 to 70,000.[2] To restless, ambitious young men laboring on the family farms of rural America, such jobs were attractive on multiple levels. Even at a low starting salary, a white-collar job provided a steady monetary income—a significant enticement to American males of the post-Civil War generation, who increasingly "measured their self-worth and status—indeed their manhood—in terms of [the] acquisition" of money.[3] And because white-collar employment was by definition non-manual employment—"employment . . . that [did] not soil the clothes . . . or the hands"—it carried with it the cachet of middle-class social respectability.[4]

In addition, since a white-collar job was almost invariably located in a city, it also offered young rural males an inviting avenue of escape from the less appealing aspects of agricultural life: the long days of "tedious and unremitting" manual labor, the mud and muck of the barnyard with its foul-smelling odors and "legions of flies," the drudgery and boredom, the social and cultural isolation.[5] By uprooting himself from the family farm and securing a white-collar position in the city, a young man could immediately transport himself into an exciting new physical and cultural environment in which the opportunities for entertainment, recreation, and intellectual stimulation seemed almost limitless, a world filled with theaters and music halls and parks and restaurants, with specialized shops selling the latest goods, a world where he could shed his "hick" image and become a more cosmopolitan, more sophisticated, more cultured person.[6] By the 1870s, as a result, midwestern farm boys by the tens of thousands were pouring into the region's cities, abandoning "the narrow scope and isolation of rustic life" for "the golden allure of the urban scene," drawn irresistibly to the "exciting new way of life" that "city jobs and wages, combined with city lights and entertainments," seemed to promise.[7]

For Thomas and Margaret's sons, as for most farm boys growing up in rural Oakland County during the 1850s and 1860s, life revolved almost entirely around the dull routines and monotonous chores of farm work, interrupted only by intermittent intervals of rudimentary education in their local district school. One Oakland County farmer's son, Mortimer Leggett, later recalled that most young people in the county had only two interesting events to look forward to each year: a "crude" three-day county fair featuring agricultural exhibits, horse races, "all kinds of little side shows, and a dance hall," and the annual New Year's ball in Pontiac, a "pretty rough affair" featuring "dancing [that] would commence at four o'clock in the afternoon and keep up until about nine the next day."[8] Most farm boys stopped attending district school when they were about 15 years of age, at which point many of them went directly into full-time farm labor or a rural trade, while those aspiring to urban employment often chose to "take a commercial course" in one of the small for-profit business colleges that were sprouting up throughout the nation to provide ambitious young Americans with training in the specialized skills they would need to compete for white-collar office jobs: bookkeeping and accounting, business writing and correspondence, banking procedures, basic principles of business law, penmanship, etc.[9]

Both Elisha Palmer Grow and his younger brother DeWitt attended business colleges after completing their district-school educations in rural Pontiac Township. In 1867, after studying at the Eastman Business College in

Poughkeepsie, New York, 19-year-old Palmer obtained a position as bookkeeper in Jacob ("Little Jake") Seligman's men's clothing store in Pontiac. DeWitt soon followed in his brother's footsteps. In 1870, after taking a commercial course in Detroit, he too went to work for Seligman as a 20-year-old bookkeeper in Little Jake's new branch store in Saginaw, 75 miles north of Pontiac.[10]

Seligman's stores exemplified the "revolution in clothing" that was taking place in the United States in the latter half of the nineteenth century. Prior to the Civil War, most men's wearing apparel was produced at home, cut and sewn by women of the household; while a small elite of wealthy, upper-class males employed tailors to make expensive custom-fitted clothing for them. During the industrial revolution, however, major advances in textile technology—the invention of high-volume power looms, heavy-grade fabric-cutting equipment, and the sewing machine—gave rise to a large, mechanized US garment industry. The Civil War, by creating a sudden need for millions of military uniforms, fueled the new industry's development, especially its capacity to produce clothing in standardized sizes corresponding to the most common body dimensions. By the mid-1860s, as a result, wholesale garment factories and sweatshops on the East Coast were shipping ever-increasing quantities of mass-produced, ready-to-wear men's clothing to new retail clothing stores like Seligman's that were springing up in cities and towns throughout the Midwest and elsewhere.

Mass production enabled the garment manufacturers to produce ready-made clothing at half the price of custom-made apparel, bringing affordable, well-fitting clothes within reach of most Americans—and not just the middle class, which regarded fashionable "proper" dress as an important status symbol, but also the heavily immigrant working classes, for whom the opportunity to wear the same types of clothes as those worn by the higher classes in society meant that they would no longer be looked down on as inferiors or foreigners on the basis of their clothing styles and outward appearance.

Soon even wealthy upper-class males were buying ready-made apparel from their cities' better shops. By 1870, as a result, men's clothing had already become the fifth-largest industry in the United States. Nine years later, a survey of American business reported that "the home-manufacture of men's garments has virtually ceased, and everyone, from ploughman to railroad president, goes to the store for his goods." By the turn of the century, according to historian Daniel Boorstin, "it had become rare for a man or boy not to be clothed in ready-made garments. . . . Not only suits and coats, but everything that people wore—hats, caps, shirts, undergarments, stockings, shoes—were now . . . bought ready-made" in stores. For Jacob Seligman, and for the two young Grow brothers who became his employees, the men's retail clothing business consequently represented an "attractive and profitable" economic opportunity.[11]

Little Jake Seligman was one of Michigan's most colorful Gilded Age entrepreneurs. A German Jewish immigrant who had come to the United States in 1859 as a boy of 16, he apprenticed for a year with a New York City tailor and then headed west to Michigan with another tailor who was starting his own tailoring shop in Pontiac. Three years later, in 1863, with savings of $100 that he had accumulated from his $4-per-week wages, 20-year-old Seligman embarked on a career as a clothing merchant by opening a retail store on Pontiac's Saginaw Street. Diminutive in stature (he was only 4' 11" tall and weighed 110 pounds), he adopted the trade name "Little Jake's"—which, thanks to Seligman's aggressive marketing and relentless self-promotion, soon became a household name in Pontiac and the surrounding region. In bombastic but highly entertaining newspaper advertisements, he proclaimed himself Pontiac's "King of Clothiers," the "Largest retail clothier in Michigan," and "The Greatest Clothier the United States has ever seen." Many of his ads directly attacked his retail competitors, accusing them of being "swindlers" who sold "shoddy clothing" at twice the prices that he charged, and guaranteeing that he would undersell any other clothier in the state, with "no jewing" over price. Colorful promotions—including public parades with brass marching bands, elephants with the name "Little Jake" emblazoned on their sides, and clowns carrying "Little Jake" sign-boards—lured customers to his store, where free food and cheap gifts were handed out as inducements to come inside and spend money. During buying trips to his wholesale suppliers in New York City, Rochester, and Boston, Seligman regularly telegraphed "news bulletins" to newspapers back in Michigan announcing that he was making remarkable deals and would soon return home with an immense stock of the "Best and Most Stylish" clothing, which he planned to sell "at prices which defy competition." As more and more of his competitors went out of business, he aggressively expanded his commercial empire—opening new branch stores in Saginaw (in 1870) and Bay City (in 1871), providing his customers with in-store banking and credit services, and investing his hefty profits in a wide range of enterprises, including urban real estate, the timber industry, a shingle mill, horse stables, and an electric streetcar line.[12]

For ambitious young men aspiring to a career in commerce, a salaried job—even a low-paying one—with a successful businessman like Seligman was often looked upon as an essential first step in acquiring the experience and skills they needed to start a business of their own.[13] As Seligman's bookkeepers, Palmer and DeWitt Grow were apparently thinking in precisely those terms, because in July 1872 they drew on their personal relationship with their employer to set themselves up as independent merchants in their own right—by purchasing Little Jake's new Bay City store from him and going into business for themselves as "Grow Brothers, The Clothiers."[14]

Fashion plates: Elisha Palmer Grow (at left) and DeWitt Grow (at right), in the early 1870s. (Undated tintypes from the author's family photograph collection.)

Bay City, Michigan, in 1872 was a rough, rapidly growing "frontier lumber town." Founded as an Indian trading post in the 1830s, and with barely 700 inhabitants by 1859, the small settlement's location at the mouth of the Saginaw River on Lake Huron's Saginaw Bay made it the beneficiary of a major lumber boom that got underway in Michigan the following decade. The Saginaw River basin at that time encompassed some 6,000 square miles of dense forests consisting predominantly of enormous white pines growing up to 175' tall and 8' in diameter. Because white pine was a soft, lightweight, relatively knot-free wood that could easily be worked, it was highly regarded as a superior building material. Consequently, when large-scale urbanization in post-Civil War America triggered a massive building boom in the nation's cities, the US construction industry's demand for white pine boards became "almost insatiable." In response, large logging companies began moving into the Saginaw River Valley in the late 1860s to harvest its seemingly inexhaustible timber resources. Every winter in November thousands of lumberjacks descended on the pine forests, setting up lumber camps and cutting the towering trees into 16'–20', 300-pound logs. Once cut, the logs were then dragged on horse-drawn sleds over the ice-covered ground to the nearest river bank, where they were stacked until the spring thaw and then floated down-river to sawmills in Saginaw and Bay City, where they were sawed into boards, dried, and eventually shipped by Great Lakes freighters to outside consumer markets.[15]

Hauling pine logs by sled during the Michigan lumber boom. (Photo reproduced courtesy of the Archives of Michigan, Lansing.)

By the 1870s, the Saginaw Valley had become the center of "a great logging industry," and Bay City had emerged virtually overnight as one of the leading sawmill centers and lumber ports in the state. In 1872, when the Grow brothers arrived, the town had thirty-six sawmills in operation, some of which were "among the largest in the country." At the peak of the lumber boom, loggers were floating 125 million pine logs a year down the Saginaw River, and Bay City's sawmills were producing more than 500 million board feet of lumber annually, while during the six-month shipping season, as many as twelve freighters—loaded with milled boards—cleared the port every day, bound for distant markets.[16]

Bay City's remarkable growth during the lumber boom (its population jumped from 800 in 1860 to 25,000 in 1874, to nearly 40,000 by 1885—an increase of nearly 5,000 percent in 25 years)[17] made it a fertile environment for retail commerce, and Little Jake Seligman, with his keen eye for business, was quick to exploit the opportunity, opening a clothing store there in 1871.

Like virtually everything else in the town, the local consumer market for men's clothing centered on the lumber industry. Sawmill owners, managers, foremen, buyers, commission agents, lumber inspectors, and mill workers all needed clothes, as did the employees—labor and management alike—of the various subsidiary enterprises that sprang up around the lumber industry: shingle mills, planing and turning mills, woodenware factories, barrel, stave, and hoop factories, shipbuilding companies, etc. But Bay City clothing merchants' most lucrative market—and the one that undoubtedly drew Seligman to the town—was the logging industry's labor force of lumberjacks, known in the Saginaw Valley as "shanty boys." Each spring in April or May when the winter logging season ended, several thousand transient shanty boys migrated out of the lumber camps and into Bay City with accumulated earnings of $200 to $400 in their pockets. For many of them, according to Jeremy Kilar, the leading authority on the Saginaw Valley lumber boom, one of their first major expenditures upon arrival was "a new set of clothes." After four or five months of rough manual labor in the woods, their workmen's apparel was invariably in urgent need of replacement. Heading for a local clothing store, they would quickly discard their tattered wool mackinaws, torn flannel pants, and worn-out boots and purchase "a new, brightly patterned, red flannel shirt, new suspenders, pants, shoes or boots, and a felt hat." Many of the shanty boys remained in Bay City working in the sawmills during the summer and fall before returning to the pine forests in November for the start of the next logging season, usually having purchased a new set of sturdy winter clothes and a pair of heavy boots before departing. That Seligman, who claimed in his ads to be the "Poor Man's Friend," was particularly intent on tapping the shanty-boy clothing market is indicated by his decision to locate his Bay City store on Water Street in the heart of the town's saloon district, a raucous "zone of vice" that catered specifically to the lumberjack trade.[18] That store, in 1872, became "Grow Brothers, The Clothiers."

Shanty boys had more on their minds than clothes-shopping when they headed to Bay City at the end of the logging season. After months of "monotonous winter labor" in the isolated lumber camps, they arrived in town "thirsting for what came in bottles and corsets," and Bay City was happy to oblige. By 1880 the town had more than 160 saloons and hundreds of prostitutes—mostly concentrated along a notoriously "wide open and wicked" stretch of Water Street known locally as "Hell's Half Mile." At the center of the vice district was the infamous "Catacombs," a seedy, four-block "tangle" of saloons, dance halls, and brothels where the shanty boys spent their time and money "drinking, fighting, and whoring." The Catacombs developed a particularly unsavory reputation for rowdiness and violence, with "drunken lumberjacks" "carousing and brawling" on a nightly basis. Nevertheless, Bay City authorities and the town's respectable businessmen tolerated the public mayhem and immorality because the shanty-boy trade was a boon to the local economy. Some, in fact, even profited directly from it. During the mid-1870s, for example, the town sheriff, D. H. McCraney, "owned a brothel" himself "and frequently spent his off-hours there." Using his powers as police chief, McCraney also extorted "operating fees" from other brothel proprietors and their prostitutes, ordering police raids on them when they failed to pay.[19]

Grow Brothers, The Clothiers, remained on Water Street for eight years.[20] Then, in December 1880, as Bay City developed a more cosmopolitan downtown business district, the store relocated to the upscale new Munger Block on Center Avenue where it continued to do business for the next decade and a half. Spread over two floors totaling some 6,400 square feet of space, and with a staff of several sales clerks, tailors, and "cutters," the store sold a full range of men's wearing apparel—"from the inexpensive to the best in quality"—including both custom-tailored and ready-made clothing, hats, and other accessories. By the late 1880s, it also carried boys' clothing in a separate "children's department."[21]

Shortly after becoming proprietary merchants, both Palmer and DeWitt also became family men. In January 1873, 25-year-old Palmer married a young Detroit woman, Nettie C. Bradford. Less than two years later, in December 1874, DeWitt, now 24, married Alice Smith, the 22-year-old daughter of a Commerce, Michigan, innkeeper, Thaddeus Smith.[22] In their marriages, both couples continued the trend toward smaller families that had been underway in American society for more than a generation. Reflecting the sharp decline of US birthrates in the second half of the nineteenth century, DeWitt and Alice had only two children, and Palmer and his wife only one—typical numbers for native-born, white middle-class families of this generation. The decision to limit themselves to so few children was based primarily on economic self-interest. In the dynamic new urban-industrial society of post-Civil War America, raising a child involved a greater commitment of time and money on the part of the parents than had been the case in previous generations. Children were no longer economic assets who could be productively employed as farm laborers or bound out as apprentices. Instead, they now required a major investment of their parents' "financial and emotional resources" to provide them with the educational training and social skills that would "prepare them for respectable careers and marriages." There was, as a result, a growing realization, particularly among young middle-class couples, that having too

Grow Brothers clothing store at its Munger Block location, 204–206 Center Avenue, Bay City, in the early 1880s. (Source: *History of Bay County, Michigan, with Illustrations and Biographical Sketches of Some of its Prominent Men and Pioneers* [Chicago: H. R. Page, 1883], 111 [illustration])

Undated *Bay City Times* photograph of Grow Brothers' Munger Block store, with Palmer and DeWitt Grow (flanking landlord James Shearer) at far right and the store's six employees at left. The wool overcoats on display were priced at $5.00 and $7.00. (Source: newspaper clipping file, Butterfield Memorial Research Library, Bay County Historical Society, Bay City, MI)

GROW BROS.

TRADE WITH

Grow Bros.,

THE CLOTHIERS.

Bay City - Mich.

Gentlemen's Furnishings.

Gent's Spring Clothing.

The new Spring blocks of the Miller hat in both Silk and Derby are now in. Most elegant and fashionable hat in all the large cities in the east and west.

Spring Overcoats.

Most elegant line ever shown in the Saginaw Valley. Spring Stock of Men's Cloth-ing now complete.

PRICES NO OBJECT.

GROW BROS.

Grow Brothers newspaper ads of the 1880s reflected the changes taking place in American advertising during a period when the US economy was becoming increasingly based on the mass production of consumer goods. The ad at left, from the *Bay City Daily Tribune* of 3 January 1880, is typical of earlier, pre-1880 advertising. It takes the form of a simple, prosaic business notice—visually dull, devoid of graphics, and no text or any mention of products or brands. The ad at right, from the 1 April 1889 *Bay City Times*, reflects the influence of an emergent US advertising industry. It combines the rhetoric of persuasion and eye-catching graphic design in a deliberate effort to attract readers' interest and entice them into buying the products described.

many children could potentially jeopardize their children's future prospects, and at the same time impede the parents' ability to enjoy a comfortable standard of living of their own. For both selfless and selfish reasons, then—a sense of parental responsibility to their progeny and their desire for an affluent lifestyle for themselves—more and more couples were deliberately choosing to limit the size of their families to one or two children.[23]

Children of DeWitt[7] and Alice (Smith) Grow, born in Bay City, MI:

> i.   Martin[8] Smith, b. 30 Jan. 1880; d. 26 Dec. 1942, Toledo, OH; m. 1909 at Saginaw, MI, Delia (Booth) Harvey.
>
> ii. Florence, b. 28 Sept. 1888; d. 14 Nov. 1976, Bay City; m. 1914 at Bay City, Dr. Van H. Dumond.

SOURCES: George W. Davis, *John Grow of Ipswich/John (Groo) Grow of Oxford*, 131; "[Toledo] Blade Obituary Index" database, Toledo-Lucas County Public Library, online at toledolibrary.org/obits (Martin S. Grow death date); "Michigan Death Index 1971–1996," online at familysearch.org/search/collection/1949333 (Florence Grow birth and death dates); "Michigan Marriages, 1868–1925," online at familysearch.org/search/collection/1452395 (Florence Grow marriage date).

For women of this period, the conditions of childbirth had changed little from those of previous generations. In the 1870s and 1880s, the vast majority of American women still delivered their babies at home, just as their maternal ancestors had done for countless generations before them. Public hospitals now existed—Bay City's opened in 1878—but conditions inside them were so appalling that they were "reviled by the middle and upper classes," and as a result "only poor and unwed mothers gave birth in hospitals." At the same time, however, procedures for home births had begun to evolve. The birth of a baby was no longer the "communal female ritual" of earlier days, when a midwife delivered the child assisted by the mother's female relatives, friends, and neighbors. Instead, a trained male doctor now came to the home to attend the expectant mother and oversee the delivery.[24]

A turn-of-the-century survey of the sex lives of women who came of age between 1850 and 1900 provides an intimate glimpse into the marital relations of couples like the Grows. The survey, which was conducted by a female physician in Philadelphia, asked forty-five married, middle-class white women—most of whom had been born before 1880—a series of detailed questions about the "sexual and reproductive" aspects of their marriages. It found, among other things, that 84 percent of the women practiced some form of birth control, with douching the most popular method, followed (in order) by "the safe method of the menstrual cycle" (or rhythm method), male withdrawal (*coitus interruptus*), and the use of condoms. Twenty-two women said that they used "female" birth control methods (mainly douches or diaphragms), while seventeen reported using "male" methods (condoms or withdrawal), and eleven employed the rhythm method. Among the twenty oldest women, all born prior to 1863, 30 percent used the rhythm method, 40 percent "practiced withdrawal," and 40 percent "employed some form of contraceptive device." When asked about the frequency of sexual intercourse with their husbands, twenty-five women responded that they had intercourse "once a week or less," ten indicated that they had it "once or twice a week," and nine said that they had it "more than twice a week" (one woman chose not to answer the question). When asked whether they "experienced orgasm during intercourse," 35 percent answered "always" or "usually," while 40 percent said "sometimes," "not always," or "no." Two-thirds of the women acknowledged feelings of sexual desire in their marriage, although a majority reported that they "felt less sexual desire than their husbands," and many indicated that they would prefer to have "less sex than they had."[25]

Gender roles were being "sharply redefined" in urban middle-class marriages of this period, a direct result of the transformations taking place in the US economy. During the preceding agrarian phase of American history, the family had essentially functioned as an integrated "economic unit" in which "husbands, wives, and children worked together as participants in a common economic

DeWitt and Alice Grow, 1883. (From the author's family photograph collection.)

enterprise": the family farm. Home and workplace were one and the same, and the family's "domestic and productive lives" overlapped so substantially that they were almost identical. Because fathers worked at home, running their farms in close proximity to their wives and children, they were a ubiquitous presence in their families' lives. After the Civil War, however, as men were drawn ever more deeply into the nation's expanding commercial-industrial economy, the middle-class husband and father assumed a new role—as a "breadwinner" and "provider" who supported his family by working in an office, store, or factory that was physically removed from his place of residence. As a result, men were now absent from their homes and families for the greater part of every workday, leaving the responsibilities for child rearing and discipline almost entirely in the hands of their wives.[26] For their part, middle-class wives now became full-time "homemakers."

Thanks to the nation's new consumer-goods industries, women had been freed from their traditional responsibilities for producing food, clothing, and other household items "from scratch," while birth control had liberated them from continual childbearing from the first year of marriage until menopause. As a result, they now devoted themselves primarily to "keeping house," shopping, and raising their few children.[27] Central to those female duties was the responsibility for maintaining the home as a place of comfort and tranquility, a peaceful, harmonious sanctuary to which the male head of the family could retreat at the end of the workday to "heal his bruised spirit" after working long, stressful hours in the cutthroat world of business in a noisy, crowded "downtown" commercial district. In the "highly sentimentalized" conception of domestic life that became deeply ingrained in middle-class culture during the late nineteenth century, the home was idealized as a safe, secure, nurturing environment of family togetherness and affection, a refuge from "the demands and pressures" of a cold, competitive, impersonal outside world—a "haven in a heartless world," in historian Christopher Lasch's lyric phrase. And it was the woman of the household who was charged with "the heavy, if not impossible, task" of trying to make that idealized vision a reality.[28]

Left to right: Alice, Florence, Martin, and DeWitt Grow, c. 1889. (From the author's family photograph collection.)

In the status hierarchies of Bay City society, DeWitt and Alice Grow and their children occupied a position in the upper stratum of the middle class. Their lifestyle—comfortable, consumption-oriented, conformist—essentially defined the provincial midwestern bourgeoisie of the late nineteenth century. In occupational terms, DeWitt, as the co-owner of a retail store, ranked in the upper 8 percent of the US labor force, which in 1870 consisted of a top tier of managers, professionals, and "proprietors" such as himself, followed by white-collar employees (12.5 percent), blue-collar workers (33.5 percent), and farmers and farm laborers (46 percent).[29] From the early 1880s onward, he and his family resided in a series of two-story Victorian houses on Fifth Street (and later around the corner on Farragut Street) in a quiet, tree-lined neighborhood favored by Bay City's merchants and professionals, approximately ten blocks from the downtown business district and the Grow Brothers clothing store.

Early Kodak snapshot of DeWitt Grow and family at home c. 1895, conveying the aura of homey domesticity and family togetherness idealized by this generation of middle-class Americans. The room furnishings (all factory-manufactured rather than handcrafted by this point in the industrial revolution) have been carefully selected to reflect the comfortable good taste that was so important to middle-class families of the period. The rocking chairs—two upholstered platform rockers and a spool-turned Colonial Revival rocker—were popular staples of middle-class living rooms of the 1880s and 1890s. (See William Seale, *The Tasteful Interlude: American Interiors through the Camera's Eye, 1860–1917*, 2nd ed. [Nashville, TN: American Association for State and Local History, 1981], 21, 23, 110, 210) According to Karen Zukowski, author of *Creating the Artful Home* (2006), both the embroidered tablecloth partially visible at right and the decorative festooning on the framed child's portrait were fashion statements that reflect the "Aesthetic Movement" style of interior decorating in vogue in the late nineteenth century. The family's wearing apparel—including the dresses with "leg o' mutton" sleeves worn by the two females—was also very much in fashion in the mid-1890s. (Personal communication with author, 9 March 2017) The pipe radiator on the rear wall is evidence of central heating, while the gas chandelier and shaded candlesticks indicate that, like 97 percent of US residences at the time, the house did not yet have electricity. (From the author's family photograph collection.)

One block south of their Fifth Street neighborhood was Center Avenue, Bay City's most prestigious residential street, where the ostentatious mansions of the city's sawmill owners and lumbermen were concentrated.[30] A mid-1890s photograph of DeWitt, Alice, and their two children posing in their living room reveals an affluent, materialistic, middle-class family attuned to the latest fashions in household furnishings and clothing.

The men's clothing business proved to be a financial success for DeWitt and Palmer. Grow Brothers, the Clothiers quickly became "one of the largest clothing establishments in Bay City," and by the late 1880s "there was scarcely a man in [the city] who did not own a suit or coat purchased at [their] store." As the business grew, the two brothers invested a portion of their profits in the timber industry. By 1883, in partnership with lumber contractor S. D. Lynes, they owned "1,800 acres of pine land" and an equal quantity of farmland along Michigan's Tobacco River north of Midland. Although Palmer eventually left the clothing business in 1891 to pursue new commercial ventures in the East, DeWitt went on to become one of Bay City's "best known" businessmen and citizens.[31]

Success did not come without serious economic challenges, however. In February 1881, nine years after selling his Bay City store to the Grows, Jacob Seligman announced plans to open a new "Little Jake's" branch in the city, with his Pontiac business partner, Frank Rossman, as its manager. Faced with a potentially devastating threat to their commercial existence—given Seligman's long history of ruthlessly underselling his competitors—DeWitt and Palmer immediately went to court seeking an injunction to block their former employer from starting a new clothing business in Bay City. To support their request, they informed the court that when they purchased their business from Seligman in 1872 "they had not only acquired his stock of goods but his good will and the right to use the name 'Little Jake.'" They also produced the following memorandum from the contract that Seligman had signed on 11 July 1872:

> For a valuable consideration, it is hereby agreed. I, Jacob Seligman, give Grow Bros. the privilege of using my trade mark "Little Jake," for their signs and advertisements, and not to sell to anyone else in Bay City, and that I will not start another store in Bay City.

Confronted with the memorandum, Seligman claimed "it had escaped his memory." When he then offered to sell the Grow brothers the stock that he had recently acquired for his proposed new clothing store, they "treated his offer contemptuously and . . . sent him an insulting reply." In March 1881, Judge Sanford Green of the Bay County Court granted the requested injunction "and forbade Little Jake from doing business in Bay City."

Jacob ("Little Jake") Seligman, detail from a portrait (present location unknown) painted by an unknown artist. (Source: Gottfried Brieger, *Pontiac, Michigan: A Postcard Album* [Chicago: Arcadia Publishing, 2000], 17; reproduced courtesy of Gottfried Brieger)

Seligman responded by attempting to circumvent the court ruling. Legally blocked from using the trade name "Little Jake" in Bay City, he defiantly proceeded to open a new store under the name "Seligman & Rossman." Its grand opening was a classic Little Jake promotional spectacle, featuring a public parade through the streets of Bay City with Seligman, his brother Joseph, and Frank Rossman riding in a "handsome cab" at the front, followed by a marching band, a large, "elegant" advertising wagon carrying a life-size portrait of Little Jake, a train of "carriages, drays, and sleighs" adorned with Little Jake advertising, and a conveyance with a black man named "Uncle Isaa" on top shouting to the spectators: "We cannot use Little Jake's name, but we have got him right ahead in person." To underscore the message that "The King of Clothiers" had returned to town, the sidewalk in front of his new store was deliberately piled high with empty packing crates affixed with large address labels reading "Little Jake & Rossman, Bay City." DeWitt and Palmer quickly returned to court, and the judge reaffirmed his original injunction, forcing Little Jake to abandon any further direct personal involvement in the Bay City clothing trade once and for all. In a final end-run around the court, however, Seligman turned the newly opened Seligman & Rossman store over to his brother Joseph and Frank Rossman to operate.[32] Nevertheless, Grow Brothers, the Clothiers had by that time apparently established a sufficient reputation in Bay City that it was able to successfully withstand the competition.

Four years later, Bay City's economy was paralyzed by a massive labor strike. US industrialization had given rise to labor-organizing activity on an unprecedented scale, leading to a series of bloody clashes between industrial workers and their employers—a nationwide railroad strike in 1877, the

"Haymarket Massacre" of 1886, the Homestead strike of 1892, the Pullman strike of 1894—that made the late nineteenth century one of the most violent periods in American history. Bay City was not immune. In 1885, the city's mill owners reacted to a temporary slump in the market price of lumber by cutting their workers' wages from the previous year's average of $1.98 per day to an average of $1.77 a day. The mill workers, who worked "six days a week, eleven or twelve hours a day," grudgingly accepted the pay cut, but in an attempt to compensate for the reduction in wages demanded that their workday be shortened to ten hours. In early July, after the mill owners refused to negotiate the issue, the workers went out on strike, adopting the slogan "Ten Hours or No Sawdust."

Eight weeks of labor violence ensued, with some 800 striking workers— mostly Polish and German immigrants armed with "clubs and. . . a few pistols"— roaming around the city, shutting down the sawmills that were the life's blood of the Bay City economy. The local police responded by beating strikers and arresting ringleaders, while the city's mill owners added to the tension by hiring their own private security force of Pinkerton detectives, who arrived in town armed with Winchester rifles and revolvers. In mid-July, Michigan governor Russell A. Alger, a "wealthy lumberman" and sawmill owner, came to Bay City to assess the situation, and, after meeting with local businessmen, ordered five companies of state militia into the city in an "effort to reopen the mills and intimidate strikers." A few weeks later, when a group of 200 strikers attempted to shut down another mill and the police responded by attacking them, gunfire broke out on both sides, leaving three strikers wounded and Bay City's sheriff with a bullet crease in his forehead. Sporadic violence continued into September, when the strikers, desperate for income, agreed to return to work on the mill owners' terms. Nevertheless, ongoing tension between "labor" and "capital" continued to disrupt the local economy "for more than a decade."[33]

Then, in the 1890s, the Bay City lumber industry completely collapsed, plunging the local economy into a deep, prolonged depression and driving the Grow Brothers clothing store out of business. The economic downturn was brought about by the rapaciousness of the region's logging companies, whose prevailing philosophy of "cutting all you can, cutting it as fast as you can, and moving on" had, in the space of two decades, reduced the Saginaw Valley's 6,000 square miles of majestic pine forests to "a desert of stumps," until by the late 1890s "there was nothing left to cut." With the valley's timber resources depleted, the logging companies shifted their operations elsewhere, and in doing so they immediately relegated Bay City to the status of a "declining mill town." By the end of the decade, half of the city's sawmills had shut down, and the local population had shrunk by 5 percent (a decline that reached 20 percent by 1910). First to leave were the lumber barons, followed by the sawmill managers and mill workers. Soon the crowds of unruly lumberjacks that had patronized the Water Street saloon district were gone, as were the throngs of immigrants normally found "milling about outside the sawmills seeking employment." As more and more mills were boarded up, "property values declined and people could not sell their homes." Meanwhile, the downtown commercial district became increasingly blighted as street maintenance was neglected and sidewalks deteriorated.[34] In the spring of 1895, with its customer base rapidly eroding and the local economy in free-fall, Grow Brothers held a going-out-of-business sale and closed its doors for good.[35]

Faced with a midlife career change at age 45, DeWitt Grow made a successful transition to employment in the coal industry. From 1900 until his death in 1921, he held a variety of mid-level positions in the Robert Gage Coal Company of Bay City, including secretary-treasurer, sales manager, accountant, bookkeeper, and salesman.[36] A lucrative new market for coal had begun to develop in the United States in the late nineteenth century, as centralized heating systems fueled by coal furnaces became standard features of houses. Robert Gage was among the first Saginaw Valley businessmen to recognize coal ore's market potential as a residential heating fuel. He began investing in coal mines in the late 1890s, and by 1915, he was one of Michigan's "biggest retailers of coal for home furnaces," operating mines throughout Bay and Saginaw counties and employing a labor force of some 1,200 men.[37] As a member of Gage's staff, DeWitt was evidently well-remunerated for his services. In the years immediately preceding World War I, he and Alice were sufficiently prosperous that they could afford to indulge each of their children with expensive one-carat diamonds at the time of their engagements, along with extensive sets of costly imported French porcelain dinnerware as wedding presents.

Saginaw County coal mine, 1908. (Reproduced courtesy of Archives of Michigan, Lansing)

American males of DeWitt's generation were subject to a variety of psychological stresses unique to the nation's late nineteenth-century modernization. The far-reaching changes that industrialization and urbanization introduced in US society were deeply unsettling to most Americans, as almost overnight their traditional agrarian world was superseded by a dynamic new commercial and metropolitan way of life. That transformation was especially abrupt and jarring for young men like DeWitt who had grown up on farms and left to pursue careers in the city. Accustomed to a stable, quiet existence in a small, culturally homogeneous, overwhelmingly Protestant farming community where everyone knew everyone else, they suddenly found themselves living and working in a chaotic, impersonal city surrounded by masses of anonymous strangers, many of them unassimilated Catholic and Jewish immigrants from southern and eastern Europe—an alien, new cultural environment rife with poverty, crime, labor violence, and class conflict.[38] To young men steeped in the conservative Protestant values of rural America, their initial exposure to the secular, money-driven, liberal values of urban society was also often disorienting and disturbing. City dwellers seemed obsessed with "getting ahead" by any means necessary. They seemed to value aggressiveness, ambition, and cunning more highly than personal integrity or moral character. Their behavior seemed to reflect more of a Darwinian "survival of the fittest" mentality than the Ten Commandments or the Golden Rule. For many newly arriving migrants from the countryside, the challenge of adapting their old-fashioned values to urban society's new-fashioned ethics added significantly to the "culture shock" of the modernization process.[39]

The social and cultural changes of the late nineteenth century were psychologically challenging in other ways as well. In the city, the pace of life was determined not by "the cycle of the seasons" as in rural areas, but by "the tempo of the time table" and the "tyranny" of "the time clock,"[40] giving urban life a hectic, frenzied quality. In many urban households, the rapid redefining of gender roles was an additional source of stress. With the husband now absent from the home during the workday, his wife became "the central and dominant figure" in the household, with primary responsibility for the care and discipline of the couple's children. As a consequence, men largely forfeited their traditional roles as family patriarchs and supervisors of their children's moral development. For some, the loss of patriarchal power and paternal authority was a traumatic challenge to their sense of male self-identity.[41] In addition, with his familial responsibilities now focused almost entirely on earning money, the man of the household inevitably felt a growing pressure to succeed and advance in his job in order to assure that he would continue to be able to provide his family with financial security and a satisfactory standard of living in the years ahead. That pressure was especially strong among middle-class men, whose families' social status by definition required high levels of spending and consumption.

With a steady stream of enticing new consumer products pouring forth from US factories every year, and with inflation pushing consumer prices steadily higher, the middle-class breadwinner faced continual pressure to earn enough money to satisfy his family's ever-increasing material aspirations for "a good life." In the vernacular of the period, he found himself under constant pressure to "bring home the bacon" so that his family would be able to "keep up with the Joneses" by purchasing the latest consumer goods and other status symbols that a respectable middle-class lifestyle demanded.[42]

But perhaps the most unsettling change faced by middle-class men of DeWitt's generation was their loss of personal autonomy. As historian David Danbom notes, farming provided American males with "a higher degree of individual independence . . . than urban occupations offered." On the farm, a man was his own boss, working on his own property and supplying most of his family's needs with his own hands. In the new commercial-industrial economy, however, he now worked for an employer, enhancing the value of someone else's property, in a pecuniary relationship that left him totally dependent on a monetary income for his and his family's sustenance.[43] That dependence on a regular monetary income in turn left him and his family dangerously vulnerable to periods of economic instability—a danger that became conspicuously evident in the 1870s, when the US economy entered a turbulent twenty-year period of financial panics, stock market crashes, recessions, and depressions that provided the American people with a painful introduction to the tumultuous and wildly unpredictable business cycles of their new industrial economy. As the collapse of the Bay City lumber industry in the 1890s graphically demonstrated, the volatile "boom and bust" nature of industrial capitalism could have catastrophic consequences for employers and employees alike. And although the economic upheavals of the late nineteenth century were relatively mild by comparison with what lay ahead in the 1930s, they were still "deeply troubling" to Americans at the time, leaving many income-earning men and their families with a growing sense of anxiety about their financial security and a disturbing feeling that they were no longer in control of their own economic lives.[44]

Economic dependence and the feelings of insecurity and vulnerability that came with it, extended into other facets of Americans' lives as well. On the farm, families were relatively self-sufficient, producing most of their food and other necessities from their own resources. Urban families, by contrast, were entirely dependent on retail merchants to supply them with the goods they needed for their day-to-day survival—goods that more often than not had been produced "by unknown hands" in faraway places and then passed from one anonymous middleman to another along a complex distribution network before reaching the consumer.[45] In addition, more and more American residences of the late nineteenth century, particularly those of the urban middle class, were physically connected to external public utilities systems—gas lines, water and sewer lines, telephone systems, and, shortly after the turn of the twentieth century, electricity grids—each of which immeasurably improved the lives of the inhabitants, but at the same time made them completely dependent on sophisticated new technologies that they did not understand but could not live without, technologies supplied by municipal and private utility companies that charged steadily rising fees for their indispensable services.[46] Consequently, in a myriad of ways, middle-class men and their families entered the twentieth century with a deepening sense that their lives were being shaped by forces beyond their control, forces they were powerless to influence.[47]

DeWitt apparently took at least two significant steps to cope with the various stresses and pressures of his times. In December 1873, a year and a half after moving to Bay City, he became a member of one of the city's Masonic lodges, Joppa Lodge No. 315.[48] The Masons—or the Ancient and Accepted Order of Freemasons, as they were formally known—were a secret, all-male fraternal organization dedicated to social fellowship, the moral "self-improvement" of their members, and charitable works in their community, including the support of widows and orphans. Lodge members convened once a week in the evening to dress in exotic costumes, listen to lectures, and participate in arcane rituals filled with references to "master builders" of the ancient past. For a young man newly arrived in town, joining the Masons had practical advantages. Because prominent local figures—politicians, clergymen, doctors, lawyers, bankers, and other "substantial men" in the community— were invariably included among a lodge's membership, becoming a Mason was an effective way to make influential contacts and acquire status as a respectable "solid citizen." And for a young businessman attempting to establish himself in local commerce, membership in the organization was particularly beneficial in developing useful business connections.[49]

But Masonry brought other benefits as well. For large numbers of uprooted rural males like DeWitt who had recently become city dwellers, membership in the Masons provided an attractive substitute for the sense of community they had left behind in their small farming towns. At a time when urbanization was radically reshaping US society and mass immigration was transforming the nation into a melting pot of ethnic and cultural diversity, Masonic lodges offered their members a comfortable, homogeneous social community, a close-knit brotherhood of like-minded men from similar backgrounds bound together by common bonds of fraternal fellowship and ritual. Although the organization imposed almost no formal restrictions on membership, the vast majority of its members were urban middle-class males employed in professional and white-collar occupations—men precisely like DeWitt Grow, in other words. For them, the local Masonic lodge performed a valuable function in the social world of late nineteenth-century urban America—by providing middle-class men with a respectable, even prestigious, gathering place for social interaction, filling the gap in their local community "between the exclusive clubs of the wealthy and the saloons of the poor." Masonry offered more than social camaraderie, however. In its literature, the organization frequently described itself as a place of "asylum" from the "confusion and strife" of "the outside world," an "oasis" of stability and order, of harmony and good will, in "an increasingly complex and disordered" urban environment. For middle-class men residing in a cold, impersonal city teeming with "strangers about whom they knew little or nothing," Masonry's spirit of brotherhood and fellowship provided a healthy antidote to the feelings of alienation and "anomie" that many of them were experiencing.[50]

The Masonic order was also a repository of traditional middle-class moral values. During a period when materialism, self-aggrandizement, and greed seemed to be eroding the moral fabric of American society, the Masons demanded that their members embody the time-honored virtues of honesty, generosity, self-restraint, and personal decency. Through secret rituals in which lodge members advanced upward through successively higher "degree" ranks, the fraternity imposed strict moral standards on its members in order to assure that they were "worthy men" of good character who would serve as positive examples to their community. And it aggressively enforced those standards by expelling members for adultery, drunkenness, fraud, and "general lascivious conduct," among other failings. According to historian Lynn Dumenil, one of the reasons why Masonry appealed to men like DeWitt Grow was because it served as a bastion of traditional morality at a time when many middle-class males were struggling to maintain their traditional values in the face of urban society's corrupting influences.[51]

And finally, the religious aspects of Masonry resonated with large numbers of middle-class men who were searching for spiritual comfort in a stressful, confusing, and increasingly secular world. The late nineteenth century was a period of "spiritual crisis" in the United States, with traditional Protestantism under attack both externally and internally. Darwinian science had effectively undermined many of Christianity's basic tenets, resulting in levels of agnosticism and atheism never before seen in American society—a trend that was eliciting public cries of alarm from ministers everywhere. Meanwhile, within the nation's mainstream Protestant churches, new liberal doctrines had taken root that bore little resemblance to the traditional fire-and-brimstone Calvinism of earlier periods. No longer did Protestant ministers interpret death as the terrifying prelude to a fateful Judgment Day when God rewarded selected Christians with life everlasting while casting sinners into the eternal fires of Hell. Instead, they now preached a milder, gentler theology, one in which the concept of Hell was largely absent and death was viewed as a welcome, even pleasant, release from life's woes, as well as the gateway to a joyous reunion with previously deceased loved ones. In addition, a massive influx of Catholic and Jewish immigrants had

Masonic Temple of Bay City, undated illustration, c. mid-1890s. (Source: *Bay City Illustrated* [Bay City, MI: C. & J. Gregory, 1898], 46)

added an element of religious diversity to American society that many native Protestants found disturbing and potentially threatening.[52]

Masonry was, in part at least, a traditionalistic response to the religious turmoil of the times. Although it was not a religion *per se*, the brotherhood incorporated numerous religious elements into its rituals and doctrines. Candidates for membership were required to formally affirm their belief in God prior to initiation, while the fraternity's rituals included prayers to the "Almighty Father," the "Divine Creator," and the "Supreme Architect of the Universe." Most Masons found the new liberal Protestantism spiritually inadequate and unfulfilling—a "watered down" theology that, in their view, seemed to suggest that all a Christian had to do in order to gain entry into Heaven was to die. Many members also complained that Sunday services in their local Protestant churches had become "tame and uninteresting." Masonry did not define itself as a Protestant, or even a Christian, organization, however, and Jesus Christ's name was nowhere to be found in the Masonic literature of the period. Instead, the fraternity espoused a more universalistic creed "that viewed all religions as equal" and centered its beliefs on "the fatherhood of God and the brotherhood of man." And yet at the same time, most Masonic rituals were also heavily infused with Christian symbolism, some of it strikingly reminiscent of Puritan Calvinism of the seventeenth and eighteenth centuries. During initiation, for example, candidates for membership were forced to confront their own mortality by undergoing a symbolic death and spiritual rebirth. Each initiate was required to slowly make his way through a darkened chamber filled with skeletons, coffins, artificial corpses, executioners' devices, and other gruesome death iconography, after which he took a symbolic "voyage through Hades" before being ceremonially "resurrected" into a new life of Masonic fellowship. His subsequent progression through the fraternity's various degree ranks represented an ongoing quest for moral purification and spiritual enlightenment that when completed would enable him "to die in the hope of a glorious immortality." By dedicating themselves to brotherly love, faith in God, personal morality, and charitable acts, most Masons believed they were "practicing a truer form of Christianity than the Protestant churches of their day"—churches that, from the fraternity's perspective, spent too much of their time fighting among themselves over obscure sectarian issues while neglecting their primary obligations to save souls, treat their fellow men with love and compassion, and aid the needy. For middle-class men who found themselves spiritually adrift in a rapidly changing world, Masonry offered an appealing alternative to the conventional forms of worship, one whose rituals incorporated a number of Calvinist precepts from earlier generations.[53]

Two decades after joining the Masons, DeWitt took an additional step to cushion himself from the stresses of late nineteenth-century life in Bay City. In 1894, at age 43, he became a born-again Christian. The only surviving record of the event is a terse hand-written notation in an old family bible, in which he is recorded as "Born April 4, 1850 . . . *again* Jan. 19—1894."[54] Nothing is known about the specific circumstances that led him to renew his commitment to Christ. He and Alice were members of Bay City's First Baptist Church,[55] but by the 1890s the emotionally intense act of spiritual rebirth would more likely have taken place during one of the evangelical revivals that itinerant preachers periodically conducted in the area. Perhaps the key to identifying the motivation behind his decision to be born again lies in its timing, because it occurred during the collapse of the Bay City lumber industry and less than eighteen months before DeWitt's Grow Brothers clothing store went out of business. Facing acute financial stress, he may have turned for emotional comfort and psychological support to the religious verities of his evangelical Baptist forefathers to help him cope with an impending business failure.

DeWitt and Alice remained in Bay City for the remainder of their lives. Alice died, at home, of heart disease on 18 December 1915, on the eve of the United States' entry into World War I. She was only 63 years old at the time.[56] Following her death, DeWitt continued to reside in the couple's Farragut Street residence, a few blocks from his daughter, Florence (Grow) Dumond, the wife of a French Canadian doctor (Van H. Dumond) who went on to become one of Bay City's wealthiest and most prominent surgeons.[57] DeWitt died, also at home, of "apoplexy" (stroke) on 24 May 1921, at age 71. Like his father, Thomas, two decades earlier, his death was front-page news in the local newspaper.[58] Both DeWitt and Alice were buried in Bay City's Elm Lawn Cemetery, with their graves marked by the simple, secular headstones increasingly preferred by middle-class Americans in the first half of the twentieth century.

Graves of Alice and DeWitt Grow, Elm Lawn Cemetery, Bay City, MI. (Photograph by the author.)

DeWitt Grow was in many respects a stereotypical upper-middle-class male of the late nineteenth and early twentieth centuries—a prosperous, locally prominent urban businessman, member of a Masonic lodge, and father of two, whose conventional, bourgeois lifestyle reflected the latest trends in clothing and household furnishings, but whose religious and moral values remained at least partially rooted in the past. Like his father, DeWitt was a transitional figure in the history of the family line, with his life spanning the period in which the United States completed its historic transformation from an agrarian nation to an urban-industrial power. In some respects, he embodied what might, in his mind, have been the best of both of those worlds. On one hand, as the owner of a Bay City clothing store and later as an official of a Saginaw Valley coal company, he reaped the financial rewards of a career in the rapidly growing white-collar world of American commerce, earning the income that provided his family with a comfortable middle-class standard of living. On the other hand, as his Masonic affiliation and decision to be born again would seem to indicate, he retained some of the core values of the traditional agrarian world in which he had been born and raised. Although he successfully exploited the opportunities available in the new commercial-industrial economy to achieve material prosperity and local status, he also fell victim to that economy's risks and dangers, particularly its volatile business cycles, when, in the mid-1890s, the Saginaw Valley lumber boom suddenly went bust, taking Bay City's economy and DeWitt's clothing business down with it. He managed to weather that economic crisis by obtaining a salaried position on the staff of a regional coal company, losing his financial independence in the process but at least managing to garner a regular source of income. Three decades later, when a massive new economic crisis known as the Great Depression crippled the United States, his son, Martin, would be considerably less fortunate.

MARTIN SMITH GROW (1880–1942)

Martin[8] Grow (*DeWitt[7], Thomas[6], Elisha[5], Thomas[4], Thomas[3], Thomas[2], John[1]*) followed in his father's footsteps by pursuing a career in commerce, as a sales manager for companies in the wholesale food and automotive service industries. For young men of Martin's generation coming of age at the turn of the twentieth century, a career in sales was a popular and logical choice. By 1900, US economic growth was increasingly centered in the nation's consumer goods industries—industries that were manufacturing an ever-widening array of brand-name products and marketing them nationally with the aid of commercial advertising agencies. As a result, by the beginning of the new century, a long and growing list of retail products—Singer sewing machines, Remington typewriters, Kodak cameras, Schwinn bicycles, Gillette razors, Borax soaps, Post and Kellogg breakfast cereals, Swift and Armour processed meats, Kraft and Borden dairy products, Pillsbury and Gold Medal flour, Jell-O gelatin, Mail Pouch tobacco, and hundreds of others, including Budweiser, Schlitz, and Pabst beer—had become household names throughout America. Inevitably, as the consumer goods sector of the economy expanded in size and influence, so too did the sales sector of the US labor force—so much so, in fact, that by the early twentieth century the United States seemed increasingly to be turning into "a nation of salesmen," as larger and larger numbers of ambitious young men aspiring to white-collar occupations and middle-class status concluded that the wellspring of economic opportunity in America, and their most promising path to a successful life, was a career on the sales staff of a US company.[1]

Martin Grow was born and raised in an upper-middle-class family in Bay City, Michigan, the only son of a prominent local businessman and his wife. Like many middle-class boys of his generation, he remained in school through the second year of high school and then dropped out at age 16 to work full-time. Taking advantage of his father's connections, he first obtained a job as a sales clerk in a Bay City men's clothing store (Oppenheim & Sons), and subsequently worked as a clerk or a traveling sales agent for several wholesale food companies that supplied local grocery stores in Bay City and neighboring Saginaw.[2]

Childhood photographs of Martin Grow: *at left*, age 2; *at right*, age 6. (From the author's family photograph collection.)

In January 1909, while employed as a clerk at the Fox & Smart Company, a Saginaw food wholesaler, 29-year-old Martin married Delia (Booth) Harvey, a 31-year-old divorcée who was born in Canada and had recently become a naturalized US citizen.[3] Delia's status as a divorced woman raised eyebrows in Martin's family, because even though US divorce rates had been rising sharply since the 1870s—a result of marital stresses brought about by urbanization, the breakdown of traditional patriarchal hierarchies, and financial pressures stemming from rampant consumerism—divorcées were still widely stigmatized as flawed women, especially in upper- and middle-class society.[4] A year and a half after their wedding, Delia gave birth to the couple's only child, a son, Martin DeWitt. Like most middle-class childbirths of the early twentieth century, the baby was born at home rather than in a hospital.[5] The couple's decision to limit the size of their family to a single child was likewise typical for middle-class couples of Martin and Delia's generation, who on average had fewer than two children—a reproductive choice made possible by the fact that the use of contraceptives for birth control was by now almost universal in middle-class marriages.[6]

Child of MARTIN[8] AND DELIA (BOOTH HARVEY) GROW:

    i.   Martin DeWitt[9], b. 12 July 1910, Saginaw, MI; d. 26 Aug. 1991 at Sacramento, CA; m. (1) 1935, Ethyl Marie Zimmerman of Swanton, OH; m. (2) 1935, Eva Modar of Toledo, OH; m. (3) 1968, Marilyn (Russell) Reynolds of Sacramento, CA.

SOURCES: George W. Davis, *John Grow of Ipswich/John (Groo) Grow of Oxford*, 160; marriage and death data from author's family history collection.

Martin's first big break in the business world came in 1912 when he obtained a position as sales manager of the Woolson Spice Company in Toledo, Ohio, 140 miles south of Saginaw. At the time, Toledo was a booming industrial city of more than 200,000 people, four times the size of Saginaw. Benefiting from its location as a midwestern rail hub and Great Lakes port, the city had developed into an important manufacturing center during the late nineteenth and early twentieth centuries, attracting factories that mass-produced bicycles, cash registers, scales, machine parts, glass, and other commodities.

By the time Martin and his family arrived, another new industry was rapidly emerging as the foundation of the local economy. In 1911, John N. Willys, a former bicycle salesman, established an automobile manufacturing company, Willys-Overland, in Toledo, and within four years the company had become the second largest car maker in the United States, surpassed only by the Ford Motor Company of Detroit. By World War I, Willys-Overland was selling 15,000 vehicles a year; its "Willys Knight" and "Overland Roadster" models were among the most popular touring cars in America, and Willys' factory alone was employing 20 percent of Toledo's labor force.[7]

Martin's new employer, the Woolson Spice Company, was one of the nation's leading wholesale coffee companies. Founded in 1882 by Toledo grocery store owner Alvin M. Woolson, the company had "revolutionized coffee merchandizing" in the United States during the late nineteenth century. At a time when consumers purchased coffee beans in bulk and ground them at home in hand-turned coffee grinders, Woolson's company roasted and ground the beans for them, packaging ready-to-brew coffee in convenient one- and two-pound containers. It also pioneered the development of innovative new marketing techniques by including a discount coupon and a collectible, lithographed trade card in each of its coffee containers. By the time Martin was hired in 1912, the Woolson Spice Company had become the second largest coffee company in America, with a diversified line of coffee, tea, and spice products distributed nationally under the popular "Golden Sun" brand name.[8]

A 1910 Woolson Spice Company advertisement. (From the author's family history collection.)

For a young man in his early thirties, securing a position as sales manager of a company the size of Woolson's was a significant professional achievement. In 1912, the company had more than 800 employees, including some 300 traveling salesmen who had succeeded in persuading more than 200,000 retail grocery stores in 41 states to stock Woolson products on their shelves. As the company's sales manager, Martin's responsibilities included hiring and firing salesmen, assigning sales territories, supervising each salesman's performance in achieving his sales quotas, and working with other company executives to develop effective marketing strategies.[9]

At Woolson's, Martin faced many of the same economic pressures and psychological stresses that men of his father's generation had experienced: pressure to succeed at his work in order to earn the income that he and his family relied on for their economic survival, feelings of insecurity stemming from the hovering fear that a sudden economic downturn could eliminate his job and reduce his family to poverty, etc. In addition, however, he also had to deal with new forms of stress intrinsic to a white-collar career in a large

Woolson Spice Company plant, Summit and Sandusky Streets, Toledo, OH, as illustrated on a 1912 postcard. (Donald D. Duhaime Collection, Ward M. Canaday Center for Special Collections, University of Toledo) Built in 1909, the facility had a weekly production capacity of 1 million pounds of roasted coffee, 100,000 pounds of tea, and 25,000 pounds of ground spices. With two railroad lines and a Maumee River loading wharf adjacent to the plant, the company bulk-shipped its products to distribution centers in Detroit, Buffalo, Cincinnati, Chicago, Minneapolis, Kansas City, St. Louis, Davenport, Memphis, Dallas, and other cities. (Scribner, *Memoirs of Lucas County and the City of Toledo*, 1: 559; "Modernity in Coffee Roasting Factories," *The Spice Mill*, vol. XXXV: no. 1 [January 1912]: 27)

twentieth-century business organization. In earlier periods, a man achieved success in the business world by displaying competence, good judgment, and a willingness to work hard. Those fundamental attributes remained essential in the twentieth century, but they no longer assured success in and of themselves. The owners and directors of large manufacturing companies like Woolson's imposed additional standards of performance on their white-collar employees as prerequisites for career advancement. To successfully climb his company's career ladder and prosper financially, an employee needed to demonstrate loyalty and a personal commitment to the organization. He had to be a solid "team player" who willingly followed orders, deferred to his superiors' decisions, and got along with his colleagues. He had to "fit in" socially by conforming to the internal "corporate culture" that the company's owners and directors had established. And he had to be a respectable family man of sound moral character who would enhance the company's public image. Executive-level employees like Martin were additionally expected to have the managerial skills—persuasive, coercive, and other manipulative abilities—needed to ensure that the employees under their supervision successfully accomplished the tasks required of them by the company.

For men who did not innately possess the interpersonal skills and other personality traits needed to succeed in a large, hierarchically structured business organization, the extra effort required on their part to satisfy their employer's expectations—by conducting themselves in ways that were contrary to their normal inclinations, pretending to be someone other than who they really were in order to "get ahead" in their jobs—could produce high levels of psychological discomfort and internal stress. In a work environment in which the subjective judgments of a man's superiors could determine his future in the company, the pressure to conform, to curry favor, to adopt a deferential manner and ingratiate himself with the men above him for the sake of his career, could leave him feeling hypocritical and untrue to himself.[10]

Meanwhile, the ongoing transformation of women's roles in American society was creating challenges of a different sort for male employees in the white-collar workplace. During the late nineteenth century, women began entering the workforce in ever-increasing numbers in response to new employment opportunities arising out of the industrial revolution. The percentage of female workers in the US labor force increased from 16 percent in 1870 to 20 percent in 1900, to 25 percent in 1910, and to nearly 40 percent by 1920. Many of the new employment opportunities for women were low-level positions in the administrative offices of business firms and manufacturing companies—positions as stenographers, typists, secretaries, file clerks, and telephone operators. As females moved into those jobs and began working in close proximity to male employees, their presence introduced a new sexual dynamic into the twentieth-century office workplace, and male employees suddenly found themselves working in a radically altered environment rife with romantic temptations and potential opportunities for extramarital involvements. The office romances that occasionally resulted were often consensual in nature, but the potential for sexual misconduct—on the part of male and female employees alike—was ever-present. Most of the women who filled the new office jobs were young, single, poor, and vulnerable to sexual harassment, while the male supervisors under whom they worked wielded enormous economic power over them. At the same time, their jobs were almost invariably low-paying, dead-end positions that "offered no prospect of advancement," and a morally unscrupulous young woman who was "on the make" and looking to improve her situation in life soon found that the office environment provided her with abundant opportunities to seduce a white-collar male employee and attempt to entice him into marriage.[11]

The new sexually charged workplace atmosphere was merely one aspect of a broader "revolution in morals" that was undermining traditional norms of behavior in the United States in the early years of the twentieth century. The materialistic, consumption-oriented values that had become so pervasive in late nineteenth-century American society—values that placed an ever-greater emphasis on the acquisition of consumer goods and the enjoyment of material possessions—fostered a widespread acceptance of self-indulgence, self-gratification, and personal fulfillment, including sexual fulfillment, as legitimate pursuits in life, while the secularizing trends of the period were simultaneously eliminating traditional religious restraints on forms of behavior that had previously been considered immoral or improper. New technological inventions—the phonograph, the automobile, "moving pictures"—helped to accelerate the process.

By the early twentieth century, there were growing indications that "a new morality" was taking root in American society. Fashionable young women were consuming alcohol, smoking cigarettes in public, wearing rouge, lipstick, and eyeliner, raising their hemlines above the ankle, and generally flaunting conventions of every sort; while young couples now went out on dates unchaperoned in automobiles, attended "petting and necking" parties, and danced the erotic new "turkey trot" and "bunny hug" to the syncopated rhythms of "ragtime" music in raucous public dance halls or at home around the family Victrola. Meanwhile, Americans of all ages and classes were being entertained, and their values heavily influenced, by the "romantic sensuous imagery" of motion pictures starring such early "sex symbols" as Theda Bara and John Barrymore. And above all, Americans were engaging in premarital and extramarital sexual activity on a scale previously unheard of. Surveys conducted during the period found that while "nearly 90 percent" of women born before 1890 were virgins at the time of their marriage, the percentage dropped to 74 percent for women born between 1890 and 1899, to 51 percent for those born between 1900 and 1909, and to just 32 percent for those born after 1910. Other studies identified "a growing trend toward adultery" in the United States, as the biblical injunction against "coveting thy neighbor's wife" (or, in the case of women, "thy neighbor's husband") fell by the wayside. Conventional historical interpretations date the decline and fall of Victorian-style morality in US society and the emergence of a sexually liberated "new woman" to the decade of the 1920s—the so-called "Roaring Twenties"—but the revolution in moral and sexual behavior to which they refer actually began "at least a decade earlier," in the years preceding World War I.[12]

The new climate of looser morality had a near-ruinous impact on Martin's life. In 1919, as he continued to reap the rewards of professional success as a Woolson Spice Company executive, it suddenly became known that he had been carrying on an extramarital affair with one of the company's female employees. The price he paid for his infidelity was a heavy one—as soon as they learned of the affair, Woolson's morally conservative directors immediately fired him for "philandering." And although his wife, Delia, chose not to terminate their marriage, she remained resentful and unaffectionate toward him for the rest of his life.

After losing his job at Woolson's, Martin bounced around for the next several years, holding a series of less prestigious positions at several smaller Toledo-area businesses. City directories for the period list him as a "department manager" at the Berdan Company (a local food wholesaler) in 1920; as the sales manager of the Smith-Kirk Candy Company in 1921 and 1922; as an "employee" of a local truck manufacturer (the Garland Motor Truck Sales Company) in 1923; and as a "salesman" for an unidentified employer in 1924.

Martin and Delia Grow, c. 1920s. (From the author's family photograph collection.)

Then, in 1925, Martin received his second big break in the business world when he was hired as sales manager of the Air-Scale Company, a recently established Toledo company that manufactured compressed-air machines for inflating automobile and truck tires. By the mid-1920s, Toledo had developed into one of the major production centers of the rapidly growing US automobile industry. The success of the Willys-Overland Company—whose Toledo factory was, for a number of years, the single "largest automobile manufacturing facility in the world"—attracted a growing number of other automobile-related businesses to the city, including Champion Spark Plug, Tillotson Carburetor, the Mather Spring Company, and some thirty other manufacturers of auto parts, while Toledo glassmakers became leading suppliers of car windshields and windows. Air-Scale was a new addition to the expanding automobile sector of the city's economy. In 1924, the company founder Earl M. Morley, a Delta, Ohio, inventor, designed and patented an air-pressure regulator that quickly became the basis for the world's first compressed-air tire-inflation device. Soon, Morley's company was marketing its "Air-Scale Automatic Tire Inflating Machine" to the thousands of gasoline filling stations, automobile service garages, car dealerships, and tire stores that were springing up across the United States as the burgeoning new "automobile age" revolutionized the nation's transportation landscape and culture. By 1928, Air-Scale was aggressively expanding its product line to include several models of freestanding and ceiling-mounted tire-inflation machines, compressed-air cleaning machines, and spray guns. In landing a position as the company's sales manager, Martin had returned to the upper echelons of his profession—as an executive of an up-and-coming company in one of the nation's fastest growing industries.[13]

The late 1920s were years of prosperity for Toledo, thanks largely to the explosive growth of the automobile industry. By the end of the decade, two out of every three American families owned cars, and Willys-Overland was setting new vehicle-production records each year. Rising incomes and a booming "bull" stock market enabled those Toledoans in the top half of local society to enjoy a standard of living vastly superior to that of earlier generations. By the end of the 1920s, most upper- and middle-class residences in the city had electricity, central heating, hot and cold running water, and bathrooms equipped with bathtubs and flush toilets, while a growing number of new electrical appliances—refrigerators, washing machines, water heaters, vacuum cleaners, toasters, etc.—were helping make life easier and more pleasant for their inhabitants.[14]

The Grows lived more comfortably than most of the city's residents. Shortly after joining Air-Scale, Martin—in a probable attempt to regain Delia's affection, and perhaps using money that he inherited at the time of his father's death five years earlier—purchased a luxurious new home in Ottawa Hills, Toledo's wealthiest and most prestigious suburb.[15] Early in the twentieth century, wealthy and middle-class Toledoans had begun moving out of the dirty, crowded, older residential neighborhoods of the city's central district and into attractive new subdivisions opening up on Toledo's far west side, essentially abandoning the residential core of the downtown area to the city's working-class population of Polish, Hungarian, and black factory workers and their families. In 1915, with the aid of a $2 million investment by John Willys, the founder and president of Willys-Overland, local real estate developer E. H. Close purchased 1,200 acres of farmland and forest west of the city, some twenty minutes by automobile from the downtown business district, and developed it into the exclusive new residential community of Ottawa Hills, a fastidiously planned upscale development deliberately designed to attract Toledo's "wealthiest and most prominent" businessmen and professionals as residents. Inspired by the concepts of Frederick Law Olmsted, the famous nineteenth-century landscape architect and urban planner, Close set out to create "a suburban Eden"—a residential village in a pastoral "park-like setting

Increase Your Sales with *Air-Scales*

GETTING motorists to stop is your biggest problem. Air Scales stop them and bring them back. That has been proven in thousands of instances!

Here's How They Do It

Air Scales are trim, business-getting equipment. Their dark blue Duco finish and bright brass and bronze fittings are attractive to everybody. Electrically lighted inside at night, they invite trade as long as your station is open.

Air Scales deliver CLEAN filtered air. No dirt, moisture or grease gets into the tire.

Air Scales are accurate and automatic. Desired pressure obtained with a turn of the wrist.

Air Scales are speedy. No guessing—no gauge necessary. Unnecessary to stop to test pressure or adjust for each tire.

Air Scales service any tire—balloon or high pressure truck. Only air machine calibrated from 20 to 130 pounds pressure.

Air Scales are always in service. Not controlled by springs. Water trap below frost line eliminates freezing of moisture in pipes in any weather.

Air Scales keep the hose and nozzle clean and always off the ground.

Air Scales are salesmen for your station. Whether the station attendant fills the tires or the motorists do it themselves, they appreciate the clean, speedy, accurate service Air Scales render. They KNOW they get right pressure because it's visible just as the gasoline or oil they buy is served visibly.

There's an Air Scale model to meet every requirement whether for inside or outside installation and with or without water attachment. Why not let Air Scales—the modern, business-getting and trouble-free equipment—increase YOUR sales and boost YOUR profits? Write today for complete information and prices.

The Air Scale Co.
802 Broadway   Toledo, Ohio

3

Exclusive
Air Scale
Features

Beam-Type
Weighing
Unit

Positive
Filter

Water Trap

NEW AND IMPROVED *Air-Scales*

Air-Scale trade publication advertisement, *National Petroleum News*, 21 September 1927, p. 193.

that would preserve the natural surroundings of the countryside." One-third of the development was set aside for parks, woodlands, and open space, while Close and his associates rejected the standard geometrical street grids found in most suburban developments in favor of winding roads and curving streets that followed the contours of the tract's rolling hills and small stream valleys. State-of-the-art sewage and drainage systems were installed and unsightly telephone and electricity lines were buried in underground conduits. Utilizing the services of Toledo's foremost architects, stately, spacious houses conveying an impression of "grandeur" and "classic elegance" were constructed on large, beautifully landscaped lots. In addition, a series of "inflexible property restrictions" were drawn up to protect homeowners from any possibility that "undesirable neighbors" might move in and damage property values. Blatantly discriminatory "restrictive ownership covenants" prevented members of lower-class ethnic groups and non-white races from purchasing property in the village, essentially preserving Ottawa Hills exclusively for white, Anglo-Saxon, Protestant residents like the Grows, while strict zoning regulations prohibited the development of the types of commercial enterprises—gas stations, retail stores, "unsightly apartments," rooming houses, "barbecue lunch stands," etc.— that had "spoiled some of the finest" neighborhoods in older sections of Toledo. Additional property restrictions enforced uniform standards of good taste by prohibiting the construction of any residences that did not harmonize with the general architectural tone of the community.[16]

Despite lingering strains in their marriage, Martin and Delia lived a life of affluence and privilege in Ottawa Hills. Their stylish, three-bedroom brick home, with 3,180 square feet of living space for two adults and one child, was 50 percent larger than the eighteenth-century Connecticut farmhouse that had been home to Deacon Thomas Grow and as many as fifteen family members four generations earlier. Further enhancing the couple's suburban lifestyle were several new recreational and leisure time activities that were becoming increasingly popular among the automobile-owning US middle class. By the 1920s, a "Sunday drive in the country" had become a weekly ritual in many middle-class families—so much so, in fact, that according to automobile historian James Flink an outing on the Sabbath in the family Model T was now "a preferable alternative to attending church" services for more and more middle-class Americans,[17] especially those in "the business classes," among whom religious skepticism and "indifference" were increasingly widespread. Historian Lynn Dumenil writes that during the 1920s most middle-class Americans were more interested in "enjoying the rapidly expanding world of consumption and leisure" than in attending church, and that religious belief had by now "become an embarrassment for the urban, middle-class male."[18]

As a case in point, there is no evidence that Martin and Delia were churchgoers. Instead, on Sundays in good weather, they frequently took a

Martin and Delia Grow's home in Ottawa Hills, at 3422 Chestnut Hill Road. (From the author's family photograph collection.)

leisurely car ride to "see the sights" on the country roads outside of Toledo. One of their favorite destinations was the Irish Hills region of southeastern Michigan, a beautiful rural area of farms and orchards, crystalline lakes, and "idyllic scenery" an hour's drive north of the city.[19] During these Sunday day-trips, the couple periodically indulged in another activity popular in middle-class society at the time: antiques collecting. Throughout the 1920s, partly in reaction to the hectic complexity of urban-industrial life and a growing concern that mass foreign immigration was destroying the nation's traditional Anglo-Saxon culture, many middle-class Americans, and particularly descendants of "old native stock" like the Grows, developed a growing interest in family history and the material culture of their ancestors. Doctors, lawyers, businessmen, and other upper-middle-class professionals with sufficient disposable income began to collect American antiques—spinning wheels, Windsor chairs, grandfather clocks, quaint old lighting devices and cooking implements, and other handcrafted household furnishings that they nostalgically associated with a simpler, slower-paced, pre-industrial past and with the lives of their own pioneer ancestors.[20] Martin and Delia apparently found the new pastime appealing, because during their Sunday drives they occasionally stopped at out-of-the-way antiques shops in Cambridge Junction, Adrian, and other small Irish Hills towns and purchased antique artifacts, including a pre-Civil War Seth Thomas mantle clock from Connecticut that they proudly displayed over the fireplace in their Ottawa Hills home.

Each year the couple also indulged in another popular new feature of middle-class life: a summer vacation. Prior to World War I, the practice of taking vacations was limited exclusively to the nation's wealthy upper-class elites. During the 1920s, however, with more money in their bank accounts and their own automobiles to transport them, increasing numbers of middle-class Americans "took to the road" on annual summer vacations that offered them a week or two of rest and relaxation from stressful jobs and "the pressures of modern life."[21] Martin and his family became part of that trend. Every summer during the late 1920s, they returned to the Irish Hills and rented a cottage on Devil's Lake, southeastern Michigan's largest inland body of water, where they enjoyed two weeks of swimming, boating, and the recreational attractions of the Devil's Lake amusement park and public dance pavilion. Consequently, as the 1920s drew to a close, the Grows were living what most middle-class Americans regarded as "the good life." Martin, now 49 years of age, was in many respects a classic upper-middle-class success story: a prosperous business executive with an impressive home in Toledo's finest suburb and a salary that enabled his family to enjoy an affluent lifestyle filled with amenities, including antiques and yearly summer vacations at a picturesque lake in Michigan.

And then, suddenly and without warning, the bottom dropped out of the US economy. A catastrophic stock market crash in October 1929 triggered a massive nationwide financial panic that quickly plunged the United States into the worst economic depression in its history. The economic carnage was staggering. Between 1929 and 1932, the US gross national product shrank by nearly 50 percent (from $104 billion to $56 billion) and stocks trading on the New York Stock Exchange lost 83 percent of their total value. By 1932, one-fifth of the nation's commercial banks had failed, wiping out the savings accounts of some 9 million American families. As factories shut down and retail businesses went bankrupt, millions of workers lost their jobs. By 1933, 25 percent of the US labor force was unemployed, and most of the remaining 75 percent were working part-time at drastically reduced wages. As more and more Americans were forced into unemployment or underemployment, they were no longer able to meet their mortgage payments and lenders began foreclosing on their houses. By the end of 1933, a majority of the nation's homeowners were in default on their mortgage loans and millions of families had become homeless.[22]

The depression had a particularly devastating impact on the US automobile industry and on the cities in which it was based. As the consumer market for new cars evaporated, the major automakers reduced production and laid off large numbers of their workers. By 1933, Detroit and Toledo were experiencing unemployment rates of 50 percent, double the national average. In 1932, total employment in Detroit's automobile factories was "less than 40 percent" of average levels of the mid-1920s, and vehicle production at Ford Motor

Company plants in the city had dropped "from over 1.5 million units in 1929 to . . . 232,000." Between 1931 and 1933, Ford recorded losses totaling $120 million. In Toledo, Willys-Overland was "nearly bankrupt" by 1932 and "went into federal receivership" the following year. In 1933, as local unemployment continued to soar, Toledo's city government "bankrupted itself trying to feed the hungry."[23]

The economic catastrophe brought hard times to the Grow family. Like many Americans, Martin lost all of his savings early in the depression and never recovered financially. And like most Americans, he and Delia experienced a painful reduction in their standard of living. Nevertheless, with a resourcefulness born of desperation, Martin managed to avoid the joblessness, homelessness, and abject poverty—the breadlines, the soup kitchens, the transience and squalor of life in a wretched "Hooverville" shantytown—that millions of other American men endured during the 1930s. Although he was gradually demoted from sales manager to salesman and eventually to "clerk," he remained on Air-Scale's payroll until 1935, when the struggling company let him go. He then obtained a series of low-level, low-paying jobs that produced a trickle of income at best. In 1936 he worked as an "outside man" at the Lang Tire Company, and in 1937 as a salesman for the same company's household-appliance store.[24] He then picked up a few temporary public-relief jobs created by the New Deal's Works Progress Administration (WPA) in Toledo, including a position as part-time librarian at the Toledo Public Library. In 1940, he was employed as a WPA-funded "research assistant," earning a total annual income of $900.[25] Two years later, he was working as an inspector on the production line of the Libby Glass Company.[26]

At several points during this long, difficult period, Martin and Delia were forced to move to progressively poorer neighborhoods in an effort to secure more affordable housing. In October 1930, at the onset of the depression, they were able to find a buyer for their Ottawa Hills home before their mortgage lender (the Prudential Insurance Company of America) foreclosed on it. Although the sale price was not recorded on the deed transfer, the money they received enabled them to purchase a small, nondescript, 1,190-square-foot house in a modest lower-middle-class neighborhood in West Toledo.[27] (For purposes of comparison, the value of that house in 1940 was $5,500, barely one-fifth of the $25,000 valuation placed on their Ottawa Hills residence a decade earlier.[28]) By the early 1940s, they were living in a shabby lower duplex in a run-down, working-class neighborhood on Toledo's north side.[29] To make ends meet, Delia was eventually forced to work as a salesclerk at LaSalle's Department Store, in the process becoming the first female in the family line to enter the workforce. Embittered by her reduced circumstances and by the disappointing way that her life was turning out, she became increasingly cold and vindictive toward Martin.

Delia and Martin Grow, c. 1930s. (From the author's family photograph collection.)

The depression dragged on for more than a decade, until massive military spending by the US government in World War II finally fueled a recovery. By then, however, the unrelenting hard work and years of financial and marital stress had taken a toll on Martin's health. In late 1942, two days before Christmas, he suffered a heart attack and was rushed to Toledo's Flower Hospital, where he died on December 26,[30] the first member of the family line to end his life in a hospital. He was only 62 years old at the time. Years later, his daughter-in-law would remember him affectionately as a quiet, refined, "sad man" who in his leisure hours could usually be found reading a book with his pet Russian wolfhound at his feet—a man who, in her decidedly unscientific view, had died not from a heart attack but from "a broken heart."

To sustain herself economically in widowhood, Delia continued working at LaSalle's into her seventies, at which point she left Toledo to live near her son in Sacramento, California—"to make him take care of me in my old age," as she put it at the time. She died on 5 October 1969 at the age of 92, after residing for many years in a Carmichael, California, nursing home. According to her death certificate, the cause of death was "pneumonia and a complete cardio-circulatory collapse" brought on by "arteriosclerosis and old age." Reflecting

Martin Grow shortly before his death in 1942. (From the author's family photograph collection.)

Martin Grow's gravestone, Swanton Cemetery, County Road 1, Swanton, OH; erroneous year of death on headstone. (Photograph by the author.)

an increasingly popular trend in American mortuary practices, her body was cremated and her ashes were scattered in the Pacific Ocean, 3 miles out from San Francisco's Golden Gate Bridge.[31]

Martin Grow was a casualty of the times in which he lived. The first generation of the family line to be born and raised in urban-industrial America, he eventually saw his life ruined by the economic and cultural upheavals that accompanied "modern progress" in the first third of the twentieth century. In his youth, he followed the conventional path to success favored by most middle-class males coming of age at the turn of the century: a business career. Economic success came quickly, but within the context of a licentious new moral climate in which rates of pre- and extramarital sexual activity were increasing measurably. Marital infidelity was of course nothing new in American history— or in the history of the Grow family for that matter, as preacher William Grow's 1784 affair with a female parishioner in the Grow Hill Baptist Church graphically illustrated. Nevertheless, the liberalized morality and sexualized work environment of the early twentieth century significantly increased the likelihood of its occurrence—with unfortunate and lasting consequences for Martin and Delia's marriage. A decade after his adulterous affair cost him his job, and with the emotional wounds from his infidelity still unhealed, he and Delia were suddenly plunged into financial ruin by the most devastating economic disaster in US history. The collapse of the nation's economy—and with it the economic growth that had become the indispensable foundation of middle-class opportunity in the United States—reduced the couple to a hand-to-mouth existence for the remainder of Martin's life. An unfortunate victim of forces beyond his control, he nonetheless managed to ensure that his son received the educational training needed to move into a white-collar profession, thereby safeguarding the next generation of the family line from the very real threat of downward social mobility.

MARTIN DEWITT GROW (1910–1991)

By the time Martin[8] and Delia Grow's son, Martin DeWitt[9] (*Martin[8], DeWitt[7], Thomas[6], Elisha[5], Thomas[4], Thomas[3], Thomas[2], John[1]*), was nearing adulthood in the late 1920s, a half century of economic expansion and wage growth had transformed the United States into an overwhelmingly middle-class society. The American middle class of the early twentieth century encompassed a wide range of occupational categories, including independent farmers and small tradesmen (the core groups of the "old" middle class) as well as salaried white-collar employees of the "new" middle class, a social sector comprised of an upper tier of doctors, lawyers, business executives, engineers, academics, and other professionals, an intermediate stratum of mid-level managers, bureaucrats, school teachers, and accountants, and a lower tier of salespeople, office workers, technicians, and foremen. Collectively, the members of this broad and diverse middle class shared a common set of values—"bourgeois" values that measured success in terms of wealth and respectability and led middle-class families to pursue a materialistic, consumption-oriented, status-driven way of life. By the 1920s, those middle-class values had become so widely accepted in US society that they were virtually "synonymous with the national culture."[1]

Middle-class families of the early twentieth century attached particular importance to education, recognizing that to obtain white-collar employment and the middle-class lifestyle that came with it their children would require formal schooling to acquire the specialized skills they needed to succeed in the highly competitive, technologically advanced US economy. By the 1920s, a high school diploma was necessary for even a low-level white-collar job, while a college degree was the minimum prerequisite for entry into a lucrative, high-status profession. In earlier, pre-Civil War generations, conscientious fathers in the Grow family gave their young adult sons a start in life by providing them with farmland. In the twentieth century, responsible middle-class fathers like Martin[8] Grow saw to it that their offspring obtained the educational training and credentials that had become "the main avenue to economic and social success" in American life.[2]

Martin DeWitt Grow was the only child of a successful Toledo, Ohio, sales executive and his homemaker wife. He was raised in an affluent upper-middle-class environment that by his mid-teens included a stately family residence in Ottawa Hills, Toledo's wealthiest, most exclusive suburb, and summer vacations at Devil's Lake in the Irish Hills of southeastern Michigan. Because Ottawa Hills had not yet developed its own school system, he attended Scott High School in Toledo's "old west end," graduating in 1928, at a time when roughly half of American adolescents between ages 14 and 17 went to high school and "fewer than 17 percent . . . graduated."[3] He was the first member of the family line to earn a high school diploma.

Childhood photograph of M. DeWitt Grow. (Unless otherwise indicated, all photographs in this chapter are from the author's family photograph collection.)

Martin DeWitt—"M. DeWitt" as he referred to himself formally, or simply "De" as he was known to his family and friends—was intelligent, artistic, and ambitious. Finding the prospect of a conventional business career unappealing, he instead decided to pursue a vocation that would not only bring him money and status, but that would also provide opportunities for intellectual creativity so that his work life would be meaningful and fulfilling in a non-monetary sense. Accordingly, he chose to seek a career in architecture, a profession that was prestigious and well-remunerated, and that would also allow him to utilize his artistic and creative talents. In 1929, with that goal in mind, he enrolled in his hometown university, the University of Toledo.

That same summer, while he and his family were spending their annual vacation at Devil's Lake, he began a romantic relationship with Ethyl Marie Zimmerman, a beautiful and stylish young woman whose family rented the cottage next door to the Grows.[4] A year later, the young couple became engaged.

In 1930, after completing a year of study at the University of Toledo, De transferred to the Carnegie Institute of Technology in Pittsburgh to work toward a degree in that university's highly regarded architecture program. The timing could not have been less auspicious, because by the time he arrived in Pittsburgh, the national economy had plunged into the most catastrophic depression in American history and his parents were facing financial ruin. Although his father did what he could to provide financial support, it was only with the aid of extensive student loans that De was able to remain at Carnegie Tech and complete his architectural training there in 1934—becoming the first member of the family line to graduate from college.

Ethyl Zimmerman and "Dewey" Grow (as M. DeWitt was known in school), Devil's Lake, Michigan, c. 1929.

Carnegie Tech commencement, June 1934—*left to right*: Martin Grow, Delia Grow, Ethyl Zimmerman, and M. DeWitt Grow.

The year 1934 was a grim time to be entering the US labor market, especially for a young, newly minted architect. The nation was mired in the depths of the Great Depression, unemployment in Toledo and other midwestern industrial cities stood at 50 percent, and housing construction was at a near standstill. Between 1928 and 1930, De had held several part-time jobs as a low-level junior draftsman for various Toledo architects (Sidney E. Aftel, Joseph C. Huber, and the firm of Britsch & Munger), however, after he graduated from Carnegie Tech, Britsch & Munger hired him as a full-time draftsman at a weekly salary of $25. The pay was paltry and the duties rudimentary, but the job gave him a foot in the door of the architecture profession. It proved to be a particularly fortuitous opportunity, because Britsch & Munger would soon become one of Toledo's leading architecture firms. Established in 1927 by Carl C. Britsch (a 1916 Carnegie Tech graduate) and his business partner, Harold H. Munger (Notre Dame class of 1915), the firm was steadily attracting clients and commissions by the late 1930s with its "modernist" designs for schools, hospitals, office and apartment buildings, churches, and residential homes throughout northwest Ohio.[5]

The following year, 1935, De and Ethyl Zimmerman were married. Like most Depression-era brides and grooms, the young couple struggled financially for several years, living on a shoestring budget and saddled with De's student loan repayments.

M. DeWitt Grow and Ethyl Zimmerman on their wedding day, 25 October 1935.

By the end of the decade, De was rapidly ascending the Britsch & Munger career ladder. In the late 1930s, the Toledo Metropolitan Housing Authority commissioned the firm to design and oversee the construction of several multi-million-dollar public housing projects funded by the New Deal's Public Works Administration (PWA). De's first major opportunity to impress his superiors came in 1937–1938 when he helped design the $2 million PWA-funded Brand Whitlock Homes, the city's "first public housing and slum clearance project." He also worked on another large PWA-funded municipal housing project—the Charles F. Weiler Homes—and several school construction projects. By 1940, his performance had earned him a promotion to the position of "chief draftsman and designer" in the firm, with an annual salary of $2,400—more than two-and-a-half-times the median national income at the time. He had also recently acquired his state license as a registered architect.[6] Still only 30 years old, he was well on his way to a successful career.

World War II proved to be a major shot in the arm for the nation's economy. Massive wartime military spending by the federal government quickly brought the depression to an end, restoring economic growth and reducing unemployment to "almost zero."[7] Like many other Toledo-area businesses, Britsch & Munger prospered from government defense contracts during the war. In 1942, the firm was awarded a War Department contract to design and construct a $5 million quartermaster's depot for the US Army Corps of Engineers in Marion, Ohio, south of Toledo, and the Federal Public Housing Authority commissioned it to build fifteen "defense housing facilities" on US

Army bases. All told, between 1941 and 1946, Britsch & Munger completed projects valued at more than $12 million.[8]

Late in the war, De and Ethyl became parents for the first and only time.[9] During the Great Depression, US birthrates had continued their decades-long decline, dropping "below the replacement level" of two children per couple "for the first time in American history,"[10] as the use of artificial birth control devices (principally diaphragms by the 1930s and 1940s) remained almost universal among middle-class couples.[11] De and Ethyl's baby—a son, Michael—was the first in the family line to be born in a hospital, a reflection of the major advances taking place in hospital-based obstetrics in the United States in the post-World War I decades. By 1945, 79 percent of American women were delivering their babies in hospitals.[12]

Child of MARTIN DEWITT[9] AND ETHYL (ZIMMERMAN) GROW:

    i.   Michael[10] Robert, b. 23 April 1944 at Toledo, OH; m. (1) 1966 at Toledo, OH, Linda Cox; m. (2) 1989 at Athens, OH, Catherine (Carbone) Russell.

SOURCE: Author's family history collection.

Ethyl's pregnancy, spanning the months from July 1943 to April 1944, came during a period of severe wartime stress for the couple. Shortly after she became pregnant, De learned that he was about to be drafted into the army. At the time, the couple owned a pleasant little home in Toledo's Minor Park neighborhood, a semi-rural suburban area on the far western outskirts of the city adjacent to Ottawa Hills; and rather than have his wife and newborn child live alone in such a secluded setting while he was serving in the military, De put the house up for sale. As soon as it sold and the couple relocated to less appealing accommodations, he received a last-minute job deferment based on Britsch & Munger's defense-related work for the War Department.

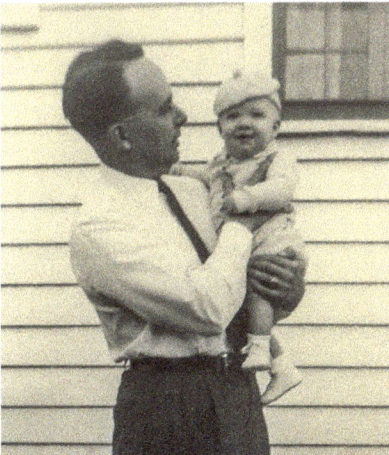

De and son Michael, 1944.

The end of the war in 1945 ushered in the "greatest period of sustained economic growth" in US history, a period that saw the nation's gross domestic product increase by 87 percent over the next ten years. Helping to fuel the dynamic postwar expansion was a massive building boom in the US housing industry. Residential construction had been largely moribund during the preceding decade and a half of depression and war, and, as a result, pent-up demand for housing was already "intense" by the end of the war when several million demobilized military veterans suddenly returned home from overseas, creating a housing shortage of "crisis proportions." By the end of 1945, "98 percent of American cities" were reporting shortages of housing.[13] To alleviate the crisis, the federal government established a series of loan programs through the Veterans Administration and the Federal Housing Administration enabling qualified borrowers to obtain government-backed, thirty-year mortgages at low (4.5 percent) interest rates, with tax-deductible interest payments. The availability of federal funds for home purchases immediately converted the housing shortage into a powerful building boom, with US housing starts "exploding" from 114,000 in 1944 to "a record 1.95 million" in 1950. Between 1946 and 1955, "nearly 15 million" new housing units were built in the United States, the majority of them single-family dwellings constructed in new suburban residential communities for the nation's steadily expanding white middle class.[14]

The postwar building boom proved to be a godsend for America's architects, and in Toledo Britsch & Munger reaped its share of the rewards. During the late 1940s, the firm designed and oversaw the construction of numerous upscale homes, along with twenty-five public school projects and two hospitals. It also began to expand its presence nationally, designing the American Legion organization's new seven-story national headquarters in Washington, DC, and the Legion's Indiana state headquarters building in Indianapolis. By 1950, the firm was growing rapidly, with a total staff of twenty-six architects, designers, engineers, draftsmen, and specifications writers.[15]

For De personally, the early postwar period was a time of significant accomplishments, professionally, economically, and socially. In 1946, at only 36 years of age, he was elevated to the position of "junior partner" in Britsch & Munger, with a partial ownership stake in the business and decision-making authority second only to that of Carl Britsch and Harold Munger, the firm's two founders and senior partners.[16] Five years later, in 1951, one of De's architectural housing designs won the American Architects Award for "Best New Residence in the State of Ohio." Built for Jules Jay Roskin, the owner of a Toledo metalworks company, and situated overlooking a picturesque ravine in Ottawa Hills, the strikingly contemporary redwood-and-glass structure incorporated many of the modernist design elements of Frank Lloyd Wright, the nation's most innovative twentieth-century architect—including an open floor plan, wood-paneled rooms with brass track lighting, an array of built-in seating and display features, and large, floor-to-ceiling windows that maximized exposure to the scenic natural environment outside.[17] That same year, De was elected to a two-year term as president of the Toledo chapter of the American Institute of Architects, the leading professional association of US architects.[18] By the early 1950s, he was clearly a rising star in his profession.

M. DeWitt Grow's award-winning 1951 house, 3921 Brookside Road, Ottawa Hills. (*Toledo Blade*, 20 July 1986, p. C-1, reproduced courtesy of the *Toledo Blade*)

Professional success was accompanied by an aggressive pursuit of upward social mobility. Throughout their marriage, De and Ethyl changed residences repeatedly, selling one house and buying a more expensive one in a relentless quest for more affluent living accommodations. In all, the couple owned seven different homes during their first fifteen years of marriage, frequently losing money as they "traded up" by selling their existing home before it had time to appreciate in value. In 1951, they realized a long-term dream by building a new home for themselves in Ottawa Hills, Toledo's "suburban mecca."[19] The house—at 2406 Hempstead Road—was a modest-sized, two-story, three-bedroom structure with a prominent bay window, located on a quiet, tree-lined street in a newer section of the village. In his floor plan for the house, De incorporated a fashionable new feature of American residential design: a small "television room" off the living room, dedicated exclusively to the viewing of a revolutionary new photo-electronic invention that would soon become the center of family life in middle-class households.[20] From De and Ethyl's standpoint, however, the most important feature of their new home was its high-status location in Ottawa Hills.

During this same period, De's earning power enabled the couple to indulge their increasingly extravagant taste for the status symbols of upper middle-class success. They purchased a cottage on a small, secluded lake a few miles north of Devil's Lake[21] and began spending their summers there, with De commuting on weekdays to his office in Toledo. They took annual winter vacations in Florida, flying on the commercial airlines that were revolutionizing postwar travel in the United States. And they became members of the Toledo Club, an exclusive private social organization whose membership included many of the city's most prominent elite families. Housed in an opulently furnished five-story mansion in downtown Toledo, the club was locally renowned for its elegant dining facilities featuring gourmet cuisine, white-gloved waiters, and silver finger-bowls for freshening club members' hands at the completion of their sumptuous multi-course meals.

Michael, Ethyl, and De at home, c. 1950.

By the early 1950s, De had achieved a notable record of success for a man of his age. Still in his early forties, he was a prosperous, award-winning architect and a junior partner in his firm, with a comfortable residence in Toledo's finest suburb and an affluent lifestyle filled with amenities, including membership in the city's most prestigious social club and a lakeside cottage in Michigan. His future, if anything, looked even brighter, with a senior partnership in Britsch & Munger, an even grander home in Ottawa Hills, and entree into the highest

De and son, Deep Lake, MI, c. 1950–1951.

circles of Toledo society well within his reach and seemingly only a matter of time. And then, in 1953, he deliberately threw it all away.

In July of 1953, in the midst of an apparent "midlife crisis" at age 43, De deserted his wife and 9-year-old son and headed west to begin a new life in California, accompanied by his 32-year-old married secretary at Britsch & Munger, Eva Modar, with whom he had been carrying on a secret extramarital affair. In a pattern strikingly reminiscent of his father's infidelity with a Woolson Spice Company coworker a generation earlier, a workplace romance in early middle age had changed his life forever.

The phenomenon known as a midlife crisis was a uniquely twentieth-century form of psychological stress that American males became susceptible to in middle age, starting around the age of 40. The jarring realization that their life was now half over, and the heightened awareness of their own mortality that came with it, triggered a natural impulse in many middle-aged men to take stock of their lives—to reassess the choices they had made and the paths they had followed that had led them to their current situations in life. That introspective process of midlife self-reappraisal could easily lead to psychologically unsettling pangs of regret over choices not made and paths not taken, over opportunities missed and alternatives ignored, over careers not pursued, lifestyles not experienced, "women not bedded." In some middle-aged men, those feelings of regret eventually reached the level of a psychological crisis—a "midlife crisis"—that left them depressed and discontented with the realities of their lives. For men in the grip of such a crisis, it was not unusual to feel trapped—trapped by the responsibilities of work and family, trapped in their assigned role as the family breadwinner, trapped in a life in which their sole purpose was to make money, a life devoted almost entirely to earning and acquiring and "keeping up with the Joneses." Increasingly preoccupied with thoughts of death, distressed by their declining vigor and other physical changes associated with middle age, bored with the monotonous routines of job and marriage, and secretly yearning for "something more" in life, something new and different, such men often daydreamed about liberating themselves from "the bondage of breadwinning" and fantasized about escaping their burdens of responsibility for a different kind of life, one filled with exciting new experiences and sexual adventures that would help them recapture their youthful vigor and ward off the anxieties of middle age. For most middle-aged men, such fantasies remained just that—fantasies and daydreams; and in the end, most men simply accepted their responsibilities and made peace with the choices they had made.[22] Some, however—including M. DeWitt Grow—instead chose to act on their fantasies by abandoning their families and careers and setting out on what they presumed would be a more personally fulfilling new path in life.

In De's case, the fact that his midlife crisis involved an extramarital affair with a younger woman is a strong indication that he was experiencing sexual and other frustrations within his marriage, although he later stated that he left Toledo in 1953 in part because "he didn't want to work all his life just to make money."[23] No longer motivated by the conventional goals of wealth and status, no longer sharing his wife's social ambitions, and apparently feeling deeply discontented and unfulfilled, he simply walked away from his established life to start a new life in the West, a region traditionally associated in the American mind with escape and new beginnings.[24] In doing so, he deliberately threw aside the traditional middle-class desire for respectability that had shaped male behavior in the family line for generations, opting instead to embark on what writer Norman Mailer has characterized as an "uncharted journey into the rebellious imperatives of the self."[25]

Traveling by automobile, De and Eva headed first to Reno, Nevada, "the divorce capital of the United States," where the local courts were notorious for granting divorce decrees on the flimsiest of legal grounds and with "assembly-line" speed and efficiency.[26] There, De quickly terminated his marriage with Ethyl on grounds of "cruelty." The compliant divorce judge also granted him an exceptionally favorable financial settlement that required him to pay Ethyl a mere $100 a month in child support and no alimony. Eva divorced her husband at the same time, also on grounds of "cruelty." As soon as their divorce papers were finalized, De and Eva married.[27]

M. DeWitt Grow, c. 1952.

Back in Toledo, meanwhile, Ethyl—blindsided and shattered by her husband's unexpected abandonment—struggled financially to maintain a comfortable standard of living for herself and her son. The cottage in Michigan was soon sold to make ends meet, and in 1958, unable to keep up her mortgage payments, she was forced to sell the Ottawa Hills house and relocate to a rented duplex apartment in West Toledo. Desperate for income, and with a well-developed eye for fashion, she obtained a job as a saleswoman in the Florence Shop, a small, upscale women's clothing store, where she worked for the next two decades before retiring in the late 1970s. In retirement, she lived entirely on her small monthly Social Security benefits, eventually moving to a rent-subsidized basement apartment in a blue-collar neighborhood on Toledo's north side. She lived there until 1984, when heart problems forced her into a Waterville, Ohio, nursing home, where she died of a "cerebral vascular accident," complicated by Alzheimer's disease, three years later, at age 79.[28] She was buried in Swanton, Ohio,[29] her birthplace, next to the grave of her father-in-law, Martin Grow.

Like most middle-class women of her generation, Ethyl had aspired to a comfortable life as the stay-at-home wife of a successful professional man.[30] With De, she succeeded in reaching that goal. When her marriage suddenly fell apart after eighteen years, however, she had few marketable skills to fall back on, and for the sake of survival was forced to work a low-paying, commission-based job in retail sales until she was in her early seventies and physically unable to continue working. After attaining a life of affluence and local social prominence as De's wife, she spent the final three decades of her life in reduced and melancholy circumstances.

The next quarter-century of De's life was a period of lessened ambitions, smaller accomplishments, and additional failed marriages. Following their wedding, De and Eva remained in Reno, where De obtained part-time employment with a local architecture firm, Ferris and Erskine.[31] In January 1955, he became the partner of long-established Reno architect David Vhay, forming the small firm of Vhay and Grow.[32] An ugly dispute with other local architects over De's proposal to streamline the construction of Reno school buildings by utilizing a single uniform design eventually led to the revocation of his Nevada state architect's license, however, and by the early 1960s, he and Eva had moved to Sacramento, California, where they initially led a threadbare existence living in a mobile home.[33] In 1963, De joined the Sacramento architecture firm of Dreyfuss & Blackford—at the time "the largest and most progressive architectural office in California's Central Valley"[34]—as a senior staff member. The salary was "average" and his duties were non-creative, consisting primarily of administration, public relations, and the overseeing of specifications, but as the firm's oldest employee, he also served as a mentor to its young architects and engineers, and he found the youthful atmosphere enjoyable.[35]

By the mid-1960s, De's marriage to Eva had soured. Alienated by her "nagging," he divorced her in May 1967, and she angrily retaliated by obtaining a punitive settlement that imposed heavy monthly alimony payments on him.[36] The following year, in August 1968, De married Marilyn Russell, a secretary at Dreyfuss & Blackford, with whom he had been having an affair. Over the course of their six-year marriage, De became increasingly "brooding" and emotionally withdrawn. According to Marilyn, he also drank "quite a bit,"

Dreyfuss & Blackford staff, c. 1974–1975; De is in back row, center.

routinely consuming two or more martinis before dinner and wine with dinner, followed by an after-dinner drink. "After four ounces of gin," she later recalled, he would often become argumentative and "pick fights."

In the early 1970s, he also began to encounter problems at work. By then in his mid-sixties, he occasionally found his competence being called into question at Dreyfuss & Blackford, an experience that left him with bitter feelings toward the firm. During that same period, he designed and built—largely with his own hands—a modest retirement house for himself and Marilyn overlooking a high valley of the Sierra Nevada mountains near Pine Grove, California, some 55 miles east of Sacramento. Increasingly reclusive, he informed Marilyn that all he now wanted was "to be left in peace," and insisted that they have no visitors or telephones in the house. When he started to become increasingly domineering and condescending toward her, Marilyn eventually divorced him in July 1974.[37]

Two years later, in 1976, De retired from Dreyfuss & Blackford at the age of 66. The final years of his life were spent in isolation and declining health in his mountaintop home in Pine Grove. He occupied his time painting pictures—a lifelong avocation—until 1978–1979, when he suffered a significant loss of eyesight due to macular degeneration. In 1981, finding him ill, nearly blind, and lonely, Marilyn returned to take care of him. She moved out again in 1988, when advancing age and illness (Guillain-Barré syndrome, Meniere's disease) accentuated the domineering, "cranky" aspects of his personality (leading to occasional outbursts of mild physical abuse of Marilyn). Before departing, she arranged for a caretaker to look in on him two to three times each week.

Three years later, on 11 July 1991, alone, deaf, and virtually blind, De suffered a cerebral hemorrhage. Three days elapsed before the caretaker discovered him. He died six weeks later, on 26 August 1991, in a Sacramento hospital, at age 81.[38] His body was cremated and his ashes scattered in the Sacramento Memorial Lawn and Crematory's "Rose Scattering Garden."[39]

Those who knew M. DeWitt Grow personally described him as "a fine gentleman," "very intelligent," and "charming," with "a fine mind and a great sense of humor"—"the finest man I've ever known," in the words of a former brother-in-law (Dale B. Henly of Toledo). His third wife, Marilyn, remembered him as "a sensitive, artistic man who cried easily." But she also described him as "very closed" and reluctant to talk about his inner feelings or his past. He was "very good at blocking out memories and experiences," she later recalled, but he also "suffered a great deal of internal anguish over the decisions of his life." Friends observed that he seemed to have "so much contained emotion" bottled up inside himself.[40] His paintings, which were largely derivative of such major twentieth-century American artists as Edward Hopper and Andrew Wyeth, frequently conveyed an empty, dark mood—a reflection, presumably, of his otherwise-unexpressed inner emotions.

Left: "War" and *Right:* "Peace" c. 1969, by M. DeWitt Grow.

In his religious values, De was spiritually adrift but retained vestigial traces of the family line's traditional Protestant values. According to Marilyn, he was not interested in any organized religion or church, but "had his own way of looking at the spiritual aspects of life"—a personal philosophy that he claimed to have come to in his twenties, based on "how you treat your fellow man." He was interested in reincarnation, dabbled briefly in Christian Science, and read the Bible from cover to cover at the age of 74 (with the aid of a magnifying glass because of his failing eyesight).[41] In 1988, he told his son: "At the time of my departure from Toledo, and in intervening years, I was, and have been, aware of a direction and guidance that I cannot explain, nor do I attempt to. Karma? I do not know."[42]

In midlife, after two decades of conventional success and achievement, he rejected financial gain and social status as motivating drives. Ultimately, however, his life was shaped to a large extent by another increasingly powerful core element of the twentieth-century American value system: the pursuit of self-gratification—a narcissistic impulse that elevated personal happiness and self-indulgence to a higher plane of importance than spiritual or family values.[43] His cultural models included the path-breaking twentieth-century architect Frank Lloyd Wright, whose libertine lifestyle and abandonment of wife and children openly defied the conventions of his day,[44] and author Ayn Rand, whose 1943 novel, *The Fountainhead*,[45] glorified creative, self-centered individualism as personified by its lead character, architect Howard Roark. When later asked how he could have abandoned his wife and young child in 1953 without making adequate provision for their future well-being, De replied: "You're telling me I didn't have a right to make a happy life for myself."[46]

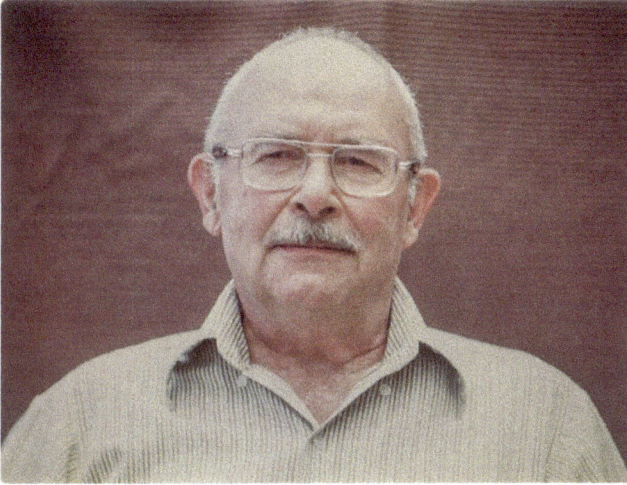

M. DeWitt Grow, 1980.

MICHAEL ROBERT GROW (1944–   )

Like his father, Michael[10] Grow (*Martin DeWitt*[9], *Martin*[8], *DeWitt*[7], *Thomas*[6], *Elisha*[5], *Thomas*[4], *Thomas*[3], *Thomas*[2], *John*[1]) grew up in an environment of upper-middle-class privilege. The only child of a prominent Toledo, Ohio, architect and a stay-at-home mother, he was raised in Ottawa Hills, Toledo's wealthiest, most exclusive suburb—a quiet, safe, beautifully manicured community where he roamed freely on his bicycle playing with children from similarly affluent families. Summers were spent at his parents' cottage on Deep Lake in the Irish Hills of Michigan, where he enjoyed a bucolic three months each year swimming, fishing, and immersing himself in nature. Every winter he and his parents escaped the snow and freezing temperatures of northern Ohio by flying south to Florida for a two-week vacation in the sun. His cultural-enrichment activities included private piano lessons beginning at age 5, and he participated in his first public recital when he was 6.

In US middle-class society of the late 1940s, a good education was considered so vital to a child's future prospects that many parents made key decisions about where to live and work based on the relative quality of the schools in their communities. Growing up in Ottawa Hills, Michael benefited from the best education that money could buy. By the time he entered kindergarten, the village's high property values and correspondingly high property taxes, combined with the residents' insistence on rigorous pedagogical standards, had produced an extremely well-funded school system with a reputation for "academic superiority"—a system in which "almost every teacher" held an advanced degree and virtually every graduating student went on to college. From the mid-twentieth century onward, in fact, the Ottawa Hills school system was consistently ranked among the best—and in some years as *the* best—in the state of Ohio.[1] In Michael's case, the elementary school's heavy emphasis on reading and writing imbued him with skills that would serve him particularly well later in life.

This relatively idyllic early phase of his life came to an abrupt and traumatic end in July 1953, shortly after his ninth birthday, when his father deserted the family and left Toledo for the West Coast accompanied by a young female secretary from work (see Generation Nine). A "quickie" divorce in Reno

Michael Grow childhood photos, *at left,* c. 1948; *at right,* Deep Lake, MI, c. 1951–1952. (All photographs in this chapter from the author's family photograph collection.)

imposed minimal child-support obligations and no alimony payments on his father, leaving Michael's mother struggling to maintain a decent middle-class standard of living for herself and her son. As a result, she was soon forced to begin selling off her tangible assets. By the time Michael was preparing to enter high school in 1958, the summer cottage and the Ottawa Hills house had both been sold, and he and his mother were living in dramatically reduced circumstances in Toledo—first in a rented duplex, then in a small, nondescript house in a crowded lower-middle-class neighborhood.

Consequently, after nine years of excellent teachers, small classes, and outstanding facilities in Ottawa Hills, Michael was suddenly thrust into a large, 3,000-student Toledo public high school (DeVilbiss) with teachers of varying abilities and students from a wide range of socioeconomic backgrounds. After four years of mediocre education and relatively mediocre grades—and with a diverse mix of friends, including college-bound "preppies," working-class "hoods," and popular "jocks"—he graduated in 1962.

By the early 1960s, a college degree had become a virtual prerequisite for white-collar employment and a middle-class lifestyle in the United States. Michael's high school record and S.A.T. college-aptitude test scores gained him admission to the University of Wisconsin-Madison, a major midwestern university with strong undergraduate programs in journalism and political science, fields of particular interest to him at the time. But his mother's modest income as a salesclerk in a women's clothing store was insufficient to cover his out-of-state tuition and living expenses. Fathers in the family line had customarily provided their sons with the essential resources they needed to succeed as adults: farmland in the eighteenth and nineteenth centuries,

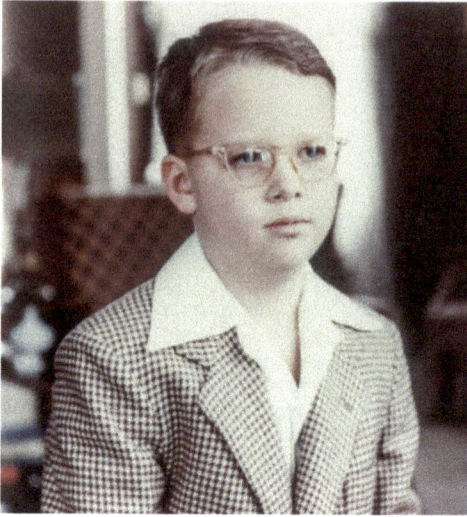

Michael Grow, c. 1954–1955.

Michael Grow, 1962 high school
yearbook photograph.

education in the twentieth century. When Michael's father abandoned his family, however, he essentially left his son to sink or swim on his own, and facing the distinct possibility of downward social mobility out of the ranks of the middle class if he was unable to obtain a college education. To spare him that fate, an older family member two generations removed suddenly and unexpectedly came to Michael's aid. In 1962, his wealthy great-aunt Florence (Grow) Dumond of Bay City, Michigan, the sister of his deceased grandfather Martin Grow, volunteered to pay his tuition through four years of college. In effect, a generous and supportive relative from the eighth generation of the family line stepped forward to fulfill the parental responsibilities abdicated by an irresponsible ninth generation by providing the upcoming tenth generation—Michael—with his essential start in life.

His four undergraduate years at Wisconsin were in many respects a stereotypical 1960s college experience. Initially his academic performance was substandard—a result of weak high school preparation, membership in a hard-drinking fraternity at a university known for its "party school" social atmosphere, and the university's rigid general-education requirements, which at the time channeled freshmen and sophomores into introductory courses emphasizing generalized theories and abstract concepts that many 18- and 19-year-old students lacked the life experiences to fully grasp. His writing ability nevertheless enabled him to keep his head above water academically, especially in journalism classes. By his junior year, Michael was allowed to take more specialized upper-level courses in subjects that interested him—literature courses, history courses, and political science courses, many of them focusing on Latin America, a subject area that he was finding increasingly interesting in the aftermath of the 1959 Cuban Revolution, the 1961 Bay of Pigs invasion, the 1962 Cuban Missile Crisis, and the 1965 US intervention in the Dominican Republic—and his grades immediately improved dramatically.

Michael Grow and Linda Cox at Phi Sigma Kappa
fraternity party, University of Wisconsin, c. 1964.

Michael completed his undergraduate studies in June 1966, graduating with a Bachelor's degree in journalism. Two months later, at age 22, he married his high school sweetheart, Linda Cox, also 22, who had grown up in a middle-class neighborhood of West Toledo, the daughter of a local Sun Oil Company office manager and his schoolteacher wife.

The period from 1966 to 1968 was a remarkably turbulent one in US history. A decade-long struggle by African Americans to achieve full civil rights and escape endemic poverty had given rise to widespread rioting and street violence in the nation's cities. Meanwhile, an ill-advised US military intervention in Vietnam was generating massive student protests on American college campuses, particularly after the US government began drafting large numbers of young men into the armed forces to sustain the war effort. At the same time, a cultural "generation gap" was creating rising tensions in American families, with many young Americans in their teens and twenties challenging what they regarded as the conformist, money-driven values, "uptight" morals, conservative politics, and racist attitudes of their parents and elders.

Facing uncertain job prospects and the near certainty that he would soon be drafted into the armed forces, Michael decided to remain in Madison and

Michael and Linda at Commencement, University of Wisconsin, 1966.

Grow-Cox wedding party, Toledo, Ohio, 20 August 1966.

seek admission to graduate school. Several factors lay behind the decision. First and foremost was the fact that graduate students at the time received automatic deferments from the military draft. In addition, however, it was only during his final two undergraduate years that Michael had begun to blossom academically, and he felt a strong desire to further his intellectual development by taking graduate-level coursework. And finally, Madison, Wisconsin, was a delightful place to live—a physically beautiful, intellectually stimulating, socially vibrant Big Ten college town that offered a comfortable refuge from an increasingly turbulent and chaotic outside world.

With an undergraduate degree in journalism, Michael's obvious choice for a graduate field of study was a Master's degree program in the School of Journalism. He was rapidly losing interest in a journalism career, however, finding the field intellectually shallow—"an inch deep and a mile wide," as he described it. Instead, his interests had gravitated toward international relations, and specifically Latin American studies. Shortly before graduating in June 1966, he had stopped by the office of the university's interdisciplinary Latin American Studies Program to inquire about his prospects for admission to its Master's program. The timing could not have been more fortuitous. By the mid-1960s, the US government was pouring money into foreign-language and area-studies programs at major universities in an effort to increase the nation's expertise in international affairs and bolster US national security in the Cold War. Meanwhile, private philanthropic organizations such as the Ford and Rockefeller foundations were augmenting those efforts with large-scale funding of their own.[2] Consequently, although Michael's cumulative undergraduate grade point average was less than impressive due to his poor grades as a freshman and sophomore, the director of Wisconsin's well-endowed and rapidly expanding Latin American Studies Program immediately admitted him to its M.A. program with a Ford Foundation fellowship for intensive summer language training in Spanish.

The next two years were enjoyable, productive, and challenging. The newlywed couple lived on Linda's salary as an eighth-grade science teacher at a Madison junior high school, supplemented by a $5,000 wedding present from Michael's great-aunt and benefactor Florence (Grow) Dumond, and by Michael's earnings as a part-time writer for the Wisconsin State Historical Society magazine. It was during that period that radical anti-war demonstrations began to seriously disrupt life on the Wisconsin campus. In April 1967, when Michael arrived at the Law School building for a job interview with visiting US Central Intelligence Agency recruiters, he was given a police escort to the interview room down a long corridor lined with hostile protestors screaming that he was a "goddamned murderer." That October, leaving Bascom Hall after a graduate seminar on landholding patterns in nineteenth-century Argentina, he found himself in the middle of a full-scale riot outside the neighboring

Commerce Building as helmeted Madison police battled several hundred students protesting the on-campus recruiting activities of the Dow Chemical Company, the manufacturer of napalm, a lethal incendiary that was being used by the US military in Vietnam.[3]

By the time he completed his M.A. in 1968, Michael had been hired as a research analyst at the Defense Intelligence Agency (DIA) of the US Department of Defense in Washington, DC. Arriving in the nation's capital in mid-June, he and Linda found the city filled with tension. An outburst of rioting in the aftermath of Martin Luther King's assassination in April had reduced large expanses of its Northeast section to smoldering rubble. Then in May, a "Poor People's March on Washington" had brought some 50,000 southern blacks to the city to demonstrate on behalf of economic justice for the poor, and they had set up a sprawling temporary shantytown on the National Mall that police and National Guardsmen removed with force at the end of June. Eight months earlier, 100,000 angry demonstrators had poured into the capital for the first in a long series of massive and increasingly violent anti-Vietnam War protests. For Michael and Linda, their initial exposure to Washington—the excitement of visiting the White House, the Capitol, and the city's imposing monuments and museums in person, the powerful sense of history, the "vibe" of revolutionary tension in the air—was an exhilarating experience.

The thrill soon wore off. Michael's work responsibilities at DIA turned out to be intellectually unchallenging. As the Uruguay/Paraguay desk analyst in the agency's Western Hemisphere/Latin America branch, he spent his work days maintaining DIA data files on the personnel, weaponry, and military capabilities of two of South America's smallest and least significant armed forces; briefing out-going US military attachés; and monitoring classified message traffic transmitted by DIA, CIA, and State Department representatives in Montevideo and Asunción. His status as a civilian employee of a conservative, military-run intelligence agency quickly proved to be psychologically stifling. And DIA immediately alienated most of the young men in its fifty-member 1968 recruiting class by informing them that it would not attempt to procure draft deferments for them—forcing most of them, Michael included, to hurriedly enlist in local Army Reserve or National Guard units in order to avoid the draft and the strong likelihood of military service in Vietnam. In Michael's case, he enlisted in the District of Columbia Air National Guard, spent six months of 1969 on active duty in the Air Force beginning with eight weeks of basic training at Lackland Air Force Base in San Antonio, Texas, and then returned to DC to serve as a "weekend warrior" in the unit's intelligence wing at Andrews Air Force Base outside Washington. During his time in the Air National Guard, he and his fellow airmen received extensive riot-control training for the suppression of anti-war demonstrations in the capital—a particularly ironic activity considering that he and most of the other Guardsmen in his unit personally sympathized with the protestors' cause. In November 1969 and May 1970, in fact, Michael and Linda themselves participated in anti-war marches around the White House.

They also found the overall quality of life in metropolitan Washington unsatisfying. Although Michael's starting salary at DIA—$8,054—was above the 1968 median US household income of $7,700,[4] and although Linda quickly obtained full-time employment as a laboratory technician in the Microbiology Department of the George Washington University School of Medicine, the high cost of living left them struggling financially on a tight, no-frills budget. Priced out of the area's inflated real estate market, they had no option but to rent a series of high-priced townhouses and small homes in the northern Virginia suburbs of Alexandria and Arlington, 6 to 8 miles outside the city. As a result, after a hellish daily commute and a long workweek, they seldom had the energy to partake of DC's many cultural attractions, even if they could have afforded tickets to concerts at the Kennedy Center for the Performing Arts or professional sporting events at RFK Stadium. Nor was Washington itself an entirely attractive model city. Its crime rate had begun to soar in the aftermath of the King assassination, and by 1969, the city was setting all-time records for homicides, rapes, and robberies.[5] Although neither Michael nor Linda was ever directly impacted personally by violent crime, the incessant daily media reports of murders, sexual assaults, muggings, multiple-fatality accidents, etc., gradually had a deleterious effect on their psyches, making them increasingly cautious and fearful and suspicious of strangers. For a young couple planning to have children, the Washington area seemed a less-than-ideal environment in which to raise a family.

Accordingly, in 1970, after less than two years in the nation's capital, they began formulating a plan to leave. Desperately missing the college town ambiance of Madison, they decided to seek a similar academic environment in which to work and start a family. According to their plan, Michael would enter a PhD program and attempt to become a college professor—employment that would provide prestige, a decent salary, intellectual creativity, personal freedom, and the opportunity to escape the dispiriting urban environment of Washington, DC, with its high cost of living, crime, racial tension, and long commutes, for a quieter, less stressful, more enjoyable life in a small college town where real estate was affordable and children could grow up safely. It took them thirteen years to achieve their goal.

In September 1970, Michael resigned from DIA and enrolled in a doctoral program in Latin American history at George Washington University. His choice of universities was an easy one, because at the time the couple lacked the financial resources to relocate from Washington, and Linda's job in the GWU Microbiology Department provided tuition benefits for employees' spouses, making Michael's pursuit of a PhD financially feasible.

His doctorate took more than six years to complete. History Department graduate fellowships provided additional financial support, and to further augment their income Michael took a variety of part-time teaching positions—as a history instructor at Northern Virginia Community College's Annandale campus and as a summer school lecturer at George Washington—slowing his academic progress but enabling him to acquire valuable teaching experience. After completing his doctoral field examinations in 1974, he embarked on his dissertation research project, a study of US-Paraguayan relations during World War II (a topic to which he had been attracted by wartime US military attaché reports on Nazi German influence in Paraguay that he had found in his files as the Paraguay desk analyst at DIA). After a year of research in US diplomatic and intelligence records at the National Archives, followed by a year of writing, he successfully defended his dissertation in 1976, and officially graduated the following year.

Unfortunately for the couple's plans, a completed PhD did not guarantee a college teaching position. Michael could not have picked a worse time to enter the academic employment market. The quarter-century from 1945 to 1970 had been a time of tremendous growth in US higher education—a "golden age" of booming undergraduate enrollments and faculty hiring. Fueled by the GI Bill in the 1950s and by a flood of "baby boomers" in the 1960s, college enrollments exploded from less than 1.5 million on the eve of World War II to 2.7 million in 1950, to 3.6 million in 1960, to over 7.9 million in 1970. As the nation's institutions of higher learning expanded to accommodate the growing tidal wave of undergraduates, they were faced with an increasingly severe shortage of qualified faculty. The existing pipeline of PhD production that supplied colleges and universities with their professors was inadequate to the task, and higher education responded with "a massive proliferation of doctoral programs nationally," as a result of which the number of doctorates awarded in the United States rose from less than 6,500 in 1950 to more than 11,000 in 1960, to nearly 30,000 by 1970. Supply nevertheless continued to lag demand, and by the mid-1960s "a new PhD from a major university" could still expect to receive "three or four tenure-track job offers."[6]

That golden age came to an end in the early 1970s, just as Michael was beginning his doctoral studies. Two decades of academic overexpansion, falling enrollments resulting from the nation's declining, post-"baby boom" birthrate, reductions in federal funding for higher education, and a severe downturn in the national economy, forced the nation's colleges and universities to retrench. By 1975–1976, student enrollments were declining by 175,000 annually, and—although Michael had no way of knowing it at the time—a fifteen-year faculty-hiring boom had become a thing of the past. Michael's discipline of history was particularly hard hit. During the 1960s, in response to market demand, the number of history doctoral programs in the United States had grown from 80 to 120, while the number of history doctorates conferred more than doubled. Consequently, by the time the hiring boom ended, the nation's history faculties were already saturated with young, tenured professors, leaving little prospect of vacancies for years to come—at precisely the time when an accelerating flow of newly minted history PhDs was entering the teaching market. By the time Michael completed his doctorate, the academic employment market in history had virtually dried up and the discipline was facing a job crisis of unprecedented proportions. In 1976–1977, there were barely 700 history teaching positions available nationwide for 1,200 newly graduated history PhDs and an enormous backlog of earlier doctoral recipients who had not yet found academic employment. In the staple fields of American and European history, it was not unusual for a single tenure-track faculty vacancy to attract 500 to 600 qualified applicants, and as a result droves of young history PhDs were being forced in desperation to search for alternative sources of employment.[7] In such a glutted and ultra-competitive environment, job candidates from Ivy League and other elite doctoral programs almost invariably had a competitive advantage; and to make matters worse, by the mid-1970s academic deans around the country were under intensifying pressure to increase their faculty diversity by hiring qualified women and minorities whenever possible. For Michael, as a white male with a doctorate from a non-elite, second-tier history department that wielded little influence in the academic marketplace, the odds were stacked heavily against him.

By the time Michael completed his PhD in 1976–1977, he and Linda were facing steadily mounting financial pressures. The 1970s had brought an end to a quarter-century of post-World War II growth and prosperity in the US economy, ushering in a painful new period of economic belt-tightening for most Americans. Massive federal spending on "Great Society" domestic programs and a war in southeast Asia, combined with a crippling energy crisis beginning in 1973, pushed the US economy into its worst downturn since the Great Depression, with stagnant wages, rising unemployment, and inflation rates that skyrocketed from 1 percent in 1964 to 12 percent in 1974, before peaking at over 13 percent in 1979.[8] In metropolitan Washington the cost of living soared, with average rents alone rising 88 percent during the 1970s.[9] Linda continued to work full-time at George Washington University, but her modest salary as a lab technician failed to keep pace with inflation, while the income that Michael was able to bring in from part-time teaching, supplemented by a series of temporary part-time research jobs in DC, did little to improve their financial situation.

Then, once again, Michael's great-aunt Florence (Grow) Dumond came to the rescue—this time literally from the grave. In September 1977, ten months after her death at age 88, Michael learned that she had bequeathed him more than $80,000 in her will.[10] The stunning inheritance came at a particularly crucial moment for the couple, because it enabled them to continue to persevere in pursuing their dream of an academic life in a college town environment. And for a couple now approaching their mid-thirties, it also provided the financial resources they needed to finally start a family before it was biologically too late. As a result, two children were born soon thereafter—a son, Nathaniel, in 1979 and a daughter, Sarah, in 1982. For a fourth consecutive generation—thanks to the ever-wider availability of effective birth control devices (by the 1960s in the form of a revolutionary new oral contraceptive known as "the pill")—the family line had produced two or fewer offspring, consistent with the national average.[11]

Children of MICHAEL[10] AND LINDA (COX) GROW:

i.   Nathaniel[11], b. 11 Oct. 1979, Arlington, VA; m. 2011, Athens, GA, Lara Wagner; currently an associate professor of business law, Kelly School of Business, Indiana University, Bloomington.

Children of Nathaniel and Lara (Wagner) Grow:

a.   *Violet Linda*, b. 18 June 2013, Athens, GA.

b.   *Henry Livingston*, b. 17 Aug. 2017, Bloomington, IN.

ii. Sarah Dumond, b. 7 May 1982, Arlington, VA; currently residing in Athens County, OH.

Children of Sarah Dumond Grow:

a.   *Garak Michael Grubb*, b. 1 Aug. 2009, Van Wert, OH.

b.   *Kira Jean Grubb*, b. 23 Aug. 2011, Van Wert, OH.

Meanwhile, a pivotal career opportunity had unexpectedly come Michael's way in mid-1977. Among his various part-time jobs, he had worked for two years as a research assistant at the Woodrow Wilson International Center for Scholars, a prestigious research center housed in the original Smithsonian Institution building (the red brick "Castle") on the National Mall. Each year, after a rigorous international competition, the Wilson Center awarded between 80 and 100 fellowships to US and foreign scholars in the humanities and social sciences, with the recipients spending a period of four months to a year in residence at the Center working on a major research project. A research assistant, usually a graduate student like Michael from a local DC university, was assigned to each of the visiting scholars to provide up to twenty hours per week of research support. The Wilson Center had recently begun to publish a book series of *Scholars' Guides to Washington, D.C.* that surveyed the wealth of resources available in the nation's capital for research on various regions of the world. A first volume, on Russia and the Soviet Union, had appeared in 1977, and the Center was seeking an author for the next scheduled volume in the series, on Latin America and the Caribbean, to be published under the auspices of the Center's newly created Latin American Program. Michael proved to be the proverbial "right person in the right place at the right time." The founding director of the Latin American Program, Abraham F. Lowenthal, an internationally prominent political scientist from Harvard University, awarded Michael the book contract along with a $9,000 stipend, and Michael then spent all of 1978 producing a manuscript. The resulting *Scholars' Guide to Washington, D.C. for Latin American and Caribbean Studies* was published by the Smithsonian Institution Press in 1979 and received wide praise within the international Latin American Studies community. Michael now had a major credential to add to his résumé.

Favorably impressed by the quality of Michael's work on the *Scholars' Guide* project, Lowenthal then added him to his staff as coordinator of the Latin American Program's "Working Papers" series, with the responsibility for editing and overseeing the printing and distribution of research papers produced by program fellows at the end of their periods in residence at the Center. The position was once again part-time in nature, providing no health insurance or retirement benefits, but it integrated Michael more fully into the Wilson Center's high-powered intellectual world, which included weekly "sherry hours" for fellows and staff, research presentations by fellows and invited speakers, and opulent dinners for visiting dignitaries. As a result, he attended events alongside prominent US politicians and media figures—Barry Goldwater, George McGovern, and Gloria Steinem, among others—personally met several Latin American heads of state,[12] and made numerous influential contacts in the field of Latin American studies. Such firsthand exposure to US intellectual life at its highest level created lasting memories (as did the frequent experience of driving home at night up Constitution Avenue past the dramatically lit White House, Washington Monument, and Lincoln Memorial after late-evening events at the "Castle").

For the next four years, Michael coordinated the Latin American Program's "Working Papers" series, taught part-time at George Washington, and applied for college teaching positions to no avail. As the teaching-vacancy rejection letters piled up and the quality of life in metropolitan Washington continued to deteriorate, he and Linda began to despair of ever leaving the area. In 1982, Michael's new parental responsibilities finally forced him to abandon the dream of an academic life and begin a search for stable full-time employment with health insurance and retirement benefits. Drawing on his DC influence networks, he soon secured job offers for two full-time positions: one as a Latin American research analyst in the US State Department's Bureau of Intelligence and Research at an annual salary of over $40,000, the other as publications coordinator for a new Center-wide "Working Papers" series at the Wilson Center at $30,000 a year. Then, late in the year, as he waited for the State

Department to complete a nine-month security background investigation of him—and he and Linda debated the relative merits of the two job offers—a new academic vacancy suddenly appeared: a joint appointment as associate professor of Latin American history and director of the interdisciplinary Latin American Studies Program at Ohio University in the rural southeastern Ohio college town of Athens. Having essentially given up on his dream of an academic career, Michael nevertheless decided to "give it one last shot."

His credentials, as it turned out, matched the specifications of the joint vacancy almost perfectly. Under the visionary leadership of Professor John Gaddis, one of the nation's preeminent diplomatic historians and a leading authority on US foreign policy in the Cold War, the Ohio University history department was at the time actively building up a core of faculty expertise in twentieth-century history with an emphasis on post-World War II international history; and Gaddis' efforts had recently secured a $500,000 John D. and Catherine T. MacArthur Foundation grant to establish a Contemporary History Institute at the university that would train graduate students to analyze current national and world events in the context of long-range historical patterns and trends. Michael's doctoral training and research interests meshed well with those initiatives. It also helped that his dissertation had been published the previous year by the Regents Press of Kansas, and by 1982 the resulting book—*The Good Neighbor Policy and Authoritarianism in Paraguay: U.S. Economic Expansion and Great-Power Rivalry in Latin America during World War II*—was receiving laudatory reviews in influential scholarly journals.[13] In addition, his *Scholars' Guide* book and his extensive exposure to the operations of the Wilson Center's high-powered Latin American Program had equipped him with at least rudimentary qualifications for running an interdisciplinary Latin American Studies program. Consequently, he was interviewed by Ohio University history department representatives at the American Historical Association convention in Washington, DC, in late December, brought to Athens for on-campus interviews and a research presentation the following February, and offered the job shortly thereafter. Although the starting salary of $26,000 was substantially lower than what he would have earned at the State Department or the Wilson Center, he and Linda unhesitatingly leaped at the opportunity to escape metropolitan Washington for the college-town lifestyle they had struggled for thirteen years to attain. Their hard work and perseverance had finally paid off.

Life in Athens was everything the couple had dreamed of. After seventeen years of marriage, they were now finally able to purchase their first home—a charming one-and-a-half-story, five-bedroom hillside house on five acres, with a large stone chimney in front and a rear fieldstone patio overlooking a heavily wooded ravine and small stream, less than a mile from the university campus. Athens itself was a classic midwestern college town, with a strikingly beautiful campus, brick streets, quaint stores, and friendly people. Crime was so uncommon that the residents seldom bothered to lock their doors. And between the town and the university, there were more enrichment activities available for the children than Michael and Linda could possibly fit into their schedules.

Campus life at the university featured the full range of events that Michael and Linda had been hungering for since leaving Madison: major college sports, annual homecoming parades led by the university marching band, an annual film festival and performing arts series, outdoor summer band concerts "under the elms" on the main campus green, and more. Professionally, the couple's first year at the university exceeded their expectations. Prior to leaving DC, Linda had completed a doctorate in biology at George Washington,[14] and in early 1984 Ohio University's Department of Zoological and Biomedical Science offered her a part-time appointment as an assistant research professor with an opportunity to teach introductory biology courses in the future. Michael, meanwhile, had made a sufficiently favorable impression in the Department of History that after one year on the faculty his new colleagues voted unanimously to award him tenure. All things considered, he and Linda could not have found themselves in a more ideal situation.

And then, a year after they arrived in Athens, tragedy struck. In late summer of 1984, Linda was diagnosed with breast cancer, one of the leading medical scourges of the twentieth century. By the time it was diagnosed, the cancer cells had metastasized to her liver, and despite six months of chemotherapy treatments at the Ohio State University Hospital in Columbus, she died on 27 January 1985, at only 40 years of age. Her death left Michael in a state of numbed grief, with two small children, ages five and two-and-a-half, to raise alone.

The next four years were an exhausting blur of work and childcare. As a single parent, Michael's highest priority was to assure that his children grew up psychologically healthy and emotionally unscarred by their mother's premature death. Accordingly, he quickly stepped down from his position as director of the university's Latin American Studies Program to devote more time to their upbringing. He also revamped his scholarly research agenda by conceiving a new book project—an analysis of Cold War US interventionism in Latin America—that could be based largely on secondary literature and not require extensive archival or field research that would take him away from Athens and his children for extended periods of time.

The enervating challenges of single-parenthood came to an end in 1989, when Michael married Catherine (Carbone) Russell,[15] a beautiful 40-year-old widow pursuing a PhD in the university's English Department. Childless from her first marriage to a much older man, Catherine quickly made the selfless

Nathaniel, Michael, and Sarah Grow, 1986.

Michael Grow, 1987.

decision to abandon her pursuit of a doctorate in order to devote full-time attention to helping raise Michael's children (although later, after the children grew older, she eventually joined the university faculty as an instructor in the English Department and Women's Studies Program).

In all, Michael spent twenty-two years on the Ohio University faculty. A popular professor, he quickly built up enrollments in the History Department's Latin American history survey courses from 15 students per course at the time of his arrival on the faculty in 1983 to nearly 100 a decade and a half later. He also taught undergraduate surveys and graduate seminars on the history of US-Latin American relations and a graduate seminar on authoritarianism in Latin America. In addition, as a member of the History Department's graduate faculty, he directed eight Master's degree thesis projects and four PhD dissertations. In 2001, he was appointed director of the university's Contemporary History Institute (CHI), the interdisciplinary graduate training center founded by John Gaddis in the early 1980s. Under Michael's leadership, the institute's visibility was elevated significantly, both on campus and nationally. A steady stream of prominent historians, political scientists, economists, and journalists visited CHI as invited speakers,[16] while annual conferences on major topics of contemporary significance—"Democracy in Post-Soviet Russia," "US Energy Consumption and the Environment," "The United States and Global Hegemony," "US Intelligence, Terrorism, and Homeland Security"—brought high-level public figures, including former US Secretary of the Interior Bruce Babbitt, Carter administration National Security Adviser Zbigniew Brzezinski, and former director of the Central Intelligence Agency James Woolsey, to campus as keynote speakers.

Grow-Russell wedding ceremony in the living room of Michael's home, Athens, Ohio, 6 August 1989, with Athens Mayor Sara Hendricker, an Ohio University colleague of Michael's from the Political Science faculty, presiding.

Four years later, burned out at age 61, he opted for early retirement—a financially attractive arrangement that enabled him to retire on a full pension with the opportunity to teach one academic quarter per year for an additional one-third of his final full-time salary on top of his pension. For the next two years, 2006–2007, his reduced early-retirement teaching load afforded him the time to finally complete his third book—*U.S. Presidents and Latin American Interventions: Pursuing Regime Change in the Cold War*—which was published by the University Press of Kansas in 2008, the capstone of a successful scholarly career.

Michael had faced a variety of hurdles in his pursuit of success. First, his abandonment by his father at age 9 had seriously jeopardized his prospects for a comfortable middle-class life. Then, in his mid-twenties, the national economy entered a long period of low growth, high inflation, and increasingly unequal income distribution that further lengthened the odds against him. By the 1980s, incomes were rising for the top tier of the US labor force—its highly educated managerial and professional sectors, including college professors—

Michael Grow in the classroom, Ohio University, c. 2004–2005.

while remaining stagnant for the bottom two-thirds. In addition, as social scientist Robert J. Gordon has noted, "the *composition* of jobs" was changing, "with more jobs created at the top and bottom of the occupational distribution and a hollowing out of the middle." In effect, the middle class had begun to shrink, with more and more of its members "slipping down the economic scale, or barely clinging to middle-class living standards," while the upper and upper-middle classes continued to prosper. Most middle-class families now found themselves in an increasingly precarious situation as they struggled financially in the face of eroding incomes, high mortgage interest rates, and rapidly rising tuitions for their college-age children. As a result, middle-class wives began entering the labor force in record numbers to provide the second incomes that their families desperately needed to maintain a middle-class standard of living. All of those trends remained prevalent into the twenty-first century.[17]

In 1982, Michael was 38 years old, with a wife, two children, and no full-time job. Thanks in large part to three key women in his life, however—a hardworking mother, a generous great-aunt, and a hardworking wife—he had been able to acquire the educational and other credentials that eventually enabled him to gain entry into his chosen profession, as a college professor. When he retired in 2005, he was earning $80,000 a year, a salary that ranked in the top 24 percent of household incomes (including dual incomes) in the United States[18] and was nearly double the 2005 median national income.[19] That

Michael Grow, director of the Contemporary History Institute, introducing former US Secretary of the Interior Bruce Babbitt at CHI conference, Memorial Auditorium, Ohio University, April 2003.

same year, his house in Athens had a market value of $255,000, some $42,000 (or almost 20 percent) above the average selling price of US homes in 2005.[20] Despite early hardships, a difficult economic environment, and many years of struggle, he had secured a position in the upper middle class,[21] continuing a long, uninterrupted tradition in the family line.

Michael was able to retire with a level of economic security unknown to previous generations. Prior to the twentieth century, most men continued to work until they were no longer physically able to do so, at which point they and their wives became dependent on their children (or local charities) for support in old age. By the early twentieth century, families had grown smaller and more geographically dispersed, and adult children consequently became a less reliable source of care for elderly parents. As a result, with government welfare programs and private pension plans virtually nonexistent, a large percentage of the nation's senior citizens lived out their lives in poverty. Then, in 1935, passage of the New Deal's Social Security Act dramatically improved the living conditions of the elderly by establishing "a nationwide old-age pension system" through which employed workers regularly contributed a portion of their paychecks and then received a "guaranteed and secure" government pension after they retired. Social Security in turn stimulated the widespread growth of "defined-benefit pension plans" for employees of private corporations and public-sector organizations, including state universities. Consequently, when Michael retired, he and Catherine could rely on a secure retirement income and old-age protection in the form of a full pension from Ohio University supplemented by monthly Social Security payments; and as soon as they turned 65 they became eligible for government-provided Medicare health insurance as well.[22]

In addition, in the late 1970s, Michael had invested $4,000 of his $80,000 inheritance from Florence (Grow) Dumond in an innovative new tax-deferred savings instrument known as an "individual retirement account" (or IRA), and by 2005, after systematically reinvesting the accrued capital gains and dividends each year for a quarter century, the value of his IRA had increased to $100,000, providing the couple with an additional cushion of financial support in retirement.

Michael's retirement was influenced by his late great-aunt in another way as well. During his childhood visits to her Bay City home in the early 1950s, she had introduced him to George W. Davis' Grow family genealogy *John Grow of Ipswich/John (Groo) Grow of Oxford*, and the book quickly instilled in him a lifelong desire to know more about the lives of his ancestors. Coming of age in the 1960s, many members of Michael's generation found life in America's secular, money-driven consumer society relatively meaningless and spiritually empty, and their search for meaning in their individual lives led them in widely differing directions. Some turned to consciousness-expanding psychedelic drugs, and some to "New Age" mysticism, Zen Buddhism, or other exotic forms of spiritual enlightenment; some dedicated themselves to the pursuit of "psychological growth" and personal self-improvement through meditation, vegetarianism, yoga, or physical fitness; and some involved themselves in the vast array of secular voluntary associations (political, environmental, etc.) that purported to provide meaning in life by working to improve the world. Others, like Michael, found meaning in "the search for ancestral roots" and the study of their family's history.[23]

In the summer of 1996, curious to see if any traces of his eighteenth- and early-nineteenth-century Connecticut ancestors still existed, Michael and Catherine spent a one-week vacation in Windham County. There, using an old map and other information from the Davis genealogy, they managed to locate the family's former Grow Hill farm and c. 1740s farmhouse, the Grow Hill Burying Ground where some fifteen members of the family lie buried, and—a few miles to the north—the ancient graves of Thomas (1684–1753) and Rebecca (1688–1762) Grow. They immediately fell in love with the area. In the late twentieth century, Windham County still retained much of its historical character, with a picturesque rural landscape of rolling hills, unpolluted brooks and streams, and third-growth forests dotted with working farms, quaint villages, historic houses, and countless miles of old, lichen-covered stone walls. Known as Connecticut's "Quiet Corner," the county remained so unspoiled by urbanization and development that in nighttime satellite photographs it appeared as a small but conspicuous oasis of darkness within the heavily illuminated East Coast "megalopolis" that stretched from Boston to Washington, DC.[24] Returning to Ohio after their initial visit, Michael and Catherine began formulating plans to eventually relocate to the Pomfret-Hampton area in retirement.

During brief follow-up visits over the next several summers, they actively explored Windham County's real estate market, and in July 2001, they purchased a small, c. 1810 historic home in Scotland, a thinly populated rural town 11 miles south of Grow Hill. Situated on 2.5 acres, with a mill stream (Merrick Brook) on one side and meadows on two others, the house retained many of its original features, including a brick fireplace in the living room, wide-plank wood floors, several interior doors with original hardware, and a dry stone, dirt-floor basement. Known locally as "the Mill House," it had originally been built as a residence for the manager of early gristmills and sawmills on Merrick Brook. Throughout much of the year, the only visible neighboring house was an eighteenth-century farmhouse several hundred yards away, while around the corner was the 1734 Reverend Ebenezer Devotion house, the home of an influential Scotland minister. The town green, featuring a general store, a post office, and an 1842 Congregational Church, was a ten-minute walk away.[25] On Sunday mornings, the church bells played traditional hymns that were heard throughout the town.

When the couple purchased the property in 2001, Michael had only recently begun his appointment as director of Ohio University's Contemporary History Institute, and he was not yet in a financial position to take early retirement. Consequently, he and Catherine returned to Ohio and rented out their Connecticut house for the next four years as absentee landlords. Then, in the summer of 2005, they sold their home in Athens and relocated to Scotland. That fall, Michael returned to the university to complete his remaining administrative and teaching duties as a full-time faculty member, and subsequently returned again in 2006 and 2007 to teach single ten-week terms as an early retiree. By 2008, the couple had paid off their Scotland mortgage and completed the extensive renovations that the Mill House required. As a result, Michael was now able to fully retire from the university and settle permanently into his home in Connecticut. Nearly 200 years and five generations after Elisha and Lois Grow sold their Abington farm and migrated west to the New York frontier, the family line had returned to Windham County.

During their Connecticut retirement, Michael and Catherine immersed themselves in the history and culture of New England. Decorating their historic

The Mill House, 39 Gager Hill Road, Scotland, Connecticut.

Yankee redux: Catherine and Michael Grow, in the Mill House living room, Christmas 2006.

home with period furnishings, they were soon drawn into the rarified world of the region's antiques collectors, attending high-end shows and auctions and forming personal friendships with prominent dealers. They became members of the Hampton, Connecticut, Cemetery Association and served as caretakers of the Grow Hill Burying Ground, keeping the cemetery clean and straightening its weathered gravestones. They traveled throughout New England exploring areas where Grow ancestors had lived and conducting family history research in a wide variety of repositories, including the Peabody Essex Museum's Phillips Library in Salem, Massachusetts, and the New England Historic Genealogical Society library in Boston. And then, after ten years of research, Michael wrote this book.[26]

The small, uninscribed gravestone marking the location where Linda (Cox) Grow's cremated remains are buried (and where Michael and Catherine Grow's ashes will eventually be placed), Grow Hill Burying Ground, Hampton, Connecticut (see Appendix D, number 7). The flag-decorated headstone to the immediate right marks the grave of revolutionary war soldier Ebenezer Grow (1755–1827).

CONCLUSION

The Grows were by no means an important or distinguished family historically. Over a span of ten generations and three and a half centuries, they produced no major political or military leaders, no wealthy business tycoons or pioneering scientists, no famous artists or popular celebrities.[1] And yet in at least two respects, the family's history reflects the very core of the American experience.

What is perhaps most striking about these ten generations of Grows is the consistency with which they lived their lives in the mainstream of American history. Generation after generation, the family's lifestyle and living conditions typified the prevailing trends of the times. The economic environment that largely shaped their lives changed profoundly over the centuries as America passed through its successive stages of historical development, but the Grow family repeatedly adapted to that changing environment by moving into new occupations that continued to position it firmly within the socioeconomic mainstream.

Like most families in the long "frontier-rural" phase of American development stretching from initial colonization to the late nineteenth century, the first six generations of Grows were farmers.[2] The first of those six generations—John Grow of Ipswich, Massachusetts—was a seaman and weaver rather than a farmer *per se,* but he and his wife and children were closely tied to the soil nonetheless. Ipswich and other early New England coastal settlements developed landholding patterns based on various combinations of traditional English open-field and enclosed-field models, with the local inhabitants living clustered together in a densely populated central village and extracting food and other essential resources from the surrounding countryside, substantial portions of which—in the form of planting fields, livestock pastures, hay meadows, and woodlands—were held "in common" for communal use by the community's eligible property owners. John Grow, as a typical Ipswich artisan and "commoner," owned a dwelling house in town, raised sheep on Ipswich's common pastures, and harvested agricultural and other resources from both the local public domain and scattered parcels of land that he owned on the outskirts of town. Like other Ipswich artisans, he was both an artisan and a small farmer.[3]

By the 1700s, these early landholding patterns had largely broken down in the face of population growth and competition for land, as enterprising townsmen acquired their communities' remaining common lands and took up residence in the outlying countryside as yeoman farmers.[4] The first five generations of John and Hannah Grow's descendants—like the overwhelming majority of Americans during the frontier-rural period—were independent family farmers who lived and worked on their own privately owned farms, farms that over some two centuries became increasingly integrated into America's expanding commercial-agricultural market economy.

A central dynamic of the frontier-rural period was pioneer migration. From the start, two of colonial America's most conspicuous features—the colonists' astonishingly high birth rates and an abundance of "cheap and empty land"— provided the impetus for powerful impulses of territorial expansionism. As early as the mid-seventeenth century, population pressures were already creating land shortages in New England's early coastal towns, forcing younger residents to uproot themselves and move into the interior wilderness to found new agricultural settlements that would provide them with farms of their own. Over time, that process became a cyclically recurring pattern. As frontier farming settlements matured into stable communities, population growth eventually constricted the amount of available land, resulting in rising land prices and the inevitable out-migration of the younger generation to undeveloped new frontier areas farther inland. That ongoing process of pioneer migration deeper and deeper into the western interior of the North American continent continued uninterrupted for more than two centuries, until by the late nineteenth century there was no more frontier land available, effectively bringing the frontier-rural phase of American history to a close.[5]

The Grows were active—in fact, classic—participants in the pioneering process. Four of the first five generations of John[1] and Hannah Grow's descendants migrated to frontier areas in search of affordable farmland for themselves and their children. In 1710, John and Hannah's son Thomas[2] (1684–1753) moved 15 miles west from overcrowded Ipswich to the new frontier farming community of Andover, Massachusetts, where he became a farmer and maltster. Two decades later, he moved his family from increasingly overpopulated Andover to a newly opened agricultural frontier in northeastern Connecticut. Thomas' son Thomas[3] (1714–1806) was, like his parents, a Connecticut pioneer farmer, who later in life accompanied one of his sons to a new farming frontier in Vermont. Two generations later, in 1812, John and Hannah's great-grandson Elisha[5] (1779–1850) migrated from increasingly land-poor Connecticut to the recently founded frontier settlement of Homer, New York, and after a quarter-century there migrated westward again—this time via the Erie Canal—to a more promising new agricultural frontier in Oakland County, Michigan. Elisha's son Thomas[6] (1818–1902) accompanied his parents to the Michigan frontier, where he too became a pioneer farmer. When Thomas and his wife retired from active farming and moved off the land in 1873, their change of lifestyles essentially symbolized the end of the frontier-rural period in American history.

By the 1870s, agriculture was rapidly giving way to urban-based manufacturing and commerce as the foundation of the American economy, and the lives of the next two generations of the family mirrored that transformation. Both DeWitt[7] Grow (1850–1921) and his son Martin[8] Grow (1880–1942) were urban businessmen who forged careers in commercial sales, DeWitt as a retail clothing store proprietor and later a coal company executive, Martin as a sales manager for national firms in the food and automobile-service industries. In other ways as well, these two generations reflected the dramatic changes taking place in American society in the late nineteenth and early twentieth centuries. They lived most or all of their lives as city dwellers. In addition, exemplifying the sharp decline in US birth rates during this period, both produced families significantly smaller in size than those of their ancestors. Whereas the first six generations of the family line in America averaged ten children per generation, the first two post-frontier-rural generations produced two and one offspring respectively.

The subsequent two generations of the family were also representative types of their times. In the technologically complex and ruthlessly competitive twentieth-century US economy, in which advanced training and technical skills were essential prerequisites for success, the ninth and tenth generations of Grows carved out careers as college-educated professionals—Martin DeWitt[9] (1910–1991) as an architect, Michael[10] (1944–) as a university professor. Both of these twentieth-century generations also continued the post-frontier-rural trend of low birth rates and small families, producing one and two offspring respectively.

Along with their mainstream profiles, what is equally notable about these ten generations of Grows is the consistency with which, generation after generation, they occupied upper-middle-class positions in their local society. According to historian Walter Nugent, the foundational "core of American culture" has been a "white, Anglo-Protestant, middle class."[6] The Grows, historically, are quintessential examples of that middle class. Ten consecutive generations of the family have situated themselves firmly within its upper echelons—first as successful members of the "old" agrarian middle class of the frontier-rural period, and more recently as equally successful members of the "new" urban, white-collar middle class of the post-1870 period, a modern new middle class headed by an upper tier of salaried "managers and professionals and academics."[7] John[1] Grow (c. 1642–1727), presumably starting from humble origins, managed to attain a "middling"-level niche in early colonial society by marrying into an influential upper-middle-class Ipswich family. Thomas[2] Grow

(1684–1753) became a prosperous pioneer farmer and large landowner on the Pomfret, Connecticut, agricultural frontier. His son Thomas[3] (1714–1806) and grandson Thomas[4] (1743–1824) were prosperous farmers, local church leaders, and town officials in neighboring Hampton, Connecticut. Pioneer farmers Elisha[5] Grow (1779–1850) and his son Thomas[6] (1818–1902) both ranked in the top 10 percent of their rural Michigan communities as measured by property ownership and taxable wealth. DeWitt[7] Grow (1850–1921) was an affluent and locally prominent Bay City, Michigan, businessman. His son, Martin[8] Grow (1880–1942), was a prosperous Toledo, Ohio, sales executive prior to being ruined financially in the Great Depression. Martin DeWitt[9] Grow (1910–1991) was an award-winning Toledo architect. His son Michael[10] (1944–   ) was a tenured professor and institute director at an Ohio public university. In every generation, the family enjoyed an affluent or at least comfortable middle-class standard of living, status in its local community, and a position of respect and even prestige in local society. (The pattern persists in the twenty-first century: Michael's son, Nathaniel[11] [1979–   ], earned a law degree at the University of Michigan and currently holds a tenured faculty position as a professor of business law at Indiana University in Bloomington.)

One of the most powerful themes in US history is upward social mobility. A fundamental element of US national self-identity and a basic component of our historical self-image as a people is the belief that in America, unlike other areas of the world, economic abundance and open, unencumbered access to opportunity have traditionally enabled individuals from lower-class backgrounds to rise as high in society as their talents and capabilities will carry them—that individual members of American society, no matter how poor or low-born they may be, have, with hard work, talent, and ambition, regularly pulled themselves up by their own bootstraps to achieve a better life for themselves and their children.[8] Although that time-honored stereotype may well apply to John Grow, the longer-range history of his descendants suggests that an alternative narrative may in fact be equally central to American history. The Grows, historically, provide an example not of upward (or downward) mobility but of uninterrupted social continuity, as a representative American family that has successfully maintained a stable, consistent position in the upper ranks of the middle class through ten consecutive generations. A major social-science research project measuring social mobility in world history recently found that in the United States, England, and elsewhere the social status of individual families has changed remarkably slowly, if at all, over the last several centuries, and that continuity rather than mobility or change in social status has been the historical norm for most American families.[9] Grow family history supports those findings. It offers a case study of the ways in which one upper-middle-class family has, generation by generation, provided the resources—land, education, and monetary inheritances, combined, perhaps, with the power of parental example and parental expectations—that consistently enabled the next generation of the family line to secure its own niche in the upper middle class and perpetuate a comfortable position in the mainstream of American society from the seventeenth century to the present.

APPENDICES

Ipswich Commoners List of 1665

Single share

Hanniel Bosworth — 77	John Sparke Tho: Bishop 74	Nicolas Marrable
Thomas Smith — 60	Henry Archer mr Symons — 18	Currimarke
Caleb Kimbal — 49	Tho Wainte osgood — 72	Joseph Goodhue
Mark Quilter — 17	Edward Bridges — 80	John Ringe Bragg
John Lord & Kimbal 16	John Smith mr Appleton 95	Willm Searle —
John Brewer — 58	widdow Quilter — 34	Thomas Clarke —
John Denison — 91	Simon Stacey — 40	Samuel younglove jun
Robert Whitman — 33	Willm Gutterson — 50	Willm Mort Carche
Walter Roper — 7	Thomas French — 97	Philip Fowler
Georg Smith — 110	Joseph Whipple — 42	Robert Kingmanfor
Edward Chapman — 5	John Safford — 54	Willm Fellows
Robert Lord Jun — 27	Jeremy Belcher — 78	Thomas Whitred
Andrew Peters — 19	Samuel younglove sen — 26	Samuel Pod
Robert Collins — 43	Thomas Manning Nord — 62	Daniel
John Caldwell — 3	Samuel Ayres — 39	Ed Deer & hir mr
mr Rufsell — 31	Nathaniel Russ — 64	John Kinlfon
Joseph Brower — 67	Ezekiel woodward — 101	max yfiling & finalis
John Brown jun — 30	Joseph Reading — 41	Ed Neland
Robert Lord Junr 98	Samuel Hunt — 45	Jenny Hove
John Edwards in vincent 47	Willm Mott — 14	widdow and Wyatt
Michael Creg — 100	Willm Warner — 68	John Gaines — 1
John Gaines — 1	Daniel Hovey — 6	Jo Reinerath for Hinder
John Newman — 46	Thomas Emerson — 107	John Newman jun
Giles Birdley — 105	Isaiah Wood — 53	Neh: Abbot
Francis Jordan — 102	Robert Fitch — 8	Kinsmen Vefs Haymonds
Thomas Harris — 64	widdow Lea 106	John Hufoll
James Chute — 28	John Marshal Brelred 85	Daniel Hovey
Obadiah wood — 92	Willm Marshal Leet — 87	Tho: Clarke tanar
John Kendricke — 2	Thomas Stacey farmr 21	Ed Heard hath preflexed
Willm Burkley — 65	John Cogswell — 12	Avon Pengry
Sam: Taylor — 56	John Knolton — 15	Scot Church an de
Willm Hodkin 66	Samuel Ingals — 76	Joseph Fellows hath yet
Bennet Puleifer — 55	Thomas Loar jun — 35	John Gibbins
Thomas Lord — 82	Daniel Davison Hublord 69	Tho: Gibbins
Robert Dutch — 99	Alexander Templton whipple 29	Thomas Brewer
John Annable — 6	John Rofs Wardwel — 103	
Andrew Hodges — 32	Willm Reynur — 104	Liberty for freewood
Jacob Foster — 38	Abram Foster — 90	& one cow
Job Bishop w Appleton 79	Isark Foster — 57	John Knowlton
Samuel Graves — 52	Henry Batchelor — 13	Obadiah Bridges
John Wyatt — 51	Reinold Foster junr — 70	John Fenke
John Pindor — 37	Thomas Lurny — 86	John Pengry
John French — 25	John Choate the Bishop 88	Sam Burtton
Willm Wallis — 63	John Jerosill — 75	John Brown
Thomas Wilson — 48	Willm Whitred Jo Perkins 82	Steeven Crose

Detail.

SOURCE: "A List of Inhabitants that have shares in Plum Island, Castle Neck, and Hog Island . . . according to the Towne order the 14 of Feb: '64," document of 20 April 1665, original manuscript from the Ipswich Town Records, archive of the Office of the Town Clerk, Ipswich, MA. (Photograph by David Stone for the Ipswich Museum.)

John Grow's Mark (1686)

We whose Names are hereunderwritten, have found
by Experience; That since our Sheep have been Folded
we have not had that profit by them, as before they
were Folded. Therefore we are Unanimously minded
to Hire a Shepheard to keep our Sheep on Jeffries
Neck, having a little house there (which may be
easily procured) for the Shepheard to lodge in
in the Night time, which shepheard by using the
Sheep on the Neck to some place to be lodged a
Nights, may with no great Trouble bring them there
lying by them there in the little house, having
a Smal Dogg or two lying without the House wch
being Wakefull, will give notice to the shepherd
if any thing comes there to Molest the sheep &c
And We conceive our sheep may be preserved
by so doing. And much bettered in the Increasing
of Wool, without which, we cannot well subsist.

Thomas Boarman
Jacob Perkins
Thomas Dale
Thomas Lovell
John Newmarch
Hopkin Davis
Thomas Harris
John Annabell
Sam Pearce
John Edwards
Caleb Emerson
Thomas Lull
Edmund Dear
John Grow
James Day
John Numan
Thomas Newman
William Hobgkins
Jacob Hix
John Newmarch Senior
Benjaman Newman
Benjamin Pulsifer
Caleb Kimball
Jeremiah
William Morton
Samuel
Samuel
John Brown
Thomas Dennis
Joseph
Thomas Percy

We whose Names are hereunder written have found
by Experience that since our Sheep have been folded
we have not had that profit by them, as before they
were Folded. Therefore we are unanimously minded
to Hire a Shepheard to keep our Sheep on Jefferie's
Neck, having a little house there (which may be
easily procured) for this Shepheard to lodge in
in the Night time, which Shepheard by [??]ing the
Sheep on the Neck to some place to be lodged at
Nights, may with no great Trouble bring them there
lying by them there in the little house, having
a Smal Dogg or two lying without the House, wch[.]
being Wakefull, will give notice to the Shepheard
if any thing comes there to Molest the Sheep, etc,
and We conceive our Sheep may be preserved
by so doing, And much bettered in the Increasing
of Wool, without which, we cannot well Subsist.

Thomas Boarman
Jacob Perkins
Thomas Dow   Thomas Lovell Senr   John Newmarch jr.
Hopkin Davis   Thomas Jacob   John Newmarch sener [X]
Saml Pearce   John Harris   Beniamen Newman
Nath. Emerson ser.   John Annabell   Beniamin Pulsifer   Jacob perkins
                      Thomas Harris   Caleb Kimball   Mathew perkins
                      John Edwards   Jerimah Dow   Corp. Tho[.] Clarke
                      Thomas Lull   William Norton
                      Edmund Dear [X]   Samuell Smith
                      john grow [X]   Samuell Chapman
                      james day   John Browne
                      John numan   Samuell graves sener
                      Thomas Newman   Samuell graves junior [?]
                      william hobykins   Robert Lord jnior
                      Jacob Foster   Thomas Dennis
                                            Edward W. Nalland [X]
                                            Joseph Quilter
                                            Thomas fossey

X = mark

SOURCE: Petition to the Ipswich, Massachusetts selectmen, 12 April 1686, "Records of the Essex County Quarterly Courts, 1636–1694," Phillips Library, Peabody Essex Museum, Salem, MA, box 46, folder 69.

Book Collection of Thomas Grow
(1743–1824)

[*Note:* The following list of Thomas Grow's books is arranged alphabetically using the abbreviated spine-label titles (in quotes) by which they were identified in his probate records, followed by full citations where possible.]

"Appol for Baptists"—probably Abraham Booth, *An Apology for the Baptists, in which they are vindicated from the imputation of laying unwarranted stress on the ordinance of baptism; and against the charge of bigotry in refusing communion at the Lord's table to Paedobaptists* (1788), a 179-page pamphlet written by English clergyman Abraham Booth (1734–1806), one of the most widely read Baptist authors of his day.

"Backus History"—Isaac Backus, *A History of New England with Particular Reference to the Denomination of Christians Called Baptists* (1777 and later editions). Backus (1724–1806) was one of eighteenth-century New England's preeminent Baptist leaders. He visited the Grow Hill farm of Thomas Grow (1714–1806) on multiple occasions and personally ordained Thomas' son William Grow as a Baptist preacher in 1776.

"Backus Sermons"—possibly Charles Backus, *Five Discourses on the Truth and Inspiration of the Bible, Particularly Designed for the Benefit of Youth* (1797). Backus was the Congregational minister of Somers, Connecticut.

"Baldwin on Baptism"—Thomas Baldwin, *The Baptism of Believers Only, and the Particular Communion of the Baptist Churches, Explained and Vindicated*, 3 vols. (1806). Baldwin (1753–1825) was a minister of the Second Baptist Church of Boston.

"Baldwin's Letters" (4 copies)—Thomas Baldwin, *A Brief Account of the Late Revivals of Religion Among the Congregationalists and Baptists, in a Number of Towns in the New-England States . . . Extracted Chiefly from Letters . . .*(1799), a 16-page pamphlet.

"Baxter's Call"—Richard Baxter, *A Call to the Unconverted, To Turn and Live, and Accept of Mercy while Mercy May be Had, as Ever They Will Find Mercy in the Day of Their Extremity, From the Living God.* Baxter (1615–1691) was a prominent seventeenth-century English Puritan minister, evangelist, and religious reformer, whose work was widely read in New England in the second half of the eighteenth century.

"Benedict's History"—David Benedict, *A General History of the Baptist Denomination in America, and Other Parts of the World,* 2 vols. (1813), by the pastor of the Pawtucket, Rhode Island, Baptist Church.

"Bibles" (five copies).

"Christians Herald"—*The Christian Herald,* a bound collection of a biweekly religious journal popular among Protestant evangelicals of the early nineteenth century.

"Duty of Man"—possibly (1) Henry Venn, *The Complete Duty of Man* (1763), by an acclaimed English preacher, evangelical minister, and abolitionist whose book was "one of the most popular . . . devotional works of the Evangelical school"; (2) Richard Allestree, *The New Whole Duty of Man Containing the Faith as well as Practice of a Christian* (1777); or (3) Charles Atmore, *The Whole Duty of Man, or the Christian's companion, containing the most important truths of our Holy religion* (1763).

"Indian Wars"—probably (1) an early nineteenth-century edition of William Hubbard, *Narrative of the Indian Wars in New England* (1677), by a Puritan minister of seventeenth-century Ipswich, Massachusetts; or (2) Daniel Sanders, *History of the Indian Wars With the First Settlements of the United States, Particularly in New England* (1812) by the president of the University of Vermont, a work that aroused bitter criticism because of its strictures on colonial bigotry and cruelty to Native Americans.

"Laws of United States."

"Life of Joseph"—John MacGowan, *The Life of Joseph the Son of Israel, in Eight Books: Chiefly Designed to Allure Young Minds to a Love of the Sacred Scriptures* (1771 and later American editions). MacGowan (1726–1780) was a Scottish Baptist minister.

"Memoirs of S. Osburn"—*Memoirs of the Life of Mrs. Sarah Osborn: Who Died in Newport, Rhode Island, on the Second Day of August 1796, in the Eighty Third Year of Her Age/ by Samuel Hopkins, D.D., Pastor of the First Congregational Church in Newport* (1799, with a later 1814 edition). The collected writings of Sarah Osborn (1714–1796), an evangelical Christian woman who led an inter-denominational, interracial revival in Newport, Rhode Island, in the 1760s.

"Morse Geography"—Connecticut minister Jedidiah Morse's *The American Geography; or, a View of the Present Situation of the United States of America* (1789 and later editions).

"Pilgrim's Progress"—John Bunyan, *The Pilgrim's Progress from This World to That Which is to Come: Delivered Under the Similitude of a Dream,* the popular Christian allegory that ranked with the Bible as the most-read book in America from its initial publication in England in the late seventeenth century to the Civil War.

"Rowe's Letters"—probably Elizabeth Rowe, *Friendship in Death: In Twenty Letters from the Dead to the Living. To which are added Letters Moral and Entertaining in Prose and Verse* (1728, with numerous later editions), a work of fiction that offers epistolary words of advice and confessional tales by the dearly departed to their friends, relatives, and love interests. Rowe (1674–1737) was an English poet, essayist, and novelist who lived in rural seclusion after the premature death of her beloved husband in 1715. Her works were hugely popular in the eighteenth and early nineteenth centuries.

"Smith and Jones Hymns"—Elias Smith and Abner Jones, *Hymns, original and selected, for the use of Christians* (numerous early nineteenth-century New England editions).

"Smith's Life"—Elias Smith, *The Life, Conversion, Preaching, Travels, and Sufferings of Elias Smith* (1816, with a second edition published in 1840). Smith (1769–1846), a Baptist preacher and religious journalist, was strongly influenced in his youth by the preaching of Elder William Grow of the Grow Hill Baptist Church (see 1816 edition, pp. 32–34, 129–133). He was also a prolific composer of religious music, publishing at least fifteen hymnals between 1804 and 1817.

"Watson's Apology"—Richard Watson, (1) *An Apology for Christianity* or (2) *An Apology for the Bible* (first American editions 1796). Watson (1737–1816), an English Anglican clergyman and Professor of Divinity at Cambridge University, was considered a radical and an advocate of religious toleration. His two *Apologies* were direct rebuttals of the secular anti-Calvinist writings of Thomas Paine and Edward Gibbon.

"Watts Hymns"—one of the many compilations of the *Psalms, Hymns, and Spiritual Songs* of Rev. Isaac Watts (1674–1748), an English Puritan minister and prolific hymn composer whose work was influential among eighteenth-century religious revivalists and who was particularly popular among Americans of the revolutionary war period.

"3 Vol. Webster"—possibly Noah Webster, *A Grammatical Institute of the English Language . . . in three parts* (1783), one of Webster's earliest dictionaries.

"Whitfield Sermons" (2 copies)—*Eighteen Sermons preached by the late Rev. George Whitefield, A.M.*, the Great Awakening preacher (various American editions 1797–early nineteenth century).

"Williams Sermons" (2 copies)—Thomas Williams, *Sermons on Important Subjects* (1810). Williams (1779–1876) was a self-described "minister of the gospel."

Unspecified "old books & pamphlets."

SOURCE: Compiled from Distribution of Thomas Grow Estate, Thomas Grow Estate Papers (Hampton 1824), Windham Probate District file no. 1706, in Probate Estate Papers, Records of the Windham District Probate Court, Windham Probate District Packets, 1719–1880 (microfilm reel 1554), Connecticut State Library, Hartford.

Grow Hill Burials

Grow Hill Burying Ground
Carter Road
Hampton, Connecticut

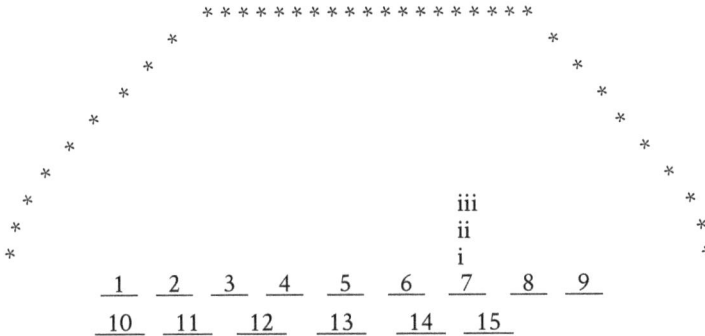

```
         * * * * * * * * * * * * * * * * *
      *                                 *
    *                                     *
  *                                         *
 *                                           *
*                                             *
*                                             *
*                  iii                        *
*                  ii                         *
*                  i                          *
     1   2   3   4   5   6   7   8   9
      10    11    12    13    14    15
```

1. Marcia Grow (1835–1857), daughter of Thomas Grow Jr.

2. Jerusha N. Grow (1798–1881), 2nd wife of Thomas Grow Jr.

3. Thomas Grow Jr. (1782–1852), son of Deacon Thomas Grow

4. Polly Grow (1798–1830), 1st wife of Thomas Grow Jr.

5. Samuel Minor Grow (1810–1811), son of Joseph Grow

6. Catherine Grow (1747–1829), wife of Ebenezer Grow

7. (i) Linda (Cox) Grow (1944–1985), (ii) Michael Grow (1944–),
   (iii) Catherine (Carbone Russell) Grow (1949–)
   [small unmarked gravestone, cremains burials]

8. Ebenezer Grow (1755–1827)

9. Joseph Grow (1787–1827), son of Deacon Thomas Grow, father of
   Galusha Grow

10. Experience Grow (1755–1835), 3rd wife of Deacon Thomas Grow

11. Deacon Thomas Grow (1743–1824)

12. Sarah Grow (1753–1819), 2nd wife of Deacon Thomas Grow

13. Experience Grow (1747–1811), 1st wife of Deacon Thomas Grow

14. Susanna Grow (1740–1749), sister of Deacon Thomas Grow

15. Timothy Grow (1751–1754), brother of Deacon Thomas Grow
    (unlocated grave) David Grow (1791–1846), son of Deacon Thomas
    Grow

ENDNOTES

PREFACE AND METHODOLOGY

1   See Francois Weil, *Family Trees: A History of Genealogy in America* (Cambridge, MA: Harvard University Press, 2013).

2   Historians are frequently criticized for failing to define their terms of analysis. As employed in *John Grow of Ipswich, Massachusetts and Some of His Descendants*, the term "middle class" refers to a combination of economic and social status distinctions based on factors of occupation, income, property ownership, standard of living, and respectability, which have historically differentiated the large intermediate stratum of the American population from a small, wealthy elite at the top of the social structure and a mass of manual workers and their families at the bottom, resulting in an intermediate stratum or middle sector that, more simply defined, is neither rich nor poor.

GENERATION ONE: JOHN GROW (c. 1642–1727)

1   Published records of the 1669 "Hackaliah Bridges v. Robert Peerce [*sic*]" court case can be found in George Francis Dow and Mary G. Thresher, eds., *Records and Files of the Quarterly Courts of Essex County, Massachusetts (1636–1692)*, 9 vols. (Salem, MA: Essex Institute, 1911–1975), vol. 4 (1667–1671): 194–195. A more complete transcription of those same records is available in a 57-volume set of bound typescripts in the collection of the Peabody Essex Museum's Phillips Library in Salem, MA: Archie N. Frost, ed., "Verbatim Transcriptions of the Records of the Quarterly Courts of Essex County, Massachusetts, 1636–1694" (Salem, MA: Works Progress Administration, 1936–1939), 15–34–5 to 15–37–4. The original seventeenth-century manuscript documents from Essex County Quarterly Court proceedings are also housed in the Phillips Library in Salem.

Use of the title "Master" in reference to a shipmaster was commonplace in the seventeenth-century English maritime vocabulary. See, for example, Bernard Bailyn, *The New England Merchants in the Seventeenth Century* (Cambridge, MA: Harvard University Press, 1955), 165.

In the seventeenth-century records, the surname "Pearce" was subject to a wide variety of alternate spellings, including "Pearse," "Peerse," "Peerce," "Peirce," "Perce," "Peres," and "Pers." "Pearce" is used herein because it appears to have been the spelling used by the family itself. (See, for example, the handwritten signature of Captain Robert Pearce's son Samuel on the 1686 Ipswich town petition reproduced in Appendix B). The commonly accepted modern spelling of the surname is "Pierce."

2   George W. Davis, *John Grow of Ipswich/John Groo (Grow) of Oxford* (Washington, D.C.: privately printed by the Carnahan Press, 1913; repr. Salem, MA: Higginson Book Company, n.d.), 5–7.

3   Frost, ed., "Verbatim Transcriptions of the Records of the Quarterly Courts of Essex County, Massachusetts," 15–37–2.

4   *Records and Files of the Quarterly Courts of Essex County, Massachusetts*, 4:422.

5   Quoted in Davis, *John Grow of Ipswich*, 13.

6   David Hackett Fischer, *Albion's Seed: Four British Folkways in America* (New York: Oxford University Press, 1989), 17; Virginia DeJohn Anderson, *New England's Generation: The Great Migration and the Formation of Society and Culture in the Seventeenth Century* (Cambridge, England: Cambridge University Press, 1991), 183; David Grayson Allen, "*Vacuum Domicilium*: The Social and Cultural Landscape of Seventeenth-Century New England," in Jonathan L. Fairbanks and Robert F. Trent, eds., *New England Begins: The Seventeenth Century* (Boston: Museum of Fine Arts, 1982), 2.

7   Davis, *John Grow of Ipswich*, 5–6; James Savage, *A Genealogical Dictionary of the First Settlers of New England*, 4 vols. (Boston: Little, Brown, 1860–1862; repr. Baltimore: Genealogical Publishing Company, 1969), II:321. According to Savage, John Grow's surname "seems much more likely to be Grove, but in the ancient form of writ. *u* for *v* it was, perhaps, pervert"—by which he meant that in sixteenth- and seventeenth-century English writing, the letter *v* was frequently represented as a *u*, resulting in the spelling of "Grove" as "Groue," and eventually, in the records of early Massachusetts Bay (where spelling was haphazard and largely based on phonetic transcriptions), as "Growe" and "Grow." Davis concurred, concluding that "it seems quite probable that John Grow of Ipswich, whether born in England, Ireland, Scotland, Salem, or Boston, substituted in his name, intentionally or otherwise, the letter *w* for *ve* in the true name, and that this spelling was afterwards persisted in by his descendants." Strengthening these early genealogists' hypotheses is compelling evidence that John Grow was illiterate and unable to write or spell his own name (see text). If, as seems likely, that supposition is correct, Essex County court clerks and Ipswich town officials would have entered his name in their records based on its oral pronunciation, resulting in spelling variations and ongoing uncertainty as to the "true" original surname.

8   Savage, *Genealogical Dictionary*, II:320; Richard S. Dunn, James Savage, and Laetitia Yeandle, eds., *The Journal of John Winthrop, 1630–1649* (Cambridge, MA: Harvard University Press, 1996), 750; Sidney Perley, *History of Salem, Massachusetts*, 3 vols. (Salem, MA: 1924–1928), I:183; Suffolk County Probate Records (1636–1894), Massachusetts State Archive, Dorchester, MA, Record Book 11, p. 53.

Circumstantial evidence invites speculation about a possible Edward Grove-John Grow father-son connection. Grove (?–1686) had extensive ties to the maritime culture of Massachusetts Bay. He was employed as a "sail-maker" in Boston and Salem, and married his first wife, Mary (1610–1683), in the latter port town. (Charles H. Pope, *The Pioneers of Massachusetts* [repr. Baltimore: Genealogical Publishing Company, 1969], 203; Perley, *History of Salem*, I:183, III:153n1; Clarence Torrey, *New England Marriages Prior to 1700* [Baltimore: Genealogical Publishing Company, 1992], 328) If he and his wife were close in age, he would have been in his early-to-mid-thirties—a peak age for male reproduction in seventeenth-century New England—at the time of John Grow's birth in 1642. His second wife, Elizabeth (Hollard) Brooking, was the widow of Grove's friend and possible business partner, "mariner" John Brooking of Boston. (*New England Historical and Genealogical Register*, vol. 63 [October 1909]: 381–383; Torrey, *New England Marriages Prior to 1700*, 328; Perley, *History of Salem*, III:153) Consequently, John Grow and Edward Grove shared a common occupational background in the Massachusetts Bay seafaring trades—Grove as a sailmaker with extensive roots in the colony's maritime community; Grow as a crew-member on an Ipswich-based sailing vessel that, as will be shown below, was active in commercial shipping along the Massachusetts coast. As the son of a Boston/Salem sailmaker, John Grow would have acquired both the skills and the contacts needed to obtain employment as a seaman. And growing up in Boston or Salem, the colony's two principal ports, he would have been advantageously positioned to do so.

Also potentially significant in that regard was John Grow's later transition from maritime employment to the occupation of weaver (also discussed below). It seems reasonable to speculate that Grow acquired knowledge of weaving prior to his transition from seafaring employment to the cloth-making trade. The fact that a portion of his testimony in the 1669 "Hackaliah Bridges v. Robert Peerce" court case centered on the ("rotten") condition of a mainsail suggests—not implausibly—that one of his functions as a member of Pearce's crew might have been to make or repair sails, activity that would have required knowledge of sewing and/or weaving. Such knowledge could have been gained through on-the-job training under Captain Pearce, or—equally plausibly—it might have been acquired while John Grow was growing up in the family of a father employed as a sailmaker.

Nonetheless, such conjectural analysis is seemingly contradicted by Edward Grove's will, which left his estate to his wife, his "Loving Daughter" Mary (Grove) Hirst, and Mary's son, Grove Hirst, and which fails to mention any other offspring. (Suffolk County Probate Records, Record Book 11, p. 53) According to Donald Deardorf, a senior research specialist on the staff of the New England Historic Genealogical Society in Boston, it would have been extremely unlikely in a seventeenth-century New England will for a father to fail to acknowledge a son, even if the two were estranged. (Personal communication to author, November 2010)

9   Davis, *John Grow of Ipswich*, 5–6; "International Genealogical Index," a data base compiled by the Church of Jesus Christ of Latter Day Saints and accessible online through its genealogical website familysearch .org; freereg.org, a British genealogical website that has extracted baptism, marriage, and burial records from English parishes back to 1538, accessible online at freereg.org.uk. A search of the freereg.org website produced the following names:

John Groue, christened 23 January 1642 in Saint Andrew, Droitwich, Worcestor; father: George Groue;

John Groue, christened 17 March 1643 in Wantage, Berkshire; father: William Groue; mother: Mary;

John Groue, christened 26 July 1643 in Saint Olave, Southwark, Surrey; father: John Groue;

John Groue, christened 22 October 1643 in Great Waldingfield, Suffolk; father: Thomas Groue;

John Grove, christened 22 August 1641 in Saints Giles, Cripplegate, London; father: John Grove;

John Grove, christened April 1642 in Rowley Regis, Staffordshire; father: Thomas Grove;

John Grove, christened 3 December 1643 in Claverley, Shropshire; father: Humphrey Grove.

10 Daniel Vickers, *Young Men and the Sea: Yankee Seafarers in the Age of Sail* (New Haven: Yale University Press, 2005), 52–56; Peter Wilson Coldham, *The Complete Book of Emigrants, 1607–1660* (Baltimore: Genealogical Publishing Company, 1987), x; David Cressy, *Coming Over: Migration and Communication between England and New England in the Seventeenth Century* (Cambridge, England: Cambridge University Press, 1987), 16, 50–51, 69, 142, 253–257; Harold A. Innis, *The Cod Fisheries: The History of an International Economy* (New Haven, CT: Yale University Press, 1940), 100, 103; Daniel Vickers, *Farmers and Fishermen: Two Centuries of Work in Essex County, Massachusetts, 1630–1850* (Chapel Hill: University of North Carolina Press, 1994), 129–133; Christine Leigh Heyrmann, *Commerce and Culture: The Maritime Communities of Colonial Massachusetts, 1690–1750* (New York: W. W. Norton, 1984), 212–213; Allan Kulikoff, *From English Peasants to Colonial American Farmers* (Chapel Hill: University of North Carolina Press, 2000), 64–65.

Thirty-one percent of immigrants arriving in Salem, MA in the 1650s were seamen; during the 1660s that figure increased to 40 percent. (Christine Alice Young, *From "Good Order" to Glorious Revolution: Salem, Massachusetts, 1628–1689* [Ann Arbor, MI: UMI Research Press, 1980], 71)

If John Grow was born in England, he conceivably could have traveled to America at a surprisingly young age. It was not uncommon in seventeenth-century English maritime culture for boys aged 15 years and younger to ship out as crewmembers on fishing boats and commercial vessels. (See, for example, Innis, *The Cod Fisheries*, 69; Heyrmann, *Commerce and Culture*, 255; Paul J. Lindholdt, ed., *John Josselyn, Colonial Traveler: A Critical Edition of Two Voyages to New-England* [Hanover, NH: University Press of New England, 1988], 146) Young boys sometimes "bound" themselves to sailors as apprentices for four years in order to learn "the art and mystery of navigation and of a mariner." (William B. Weeden, *Economic and Social History of New England, 1620–1789* [Boston: Houghton, Mifflin, 1890], 259) It should also be noted that by the late 1640s English sponsors were transporting groups of "poor children" to New England to work as indentured servants in colonial households. (Cressy, *Coming Over*, 57–58)

11 Cressy, *Coming Over*, 50; David Grayson Allen, *In English Ways: The Movement of Societies and the Transfer of English Local Law and Custom to Massachusetts Bay in the Seventeenth* Century (Chapel Hill: University of North Carolina Press, 1981), 196–198, 203; Anthony Salerno, "The Social Background of Seventeenth-Century Emigration to America," *Journal of British Studies*, 19:1 (Autumn 1979): 33.

Puritan William Pierce was one of the leading English ship captains of the Great Migration. (Cressy, *Coming Over*, 163) Shipmaster Robert Pearce's brother John was a mariner in Boston (Savage, *Genealogical Dictionary*, III:428; Frank R. Holmes, comp., *Directory of the Ancestral Heads of New England Families, 1620–1700* [New York: American Historical Society, 1923; repr. Baltimore: Genealogical Publishing Company, 1964], clxxxviii). Several of Robert's sons also followed their father to sea. (Alison I. Vannah, "'Crochets of Division': Ipswich in New England, 1633–1679" [PhD dissertation, Brandeis University, 1999], 789, 1099)

12 Thomas Franklin Waters, *Ipswich in the Massachusetts Bay Colony*, 2 vols. (Ipswich, MA: Ipswich Historical Society, 1905, 1917), I:9–10, 61, 80; II:230; Allen, *In English Ways*, 119, 132–133; Vannah, "'Crochets of Division': Ipswich in New England, 1633–1679," 17–19, 182; Robert Tarule, *The Artisan of Ipswich: Craftsmanship and Community in Colonial New England* (Baltimore: Johns Hopkins University Press, 2004), 10, 61; Joseph B. Felt, *History of Ipswich, Essex, and Hamilton* (Cambridge, MA: C. Folsom, 1834; repr. Ipswich, MA: The Clamshell Press, 1966), 108.

13 Vannah, "'Crochets of Division': Ipswich in New England, 1633–1679," 237n10, 358–364. For the broader historical context of the Ipswich Company, see Vickers, *Young Men and the Sea*, 28–29.

14 Tarule, *Artisan of Ipswich*, 34, 58, 61; Allen, *In English Ways*, 119; Susan L. Norton, "Population Growth in Colonial America: A Study of Ipswich, Massachusetts," *Population Studies*, 25:3 (November 1971): 434–435; Waters, *Ipswich in the Massachusetts Bay Colony*, II:230–234; Henry W. Belknap, *Trades and Tradesmen of Essex County, Massachusetts, Chiefly of the Seventeenth Century* (Salem, MA: Essex Institute, 1929), 18, 36–38, 44; Vannah, "'Crochets of Division': Ipswich in New England, 1633–1679," 59, 396, 460–461, 785, 791. A superb overview of the development of maritime commerce in seventeenth-century Massachusetts Bay, with particular focus on the coasting trade, can be found in Vickers, *Young Men and the Sea*, chs. 1–2; also

see Darrett B. Rutman, "Governor Winthrop's Garden Crop: The Significance of Agriculture in the Early Commerce of Massachusetts Bay," in Alden T. Vaughan and Francis J. Bremer, eds., *Puritan New England: Essays on Religion, Society and Culture* (New York: St. Martin's Press, 1977), 155–171. Chapter three of Daniel Vickers' *Farmers and Fishermen* analyzes the economic dynamics of the county's seventeenth-century fishing industry. For the commercial linkages between local agricultural production and outside markets in Ipswich and other early Massachusetts Bay towns, see James E. McWilliams, *Building the Bay Colony: Local Economy and Culture in Early Massachusetts* (Charlottesville: University of Virginia Press, 2007), 17–20, 51–52, 54–56, 75–76, 82–83, 105–106, 111–112, 115, 134–137, 145–146, 150–162.

15   Tarule, *Artisan of Ipswich*, 61; Vannah, "'Crochets of Division': Ipswich in New England, 1633–1679," 788, 908; Waters, *Ipswich in the Massachusetts Bay Colony*, I:79–82, II:231–234; *Records and Files of the Quarterly Courts of Essex County, Massachusetts*, 4:221, 333; 5:7, 226, 288–289, 442; 6:67, 240; 7:177; 8:11, 164. Also see Vickers, *Young Men and the Sea*, 45–47. For their transportation services, Pearce and the town's other commercial shippers earned an estimated "£6 to £15 a month." (Vannah, "'Crochets of Division': Ipswich in New England, 1633–1679," 788) Ipswich shipmasters were frequently paid not in hard currency but in trade goods, which they bartered or retailed in local markets. Pearce, for example, was described as a "retailer of wine" in a 1673 document. (*Records and Files of the Quarterly Courts of Essex County, Massachusetts*, 5:223)

16   This overview of Ipswich's social origins is drawn from broader interpretations of early Massachusetts Bay social history in the following sources: Allen, *In English Ways*, 132, 202–203; Anderson, *New England's Generation*, 34–35; John Demos, *Entertaining Satan: Witchcraft and the Culture of Early New England* (New York: Oxford University Press, 1982), 84, 292; Joseph A. Conforti, *Imagining New England: Explorations of Regional Identity From the Pilgrims to the Mid-Twentieth Century* (Chapel Hill: University of North Carolina Press, 2001), 12–13; Fischer, *Albion's Seed*, 176–180. Also useful are T. H. Breen and Stephen Foster, "Moving to the New World: The Character of Early Massachusetts Immigration," *William and Mary Quarterly*, 30:2 (April 1973): 197–199; and Mildred Campbell, "Social Origins of Some Early Americans," in James Morton Smith, ed., *Seventeenth-Century America: Essays in Colonial History* (Chapel Hill: University of North Carolina Press, 1959), 65–76.

Several scholars have cautioned that the concept of "class"—because of its nineteenth- and twentieth-century Marxist connotations—can be misleading in a seventeenth-century context, and that the terms "rank" or "status" would have been much more readily understood by Englishmen of the period. (Mary Beth Norton, *Founding Mothers and Fathers: Gendered Power and the Forming of American Society* [New York: Knopf, 1996], 18; Demos, *Entertaining Satan*, 84)

David Hackett Fischer explains the transfer of hierarchical social values from England to Massachusetts Bay as follows: "the founders" came predominantly from "the middling strata" of East Anglian society, and although they "sought to eliminate extremes of rank from their society, they were far from being egalitarian. Most Massachusetts towns deliberately preserved inequalities of status and wealth within a narrow range . . . [M]ost communities deliberately attempted to preserve the system of social ranks which had existed within the small villages of East Anglia. The Kings, peers, great gentry, landless laborers and wandering poor were all outsiders to those little communities. Most actual members belonged to three ranks—the lesser gentry, yeomanry and cottagers. These people lived, worked and worshipped together in ways that were bound by ancient customs of stratification which had existed from 'tyme out of mind' in East Anglian communities." These traditional "social distinctions between . . . gentry, yeomen and laborers were reproduced in Massachusetts and maintained for many generations." (*Albion's Seed*, 177, 179)

17   The population estimate of 1,700 townspeople in 1669 is at best an educated guess based on demographic calculations for earlier and later years. According to Edward Perzel, the town had a population of "approximately 800 people" in 1641. ("The First Generation of Settlement in Colonial Ipswich, Massachusetts, 1633–1660" [PhD dissertation: Rutgers University, 1967], 121) Alison Vannah calculates that the population "doubled" between 1641/1642 and 1664/1665. ("'Crochets of Division': Ipswich in New England, 1633–1679," 584) And in Arlin Ginsburg's estimate: "By 1675 the town contained 400 houses, which at five persons per house would yield a population of 2,000." ("The Franchise in Seventeenth-Century Massachusetts: Ipswich," *William and Mary Quarterly*, 34:3 [July 1977]: 451) Consequently, a figure of 1,700 for 1669 would seem to be a reasonable extrapolation.

18   Vannah, "'Crochets of Division': Ipswich in New England, 1633–1679," 75–76n42, 189–198, 532–534, 583–584, 594n8, 877n4, 1037–1139; Perzel, "The First Generation of Settlement in Colonial Ipswich, Massachusetts, 1633–1660," ch. 5; Allen, *In English Ways*, 133–134, 136; Campbell, "Social Origins of Some Early Americans," 68; Tarule, *Artisan of Ipswich*, ch. 4; Waters, *Ipswich in the Massachusetts Bay Colony*, I:73–86, 505, II:210–211, 219–227; Cressy, *Coming Over*, 52–68.

19   Allen, *In English Ways*, 134, 136; Robert von Friedeburg, "Social and Geographic Mobility in the Old World and New World Communities: Earls Coln, Ipswich and Springfield, 1636–1685," *Journal of Social History*, 29:2 (Winter 1995): 382. Also see Vannah, "'Crochets of Division': Ipswich in New England, 1633–1679," 587.

20   Allen, *In English Ways*, 132, 136–138; Ginsburg, "The Franchise in Seventeenth-Century Massachusetts: Ipswich," 448; Waters, *Ipswich in the Massachusetts Bay Colony*, I:106. "In towns like Dedham and Ipswich," Robert Gildrie writes, "men of 'landed estates' enjoyed almost a monopoly of local power." (*Salem, Massachusetts, 1626-1683: A Covenant Community* [Charlottesville: University Press of Virginia, 1975], 58)

21   Fischer, *Albion's Seed*, 179; Vannah, "'Crochets of Division': Ipswich in New England, 1633–1679," 580–583; Waters, *Ipswich in the Massachusetts Bay Colony*, I:11; Campbell, "Social Origins of Some Early Americans," 68.

22   Vannah, "'Crochets of Division': Ipswich in New England, 1633–1679," 476, 620, 829, 831–833. Also see Waters, *Ipswich in the Massachusetts Bay Colony*, I:280; Demos, *Entertaining Satan*, 22; Stephen Innes, *Creating the Commonwealth: The Economic Culture of Puritan America* (New York: W. W. Norton, 1995), 101–103; James Axtell, *The School Upon a Hill: Education and Society in Colonial America* (New York: W. W. Norton, 1974), 159–160.

23   Anderson, *New England's Generation*, 166; Waters, *Ipswich in the Massachusetts Bay Colony*, I:110, 113–115, 118, II:1–9; Demos, *Entertaining Satan*, 19–20; Vannah, "'Crochets of Division': Ipswich in New England, 1633–1679," 206, 808–810, 817. Gary Nash writes: "A Puritan never entered his church without being reminded where he and each of his fellow-worshippers stood in the ranks of the community." (*Class and Society in Early America* [Englewood Cliffs, NJ: Prentice Hall, 1970], 6)

24   Vannah, "'Crochets of Division': Ipswich in New England, 1633–1679," 584, 1072.

25   Grow's wage rate of 2 shillings per day was calculated from a "Bill of Cost" submitted to the Essex County Quarterly Court by Robert Pearce as part of the 1669 "Hackaliah Bridges v. Robert Peerce" case. In the document, Pearce requested reimbursement of 12 shillings for expenses incurred in sending "two witnesses"— his employees John Grow and John Berry—to Salem for "3 days apeece" to testify on his behalf. (Frost [ed.], "Verbatim Transcriptions of the Records of the Quarterly Courts of Essex County, Massachusetts," 15–37-1) For average worker's wages in seventeenth-century New England, see Roger Thompson, *Divided We Stand: Watertown, Massachusetts, 1630–1680* (Amherst: University of Massachusetts Press, 2001), 230n45; David Freeman Hawke, *Everyday Life in Early America* (New York: Harper & Row, 1988), 152; Axtell, *The School Upon a Hill*, 119. According to Axtell, average daily wages of 2 shillings were "from 30 to 100 percent higher than the wages of contemporary English workmen"—a point of potential significance in explaining John Grow's presence in America.

26   Vickers, *Young Men and the Sea*, 37–41 and *Farmers and Fishermen*, 96–97, 138–140, 189; Charles E. Clark, *The Eastern Frontier: The Settlement of Northern New England, 1610–1763* (Hanover, NH: University Press of New England, 1983), 27–31, 34–35; Richard Godbeer, *Sexual Revolution in Early America* (Baltimore: Johns Hopkins University Press, 2002), 22–23; Lyle Koehler, *A Search for Power: The "Weaker Sex" in Seventeenth-Century New England* (Urbana: University of Illinois Press, 1980), 424, citing Cotton Mather, *The Religious Marriner* (Boston, 1700), 5, 15–18.

The fishing center at the Isles of Shoals, which John Grow presumably visited often as a crewman for Robert Pearce, had a particularly seamy reputation as a "lawless and squalid" place inhabited by a "motley population" of drunken, brawling fishermen and foul-mouthed fishwives. (Clark, *Eastern Frontier*, 32; John Jenness, *The Isles of Shoals: An Historic Sketch* [Boston: Houghton Mifflin, 1898], 138–142, 171–172, 175)

In 1650, the Massachusetts Bay General Court complained about the "many and great miscariages [being] committed by saylors." Four years earlier, Governor John Winthrop had written about an epidemic of venereal disease that was spreading through Boston from a local seaman. (Darrett B. Rutman, *Winthrop's Boston: A Portrait of a Puritan Town, 1630-1649* [New York: W. W. Norton, 1965], 242)

In Cotton Mather's opinion, the sea was "a School of Vice." (Koehler, *A Search for Power*, 242)

27   Waters, *Ipswich in the Massachusetts Bay Colony*, I:116, 286, II:70, 73–74; Vickers, *Young Men and the Sea*, 37-38; Vannah, "'Crochets of Division': Ipswich in New England, 1633–1679," 831; Frost, ed., "Verbatim Transcriptions of the Records of the Quarterly Courts of Essex County, Massachusetts," 52–112-1; Abraham Hammatt, comp., *The Hammatt Papers: Early Inhabitants of Ipswich, Massachusetts, 1633–1700* (Ipswich, 1899; repr. Baltimore: Genealogical Publishing Co., 1980), 38, 187.

28   Fischer, *Albion's Seed*, 88–89; *Records and Files of the Quarterly Courts of Essex County, Massachusetts*, 5: 143–147. Technically, Roe was convicted of the lesser crime of "unlawful familiarity," because the court, despite a mass of sordid testimony, could not produce the two eyewitnesses needed to legally convict her of adultery.

29   Vannah, "'Crochets of Division': Ipswich in New England, 1633–1679," 815–817, 824–826n16.

30   Frost, ed., "Verbatim Transcriptions of the Records of the Quarterly Courts of Essex County, Massachusetts," 19–98–3.

31   Vannah, "'Crochets of Division': Ipswich in New England, 1633–1679," 435–437. The connection between literacy and the use of marks in seventeenth-century New England remains murky. On deeds and wills, Vannah suggests, "a recognizable mark would do just as well as a signature" because the scribe who drew up the document—usually a local clerk or lawyer—had already written the names of the signatories on it, and those signatories only needed to add their marks to make the document official (the equivalent of initialing a modern document next to one's printed name). Petitions, on the other hand, did not include the names of the signatories prior to signing, and "would not be much good" without the signer's full name. As a result, illiterate petitioners—to fully identify themselves and legitimize their marks—needed a literate person to record their full names on the document next to their marks. (Ibid., 437)

32   Petition to the Ipswich, Massachusetts selectmen, 12 April 1686, "Records of the Essex County Quarterly Courts, 1636–1694," Phillips Library, Peabody Essex Museum, Salem, MA, box 46, folder 69. The substance of the petition is discussed in the text. The full petition is reproduced in Appendix B.

33   Kenneth Lockridge, *Literacy in Colonial New England* (New York: W. W. Norton, 1974), 22; Fischer, *Albion's Seed*, 132n8; Vannah, "'Crochets of Division': Ipswich in New England, 1633–1679," 436. Also see Cressy, *Coming Over*, 217. There is also the possibility that John Grow could read but not write. According to David D. Hall, "when defined as the skill of reading English, literacy was almost universal in Puritan New England. This was so largely because reading had such a high importance in the religious system." Puritanism placed great emphasis on the ability to read "the Word," and as a result even "ordinary people . . . were comfortably acquainted with the language of their Bibles." "Wealth and occupation were significant in sorting out mere readers from those who learned to write as well: every minister in New England possessed both skills, as did merchants and magistrates. But in trades where writing did not play a major role, people often stopped with learning how to read." (*Worlds of Wonder, Days of Judgment: Popular Religion in Early New England* [New York: Knopf, 1989], 32) Vannah concurs that "more people could read than could write." (436) The consensus among most scholars of the period, however, is that, as David Cressy puts it, "at least two-fifths of the male colonists and two-thirds of the women" were illiterate. (*Coming Over,* 217)

34   Davis, *John Grow of Ipswich*, 13; Perzel, "The First Generation of Settlement in Colonial Ipswich, Massachusetts, 1633–1660," 186–187; Edmund S. Morgan, *The Puritan Dilemma: The Story of John Winthrop* (Boston: Little, Brown, 1958), 169–173; Waters, *Ipswich in the Massachusetts Bay Colony*, I:45–48, 504–507. On the "Body of Liberties," also see Innes, *Creating the Commonwealth*, 210–212, 371–372nn77–79.

35   Robert Charles Anderson, *The Great Migration: Immigrants to New England, 1634–1635*, Vol. IV, I–L (Boston: New England Historic Genealogical Society, 2005), 325–330; "Lord Family Album," genealogical website created by a Lord descendant (bwlord.com), accessed July 2011; Allen, *In English Ways*, 138; Perzel, "The First Generation of Settlement in Colonial Ipswich, Massachusetts, 1633–1660," 109, 137, 142, 154, 178–179; Perzel, "Landholding in Ipswich," *Essex Institute Historical Collections*, 104 (1968): 308; George A. Schofield, *The Ancient Records of the Town of Ipswich, From 1634 to 1650* (Ipswich: privately printed, 1899), 29; Waters, *Ipswich in the Massachusetts Bay Colony*, II:107–108; Felt, *History of Ipswich, Essex, and Hamilton*, 167.

36   Vannah, "'Crochets of Division': Ipswich in New England, 1633–1679," 1025, 1047, 1097; Perzel, "Landholding in Ipswich," 309, 323; Perzel, "The First Generation of Settlement in Colonial Ipswich, Massachusetts, 1633–1660," 36, 104–105, 154, 173, 179–181, 186; Allen, *In English Ways*, 136n25; Anderson, *New England's Generation*, 162n59; "Lord Family Album"; Tarule, *Artisan of Ipswich*, 56, 82.

37   Vannah, "'Crochets of Division': Ipswich in New England, 1633–1679," 362; Perzel, "The First Generation of Settlement in Colonial Ipswich, Massachusetts, 1633–1660," 170, 176–179, 184; Waters, *Ipswich in the Massachusetts Bay Colony*, I:128–134; Allen, *In English Ways*, 136–137; *Records and Files of the Quarterly Courts of Essex County, Massachusetts*, 1:368.

38   As late as the 1670s, political power in Ipswich remained firmly in the hands of the town's founding families. Ninety percent of eligible voters were members of families like the Lords that had settled in the

town during its first seven years of existence. (Vannah, "'Crochets of Division': Ipswich in New England, 1633–1679," 871)

39 Perzel, "Landholding in Ipswich," 309–311, 318, 328; Tarule, *Artisan of Ipswich*, 13, 34–36; Anderson, *New England's Generation*, 95; Vannah, "'Crochets of Division': Ipswich in New England, 1633–1679," ch. 4 and 1022; Perzel, "The First Generation of Settlement in Colonial Ipswich, Massachusetts, 1633–1660," 37–42, 45–58, 183–184; Waters, *Ipswich in the Massachusetts Bay Colony*, I:48, 76; Allen, *In English Ways*, 119.

40 Vannah, "'Crochets of Division': Ipswich in New England, 1633–1679," 135; Tarule, *Artisan of Ipswich*, 41.

41 Perzel, "The First Generation of Settlement in Colonial Ipswich, Massachusetts, 1633–1660," 51–52; Perzel, "Landholding in Ipswich," 328; Tarule, *Artisan of Ipswich*, 13–14; Sumner Chilton Powell, *Puritan Village: The Formation of a New England Town* (Middletown, CT: Wesleyan University Press, 1963), 7–11; Waters, *Ipswich in the Massachusetts Bay Colony*, I:60–61, 68–69. For English commonage traditions and their transfer to early Massachusetts Bay, also see Allen, *In English Ways*, passim.

42 Tarule, *Artisan of Ipswich*, 13; Vannah, "'Crochets of Division': Ipswich in New England, 1633–1679," 212, 587, 641; Perzel, "Landholding in Ipswich," 325; Allen, *In English Ways*, 142. In accordance with modern practice, dates of Ipswich commoners lists and other seventeenth-century town records are herein rendered in "New Style," reflecting the Gregorian calendar currently in use, in which years begin on 1 January. Under the "Old Style" Julian calendar used in New England until 1752, each year began on 25 March, and documents written between 1 January and 24 March bore the same year's date as those written during the preceding nine months. As a result, Ipswich's first commoners list, prepared under the "Old Style" Julian calendar, was originally dated 28 February 1641 (sometimes rendered as 28 February 1641/42), but is here dated 28 February 1642 after conversion to "New Style" usage.

43 Vannah, "'Crochets of Division': Ipswich in New England, 1633–1679," 522–523, 531, 536–537, 568–569, 584, 641, 658, 688, 727; John Frederick Martin, *Profits in the Wilderness: Entrepreneurship and the Founding of New England Towns in the Seventeenth Century* (Chapel Hill: University of North Carolina Press, 1991), 223; Tarule, *Artisan of Ipswich*, 31–41.

44 Felt, *History of Ipswich, Essex, and Hamilton*, 16; Perzel, "Landholding in Ipswich," 325; Vannah, "'Crochets of Division': Ipswich in New England, 1633–1679," 524; Martin, *Profits in the Wilderness*, 186–193. Lord and four of his fellow selectmen informed the Massachusetts Bay General Court that the March 1660 restriction on commonage was necessary, in order that "being already over burdened we may not so multiply commoners and be thereby made more uncapable [*sic*] of subsisting." (Vannah, "'Crochets of Division': Ipswich in New England, 1633–1679," 524)

45 Anderson, *New England's Generation*, 97–98; Felt, *History of Ipswich, Essex, and Hamilton*, 16; Vannah, "'Crochets of Division': Ipswich in New England, 1633–1679," 577–578, 641–642, 644, 656–658, 688, 706; Perzel, "Landholding in Ipswich," 327; Waters, *Ipswich in the Massachusetts Bay Colony*, I:69–70. In adopting their restrictive new land policies, Ipswich's leaders and established families undoubtedly believed that they were acting as responsible stewards of the town's public domain by protecting it from overuse. As the town's founders and early settlers, it was also only natural for them to believe that they and their descendants should reap the benefits of the enterprise that their physical labors and financial investments had built (Martin, *Profits in the Wilderness*, 191–192), and that they were consequently justified in limiting the number of townspeople "who could partake of the same advantages they enjoyed." (Anderson, *New England's Generation*, 97)

46 Anderson, *New England's Generation*, 97–98; Vannah, "'Crochets of Division': Ipswich in New England, 1633–1679," 526, 533, 640, 644, 657–658, 706, 866. Rights of commonage could also occasionally be purchased, but the purchase price—ranging from £15 to £20—was well beyond the reach of most townspeople in the lower and middle ranks. (Vannah, "'Crochets of Division': Ipswich in New England, 1633–1679," 728; Waters, *Ipswich in the Massachusetts Bay Colony*, I:68)

47 Thomas Franklin Waters, "Jeffrey's Neck and the Way Leading Thereto, with Notes on Little Neck" (Ipswich, MA: Ipswich Historical Society publication XVIII, 1912), 59; Waters, *Ipswich in the Massachusetts Bay Colony*, I:70; Nathaniel Farley, trans., "Records of the Town of Ipswich from 1634 to 1720" (three-volume handwritten transcription of Ipswich's early town records, in the archive of the Office of the Ipswich Town Clerk), vol. 1 (1634–1673): 263, 311, 345, 353; "A List of the Inhabitants that have shares in Plum Island, Castle Neck, and Hog Island . . . according to the Towne order the 14 of Feb: '64" (20 April 1665) [hereinafter referred to as "Commoners List of 1665"], original manuscript, Ipswich Town Records, archive of the Office of the Town Clerk, Ipswich, MA (reproduced in Appendix A). On 15 March 1670, the town of

Ipswich granted Obadiah Bridges and John Knowlton "the like liberty of firewood and feed for one cow, so long as they follow there [*sic*] trades as the fishermen, and not otherwise." (Farley, "Records of the Town of Ipswich from 1634 to 1720," 1:311) Two years later, on 11 February 1672, John Grow was granted "the like preveledge [*sic*] of the commonage as other tradesmen, as John Knowlton and Obadiah Bridges." (Ibid., 345) Read in the context of the support that the town government was extending to Ipswich's maritime workers in the years 1670–1673, it seems clear that the "privilege" extended to Grow in 1672, like the "liberty" granted to Bridges and Knowlton two years earlier, consisted of limited *access* to the commons rather than full rights of commonage.

It should be noted that two important sources—the 1913 George W. Davis genealogy *John Grow of Ipswich* (p. 13) and Edward Perzel's 1967 Rutgers University dissertation "The First Generation of Settlement in Colonial Ipswich, Massachusetts, 1633–1660" (383–385)—identify John Grow as an Ipswich commoner in 1664–1665. Both authors based their interpretations on the Ipswich "Commoners List of 1665," which recorded the names of all town residents possessing commonage rights in 1664 for the purpose of determining who was eligible to receive shares of the 800 acres of common land that were to be distributed in 1665. At the end of the "Commoners List of 1665," in the lower right corner of its third and final page under the subheading "liberty for firewood & one cow," are recorded the names of Grow and the seven other Ipswich maritime workers who were granted limited and conditional access to the commons in 1670–1673. (See Appendix A.) Because Grow's name appears on the 1665 list, it was only logical to conclude that he was one of the town's commoners in 1664–1665. A close examination of that document, however, indicates that the names of the eight men receiving "liberty for firewood & one cow" were added at a later date, probably c. 1673, and by a different hand with conspicuously different penmanship than the scribe who recorded the 1665 commoners list. (Vannah, "'Crochets of Division': Ipswich in New England, 1633–1679," 641, 753, 981–984) In addition, several names appearing higher up in the same column of the document, above the subgroup awarded "liberty for firewood & one cow," were Ipswich residents who successfully appealed their initial exclusion from the 1665 commoners list, and whose names were subsequently appended to the document in the late 1660s and early 1670s, in a third scribe's handwriting. (Ibid., 983) Perhaps the most conclusive evidence that the names of Grow and his fellow workers were added to the "Commoners List of 1665" at a later date is the fact that five of the eight men—Bridges (born 1646), Cross (born 1646), Knowlton (born 1645), John Dutch (born 1646), and Samuel Dutch (born 1650)—were still teenagers in 1664–1665 and not legally old enough at that time to possess commonage rights. (Ibid., 1042, 1056, 1092, 1111, 1118; Massachusetts Vital Records to 1850 [online database, AmericanAncestors.org]: Gloucester Births, 232) Consequently, the mistaken claim that John Grow was an Ipswich commoner in 1664–1665 probably stems from the traditional New England virtue of frugality: town officials of the late 1660s-early 1670s, finding blank space still available in the bottom right corner of the town's original copy of the "Commoners List of 1665," used that space to record the names of local residents who were subsequently granted rights and lesser privileges of commonage over the course of the next decade. Why waste blank space? Why waste additional paper when there was still open space available on the 1665 document?

Because the original "Commoners List of 1665" manuscript is smudged in places and difficult to read, modern transcriptions of the document contain several errors. Perzel transcribed the subheading "liberty for firewood & one cow" as "Liberty for free wood and one cow" and misread the name "Giles Cowes" as an additional subhead "Only cows." ("The First Generation of Settlement in Colonial Ipswich, Massachusetts, 1633–1660," 385) Vannah failed to include John Dutch's name in her transcription of the list. ("'Crochets of Division': Ipswich in New England, 1633–1679," 984) Nathaniel Farley's transcription ("Records of the Town of Ipswich from 1634 to 1720," 1:311) was accurate in content but failed to denote any evidence that the final two subgroups of names on the original document were later additions.

48   Ipswich Deeds, Mortgages, Wills, 1639–1695, Family History Library (Church of Jesus Christ of Latter-Day Saints, Salt Lake City, UT), microfilm 873019, 4:336; Waters, *Ipswich in the Massachusetts Bay Colony*, I:392; Davis, *John Grow of Ipswich*, 17; Vannah, "'Crochets of Division': Ipswich in New England, 1633–1679," 1127, 1146. "Ye Widdow Woodham" was Mary Woodham (or Woodam), whose husband John, a "bricklayer," died in 1678.

Prior to a marriage in seventeenth-century Ipswich, the parents customarily "covenanted to provide a home for the young couple." (Waters, *Ipswich in the Massachusetts Bay Colony*, I:383) Lord also acquired houses in Ipswich for two of his sons. (Vannah, "'Crochets of Division': Ipswich in New England, 1633–1679," 596n16) During the first ten years of their marriage, John and Hannah might have lived with Hannah's parents, whose large house (today known as the "Kingsbury-Lord House") still stands at 52 High Street, showing clear evidence of numerous expansions to accommodate a growing family. (Ibid., 336; Waters, *Ipswich in the Massachusetts Bay Colony*, I:363) Prior to his marriage, John probably boarded with a local family, perhaps employer Robert Pearce and his wife, in accordance with a local law requiring all single males to live "under family government," "in well-governed families," to prevent the "disorder" that was presumed to accompany solitary life. (Norton, *Founding Mothers and Fathers*, 41; Farley, "Records of the Town of Ipswich from 1634 to 1720," vol. 2 (1674–1696), 103–104; Vannah, "'Crochets of Division': Ipswich in New England, 1633–1679," 336; Fischer, *Albion's Seed*, 73; Vickers, *Farmers and Fishermen*, 59)

49   Several sources, by failing to convert the "Old Style" Julian-calendar date of the 1679 Ipswich commoners list to "New Style" (see endnote 42), have assigned a date of 13 (or 18) February 1678 to the document. (Waters, *Ipswich in the Massachusetts Bay Colony*, I:93–98; "Materials for the History of Ipswich," *New England Historical and Genealogical Register*, VII:1 [January 1853]: 77–79; Davis, *John Grow of Ipswich*, 13) Nevertheless, the town committee appointed to determine "who are commoners" was constituted on 4 February 1679, and its findings were recorded on 2 December 1679. (Vannah, "'Crochets of Division': Ipswich in New England, 1633–1679," 864; also see Allen, *In English Ways*, 215n25)

50   For Grow's land acquisitions from the 1709 division of the commons, see his deed transfers of 10 April 1712 and 18 March 1724, in Essex County Deeds (Registry of Deeds, Salem, MA), 31:64–65, 49:5–6, 57:150–151, 154–155.

51   Martin, *Profits in the Wilderness*, 197n19, 228, 241; Vannah, "'Crochets of Division': Ipswich in New England, 1633–1679," 526. Although the population of Ipswich was doubling at roughly fifteen-year intervals during the second half of the seventeenth century, the number of commoners increased only minimally, from 203 in 1665 to 224 in 1679. (Norton, "Population Growth in Colonial America: A Study of Ipswich, Massachusetts," 435; Waters, *Ipswich in the Massachusetts Bay Colony*, I:70, 98, 106)

52   Norton, "Population Growth in Colonial America: A Study of Ipswich, Massachusetts," 445; Anderson, *Great Migration: Immigrants to New England, 1634–1635*, IV:329.

53   Davis, *John Grow of Ipswich*, 15; Fairbanks and Trent, eds., *New England Begins*, 7; John Demos, *A Little Commonwealth: Family Life in Plymouth Colony* (New York: Oxford University Press, 1970), 68; Philip J. Greven Jr., *Four Generations: Population, Land, and Family in Colonial Andover, Massachusetts* (Ithaca: Cornell University Press, 1970), 201.

54   Kenneth A. Lockridge, *A New England Town: The First Hundred Years* (New York: W. W. Norton, 1970), 68.

55   Demos, *A Little Commonwealth*, 68–69; Norton, *Founding Mothers and Fathers*, 222.

56   Hall, *Worlds of Wonder, Days of Judgment*, 10; Fischer, *Albion's Seed*, 94–96. John was the most popular boy's name during the period, followed by Joseph and Samuel. For female children, Mary, Hannah, Elizabeth, Sarah, Abigail, Rebecca, and Ruth were favorite choices.

57   David E. Stannard, *The Puritan Way of Death* (New York: Oxford University Press, 1977), 54–57; Davis, *John Grow of Ipswich*, 15, 17–18. Giving their thirdborn son John the same name as their deceased first son was another typical seventeenth-century practice. According to David Hackett Fischer, "When New England families lost a child, its name was used again in 80 percent of all cases where another baby of the same sex was born." (*Albion's Seed*, 96)

58   Along with the aforementioned three sons and one daughter, their second son Samuel, although still living in 1712, seems not to have been alive by 1724–1725, when his name is absent on a series of property documents requiring the signatures of John, Hannah, and their offspring. Instead, the only names that appear on any of those documents are the two parents and their sons Joseph, Thomas, and William. (Davis, *John Grow of Ipswich*, 14–18)

59   Ibid., 13; Waters, *Ipswich in the Massachusetts Bay Colony*, I:392.

60   Anderson, *Great Migration: Immigrants to New England, 1634–1635*, IV:329.

61   Vannah, "'Crochets of Division': Ipswich in New England, 1633–1679," 19–21, 199, 794–795, 1145–1146; Waters, *Ipswich in the Massachusetts Bay Colony*, I:65, 82, map following 386, 392–393, 434; Tarule, *Artisan of Ipswich*, 57 (map), 69–71, 78.

62   In 1669, Thomas Dennis received permission from the Ipswich selectmen to cut down "6 trees for his trade" from the town's common forests. A year later, however, one of Dennis' employees, Josias Lyndon, informed the town government that Dennis illegally felled an additional 12 trees at the time of the cutting. After confirming Lyndon's accusation, the town levied a steep fine on Dennis, half of which by law was to go to his accuser. When Dennis refused to pay Lyndon his share of the fine, Lyndon sued. (Tarule, *Artisan of Ipswich*, 42–43, 51, 55–59) Among the witnesses who testified in the ensuing 1671 court case, "John Grow, aged about twenty-nine years, deposed that he heard Josias Lyndon at Thomas Denis' house demand payment of [Dennis], and the latter refused." (*Records and Files of the Quarterly Courts of Essex County, Massachusetts*, 4:422)

63   Waters, *Ipswich in the Massachusetts Bay Colony*, I:75, 392.

64   Essex County Deeds, 66:261; Tarule, *Artisan of Ipswich*, 47.

65   Unless otherwise noted, the following hypothetical sketch of John and Hannah's residence is based on Waters, *Ipswich in the Massachusetts Bay Colony*, I:22–33; Tarule, *Artisan of Ipswich*, 43–44, 60–61; Demos, *Little Commonwealth*, 29–34, 38–47; and Robert Blair St. George, "'Set Thine Own House in Order': The Domestication of the Yeomanry in Seventeenth-Century New England," in Fairbanks and Trent, eds., *New England Begins*, 161–173.

66   For evidence that the Grows owned sheep, see Appendix B. According to the Ipswich town records, sons Samuel and John "had horses on the common" in 1697. (Davis, *John Grow of Ipswich*, 15)

67   Laurel Thatcher Ulrich, *Good Wives: Image and Reality in the Lives of Women in Northern New England, 1650–1750* (New York: Vintage Books, 1991), ch. 1; Norton, *Founding Mothers and Fathers*, 222; Roger Thompson, *Divided We Stand: Watertown, Massachusetts, 1630–1680* (Amherst: University of Massachusetts Press, 2001), 130.

68   Petition to the Ipswich, Massachusetts selectmen, 12 April 1686, "Records of the Essex County Quarterly Courts, 1636–1694," Phillips Library, Peabody Essex Museum, Salem, MA, box 46, folder 69. For the full text of the original petition, see Appendix B.

69   Davis, *John Grow of Ipswich*, 13–14. The source of John Grow's training as a weaver is anyone's guess. If he was born in England, he might have come from a family background and/or an apprenticeship experience in one of the many cloth-making towns of East Anglia, a region that produced a large percentage of Ipswich's early settlers. (Allen, *In English Ways*, 117, 184–191, 194–195, 200–201; Anderson, *New England's Generation*, 31–32; Kulikoff, *From British Peasants to Colonial American Farmers*, 25–26) He could also have acquired a rudimentary knowledge of the craft while employed as a seaman (see note 8). For a discussion of weavers' training in seventeenth-century Massachusetts, see Susan M. Ouellette, *U.S. Textile Production in Historical Perspective: A Case Study from Massachusetts* (New York: Routledge, 2007), 56–57.

70   George Francis Dow, ed., *Probate Records of Essex County, Massachusetts (1635–1681)*, 3 vols. (Salem, MA: Essex Institute, 1916–1920), III:291–293.

71   Tarule, *Artisan of Ipswich*, 127; Vannah, "'Crochets of Division': Ipswich in New England, 1633–1679," 17; Clark, *Eastern Frontier*, 65; Vickers, *Farmers and Fishermen*, 144–153.

72   Vickers, *Farmers and Fishermen*, 89, 93–97, 119–124, 137, 182–186; Vickers, *Young Men and the Sea*, 3. For a suggestive description of the hardships of life at sea, see Marcus Redicker's study of early eighteenth-century Anglo-American seamen, *Between the Devil and the Deep Blue Sea: Merchant Seamen, Pirates, and the Anglo-American Maritime World, 1700–1750* (Cambridge, U.K.: Cambridge University Press, 1987), 1–3, 154, 159–160.

73   Anderson, *New England's Generation*, 134–138; Bailyn, *New England Merchants of the Seventeenth Century*, 71–74; Waters, *Ipswich in the Massachusetts Bay Colony*, I:85–86; Ouellette, *U.S. Textile Production in Historical Perspective*, 12–13, 15, 24, 65–66. In 1645 the Massachusetts Bay legislature observed that as a consequence of inadequate supplies of warm woolen clothing, "many pore people have suffered much could and hardship, to the impairing of some of their healths," and that many of their children had been "much scorched with fire" and several "burnt to death" trying to keep warm. (Quoted in Anderson, *New England's Generation*, 134)

74   Tarule, *Artisan of Ipswich*, 47, 61; Waters, "Jeffrey's Neck and the Way Leading Thereto," 56–57; Waters, *Ipswich in the Massachusetts Bay Colony*, I:71–72; Ouellette, *U.S. Textile Production in Historical Perspective*, 12; Vannah, "'Crochets of Division': Ipswich in New England, 1633–1679," 433, 795, 916, 917.

75   Farley, "Records of the Town of Ipswich from 1634 to 1720," vol. 3 (1696–1720): 32. By town order, ewes and rams were to be kept separated on the commons from 1 August to 15 November. (Ibid., 53) The measure was part of the town's effort to regulate the breeding cycles of its common sheep flocks. According to Susan Ouellette, lambs that were born too early in the birthing season "risked freezing in the late winter cold, while those who survived had to be fed precious stocks of hay when weaned before spring grass sprouted. Lambs born too late in the season were also a problem since they continued to nurse their mothers after the time when the flocks [needed to] be culled and separated." They also ran greater risk of contracting "warm weather diseases." In addition, late lambs interfered with the sheep owners' preferred shearing time and also "disrupted the seasonal breeding cycle by delaying ewes' lactation and estrus in the following season." By ordering the separation of ewes and rams, therefore, the town "hoped to preserve a balance in their flocks' reproductive cycle and in the farmers' seasonal labor requirements." (*U.S. Textile Production in Historical Perspective*, 20)

76   Tarule, *Artisan of Ipswich*, 61–62, 65–66; Waters, *Ipswich in the Massachusetts Bay Colony*, I:83, 452; Perzel, "The First Generation of Settlement in Colonial Ipswich, Massachusetts, 1633–1660," 82; Vannah, "'Crochets of Division': Ipswich in New England, 1633–1679," 794; Ouellette, *U.S. Textile Production in Historical Perspective*, 76; Allen, *In English Ways*, 133.

77   William I. Davisson, "Essex County Price Trends: Money and Markets in 17th Century Massachusetts," *Essex Institute Historical Collections*, CIII: 4 (October 1967): 180–182.

78   Ouellette, *U.S. Textile Production in Historical Perspective*, 72–74. Among the items listed in the 1679 estate inventory of William Symonds of Ipswich was an unspecified quantity of "woollen yarne at the wevers" valued at more than £43. (Dow, *Probate Records of Essex County, Massachusetts* [1635–1681], III:304)

79   Gloria L. Main, "Gender, Work, and Wages in Colonial New England," *William and Mary Quarterly*, 51:1 (January 1994): 61; Abraham Howe account book, Ipswich Museum, Ipswich, MA; Waters, *Ipswich in the Massachusetts Bay Colony*, II:253. "Linsey-woolsey" was a coarse linen fabric made of wool and flax fiber, commonly used in homemade wearing apparel. In the late 1670s, Suffolk County, Massachusetts weaver Samuel Ruggles was earning an annual income of £17 from the weaver's trade. (Gloria L. Main, *Peoples of a Spacious Land: Families and Cultures in Colonial New England* [Cambridge, MA: Harvard University Press, 2001], 161.) "[W]ith little time to keep up with farming duties," Ipswich weavers regularly traded their goods and services to obtain needed supplies of corn, wheat, barley, hay, wood, and boards from local commercial farmers such as John Burnham. (McWilliams, *Building the Bay Colony*, 111–112)

80   Thomas Franklin Waters, "Glimpses of Everyday Life in Old Ipswich" (Ipswich, MA: Publications of the Ipswich Historical Society, 1925), 12–13; George Francis Dow, *Everyday Life in the Massachusetts Bay Colony* (Boston: Society for the Preservation of New England Antiquities, 1935), 94; Waters, *Ipswich in the Massachusetts Bay Colony*, I:83. For the common varieties of wool fabric woven in seventeenth-century Massachusetts Bay, see Ouellette, *U.S. Textiles in Historical Perspective*, 30–31.

81   Vickers, *Farmers and Fishermen*, 14–23; Innes, *Creating the Commonwealth*, 64–65. Also see Anderson, *New England's Generation*, 172–173.

82   Edmund S. Morgan, *The Puritan Family: Religion and Domestic Relations in Seventeenth-Century New England* (New York: Harper & Row, 1944), 1–21; Stannard, *Puritan Way of Death*, 32–33, 36; Andrew DelBanco, *The Real American Dream: A Meditation on Hope* (Cambridge, MA: Harvard University Press, 1999), 20–21, 23; Anderson, *New England's Generation*, 175, 194–196; Demos, *Entertaining Satan*, 373–379; Hall, *Worlds of Wonder, Days of Judgment*, 71–94, 118–119, 121, 202, 222; Fischer, *Albion's Seed*, 104; Richard Godbeer, *The Devil's Dominion: Magic and Religion in Early New England* (New York: Cambridge University Press, 1992), 130; Conforti, *Imagining New England*, 50–51.

83   Perzel, "The First Generation of Settlement in Colonial Ipswich, Massachusetts, 1633–1660," 191.

84   Davis, *John Grow of Ipswich*, 13.

85   Waters, *Ipswich in the Massachusetts Bay Colony*, II:8.

86   Hall, *Worlds of Wonder, Days of Judgment*, 15–16, 119, 130–131, 136, 138–139, 164; Cressy, *Coming Over*, 83; Morgan, *Puritan Family*, 8–9, 170–171; David Thomas Konig, *Law and Society in Puritan Massachusetts: Essex County, 1629–1692* (Chapel Hill: University of North Carolina Press, 1979), 3; Francis J. Bremer, *The Puritan Experiment: New England Society from Bradford to Edwards* (New York: St. Martin's Press, 1976), 102.

87   *Records and Files of the Quarterly Courts of Essex County, Massachusetts*, 8:309–311. Among the Ipswich residents who contributed to the elder's salary were Robert Lord Sr., Robert Lord Jr., "widow Peirce and her son," Thomas Dennis, and two of John Grow's former maritime colleagues, John Berry and Samuel Dutch.

88   Waters, *Ipswich in the Massachusetts Bay Colony*, I:116, 276–277, II:2–4, 67–68. Also see Vannah, "'Crochets of Division': Ipswich in New England, 1633–1679," 812–815.

89   Konig, *Law and Society in Puritan Massachusetts*, 106; Perzel, "Landholding in Ipswich," 322; Vannah, "'Crochets of Division': Ipswich in New England, 1633–1679," 862–863, 1038. Hubbard was minister of the Ipswich church from 1656 to 1703. (Waters, *Ipswich in the Massachusetts Bay Colony*, II:9)

90   Waters, *Ipswich in the Massachusetts Bay Colony*, I:67, 117, 277; Vannah, "'Crochets of Division': Ipswich in New England, 1633–1679," 828, 874–876; Konig, *Law and Society in Puritan Massachusetts*, 134.

91   Hall, *Worlds of Wonder, Days of Judgment*, 7, 19, 58–60, 71–72, 76, 85–86, 88, 98–101, 108–109, 115; Godbeer, *Devil's Dominion*, 5–8, 24–54, 61, 66–67, 71, 122–152, 171; Stannard, *Puritan Way of Death*, 36,

66–67; Mary Beth Norton, *In the Devil's Snare: The Salem Witchcraft Crisis of 1692* (New York: Vintage Books, 2002), 5–6; Demos, *Entertaining Satan,* 9.

92   Lyle Koehler, *A Search for Power: The "Weaker Sex" in Seventeenth-Century New England* (Urbana: University of Illinois Press, 1980), 390–392. Also see Demos, *Entertaining Satan,* 402–408; Godbeer, *Devil's Dominion,* 235–237.

93   Norton, *In the Devil's Snare,* chs. 1–2, 4–7; Paul Boyer and Stephen Nissenbaum, *Salem Possessed: The Social Origins of Witchcraft* (Cambridge, MA: Harvard University Press, 1974), 1–21; Godbeer, *Devil's Dominion,* 80–82, 179–180.

94   Waters, *Ipswich in the Massachusetts Bay Colony,* I:295–296. In addition to Mary Easty, Robert Lord Jr. also shackled another accused witch from Salem Village, Sarah Cloyce, and two Haverhill women, Hannah Bromage and Mary Green. Although Easty's legal defense strategy failed to prevent her execution, it had an influential impact on the Salem court's subsequent attitude toward witchcraft prosecutions. See Bernard Rosenthal, *Salem Story: Reading the Witch Trials of 1692* (New York: Cambridge University Press, 1993), 174–182.

95   Norton, *In the Devil's Snare,* 183–184, 226–227, 319; Carol F. Karlsen, *The Devil in the Shape of a Woman: Witchcraft in Colonial New England* (New York: Vintage, 1989), 131, 133–134, 147; Waters, *Ipswich in the Massachusetts Bay Colony,* I:293; Bernard Rosenthal, ed., *Records of the Salem Witch Hunt* (New York: Cambridge University Press, 2009), 419–420, 438; Paul Boyer and Stephen Nissenbaum, eds., *The Salem Witchcraft Papers: Verbatim Transcriptions of the Court Records,* 3 vols. (New York: Da Capo Press, 1977), 2:437, 450–451 [available online at etext.virginia.edu/salem/witchcraft/texts/]. The case of Rachel Clinton is discussed in detail in Demos, *Entertaining Satan,* 19–35; and Karlsen, *Devil in the Shape of a Woman,* 108–110, 140, 259–260.

96   Norton, *In the Devil's Snare,* 254–258, 260–262; Sarah Loring Bailey, *Historical Sketches of Andover, Massachusetts* (Boston: Houghton, Mifflin, 1880), 197–201; Boyer and Nissenbaum, eds., *Salem Witchcraft Papers,* 2:335, 615–616, 3:971–972; Rosenthal, ed., *Records of the Salem Witch-Hunt,* 608–609, 647–648, 660–661, 737–738, 963.

97   Boyer and Nissenbaum, eds., *Salem Witchcraft Papers,* 2:618–620, 3:855, 971–972; Rosenthal, ed., *Records of the Salem Witch Hunt,* 693–694, 737–740; Norton, *In the Devil's Snare,* 161, 248, 256–257, 262–264, 302–303; Bailey, *Historical Sketches of Andover,* 216–218; Godbeer, *Devil's Dominion,* 204, 208–210; Chadwick Hansen, "Andover Witchcraft and the Causes of the Salem Witchcraft Trials," in Howard Kerr and Charles L. Crow, eds., *The Occult in America: New Historical Perspectives* (Urbana: University of Illinois Press, 1983), 51; Elizabeth Reis, *Damned Women: Sinners and Witches in Puritan New England* (Ithaca: Cornell University Press, 1997), 121, 124, 152–154; Karlsen, *Devil in the Shape of a Woman,* 39.

98   Norton, *In the Devil's Snare,* 266–267, 278–281, 287; Rosenthal, ed., *Records of the Salem Witch Hunt,* 688, 693, 707–708, 738–740, 884–885; Boyer and Nissenbaum, eds., *Salem Witchcraft Papers,* 2:620–621, 3:855–856, 875–876, 878–879, 1004, 1009; Charles W. Upham, *Salem Witchcraft: With an Account of Salem Village and a History of Opinions on Witchcraft and Kindred Subjects* (Boston: Wiggin and Lunt, 1867; repr. Mineola, New York: Dover Publications, 1978), 591; "Sarah Lord Wilson: Witch of Andover," accessed online at homepages.rootsweb.ancestry.com/~sam/wilson/sarah.html on 28 March 2012. Sarah's 14-year-old daughter Sarah Wilson Jr., the niece of John and Hannah Grow, was also arrested on witchcraft charges, confessed, and spent six weeks in the Salem jail before being released. (Ibid.)

99   Waters, *Ipswich in the Massachusetts Bay Colony,* I:159–224, II:31–35; Godbeer, *Devil's Dominion,* 182–183; Anderson, *New England's Generation,* 194; Kyle F. Zelner, *A Rabble in Arms: Massachusetts Towns and Militiamen during King Philip's War* (New York University Press, 2009), 54–55, 59–60, 68, 71–80, 165, 166; also see Vannah, "'Crochets of Division': Ipswich in New England, 1633–1679," 839. Estimates of the number of Ipswich soldiers killed in the war range from seven (Zelner, *Rabble in Arms,* 73, 203) to sixteen (Vannah, "'Crochets of Division': Ipswich in New England, 1633–1679," 842).
       Military records from King Philip's War identify a "Simon Grow" or "Simon Groe," purportedly of Ipswich, as serving in "Captain Brocklebank's company" and "Captain Hinchman's company" in 1676. (George M. Bodge, *Soldiers in King Philip's War,* 3rd ed. [Boston: privately printed, 1906], 207, 370; Waters, *Ipswich in the Massachusetts Bay Colony,* I:220; Zelner, *Rabble in Arms,* 221) George W. Davis believed that the soldier in question was probably named "Simon Grove" or "Simon Groves." (*John Grow of Ipswich,* 6) However, there is no record of a Simon Grow, Simon Groe, Simon Grove, or Simon Groves in seventeenth-century Ipswich. Zelner speculates that Simon Grow/Groe might have been one of several men with "no

known connection" to Ipswich who were impressed by local authorities while visiting the town on business or while hiding out there in an effort to avoid conscription in their hometowns. (*Rabble in Arms,* 78, 262n54)

Although Thomas Franklin Waters includes Robert Lord's son Nathaniel on a list of Ipswich men who participated in the war (*Ipswich in the Massachusetts Bay Colony,* I:221), it is likely that Nathaniel Lord's name appears in the military records because he was one of many men who received compensation for some non-military service that they performed during the war, "such as providing troops with military supplies," but who "cannot be placed in an actual fighting or garrison company." (Zelner, *Rabble in Arms,* 15, 260n21)

100 Waters, *Ipswich in the Massachusetts Bay Colony,* I:225–271; Francis J. Bremer, *The Puritan Experiment* (New York: St. Martin's, 1976), 155–165.

101 Norton, "Population Growth in Colonial America," 435; Waters, *Ipswich in the Massachusetts Bay Colony,* I:70–73; Waters, "Jeffrey's Neck and the Way Leading Thereto," 60–63; Vannah, "'Crochets of Division': Ipswich in New England, 1634–1679," 135, 867–868, 917. According to the distribution formula, two-fifths of the 6,000 acres were awarded "to ye ancient Commoners" and the remaining three-fifths were divided among "ye antient Commoners & new Commoners alike." Parcels of "upland" awarded to old commoners contained on average "about 136 rods" each, while portions distributed to new commoners measured "about 60 rods" each. (Waters, "Jeffrey's Neck and the Way Leading Thereto," 61, 63) Of the approximately 1,000 acres of common land not distributed in 1709, most were apparently retained as sheep pastures. For the broader context of political contention over the proprietorship of common lands in Massachusetts Bay during the late seventeenth and early eighteenth centuries, see Martin, *Profits in the Wilderness,* 290–300, and Allen, *In English Ways,* 217.

102 Davis, *John Grow of Ipswich,* 14–15, 17–18. The couple obtained legal title to the Brook Street house lot in 1683. After Robert Lord bought the property from Mary Woodham in 1679, John reached an agreement with Lord to "purchase…the house and lot" on installment "and occupied the premises." By 1683, when Lord died, John had given him partial payments totaling £22.10s. In his will, Lord bequeathed to "my daughter Hannah Grow and her children the house & land I bought of the widow Woodam wherein they now dwell & also my parcel of marsh at the hundreds [16 acres, valued at £64 in 1683] provided they pay unto their sister Susannah Osgood & her children twenty pounds." The will also returned to John his £22.10s in partial payments. (Davis, *John Grow of Ipswich,* 17; Anderson, *The Great Migration: Immigrants to New England, 1634–1635,* IV:327–328) When John and Hannah inherited the Brook Street property in 1683, it was valued at £70. In 1733, a few years after their deaths, their son Joseph sold it to fisherman Nathaniel Jones for £155. (Davis, *John Grow of Ipswich,* 15; Essex County Deeds, 66:261)

"The hundreds" was a tract of salt marsh along the Egypt River in the northern portion of Ipswich near the Rowley line. It was a source of salt hay, a livestock fodder that the town's residents used to feed their cattle and sheep during the winter months. (Waters, *Ipswich in the Massachusetts Bay Colony,* II:252)

In the 1712 transaction, John and his four surviving sons (Samuel, Joseph, Thomas, and William) appear to have traded the 8-acre Chebacco woodlot obtained in 1709 to "yeoman" John Andrews for a separate woodlot (also in Chebacco) and the two parcels of "new upland" on Jeffrey's Neck. (Davis, *John Grow of Ipswich,* 14; Essex County Deeds, 31:64–65, 57, 150–151, 154–155)

103 Davis, *John Grow of Ipswich,* 14, 17–18; Essex County Deeds, 44:46–47, 47:197–198, 49:5–6. In 1722, John—for reasons unknown—also transferred the southern half of the Brook Street house lot to his son Joseph. (Davis, *John Grow of Ipswich,* 13–14; Essex County Deeds, 41:70; Waters, *Ipswich in the Massachusetts Bay Colony,* I:392)

According to John Demos, "The average 'Puritan' man or woman continued with childbearing until, or even past, the age of forty; as a result, there were small children underfoot in many colonial households until the parents were in their fifties." (*Past, Present, and Personal: The Family and the Life Course in American History* [New York: Oxford University Press, 1986], 121)

On male employment in old age, see ibid., 166–171, and Lisa Wilson, *Ye Heart of a Man: The Domestic Life of Men in Colonial New England* (New Haven: Yale University Press, 1999), 171.

104 Davis, *John Grow of Ipswich,* 13–15; Essex County Deeds, 57:149–150. Average life expectancy figures are from Innes, *Creating the Commonwealth,* 23. Women during the period lived, on average, about 65 years.

105 Arthur Warren Johnson and Ralph Elbridge Ladd Jr., comps., *Memento Mori: An Accurate Transcription of the Tomb-Stones, Monuments, Foot-Stones, and Other Memorials in the Ancient Old North Burial Yard in the Town of Ipswich, County of Essex, Massachusetts, From its Beginnings in the Year Anno. Dom. 1634 to the Present Day, With a Chart of the Location of the Same that any Grave Therein May be Located With Ease and Accuracy, Together with a History and Description of this Ancient Burial Yard* (Ipswich Historical Society Publication 29, 1935).

106 Vannah, "'Crochets of Division': Ipswich in New England, 1633–1679," 533.

107 For the occupations of Thomas and William Grow, see Davis, *John Grow of Ipswich,* 18–19. According to a deed of 30 April 1730, "Joseph Grow of Ipswich (laborer)" transferred "lots in Jeffries Neck" to Thomas Treadwell Jr. (Ibid., 15)

GENERATION TWO: THOMAS GROW (1684–1753)

1   See, for example, Kenneth Lockridge, "Land, Population, and the Evolution of New England Society, 1630–1790," in Stanley N. Katz, ed., *Colonial America: Essays in Politics and Social Development* (Boston: Little, Brown, 1971), 468, 489; Allan Kulikoff, *From British Peasants to Colonial American Farmers* (Chapel Hill: University of North Carolina Press, 2000), 3, 125–130, 135, 137, 139, 145–149, 212, 240; Virginia DeJohn Anderson, *New England's Generation: The Great Migration and the Formation of Society and Culture in the Seventeenth Century* (New York: Cambridge University Press, 1991), 49, 105–108. Anderson estimates that "over 90 percent of the population" of seventeeth-century New England "was primarily engaged in agriculture." (145n25)

2   Sanborn Connor Brown, *Wines and Beers of Old New England* (Hanover, NH: University Press of New England, 1978), 48, 51–54, 62–63; Laurel Thatcher Ulrich, *Good Wives: Image and Reality in the Lives of Women in Northern New England, 1650–1750* (New York: Vintage Books, 1991), 23. Colonial maltsters could aptly be described as "farmers with a trade or artisans with a farm." (Jackson Turner Main, *The Social Structure of Revolutionary America* [Princeton, NJ: Princeton University Press, 1965], 17)

3   Alison I. Vannah, "'Crochets of Division': Ipswich in New England, 1633–1679" (PhD dissertation, Brandeis University, 1999), 916. In 1696, the Ipswich town government granted James Burnham permission "to have a malt-house near the old gravel-pit," now that "John Lowe had done making malt." (Joseph B. Felt, *History of Ipswich, Essex, and Hamilton* [Ipswich, MA: The Clamshell Press, 1966], 97)

4   *Vital Records of Ipswich, Massachusetts, to the End of the Year 1849,* 3 vols. (Salem, MA: Essex Institute, 1910–1919), 1:197. The couple's marriage intentions were recorded in Ipswich on 31 June 1710 (ibid.) and in Andover on 1 July 1710 (*Vital Records of Andover, Massachusetts, to the End of the Year 1849,* 2 vols. [Topsfield, MA: Topsfield Historical Society, 1911–1912], 2:160), evidence that Thomas was still residing in Ipswich at the time of his marriage. (Susan L. Norton, "Marital Migration in Essex County, Massachusetts, in the Colonial and Early Federal Periods," in Maris A. Vinovskis, ed., *Studies in American Historical Demography* [New York: Academic Press, 1979], 149)

5   Philip J. Greven Jr., "Family Structure in Seventeenth-Century Andover, Massachusetts," in Michael Gordon, ed., *The American Family in Social-Historical Perspective,* 2nd ed. (New York: St. Martin's Press, 1978), 28–29; Greven, *Four Generations: Population, Land, and Family in Colonial Andover, Massachusetts* (Ithaca, NY: Cornell University Press, 1970), 46–47, 59–60, 88–92; Greven, "Old Patterns in the New World: The Distribution of Land in 17th Century Andover," *Essex Institute Historical Collections* (Salem, MA: Essex Institute, 1965), 146. In 1705, Nicholas Holt's second son Henry was the second wealthiest man in Andover as measured by his taxable possessions. (Greven, "Four Generations: A Study of Family Structure, Inheritance, and Mobility in Andover, Massachusetts, 1630–1750" [PhD dissertation, Harvard University, 1964], 346)

6   Daniel S. Durrie, *A Genealogical History of the Holt Family in the United States: more particularly its descendants of Nicholas Holt of Newbury and Andover, Mass., ...* (Albany, NY: J. Munsell, 1864), 12, 16; Charlotte Helen Abbott, "Early Records of the Holt Family of Andover," unpublished genealogy in the "Abbott Genealogies" collection of Memorial Hall Library, Andover, MA [accessible online at mhl.org/andover/abbott], 2, 6. The farm of James and Hannah Holt was located on the south side of Holt Hill. (Ibid., 2)

7   Carol F. Karlsen, *The Devil in the Shape of a Woman: Witchcraft in Colonial New England* (New York: Vintage Books, 1989), 98–100; Charlotte Helen Abbott, "Early Records of the Allen Families of Andover," unpublished genealogy in the "Abbott Genealogies" collection of Memorial Hall Library, Andover, MA (see preceding note), 1; Abbott, "Early Records of the Holt Family of Andover," 6. For Toothaker sources, see endnote 9.

8   Karlsen, *The Devil in the Shape of a Woman,* 99–100; Mary Beth Norton, *In the Devil's Snare: The Salem Witchcraft Crisis of 1692* (New York: Vintage Books, 2003), 182–183, 233–235, 241–242, 254–256; Sarah Loring Bailey, *Historical Sketches of Andover, Massachusetts* (Boston: Houghton Mifflin, 1880), 203–209; Richard Latner, "'Here Are No Newters': Witchcraft and Religious Discord in Salem Village and Andover," *New England Quarterly,* 79:1 (March 2006): 111; Bernard Rosenthal, ed., *Records of the Salem Witch-Hunt* (New York: Cambridge University Press, 2009), 335–337.

Interpretations of Martha Carrier have changed radically over the course of three centuries. In 1692, Cotton Mather and other members of the Massachusetts Bay elite regarded her as a "Rampant hag." (Norton, *In the Devil's Snare*, 241) Present-day observers are more inclined to view her as a strong, feisty, even noble American heroine who, in the face of acute persecution, maintained her moral integrity by refusing to confess to witchcraft and rejecting the expedient alternative: a guilty plea that presumably could have saved her life. During a volatile court examination in May, several of her allegedly afflicted victims feigned violent fits, claiming that her specter was torturing them in the courtroom and that they could see Satan whispering in her ear. "It is false the Devil is a liar," Carrier vehemently informed the court, and she went on to scold the presiding magistrate: "It is a shamefull thing that you should mind these folks that are out of their wits." (Rosenthal, *Records of the Salem Witch-Hunt*, 335–336)

Prior to her August trial, Carrier's children (Rebecca Holt's first cousins) were forced to provide incriminating testimony against their mother. Initially, her two teenage sons, Richard and Andrew, were unforthcoming under interrogation, but after being taken from the courtroom and subjected to brutal physical torture they proved to be much more cooperative. According to the account of accused witch John Proctor, who was already in jail, the two Carrier boys "would not confess any thing till they tyed them Neck and Heels till the Blood was ready to come out of their Noses, and . . . this was the occasion of making them confess . . . they said one had been a Witch a Month, and the other five Weeks, and that their mother had made them so . . ." (Bernard Rosenthal, *Salem Story: Reading the Witch Trials of 1692* [New York: Cambridge University Press, 1993], 61; Norton, *In the Devil's Snare*, 234–236) Ten-year-old Thomas Carrier Jr. and his 7-year-old sister Sarah were also pressured into confessing that they were witches and that it was their mother who had recruited them into Satan's ranks. (Norton, *In the Devil's Snare*, 254–255) The four children avoided conviction.

Martha Carrier's arrest in May quickly unleashed a torrent of additional witchcraft accusations in Andover. In all, at least forty-three of the town's inhabitants were accused and thirty or more confessed— by far the largest numbers of accused and confessed witches in any Essex County town during the crisis. (Chadwick Hansen, "Andover Witchcraft and the Causes of the Salem Witchcraft Trials," in Howard Kerr and Charles L. Crow, eds., *The Occult in America: New Historical Perspectives* [Champaign, IL: University of Illinois Press, 1983], 46, 50; Latner, "'Here Are No Newters,'" 106)

9   Norton, *In the Devil's Snare*, 172, 182, 239–241, 291, 376n36, 407n56; "Roger Toothaker II (1634–1692)," online at Wikitree.com/wiki/Toothaker-2; Richard Godbeer, *The Devil's Dominion: Magic and Religion in Early New England* (New York: Cambridge University Press, 1992), 215; Rosenthal, *Salem Story*, 52.

10   Charlotte Helen Abbott, "Early Records of the Allen Families of Andover," 1, "Early Records of the Holt Family of Andover," 6, and "Early Records of the Abbott Family of Andover," 2, 9–15, unpublished genealogies in the "Abbott Genealogies" collection of Memorial Hall Library, Andover, MA (see endnote 6); Essex County, MA: Probate File Papers, 1638–1804, file 13685 (online database, AmericanAncestors .org, New England Historic Genealogical Society, 2013); Greven, *Four Generations*, 142. Rebecca's 17-year-old sister, Lydia, was placed with the family of Benjamin Abbott and her 14-year-old brother, Timothy, with the William Lovejoy family. Initially, Rebecca's wealthy uncle Henry Holt assumed guardianship over her 13-year-old brother, Joseph, but in April 1700 that guardianship was transferred to Benjamin Abbott. John Abbott, Benjamin Abbott, and William Lovejoy ranked second, thirteenth, and fifteenth, respectively, out of 77 taxpayers on the 1699 Andover tax list. (Elinor Abbott, *Our Company Increases Apace: History, Language, and Social Identity in Early Colonial Andover, Massachusetts* [Dallas, TX: SIL International, 2007], 196–198)

11   Greven, *Four Generations*, 41–62, 88, 128, 176, 179; Greven, "Old Patterns in the New World," 134–147. Indians struck the town in 1676, 1689, 1696, and 1697. (Abbot, *Our Company Increases Apace*, 127) As late as 1713, Andover's selectmen complained that good teachers were afraid to settle in the town because "we doe Ly so exposed to our Indgon enemys." (Quoted in James Axtell, *The School Upon a Hill: Education and Society in Colonial New England* [New York: W. W. Norton, 1974], 191)

12   William B. Grow, *Eighty Five Years of Life and Labor* (Carbondale, PA: privately printed by Mount Pleasant Press, 1902), 2.

13   George W. Davis, *John Grow of Ipswich/John (Groo) Grow of Oxford* (Washington, D.C.: privately printed by the Carnahan Press, 1913; repr. Salem, MA: Higginson Book Company, n.d.), 18.

14   Essex County Deeds (Registry of Deeds, Salem, MA), 47:191; Marilynne K. Roach, *Six Women of Salem: The Untold Story of the Accused and Their Accusers in the Salem Witch Trials* (Philadelphia: Da Capo Press, 2013), 299; Paul Boyer and Stephen Nissenbaum, eds., *The Salem Witchcraft Papers: Verbatim Transcripts of the Legal Documents of the Salem Witchcraft Outbreak of 1692*, 3 vols. (New York: Da Capo Press, 1977), I:203 [available online at etext.virginia.edu/salem/withcraft/texts/].

15   Essex County Deeds, 58:271–272, 89:218–219.

16   The possible location of Thomas and Rebecca Grow's homestead was extrapolated from maps produced by S. Forbes Rockwell of the North Andover Historical Society of North Andover, MA. Rockwell's maps, which were based on land deeds and site investigations, have been incorporated into the North Andover Historical Society's photostatic copy of Andover Town Records, "Accepted Town Roads, 1703–1851," 8129, 8134–8135. It is possible that the couple resided in more than one location during their two decades in Andover.

17   Essex County Deeds, 47:192–193.

18   Andover Town Records, "Proprietors Records," North Andover Historical Society, North Andover, MA, 1st Book, 651, 2nd Book, 1006–1007.

19   Allan Kulikoff, *The Agrarian Origins of American Capitalism* (Charlottesville: University Press of Virginia, 1992), 47; Anne S. Lombard, *Making Manhood: Growing Up Male in Colonial New England* (Cambridge, MA: Harvard University Press, 2003), 110–111; Daniel Vickers, *Farmers & Fishermen: Two Centuries of Work in Essex County, Massachusetts, 1630–1850* (Chapel Hill: University of North Carolina Press, 1994), 221; Gloria L. Main, *Peoples of a Spacious Land: Families and Cultures in Colonial New England* (Cambridge, MA: Harvard University Press, 2001), 107, 144–145, 209–210, 213, 235; Joseph F. Kett, "The Stages of Life," in Gordon, ed., *The American Family in Socio-Historical Perspective,* 170; John Demos, *Past, Present, and Personal: The Family and the Life Course in American History* (New York: Oxford University Press, 1986), 97; Anderson, *New England's Generation,* 157–158; Philip J. Greven Jr., "Youth, Maturity, and Religious Conversion: A Note on the Ages of Converts in Andover, Massachusetts, 1711–1749," *Essex Institute Historical Collections,* CVIII (1972): 119–120; Kulikoff, *From British Peasants to Colonial American Farmers,* 244–246; Stephanie Grauman Wolf, *As Various as Their Land: The Everyday Lives of Eighteenth-Century Americans* (New York: HarperCollins, 1994), 140; Ulrich, *Good Wives,* 13–15, 45.

20   James A. Henretta, "Families and Farms: *Mentalité* in Pre-Industrial America," *William and Mary Quarterly,* 35:1 (January 1978): 12–20; Richard L. Bushman, "Markets and Composite Farms in Early America," *William and Mary Quarterly,* 55:3 (July 1998): 362–367; Bushman, *From Puritan to Yankee: Character and the Social Order in Connecticut, 1690–1765* (New York: W. W. Norton, 1967), 26, 30; Toby L. Ditz, *Property and Kinship: Inheritance in Early Connecticut, 1750–1820* (Princeton, NJ: Princeton University Press, 1986), 7–8, 11–12, 117; Vickers, *Farmers & Fishermen,* 206–208, 221, 245–246; James A. Henretta, *The Evolution of American Society, 1700–1815: An Interdisciplinary Analysis* (Lexington, MA: D. C. Heath, 1973), 15, 18; Jackson Turner Main, *Society and Economy in Colonial Connecticut* (Princeton, NJ: Princeton University Press, 1985), ch. 6; Main, *The Social Structure of Revolutionary America* (Princeton, NJ: Princeton University Press, 1965), 149–150; Kulikoff, *From British Peasants to Colonial American Farmers,* 204, 206–207, 217; Bruce C. Mann, *Neighbors and Strangers: Law and Community in Early Connecticut* (Chapel Hill: University of North Carolina Press, 1987), 12–14; Greven, *Four Generations,* 68–69.

21   Greven, *Four Generations,* 117; Main, *Peoples of a Spacious Land,* 210.

22   Walter Nugent, *Structures of American Social History* (Bloomington: Indiana University Press, 1981), 46.

23   David Hackett Fischer, *Growing Old in America* (New York: Oxford University Press, 1978), 56n61.

24   Kenneth A. Lockridge, *Literacy in Colonial New England: An Enquiry into the Social Context of Literacy in the Early Modern West* (New York: W. W. Norton, 1974), 21; Steven Mintz and Susan Kellogg, *Domestic Revolutions: A Social History of American Family Life* (New York: The Free Press, 1988), 56; Essex County Deeds, 58:272.

25   David E. Stannard, *The Puritan Way of Death: A Study in Religion, Culture, and Social Change* (New York: Oxford University Press, 1977), 55.

26   In March 1746, Andrew Allen conveyed to Elizabeth Allen for £250 "Certain pieces or parcels of land situate in Andover . . . the first [of which was] that Land which was Thomas Grows houselot containing by estimation ten acres of land . . . lying by the west side of the way that leads from Joseph Lovejoys to Abraham Fosters." (Essex County Deeds, 89:218–219)

27   S. Forbes Rockwell map incorporated into the North Andover Historical Society's photostatic copy of Andover Town Records, "Accepted Town Roads, 1703–1851" [see endnote 16], 8134.

28   Brown, *Wines and Beers of Old New England,* 48, 51, 54, 56, 62–63; Ulrich, *Good Wives,* 23. For evidence that colonial maltsters grew their own barley, see Howard S. Russell, *A Long, Deep Furrow: Four Centuries of Farming in New England* (Hanover, NH: University Press of New England, 1976), 193–194.

29   Mark Edward Lender and James Kirby Martin, *Drinking in America: A History* (New York: Free Press, 1982), 1–21; Stanley Baron, *Brewed in America: A History of Beer and Ale in the United States* (Boston: Little, Brown, 1962), 6, 12, 31; Bruce C. Daniels, *Puritans at Play: Leisure and Recreation in Colonial New England* (New York: St. Martin's Griffin, 1995), 8, 142–146; Dick Cantwell, "Brewing in Colonial America," in Garrett Oliver, ed., *The Oxford Companion to Beer* (New York: Oxford University Press, 2012), 164–165; Ulrich, *Good Wives*, 23; Brown, *Wines and Beers of Old New England*, 48, 54; James E. McWilliams, "Brewing Beer in Massachusetts Bay, 1640–1690," *New England Quarterly*, 71:4 (December 1998): 543–549, 561–564, 568; Vickers, *Farmers & Fishermen*, 219.

30   Daniel Vickers found evidence that Essex County boys were "grinding malt and carting it to town" for their fathers "by twelve years of age at the latest." (*Farmers & Fishermen*, 221)

31   Lombard, *Making Manhood*, 36–37, 73–74; Mintz and Kellogg, *Domestic Revolutions*, 18; Anderson, *New England's Generation*, 157–158; Kulikoff, *Agrarian Origins of American Capitalism*, 47; Ditz, *Property and Kinship*, 185n16; Main, *Society and Economy in Colonial Connecticut*, 202; Kulikoff, *From British Peasants to Colonial American Farmers*, 240; James A. Henretta, "The Morphology of New England Society in the Colonial Period," *Journal of Interdisciplinary History*, 2:2 (Autumn 1971): 390.

32   Greven, *Four Generations*, 103–106, 124, 127–129, 176, 179 (table 13); Henretta, "Morphology of New England Society in the Colonial Period," 390; Mintz and Kellogg, *Domestic Revolutions*, 18.

33   Mintz and Kellogg, *Domestic Revolutions*, 18; Lombard, *Making Manhood*, 73–74; Kulikoff, *Agrarian Origins of American Capitalism*, 46; Kulikoff, *From British Peasants to Colonial American Farmers*, 240.

34   Greven, *Four Generations*, 123, 156–157, 162–167; Greven, "Four Generations: A Study of Family Structure, Inheritance, and Mobility in Andover, Massachusetts," 271–282, 312–314, 318, 320–322 (Greven quote: 322n17); Charlotte Helen Abbott, "Early Records of the Holt Family of Andover," 3–6 and "The Preston Family of Andover," 2–4, unpublished genealogies in the "Abbott Genealogies" collection of Memorial Hall Library, Andover, MA [see endnote 6]. For chain migration, see Kulikoff, *From British Peasants to Colonial American Farmers*, 149–150; Greven, *Four Generations*, 162; Greven, "Four Generations: A Study of Family Structure, Inheritance, and Mobility in Andover, Massachusetts," 273–275, 314–315. Among the Holt kin who emigrated from Andover to Windham County in the first three decades of the eighteenth century were John Preston (Rebecca's uncle by marriage); four sons (Abiel, Joshua, Robert, Daniel) and two daughters (Debora, Abigail) of her uncle Nicholas Holt II, and three of her uncle Henry Holt's children (sons George and Paul and daughter Katurah). Another of her cousins, John Preston's daughter Rebecca, was married to Robert Holt of Windham.

35   Greven, *Four Generations*, 156–157, 163, 166; Greven, "Four Generations: A Study of Family Structure, Inheritance, and Mobility in Andover, Massachusetts," 272, 275, 280, 312.

36   Essex County Deeds, 58:271–272.

37   Essex County Deeds, 89:218–219.

38   Pomfret Land Records (Town Hall, Pomfret, CT), 2:48–49, 81.

39   Wolf, *As Various as Their Land*, 145. Allan Kulikoff writes: "Only families with assets . . . could afford to move long distances. Frontier migration required money for lodging, a wagon, livestock, and farm tools as well as food to feed the family until the first crop came in." (*From British Peasants to Colonial American Farmers*, 145)

40   Harral Ayres, *The Great Trail of New England* (Boston: Meador Publishing Co., 1940), 206–207, 267; George Francis Marlowe, *The Old Bay Paths* (New York: Hastings House, 1942), passim; "The Connecticut Path: A Preliminary Report on its Route and History" (Hartford: Connecticut Historical Commission, 1998), 9, 27–28.

41   Ellen D. Larned, *History of Windham County, Connecticut*, 2 vols. (Worcester, MA: published by the author, 1874, 1880), I:16–18, 181–192; *Historical and Architectural Survey of Abington in the Town of Pomfret, Connecticut* (Pomfret Historical Society and Connecticut Historical Commission, May 1998), 25–26.

42   Larned, *History of Windham County*, I:187, 188; Charlotte Helen Abbott, "Early Records and Notes of the Chandler Family of Andover," "Abbott Genealogies" [see endnote 6], 4; Pomfret Land Records, 1:21–23, 2:81. Davis, *John Grow of Ipswich*, frontispiece map. Philemon Chandler (1671–c. 1740) was a prominent member of the Pomfret community, serving as a deacon in the Congregational church, a lieutenant in the local militia, and a town selectman. (Abbott, "Early Records and Notes of the Chandler Family of Andover," 4; Larned, *History of Windham County*, I:201, 202)

43   Larned, *History of Windham County,* I:190–191, 203–206.

44   Ibid., I:99–100, 187, 189; Pomfret Land Records, 2:48–49; Abbott, "Early Records of the Holt Family of Andover," 3–6. Among the Andover Holts living in Windham Village in 1731 were six children (sons Abiel, Joshua, Robert, and Daniel, and daughters Debora and Abigail) of Rebecca's uncle Nicholas Holt II, along with two sons (George and Paul) and one daughter (Katurah) of her uncle Henry Holt.

45   Larned, *History of Windham County,* I:188–191, 199, 201, 206, 210, 341, 343. Pomfret's 129 landowners of 1731 are identified in "A True List of the Rateable Estate of the Town of Pomfret for the Year 1731," Pomfret Papers and Records, 1742–1841, MS 68729, Connecticut Historical Society, Hartford. Between 1727 and 1730, four Pomfret men—Amos Dodge, Abiel Cheney, Ebenezer Cheney, and John Brooks—obtained tavern licenses. (Marcella Pasay, *The Windham County, CT County Court Records, 1726–1732: Abstracts of Volume 1* [Bowie, MD: Heritage Books, 2000], 22, 56, 109)

46   John C. Pease and John M. Niles, *A Gazetteer of the States of Connecticut and Rhode Island* (Hartford: William S. Marsh, 1819), 218–219; Albert Laverne Olson, *Agricultural Economy and the Population in Eighteenth-Century Connecticut,* Tercentenary Commission of the State of Connecticut No. 40 (New Haven: Yale University Press, 1935), 4–5; Mann, *Neighbors and Strangers,* 30–31; Bruce C. Daniels, "Economic Development in Colonial and Revolutionary Connecticut: An Overview," *William and Mary Quarterly,* 37:3 (July 1980): 432.

47   Bushman, "Markets and Composite Farms," 351; Ditz, *Property and Kinship,* xiv.

48   Larned, *History of Windham County,* I:206; *Historical and Architectural Survey of Abington,* 26; Bushman, *From Puritan to Yankee,* 126, 134.

49   Larned, *History of Windham County,* I:280; Susan Jewett Griggs, *Folklore and Firesides of Pomfret, Hampton and Vicinity* (Abington, CT: privately published, 1950), Pomfret: 111, Hampton: 25; Howard S. Russell, *A Long, Deep Furrow: Three Centuries of Farming in New England* (Hanover, NH: University Press of New England, 1976), 271.

50   Pomfret Land Records, 2:105.

51   See, for example, Ditz, *Property and Kinship,* 73. Also see Bushman, "Markets and Composite Farms," 364–367; Main, *Social Structure of Revolutionary America,* 105; Main, *Society and Economy in Colonial Connecticut,* 206, 217, 221.

52   Pomfret Land Records, 2:81, 105, 179; 3:194; 4:14, 44–45.

53   Pomfret Land Records, 6:125.

54   Anonymous Account Book, 1740–1752, MS 78603, Connecticut Historical Society, Hartford, 40, 222.

55   Pomfret Land Records, 3:169; Larned, *History of Windham County,* I:201, 208. The property was located on Mashamoquet Brook and bounded on the northwest by land owned by Anthony David and William Stoddard of Boston.

56   Greven, *Four Generations,* 63; Main, *Society and Economy in Colonial Connecticut,* 17, 30–31. Andover and Pomfret taxable-wealth percentages calculated from tax lists referenced in endnotes 57–59.

57   Andover Town Records: "Town and County Tax Lists, North and South End, 1717–1766," microfilm collection, Memorial Hall Library, Andover, MA, reel 4: frames 1085–1086, 1141–1142. (Copies of Andover's early tax lists are also available at the North Andover Historical Society, North Andover, MA.)

58   "A True List of the Rateable Estate of the Town of Pomfret for the Year 1731," Pomfret Papers and Records, 1742–1841, MS 68729, Connecticut Historical Society, Hartford.

59   "A List of ye Rateable Estate of ye Town of Pomfrett for Year 1747" and "List of the Rateable Estate of the Town of Pomfret for the Year 1748," Town Hall, Pomfret, CT.

60   Main, *Society and Economy in Colonial Connecticut,* 208 and 160–161, appendix 4H. If, as Jackson Turner Main has calculated, the true value of a colonial Connecticut taxpayer's wealth was seven times greater than his tax assessment (ibid., 39), Thomas Grow had an estimated net worth of approximately £917 in 1748, based on his assessment of £131-10-0 for that year.

61   Ibid., 63–64, 130, 132, 136–137, 379; Main, *Social Structure of Revolutionary America,* 18, 27; Jackson Turner Main, *Connecticut Society in the Era of the American Revolution* (Hartford: American Revolution Bicentennial Commission of Connecticut, 1977), 12–13; Larned, *History of Windham County,* I:282, 354, 570; Griggs, *Folklore and Firesides of Pomfret, Hampton and Vicinity,* Pomfret: 19; Edward M. Cook Jr., *The Fathers of the Towns: Leadership and Community Structure in Eighteenth-Century New England* (Baltimore: Johns Hopkins University Press, 1976), 75, 116; Ditz, *Property and Kinship,* 8–9, 44.

62   Larned, *History of Windham County,* I:262–263; Main, *Society and Economy in Colonial Connecticut,* 144–145, 211–212, 217–233, 379; Bushman, *From Puritan to Yankee,* 180; Bushman, "Markets and Composite Farms," 365–366; Henretta, "Families and Farms," 19–27.

63   Main, *Society and Economy in Colonial Connecticut,* 220–221.

64   Anonymous Account Book, 1740–1752 [see endnote 54], 10, 40, 46, 143, 158, 197, 207, 222, 228, 234; Laura Johnson (Associate Curator for Textiles, Historic New England, Haverhill, MA), email communication to author, 24 January 2014.

65   Main, *Society and Economy in Colonial Connecticut,* 31, 53–55, 373; Cook, *Fathers of the Towns,* 10, 27; Bruce C. Daniels, *The Connecticut Town: Growth and Development, 1635–1790* (Middletown, CT: Wesleyan University Press, 1979), 66; Ditz, *Property and Kinship,* 9.

66   Pomfret Town Meeting Records, 1719–1788, in "Copy of First Records," Town Hall, Pomfret, CT, 90, 94, 96, 98, 99, 101, 111, 117, 118, 123, 127, 134, 152; Pasay, *Windham County Connecticut: County Court Records, 1732–1736,* 182–201; Cook, *Fathers of the Towns,* 23–27, 32; Daniels, *Connecticut Town,* 72–73, 87–90; Main, *Society and Economy in Colonial Connecticut,* 55. According to town historian Walter Hinchman, Pomfret's first church was located at the northeast corner of the intersection of present-day State Route 169 and Needle's-Eye Road.

67   Larned, *History of Windham County,* I:356–358.

68   Daniels, *Puritans at Play,* 20–23, 221; Joseph A. Conforti, *Imagining New England: Explorations of Regional Identity From the Pilgrims to the Mid-Twentieth Century* (Chapel Hill: University of North Carolina Press, 2001), 68–70, 73.

69   Daniels, *Puritans at Play,* 178–179.

70   Ibid., 196–197.

71   Richard Godbeer, *Sexual Revolution in Early America* (Baltimore: Johns Hopkins University Press, 2002), 227–230; Lombard, *Making Manhood,* 84; Michelle Marchetti Coughlin, *One Colonial Woman's World: The Life and Writings of Mehetabel Chandler Coit* (Amherst: University of Massachusetts Press, 2012), 122; Daniels, *Puritans at Play,* 129; Ulrich, *Good Wives,* 122.

72   Godbeer, *Sexual Revolution in Early America,* 230–231; Daniels, *Puritans at Play,* 21–22; Bushman, *From Puritan to Yankee,* 135–137, 143; Sarah Loring Bailey, *Historical Sketches of Andover, Massachusetts* (Boston: Houghton, Mifflin, 1880), 435–436.

73   George Mooar, *Historical Manual of the South Church in Andover, Mass.* (Andover, MA: printed by Warren F. Draper, 1859), 95–100; "South Church Records—Historical Note" (MS 665), Andover Historical Society, Andover, MA; Claude M. Fuess, *Andover: Symbol of New England* (Andover, MA: Andover Historical Society and North Andover Historical Society, 1959), 105, 123, 156–157; Helen M. Wall, *Fierce Communion: Family and Community in Early America* (Cambridge, MA: Harvard University Press, 1990), 13; Bailey, *Historical Sketches of Andover,* 435–436, 443–444.

74   Quoted in Phillip J. Greven Jr., *The Protestant Temperament: Patterns of Child-Rearing, Religious Experience, and the Self in Early America* (New York: Alfred A. Knopf, 1977), 103.

75   Greven Jr., "Youth, Maturity, and Religious Conversion," 119–125; Coughlin, *One Colonial Woman's World,* 2; Greven, *Protestant Temperament,* 258; Andover South Church Newsletter (27 February 2012).

76   Mooar, *Historical Manual of the South Church,* 121–192; Rev. Samuel Phillips Record Book, 1711–1771 (MS 665, box I-A), Andover Historical Society, Andover, MA.

77   Rev. Samuel Phillips Record Book, 11, 16, 20, 24, 25; Andover South Church Newsletter (27 February 2012). Thomas and Rebecca's children were baptized on the following dates: Joseph, 20 October 1717; Ruth, 7 August 1720; Hannah, 10 November 1723; James, 29 October 1727; and Rebecca, 28 January 1728. Rebecca, the couple's first child, "recognized the Baptismal Covt" along with at least seventy-six other residents of the parish in the aftermath of a severe earthquake that shook Andover on 21 December 1727, spreading fear throughout the community.

78   Assessor's Rate Book, South Parish, Andover, 1710–1749 (MS 665, box II-B) and Deacon's Account Book, South Church, Andover, 1711–1755 (MS 665, box I-B), Andover Historical Society, Andover, MA.

79   Rev. Samuel Phillips Record Book, 11, 16, 20, 24, 25.

80   Charlotte Helen Abbott, "The Grow Family of Andover: Notes on Paternity of John Grow and Mary Farrington," unpublished genealogy in the "Abbott Genealogies" collection of Memorial Hall Library, Andover, MA [see endnote 6], 1–5 and Addendum: memorandum by George W. Davis, 29 April 1915.

81   Ibid., 4–5 and Addendum: Davis memorandum; Andover Town Records, "Town Meeting Records, 1709–1773," typewritten transcripts, North Andover Historical Society, North Andover, MA, 5139; Davis, *John Grow of Ipswich*, 15–16, 23–24.

82   Greven, *Four Generations*, 213n20; Abbott, "Grow Family of Andover," Addendum: Davis memorandum.

83   Abbott, "Grow Family of Andover," 3–5.

84   Larned, *History of Windham County*, I:342, 351; Pomfret Town Records: "First Society Record, 1733–1799," (Town Hall, Pomfret, CT), 3, 34, 37, 42; Pomfret Town Meeting Records, vol.1, entry for 2 December 1754; Daniels, *Connecticut Town*, 88; Cook, *Fathers of the Towns*, 25.

85   Larned, *History of Windham County*, I:281.

86   Ibid., I:281–282.

87   Coughlin, *One Colonial Woman's World*, 106.

88   Cornelia Hughes Dayton, "Taking the Trade: Abortion and Gender Relations in an Eighteenth-Century New England Village," *William and Mary Quarterly*, XLVIII:1 (January 1991): 19–49.

89   Main, *Society and Economy in Colonial Connecticut*, ch. 6; Fischer, *Growing Old in America*, 53–55; Ditz, *Property and Kinship*, 158–159.

90   Ditz, *Property and Kinship*, 107n10. See also Henretta, "Morphology of New England Society in the Colonial Period," 390. In Andover, fathers were selling portions of their estates to their sons (usually their eldest sons) from 1720 onward. See Greven, *Four Generations*, 131–137.

91   Toby Ditz (Professor of History, Johns Hopkins University, Baltimore, MD), email communication to author, 9 April 2014.

92   Pomfret Land Records, 3:186.

93   Pomfret Land Records, 3:194.

94   Pomfret Land Records, 4:44–45.

95   Pomfret Land Records, 4:44.

96   Larned, *History of Windham County*, I:521–522.

97   John Duffy, *Epidemics in Colonial America* (Baton Rouge: Louisiana State University Press, 1953), 184–201. In treating pleurisy, rural New England doctors at the time commonly relied on a "vigorous use of bleeding," extracting up to forty ounces of blood from their already weakened patients. (Laurel Thatcher Ulrich, *A Midwife's Tale: The Life of Martha Ballard, Based on Her Diary, 1785–1812* [New York: Vintage Books, 1991], 258) As one historian notes, "About all that the doctors" of this period "knew how to do was to abuse the bodies of the sick 'with frequent and full bleedings; often three times in as many days; with frequent emetics and cathartics, blistering, sweating, etc.' The cure was as bad as the disease." (Lewis D. Stilwell, *Migration from Vermont* [Montpelier: Vermont Historical Society, 1948], 108)

98   Ditz, *Property and Kinship*, 52, 70, 129–130, 132–133, 159; Ulrich, *Good Wives*, 37, 148. According to Ulrich, the prevailing inheritance pattern in eighteenth-century New England was "land for sons, movables for daughters, and for widows a carefully defined dependency." (Ibid., 148)

99   Pomfret Land Records, 4:125–126.

100 Pomfret Land Records, 4:128.

101 Davis, *John Grow of Ipswich*, 19.

102 Main, *Society and Economy in Colonial Connecticut*, 55, 373; Main, *Connecticut Society in the Era of the American Revolution*, 11, 22. The "continuous geometric coils" that decorate the vertical side panels of Thomas' headstone "dotted the burial grounds of the Connecticut Valley" from the 1720s onward. (Allan I. Ludwig, *Graven Images: New England Stonecarving and its Symbols, 1650–1815*, 3rd ed. [Hanover, NH: University Press of New England, 1966], 394, 396 [plate 234D], 398 [plate 235B])

103 Ludwig, *Graven Images*, 67–77, 225–226, 232; Stannard, *Puritan Way of Death*, 156–159, 161, 181; Mintz and Kellogg, *Domestic Revolutions*, 20; James Deetz, *In Small Things Forgotten: An Archeology of Early American*

Life, rev. ed. (New York: Doubleday, 1996), 98, 105. Rebecca's gravestone might have been carved by Richard Kimball (1722–1810), whose place of residence was a short distance from Thomas Grow's property in southwestern Pomfret. See James A. Slater, *The Colonial Burying Grounds of Eastern Connecticut and the Men Who Made Them,* rev. ed. (Hamden, CT: Archon Books for the Connecticut Academy of Arts & Sciences, 1996), 34, 237–239, and figures 24, 136.

GENERATION THREE: THOMAS GROW (1714–1806)

1   George W. Davis, *John Grow of Ipswich/ John (Groo) Grow of Oxford* (Washington, D.C.: privately printed by the Carnahan Press, 1913; repr. Salem, MA: Higginson Book Company, n.d.), 29; Clarence Winthrop Bowen, *The History of Woodstock, Connecticut: Genealogies of Woodstock Families,* 8 vols. (Norwood, MA: privately printed by the Plimpton Press, 1935), 6:381. Susanna Eaton's birth date is a matter of some confusion. George W. Davis, in his Grow family genealogy, erroneously recorded it as 28 November 1712, which, as Bowen points out in his *History of Woodstock* (6:381), was the birth date of Susanna's sister Alice Eaton. According to Bowen, Susanna's actual birth date was 18 April 1715 (ibid.). In his genealogy *Eaton Family of Dedham and the Powder House Rock* (Dedham, MA: privately printed, 1900), John Eaton Alden identifies Susanna's birth date as 18 April 1715 (53–54). Susanna's eldest sister Lydia (1707–?) was the wife of Philemon Chandler, the prominent Pomfret landowner from whom Thomas' father purchased property in 1731 (ibid.).

2   WPA Architectural Survey—Census of Old Buildings in Connecticut: Hampton Historical Building #031a, Connecticut State Library Digital Collections online at cslib.org, accessed August 2013; J. Frederick Kelly, *Early Domestic Architecture of Connecticut* (New York: Dover Publications, 1963), ch. II; *Historic and Architectural Survey of Abington in the Town of Pomfret, Connecticut* (Pomfret Historical Society and Connecticut Historical Commission, May 1998), 73. Dimension measurements by author.

3   WPA Architectural Survey; Kelly, *Early Domestic Architecture of Connecticut,* 102, 120, 167, 173, 187.

4   Philip J. Greven Jr., *Four Generations: Population, Land, and Family in Colonial Andover, Massachusetts* (Ithaca, NY: Cornell University Press, 1970), 131–137; Gordon S. Wood, *The Radicalism of the American Revolution* (New York: Vintage, 1993), 50; Pomfret Land Records, Town Hall, Pomfret, CT, vol. 3, p. 186; vol. 4, p. 44.

5   See Generation Two.

6   Pomfret Land Records, vol. 3, p. 186; vol. 5, pp. 25, 31; vol. 6, pp. 21, 188.

7   Sarah F. McMahon, "A Comfortable Subsistence: The Changing Composition of Diet in Rural New England, 1620–1840," *William and Mary Quarterly,* 42:1 (January 1985): 42–43, 45; Howard S. Russell, *A Long, Deep Furrow: Three Centuries of Farming in New England* (Hanover, NH: University Press of New England, 1976), 146; Bruce C. Daniels, "Economic Development in Colonial and Revolutionary Connecticut: An Overview," *William and Mary Quarterly,* 37:3 (July 1980): 441.

8   Richard L. Bushman, *From Puritan to Yankee: Character and the Social Order in Connecticut, 1690–1765* (New York: W. W. Norton, 1967), 135; Jackson Turner Main, *Society and Economy in Colonial Connecticut* (Princeton, NJ: Princeton University Press, 1985), 118–119; Bruce H. Mann, *Neighbors and Strangers: Law and Community in Early Connecticut* (Chapel Hill: University of North Carolina Press, 1987), 64; Russell, *Long, Deep Furrow,* 116, 122–123, 271; Wood, *Radicalism of the American Revolution,* 134–135; Ellen Larned, *History of Windham County, Connecticut,* 2 vols. (Worcester, MA: published by the author, 1874, 1880), II:47; Susan Jewett Griggs, *Folklore and Firesides of Pomfret, Hampton and Vicinity* (Abington, CT: privately printed, 1950), Pomfret: 136, Hampton: 50. At least one Pomfret-area farmer, Israel Putnam, dealt "directly with Boston merchants," finding "a ready market for all the meat on the hoof he could produce." (John Niven, *Connecticut Hero: Israel Putnam* [Hartford: American Revolution Bicentennial Commission of Connecticut, 1977], 20)

9   Pomfret Land Records, vol. 6, p. 136.

10   A List of the Ratable Poles and Ratable Estate of the Third Society of the Town of Pomfret for the Year 1771, Town Hall, Pomfret, CT. Thomas' 1771 tax assessment was £113.

11   List of the Poles and Ratable Estate of the Society of Abington . . . for the Year 1777, Town Hall, Pomfret, CT; Pomfret Land Records, vol. 6, pp. 136, 188; vol. 7, pp. 128–129. In 1777, Thomas' tax assessment was £104-04-00, while his sons Thomas[4] and Nathaniel, who by now had both acquired portions of their father's land, were assessed at £123–15–00 and £35–00–00 respectively.

12   Jackson Turner Main, "Standards of Living and the Life Cycle in Colonial Connecticut," *Journal of Economic History,* 43:1 (March 1983): 162, table 2; Main, *Society and Economy in Colonial Connecticut,* 116 and table 4.1.

13   Wood, *Radicalism of the American Revolution,* 134–135; Laurel Thatcher Ulrich, *A Midwife's Tale: The Life of Martha Ballard, Based on Her Diary, 1785–1812* (New York: Vintage, 1991), 389n10; Gloria L. Main, "The Distribution of Consumer Goods in Colonial New England: A Subregional Approach," in Peter Benes, ed., *Early American Probate Inventories* (Boston: Boston University for the Dublin Seminar for New England Folklife Annual Proceedings, 1987), 164–165, 168; Jackson Turner Main and Gloria L. Main, "Economic Growth and the Standard of Living in Southern New England, 1640–1774," *Journal of Economic History,* 48:1 (March 1988): 28–29, 37–45; Gloria L. Main, *Peoples of a Spacious Land: Families and Cultures in Colonial New England* (Cambridge MA: Harvard University Press, 2001), 222, 225; Bushman, *From Puritan to Yankee,* 108; Joseph A. Conforti, *Imagining New England: Explorations of Regional Identity from the Pilgrims to the Mid-Twentieth Century* (Chapel Hill: University of North Carolina Press, 2001), 68–69.

14   Abel Clark Account Book, 1772–1773, Connecticut Historical Society, Hartford, CT, pp. 96, 156, 165.

15   Pomfret Town Meeting Records, 1719–1788, in Copy of First Records, Town Hall, Pomfret, CT, pp. 99, 111, 117, 134, 159.

16   Hampton Town Records, Book A, Town Hall, Hampton, CT, p. 4.

17   Edward M. Cook Jr., *Fathers of the Towns: Leadership and Community Structure in Eighteenth-Century New England* (Baltimore: Johns Hopkins University Press, 1976), 2, 3, 6, 10, 26, 45.

18   C. C. Goen, *Revivalism and Separatism in New England, 1740–1800* (New Haven: Yale University Press, 1962), 1–6, 37, 39, 41, 130, 139, 208; Douglas L. Winiarski, *Darkness Falls on the Land of Light: Experiencing Religious Awakenings in Eighteenth-Century New England* (Chapel Hill: University of North Carolina Press, 2017), 128–130, 134; Alan Heimert, *Religion and the American Mind: From the Great Awakening to the Revolution* (Cambridge, MA: Harvard University Press, 1966), 3–6, 27, 29, 160, 210; William G. McLoughlin, *Soul Liberty: The Baptists' Struggle in New England, 1630–1833* (Hanover, NH: University Press of New England, 1991), 105, and McLoughlin, *New England Dissent, 1630–1833: The Baptists and the Separation of Church and State* (Cambridge, MA: Harvard University Press, 1971), 279, 342, 350, 353; Edwin S. Gaustad, *The Great Awakening in New England* (New York: Harper, 1957), 11–12, 14, 30, 107; Harry S. Stout, *The New England Soul: Preaching and Religious Culture in Colonial New England* (New York: Oxford University Press, 1986), 180, 192–193, 197; James A. Henretta, *The Evolution of American Society, 1700–1815: An Interdisciplinary Analysis* (Lexington, MA: D. C. Heath, 1973), 130–131; Bushman, *From Puritan to Yankee,* 178–179, 202; Larned, *History of Windham County,* I:394, II:101; James Oliver Robertson and Janet C. Robertson, "The Devotion Family in Eastern Connecticut," in Lance Mayer and Gay Myers, eds., *The Devotion Family: The Lives and Possessions of Three Generations in Eighteenth-Century Connecticut* (New London, CT: Lyman Allyn Art Museum, 1991), 28.

19   Goen, *Revivalism and Separatism in New England,* 7–8, 13–14; McLoughlin, *New England Dissent,* 352; Stout, *New England Soul,* 188–189; Gaustad, *Great Awakening in New England,* 19–20, 23, 106. Edwards' block quote from "The Eternity of Hell Torments," (Sermon XI) in Jonathan Edwards, *Works,* 10 vols. (New York: S. Converse, 1829–1830), vol. VI:122–123.

20   Goen, *Revivalism and Separatism in New England,* 9, 15–16, 18; Gaustad, *Great Awakening in New England,* 24–26, 28; Heimert, *Religion and the American Mind,* 35, 37, 160, 208–209, 228–229; Stout, *New England Soul,* 189–193; Winiarski, *Darkness Falls on the Land of Light,* 133–141, 143, 512.

21   Goen, *Revivalism and Separatism in New England,* 9–10, 16–17, 29, 31, 136, 174; Stout, *New England Soul,* 189, 200; Gaustad, *Great Awakening in New England,* 72; Henretta, *Evolution of American Society,* 131, 134–135; Heimert, *Religion and the American Mind,* 93; McLoughlin, *New England Dissent,* 136; Winiarski, *Darkness Falls on the Land of Light,* 138–139, 141–142, 146–181, 186–194, 287–290, 322–333, 387–389.

22   Gaustad, *Great Awakening in New England,* 35, 38; Goen, *Revivalism and Separatism in New England,* 21–22, 48–52; Heimert, *Religion and the American Mind,* 54; Stout, *New England Soul,* 194–195; McLoughlin, *New England Dissent,* 349–350; Winiarski, *Darkness Falls on the Land of Light,* 144–146, 333–342.

23   William McLoughlin, *Isaac Backus and the American Pietistic Tradition* (Boston: Little, Brown, 1967), 45.

24   Heimert, *Religion and the American Mind,* 164, 177; Goen, *Revivalism and Separatism in New England,* 10, 12, 54–55, 57–62; Gaustad, *Great Awakening in New England,* 78, 103; Stout, *New England Soul,* 195; Winiarski, *Darkness Falls on the Land of Light,* 267–268, 274–276, 299–301; Bushman, *From Puritan to Yankee,* 186–187.

25   Goen, *Revivalism and Separatism in New England*, vii, 35–36, 66–67; McLoughlin, *New England Dissent*, 346–349; Winiarski, *Darkness Falls on the Land of Light*, 304–305, 358–364, 372–384, 494–496.

26   Goen: *Revivalism and Separatism in New England*, 39, 154–155, 164; Stout, *New England Soul*, 210; Heimert, *Religion and the American Mind*, 25, 29, 93, 162, 193, 195; McLoughlin, *New England Dissent*, 120, 216, 341, 345–346, 348–349, 574; Winiarski, *Darkness Falls on the Land of Light*, 382, 393, 396–399. "Evangelicalism," historian Catherine Brekus writes, "remained closely connected to older forms of Puritanism, and . . . there were clear continuities between seventeenth-century Puritans and their eighteenth-century evangelical descendants." (*Sarah Osborn's World: The Rise of Evangelical Christianity in Early America* [New Haven, CT: Yale University Press, 2013], 11)

27   McLoughlin, *New England Dissent*, 345–346, 348, 359, 361–363, 366, 371, 374, 483, 1002; Heimert, *Religion and the American Mind*, 164; Goen, *Revivalism and Separatism in New England*, 10, 22–23, 39–40, 58–59, 67n79, 134, 141–142, 195, 202; Larned, *History of Windham County*, I:478–479; Gaustad, *Great Awakening in New England*, 74–75, 109; Winiarski, *Darkness Falls on the Land of Light*, 393.

28   McLoughlin, *New England Dissent*, vii, xvi, xx, 2–4, 16–21, 206–212, 214, 222, 233, 243, 257–259, 269, 273, 275, 279–280, 282, 348, 422–423, 425, 428, 438, 551, 553, 559; Goen, *Revivalism and Separatism in New England*, 206; Winiarski, *Darkness Falls on the Land of Light*, 400–401; Gaustad, *Great Awakening in New England*, 120–123; Henretta, *Evolution of American Society*, 136; Bushman, *From Puritan to Yankee*, 222; McLoughlin, *Soul Liberty*, 3–4, 6–9.

29   Pomfret Town Records, First Society Record, 1733–1799, Town Hall, Pomfret. CT, pp. 9–10; Larned, *History of Windham County*, I:508–516, 552; J. Frederick Kelly, *Early Connecticut Meetinghouses* (New York: Columbia University Press, 1948), 3; *Historic and Architectural Survey of Abington in the Town of Pomfret*, 31–32.

30   Larned, *History of Windham County*, I:393–485 (Windham Village: 434; Pomfret: 464), 515–516 (Abington).

31   Goen, *Revivalism and Separatism in New England*, 228–229; Isaac Backus, *A History of New England, with Particular Reference to the Denomination of Christians Called Baptists*, 2 vols., 2nd ed. (Newton, MA: Backus Historical Society, 1871; repr. New York: Arno Press, 1969), II:521–522; McLoughlin, *New England Dissent*, 949–950; Larned, *History of Windham County*, II:100. Ledoyt's age in 1763 was calculated from his gravestone inscription, which states that he "died at Woodstock March 24th 1813 in the 70th year of his age." ("Cemetery Transcriptions from the NEHGS Manuscript Collections," New England Historic Genealogical Society, 2002, online database, accessed at AmericanAncestors.org, September 2014)

32   Ledoyt letter to Isaac Backus, undated, in Backus, *History of New England*, II:522-523n1.

33   Backus, *History of New England*, II:521–524; Goen, *Revivalism and Separatism in New England*, 228–229; Larned, *History of Windham County*, II:100–103; McLoughlin, *New England Dissent*, 949–950.

34   I am greatly indebted to the late Bruce Steiner, professor emeritus of history at Ohio University and a leading authority on eighteenth-century Connecticut church history, for his insights into the conditions that might have caused the Grow family to separate from the Abington Congregational Church and help launch a rival Separate Baptist church in the Grow Hill area of Abington. In a 3 November 2014 letter to the author, Professor Steiner called my attention to evidence of the discontents simmering in the Abington and Windham Village Congregational churches c. 1770.
        According to a 1781 Abington Congregational Church document, for example, Reverend Ripley had been unable to fulfill his regular ministerial duties "*for years*" (emphasis added). "[B]y the frequent Returns of an Inveterate Malody which Increased upon him . . . he hath Every year been Confined for weeks to his Bed and for Months to his house." (Connecticut Archives, Ecclesiastical Affairs [MS. F91/C56, Connecticut State Library, Hartford], 15:49) For efforts by Ripley's congregation to withhold his salary and dismiss him, see ibid., 15:35–36; and Larned, *History of Windham County*, II:196–197.
        A 1783 Windham Village Congregational Church document noted that Reverend Mosely "*for some time past* through Bodily infirmity has been wholly unable to perform Ministerial Duties," and "*for many years past* has for a considerable part of the time been wholly unable to perform Publick Preaching whereby this Society have been put to great Expence to procure preaching among us and a considerable part of the time have been without the dispensation of the Gospel." (Hampton, CT First Congregational Church Records [ms. 974.62/ H181cr, Connecticut State Library, Hartford], vol. III:67–68), (emphasis added). For Mosely's disputes with members of his congregation, see Franklin Bowditch Dexter, ed., *Literary Diary of Ezra Stiles*, 3 vols. (New York: Scribner's Sons, 1901), I:147–149; and Larned, *History of Windham County*, II:60–67. Among the charges against him was the classic Separatist complaint that he did "very much err in opening the door so

wide into the church as to admit members without some satisfying account of a work of grace on their hearts, and without the consent of the church, merely because they say they are of a mind to come. We think, sir, it is the right way to let Anti-Christ into the church full breast, for certain unclean persons and hypocrites have no right in Christ's church." (Ibid., II:63) The names of some of the critics within his congregation (or their sons)—men like Ebenezer Griffin and George Martin—later appear in the membership records of the Grow Hill Baptist Church. (Hampton Baptist Church Records, 1770–1852 [Connecticut State Library, Hartford], vol. 3, part 1: "Meeting House Subscriptions 1791," [unpaginated], and vol. 4: "Subscriptions, 1796–1817," 12–16; also see note 37)

35 Bruce Steiner, letter to author, 3 November 2014. According to Professor Steiner, "Generally speaking, Connecticut's ecclesiastical societies functioned effectively only within a 3-mile radius of the meetinghouse. Beyond that invisible circle, people attended Sabbath services less frequently [and] got less for their ministerial taxes, as it were, than those more conveniently situated. The 3-mile radius assumes a topography making for relatively easy travel; if, however, the landscape was especially hilly, or if travel was clogged by swamps or streams and necessitated a roundabout route, requiring a journey by road much longer than the straight-line distance from homestead to meetinghouse, the system could function poorly even within the 3-mile radius." "It appears," Steiner concludes, "that the Abington/[Windham Village] borderland had a to-meetinghouse travel-time/mileage problem."

36 Ibid.

37 Unless otherwise noted, this historical sketch of the Grow Hill Baptist Church and the Grow family's involvement in it is drawn from volume one ("Meetings of the Church, 1770–1817") of the church's original records, a five-volume collection catalogued as Hampton Baptist Church Records, 1770–1853 (ms. 974.62/H182b) in the Connecticut State Library, Hartford. The other members of the founding group were James Raymond Jr. (who hosted the meeting), Nathan Dean, Silas Record, Abayal Lyon, and Nehemiah Dodge.

38 According to William McLoughlin, "Most Separate churches began worship in private homes or barns." *New England Dissent*, 346–347.

39 According to a manuscript document in the Isaac Backus Papers (Andover Newton Theological School, currently on loan to Brown University) listing the dates when New England Baptist churches were founded and their elders ordained, "A Church was gathered at Abington in Pomfret[,] Jan[.], 18, 1776, by 10 males and 4 females. In June 1776 [at the time of William Grow's ordination] they were 25." Copy of document attached to a personal letter from Bruce Steiner to the author, 3 November 2014.

40 McLoughlin, *Soul Liberty*, 270, and *New England Dissent*, 742.

41 Main, *Society and Economy in Colonial Connecticut*, 53, 317. Main elsewhere describes deacons as "men of local consequence." (*Connecticut Society in the Era of the American Revolution* [Hartford: American Revolution Bicentennial Commission of Connecticut, 1977], 69)

42 Hampton Baptist Church Records, vol. 3, part 1 ("Meeting House Subscriptions, 1791"). On 1 June 1791, according to the Hampton Town Records, "Thomas Grow and Nathaniel Grow of Hampton quit-claimed unto the first Baptist Church and their Society in the Town of Hampton a tract of land . . . to build a public meeting house thereon and also a meeting house green, beginning at a stake and stones on the South Side of the highway leading from Hampton to Pomfret and at the northeast corner of a certain tract of land formally owned by Jordan Dodge now owned by Jacob Holt and wife . . ." (Hampton Town Records, Book C, p. 316, Town Hall, Hampton, CT) From 1785 onward, Thomas and his son Nathaniel were co-owners of a substantial portion of the family's Grow Hill farm.

43 William G. McLoughlin, ed., *The Diary of Isaac Backus*, 3 vols. (Providence: Brown University Press, 1971), II:889–890; Goen, *Revivalism and Separatism in New England*, 223, 269, 273; McLoughlin, *Soul Liberty*, 270–271.

44 Davis, *John Grow of Ipswich*, 36–37; Goen, *Revivalism and Separatism in New England*, 243, 275–276; Gaustad, *Great Awakening in New England*, 109; McLoughlin, *Soul Liberty*, 270–271. As Davis noted, there is no evidence that William Grow graduated from Rhode Island College. That he was residing in Providence in 1774, however, is confirmed by his membership in that town's First Baptist Church, of which James Manning was the pastor. ("Providence, Rhode Island: Catalog of the Members of the First Baptist Church," New England Historic Genealogical Society, 2003, online database, AmericanAncestors.org. Originally published as *Historical Catalogue of the Members of the First Baptist Church in Providence, Rhode Island* by Henry Melville King [Providence: F. H. Townsend, 1908]) According to McLoughlin, Manning's Rhode Island College graduated fewer than twenty students per year until the 1790s. (*New England Dissent*, 770)

45   Hampton Baptist Church Records, vol. 1; McLoughlin, ed., *Diary of Isaac Backus*, II:960–961.

46   Davis, *John Grow of Ipswich*, 30; Michael G. Kenny, *The Perfect Law of Liberty: Elias Smith and the Providential History of America* (Washington, D.C.: Smithsonian Institution Press, 1994), 42, 46, 276–277n30.

47   The "Articles of Belief" are included in volume five ("Covenant and Members, 1813–1814, 1823–1844") of the Hampton Baptist Church Records.

48   McLoughlin, *New England Dissent*, 259–260, 273.

49   Hampton Baptist Church Records, vol. 5

50   McLoughlin, *New England Dissent*, 274–275; Hampton Baptist Church Records, vol. 5.

51   McLoughlin, *New England Dissent*, 211–212, 422; Hampton Baptist Church Records, vol. 5.

52   Hampton Baptist Church Records, vols. 1, 5.

53   Ibid., vol. 5; McLoughlin, *New England Dissent*, 274–275; McLoughlin, *Soul Liberty*, 270; Bushman, *From Puritan to Yankee*, 212.

54   McLoughlin, *New England Dissent*, 772–773.

55   Heimert, *Religion and the American Mind*, 59–62, 66–67; Jon Butler, *Awash in a Sea of Faith: Christianizing the American People* (Cambridge, MA: Harvard University Press, 1990), 216–217; McLoughlin, *New England Dissent*, 358, 576.

56   Heimert, *Religion and the American Mind*, 62. In 1997, during one of the author's initial research visits to the Abington area, Wendell Davis, a local-history enthusiast who resided in the Grow Hill neighborhood, informed him that based on local oral history tradition, "Deacon Thomas Grow" (whether father or son is unclear) was an avid student of the Bible who at one point calculated the exact date of Jesus' second coming. On the morning of that day, he dressed himself entirely in white and climbed to the highest point of his barn roof in order to be as close to Heaven as possible when the Savior arrived. At day's end, he climbed down again, announcing—presumably with disappointment—that "nothing happened." On a subsequent research visit a year or two later, a staff member of the Sharpe Hill Vineyard (located on a neighboring hilltop a half-mile southeast of Grow Hill) told the author a virtually identical story about the patriarch of the Sharpe family who owned the property in the eighteenth century. Adding to the unreliability of the story is a third version included in Susan Griggs' *Folklore and Firesides: Pomfret, Hampton and Vicinity*. Griggs describes "two amusing incidents" which "have come down to us" from the mid-nineteenth century about evangelical farmers along "the Hampton-Pomfret line" "who proclaimed the second coming of Christ and the end of the world . . . Certain members of the Kimball family [who lived on Kimball Hill, a hilltop farm adjacent to Grow Hill and Sharpe Hill] robed themselves in white on the day appointed for the 'Judgment,' and spent the day on a shed roof awaiting the 'last Trumpet'; so, also, Reuben Elliot—who . . . lived [in a Grow Hill house formerly owned by the Grows]—dressed in white and climbed a tall pole to be ready for the 'coming.'" (Hampton: 99) The lesson is clear: no matter how colorful or charming, local oral history traditions are to be treated with considerable caution as sources of family history information.

57   McLoughlin, *New England Dissent*, 773.

58   Hampton Baptist Church Records, vol. 5.

59   McLoughlin, *Soul Liberty*, 157, 159, 290; McLoughlin, *New England Dissent*, 922, 923.

60   Abington Congregational Church Records, Connecticut State Library, Hartford, I:66, 78; Hampton First Congregational Church Records, III:58. I am indebted to Professor Bruce Steiner (see note 34) for calling my attention to these references.

61   McLoughlin, *Soul Liberty*, 157–161, 166, 174–175, 231–232, 252, 262–263; McLoughlin, *New England Dissent*, 447, 450, 542, 547–554, 946; Winiarski, *Darkness Falls on the Land of Light*, 517. Critics claimed that Baptist dissenters "get under water to wash away their *minister's rates*." (Ibid., 401)

62   Griggs, *Folklore and Firesides of Pomfret, Hampton and Vicinity*, Hampton: 96–97.

63   McLoughlin, *New England Dissent*, 751–752.

64   Ibid., 339–341, 354–355, 358, 438, 551, 553, 559, 564, 572–575, 585–586; Goen, *Revivalism and Separatism in New England*, 28, 50, 53, 128, 269; Henretta, *Evolution of American Society*, 136–137; Heimert, *Religion and the American Mind*, 12, 203. Heimert writes that the evangelical religion of the Separate Baptists "embodied a radical and even a democratic challenge to the standing order of colonial America," (ibid., 12), and that "The ultimate goal of those who demanded religious liberty in the decades before the Revolution was, in the

profoundest sense, freedom of speech—the right of as many Americans as possible to hear not merely the doctrines, but the voices, of the evangelical clergy. The quest for religious freedom, involved as it came to be with the economic and political question of taxes, poured much of the energy of evangelical religion directly into the movement that became the American Revolution." (Ibid., 207) In Douglas Winiarski's view, "the Separate movement later served as a proving ground for Revolutionary radicalism." (*Darkness Falls on the Land of Light*, 380)

65   Larned, *History of Windham County*, II:144–161; Henry P. Johnston, ed., *Record of Service of Connecticut Men in the War of the Revolution, 1775–1783* (Hartford: Case, Lockwood & Brainard Co., 1889), 58.

66   "Muster and Pay Rolls of the War of the Revolution, 1775–1783: Miscellaneous Records," online database at ancestry.com, accessed May 2008, records 1,049–1,058, 1,130–1,139; Richard Buel Jr., *Dear Liberty: Connecticut's Mobilization for the Revolutionary War* (Middletown, CT: Wesleyan University Press, 1980), 73–75. On 14 September 1776, Nathaniel Grow marched to West Chester, NY, as a private in the 11th Connecticut Militia Regiment's 3rd Company ("of Killingly"), under the command of Captain Joseph Cady. (Johnston, *Record of Service of Connecticut Men in the War of the Revolution*, 461)

67   Albert Carlos Bates, ed., *Rolls and Lists of Connecticut Men in the Revolution, 1775–1783 (Collections of the Connecticut Historical Society, Vol. 8)* (Hartford: Connecticut Historical Society, 1901), p. 149; repr. Bowie, MD: Heritage Books, 2000.

68   Charles P. Neimeyer, *The Revolutionary War* (Westport, CT: Greenwood Press, 2007), 4.

69   Thomas Grosvenor deposition, 28 September 1818, Ebenezer Grow Pension File, No. 36566, "Revolutionary War Pensions," online database at footnote.com, accessed August 2009. According to historian Stephanie Wolf, "what we call 'mental illness'" was "referred to by eighteenth-century people as 'insanity,' 'madness,' or sometimes 'derangement.' Before the Revolution, there was actually a rather tolerant attitude toward madness. It was seen as a recurring rather than a continuous state, so that between bouts of its outbreak, the individual was expected to perform usefully in society... Colonists found the insane to be 'irritating nuisances' [but not] persons to be controlled, confined, or cured." (*As Various as Their Land: The Everyday Lives of Eighteenth-Century Americans* [New York: HarperCollins, 1993], 244)

70   In his sixties, Ebenezer was still signing legal documents with a "mark" rather than a signature, a strong indication of illiteracy. See the documents of March and April 1818 that he submitted in support of his request for a revolutionary war pension, in the online collection "Revolutionary War Pensions" cited in the preceding endnote. A 1780 document acknowledging his receipt of a reenlistment bounty contains what might be his signature, but with the name "Ebenezer" misspelled "Ebaezer." ("Zebediah Ingalls Collection," Revolutionary War Miscellaneous Collection, 1774–ca.1847, New-York Historical Society, New York, NY)

71   Charles Neimeyer, *America Goes to War: A Social History of the Continental Army* (New York: New York University Press, 1996), 8–18, 109; John Ferling, *Almost a Miracle: The American Victory in the War of Independence* (New York: Oxford University Press, 2007), 340. Also see Robert A. Gross, *The Minutemen and Their World* (New York: Hill and Wang, 1976), 146–152.

72   Davis, *John Grow of Ipswich*, 40.

73   Ibid.

74   Ibid.; Johnston, *Record of Service of Connecticut Men in the War of the Revolution*, 461; Buel, *Dear Liberty*, 76–77; Larned, *History of Windham County*, II:164–168; Ferling, *Almost a Miracle*, ch. 6. British forces killed, wounded, or captured one-third of the 3,500 American troops deployed against them during the Long Island engagement. (Ira D. Gruber, "America's First Battle: Long Island, 27 August 1776," in Charles E. Heller and William A. Stofft, eds., *America's First Battles, 1776–1965* [Lawrence: University Press of Kansas, 1986], 25; also see Joseph J. Ellis, *Revolutionary Summer: The Birth of American Independence* [New York: Knopf, 2013], ch. 6.) Among the Connecticut officers commanding American units in the fighting were General Israel Putnam, General Samuel Holden Parsons, and Colonel Gold S. Silliman. (Ibid., 21, 28)

75   Ebenezer Grow pension petition, 18 March 1818, Ebenezer Grow Pension File, No. 36566, "Revolutionary War Pensions"; Johnston, *Record of Service of Connecticut Men in the War of the Revolution*, 253, 255–256; Tom Jones and John R. Elting, "Sherburne's Additional Continental Regiment, 1779," *Military Collector and Historian*, 31:1 (Spring 1979): 19.

76   Johnston, *Record of Service of Connecticut Men in the War of the Revolution*, 245, 253; Jones and Elting, "Sherburne's Additional Continental Regiment"; Francis A. Galgano, "The Revolutionary War in the Hudson Highlands: Fortifying West Point, 1775–1779," *Middle States Geographer*, 43 (2010): 60–71; Neimeyer, *Revolutionary War*, 32–34, 44–48; Buel, *Dear Liberty*, 116; Ferling, *Almost a Miracle*, 120. George

Washington called the Hudson River the "Key to America," while West Point was generally regarded as "America's Gibralter." (Alfred F. Young, *Masquerade: The Life and Times of Deborah Sampson, Continental Soldier* [New York: Knopf, 2004], 94–95) For a detailed history of the Hudson Highlands in the revolution, see Dave Richard Palmer, *The River and the Rock: The History of Fortress West Point, 1775–1783* (New York: Greenwood Publishing Co., 1969).

77 Jones and Elting, "Sherburne's Additional Continental Regiment"; Johnston, *Record of Service of Connecticut Men in the War of the Revolution*, 131. In the Battle of Rhode Island, Sherburne's Regiment fought as a component of Varnum's Brigade, a 998-man unit commanded by Brigadier General James Varnum of Rhode Island and that also included the First Rhode Island Regiment consisting of some 250 freed Rhode Island slaves. During the battle, British Hessian mercenaries repeatedly assaulted American forces on the immediate left and right flanks of Varnum's Brigade, bayoneting wounded American soldiers as they advanced, before being driven back. See Paul F. Dearden, *The Rhode Island Campaign of 1778: Inauspicious Dawn of Alliance* (Providence: Rhode Island Bicentennial Foundation, 1980), 23, 37, 43n86, 113–128; Ferling, *Almost a Miracle*, 309–313, 342; Neimeyer, *Revolutionary War*, 152–154; and two online articles prepared by the Rhode Island Society of the Sons of the American Revolution: "The Battle of Rhode Island" and "Rhode Island Units in the Revolutionary War," online at rhodeislandsar.org, accessed November 2014.

78 Jones and Elting, "Sherburne's Additional Continental Regiment"; Johnston, *Record of Service of Connecticut Men in the War of the Revolution*, 131; Colonel David Humphreys, *An Essay on the Life of the Honorable Major-General Israel Putnam: Addressed to the State Society of the Cincinnati in Connecticut* (Middletown, CT: 1794), 164; Griggs, *Folklore and Firesides of Pomfret, Hampton and Vicinity*, Pomfret: 104; Niven, *Connecticut Hero*, 82; Davis, *John Grow of Ipswich*, 40. According to most sources, Putnam was riding alone when he made his dramatic downhill escape; local Greenwich historian Joseph Zeranski, however, writes in his detailed study of the episode that some of Putnam's soldiers also "headed down the brush-covered, rocky precipice" with him. (*General Putnam's Horseneck Confrontation with the British* [Horseneck, CT: Dumpling Pond Press, 2001], 17)

79 Johnston, *Record of Service of Connecticut Men in the War of the Revolution*, 132, 134, 253.

80 *Muster and Pay Rolls of the War of the Revolution, 1775–1783* (New York: Collections of the New-York Historical Society, 1916), 68–69.

81 Ibid., 89–91.

82 Palmer, *The River and the Rock*, 293–299; "Pay Roll, Maj. Throop's Comp'y," 28 April 1781, in "Revolutionary War Service Records," online database at footnote.com, accessed August 2009.

83 Johnston, *Record of Service of Connecticut Men in the War of the Revolution*, 301–306, 315. Troops stationed at the Highlands engaged in at least two military skirmishes with British forces in 1782–1783. (Ferling, *Almost a Miracle*, 330)

84 Ibid., 359; Ebenezer Grow pension petition, 18 March 1818, Ebenezer Grow Pension File, No. 36566, "Revolutionary War Pensions."

85 Charles Royster, *A Revolutionary People at War: The Continental Army and the American Character, 1775–1783* (Chapel Hill: University of North Carolina Press, 1979), 131; letter, Colonel Henry Sherburne to George Washington, 23 May 1777, Founders Online, National Archives and Records Service, online at founders.archives.gov/documents/Washington/03-09-02-0503, accessed 15 October 2014.

86 Buel, *Dear Liberty*, 221, 235, 250.

87 Neimeyer, *Revolutionary War*, 149; "Pay Abstract of Capt. Amos Stanton's Company, Col. Sherburne's Regt. for the month of November 1779," in "Revolutionary War Rolls," online database at footnote.com, accessed August 2009; "Pay Roll, Maj. Throop's Comp'y," 28 April 1781, and "Pay Roll, Capt. Bulkley's Comp'y," undated 1783, in "Revolutionary War Service Records," online database, footnote.com, accessed August 2009.

88 Neimeyer, *America Goes to War*, 124–126; Ferling, *Almost a Miracle*, 348–349, 351; Buel, *Dear Liberty*, 118; Neimeyer, *Revolutionary War*, 147, 149–151, 157.

89 George E. Scheer, ed., *Private Yankee Doodle: Being a Narrative of Some of the Adventures, Dangers and Sufferings of a Revolutionary Soldier* (Boston: Little, Brown, 1962), passim; Buel, *Dear Liberty*, 181–183, 231, 235–236; Larned, *History of Windham County*, II:178–179, 189, 261; Neimeyer, *Revolutionary War*, 12–13, 75, 78, 80, 104–109, 147, 151–152; Royster, *A Revolutionary People at War*, 32, 34, 60–61, 130–131; Ferling, *Almost a Miracle*, 332–333, 559. According to Ferling, "For every soldier killed in combat, more than two died of disease." (333)

90 Buel, *Dear Liberty,* 179; Ferling, *Almost a Miracle,* 195, 197; Gross, *Minutemen and Their World,* 146–152. Gross writes, "From 1777 on, the Continental ranks were manned largely by the lower social orders." (150)

91 Letter, Col. Henry Sherburne to George Washington, 23 May 1777 (see endnote 85). By 1777, Ebenezer already had been exposed to widespread disease as a member of the 11th Connecticut Militia Regiment at New York the previous autumn. In a letter home dated September 1776, one of his fellow militiamen, Thomas Dike of Thompson, wrote that "It is very sickly here among the militia," while a month later, Oliver Grosvenor of Pomfret, the 11th Regiment's commissary officer, informed his wife that "The sick daily increases [*sic*] in numbers: some companies not more than two or three . . . fit for duty: the rest sick and taking care of the sick. . . . It is not in my power to paint you the doleful scenes I behold every hour: neither did I believe that rational creatures could be divested of that humanity that I find they are subject to in the camps, where sickness and sin so much prevail. Alas for our land which now mourns beneath the horrors and distresses of our present war. . . .Six of our regiment have died since the day before yesterday and now there are a number I expect to hear are dead in the morning." (Ellen Larned, *Historic Gleanings in Windham County, Connecticut* [Providence, RI: Preston and Rounds Co., 1899], 112–113)

Oliver Grosvenor's mention of "sin" probably referred to the prostitution that flourished on the outskirts of Continental Army camps. In his wartime diary, Benjamin Gilbert, a young Massachusetts officer stationed at the Hudson Highlands during the period that Ebenezer Grow was deployed there, recorded at least sixteen visits to "Wyoma," a brothel featuring "super fine Kippen" (whores) located a short distance north of his encampment. In a 1782 letter to a friend, Gilbert wrote that at the Highlands "Nothing is wanting on my part as a soldier to make me happy, but Cunt Cash and New Clothes." (John Shy, ed., *Winding Down: The Revolutionary War Letters of Lieutenant Benjamin Gilbert of Massachusetts, 1780–1783* [Ann Arbor: University of Michigan Press, 1989], 54, 86–87nn187–188)

92 Letter, Major General John Sullivan to George Washington, 4 September 1778, *Calendar of the Correspondence of George Washington, Commander in Chief of the Continental Army with the Officers* (Washington, D.C.: Library of Congress, 1915), 728.

93 Buel, *Dear Liberty,* 181.

94 Scheer, ed., *Private Yankee Doodle,* 171; Neimeyer, *Revolutionary War,* 155.

95 Johnston, *Record of Service of Connecticut Men in the War of the Revolution,* 135–136; Ferling, *Almost a Miracle,* 412–413. Visiting Morristown at the end of May 1780, the Marquis de Lafayette found "An Army that is reduced to nothing, that wants provisions, that has not one of the necessary means to make war, such is the situation wherein I found our troops and however prepared I could have been to this unhappy sight by our past distresses I confess I had no idea of such an extremity." (Quoted in George F. Scheer and Hugh F. Rankin, *Rebels and Redcoats* [Cleveland and New York: World Publishing Co., 1957], 373)

96 Buel, *Dear Liberty,* 224.

97 Scheer, ed., *Private Yankee Doodle,* 172. See also letter, James Fairlie, an American army major at Morristown, to Charles Tillinghast, 12 January 1780, in which Fairlie wrote that "During our hungry time, I Eat [*sic*] several meals of Dogg, and it Rellish'd very well." (Dennis P. Ryan, ed., *A Salute to Courage: The American Revolution as Seen Through Wartime Writings of Officers of the Continental Army and Navy* [New York: Columbia University Press, 1979], 178)

98 Royster, *A Revolutionary People at War,* 299.

99 Jones and Elting, "Sherburne's Additional Continental Regiment."

100 Palmer, *The River and the Rock,* 292–295, 334–336, 348; Scheer, ed., *Private Yankee Doodle,* 275; Ryan, *Salute to Courage,* 213–214; Young, *Masquerade,* 96, 107; Ferling, *Almost a Miracle,* 466–467, 469.

101 Buel, *Dear Liberty,* 164, 168, 177; Larned, *History of Windham County,* II:175, 179; Griggs, *Folklore and Firesides of Pomfret, Hampton and Vicinity,* Pomfret: 121.

102 Main, *Connecticut Society in the Era of the American Revolution,* 54–55, 62; Buel, *Dear Liberty,* 140, 149–150, 240–242; Daniels, "Economic Development and Colonial and Revolutionary Connecticut," 437; Russell, *Long, Deep Furrow,* 224–225; Larned, *History of Windham County,* II:200. In neighboring Massachusetts, "Beef cost $.04 a pound in 1777; three years later, it stood at $1.69 and was still rising." (Gross, *Minutemen and Their World,* 141)

103 "Pomfret Soldiers in the War of the American Revolution in the Pomfret Selectmen's Account, 1781–1848" (Hartford: Connecticut State Library, 1928), [copy in Pomfret Town Hall, pp. 5, 7]; Pomfret Town Meeting Records, 1719–1788 in Copy of First Records, Town Hall, Pomfret. CT, p. 140.

104 Larned, *History of Windham County*, II:243; Richard M. Bayles, ed., *History of Windham County, Connecticut* (New York: W. W. Preston, 1889), 376–377; Miscellaneous Town Records, 1789–1813, Town Hall, Hampton, CT, pp. 1, 7; Marilyn Labbe, *The Poor and Others to be Pitied: Eighteenth and Nineteenth Century Selectmen's Records of Town Welfare Cases—Windham County, Connecticut* (Westminster, MD: Heritage Books, 2005), 291.

105 Hampton Baptist Church Records, vol. 1, pp. 45-47; Davis, *John Grow of Ipswich*, 37; McLoughlin, *Diary of Isaac Backus*, II:961. It appears that Eunice Abbott remained in Hampton, unmarried and living in poverty. During the early 1820s, William's brother Thomas was supporting her economically. (Miscellaneous Town Records: 1812–1854, Town Hall, Hampton, CT, p. 62) The illegitimate child's birth went unrecorded in the Pomfret and Windham Village town records—according to historian Jack Larkin, "even those American communities known for meticulous record-keeping often failed to record illegitimate births" (*The Reshaping of Everyday Life, 1790–1840* [New York: Harper & Row, 1988], 198)—and the child's fate is unknown. According to Grow family genealogist George W. Davis, one of William's offspring—a son named George whose birth date apparently went unrecorded—was of "uncertain" parentage. (*John Grow of Ipswich*, 39) Eunice might have been related to the William Abbott who was a member of the Grow Hill Baptist Church in the 1780s and 1790s. (Hampton Baptist Church Records, vol. 1, pp. 53, 60; vol. 3, part 1)

At the time of his fall from grace, William Grow was an up-and-coming Baptist minister with a growing reputation for eloquent and dynamic preaching that extended well beyond Abington. In August 1781, he preached at the Atherton farm in Andover, Connecticut, some 25 miles west of Abington. Elias Smith, a 12-year-old boy from neighboring Hebron, was in attendance, and later described the profound spiritual impact that Grow's preaching had upon him:

> We heard that a young man was to preach there by the name of *William Grow* from *Abington* in Connecticut. My desire to hear him was very great, I walked on foot early to hear all that he preached. In the forenoon he preached in the house; how he preached, I do not remember. The assembly was so large in the afternoon, that the meeting was held in an orchard. Every thing about the preacher drew my attention to him. He was young, decently dressed, had a melodious and commanding voice; his being in early life engaged in preaching Christ; having left all for him; all these things led me to admire him. I considered him the happiest man on earth, and one whom God delighted to honor. I . . . remember his subject, and believe [I] shall [do] so [as] long as my Memory retains any thing. It was this— "*The glory of Christ, as the judge of the world.*" His description of Christ was new to me, and glorious beyond all I had ever heard before. He described him from the manger to the cross; from the cross to the throne; and from the throne to the judgment seat. After describing the glory of Christ in a manner to me then beyond all I had ever imagined, he said:
>
> > *"All over glorious is my Lord;*
> > *Must be belov'd and yet ador'd;*
> > *His worth if all the nations knew,*
> > *Sure the whole earth would love him too."*
>
> When he came to describe the last judgment, I seemed for a while to forget the preacher, myself, and every thing earthly. O, to what a pitch of wonder, grief, and desire was my mind wrought up, when he described the state of the immortal saints, at the time Christ will say, "Come ye blessed of my father, inherit the kingdom prepared for you from the foundation of the world!" Then, said he, it will be glory to God; glory to Christ; glory to angels; glory to the apostles; glory to martyrs; glory to saints; glory to parents; and glory to *William Grow.* O how these things sounded in my ears, and to my heart.

(Elias Smith, *The Life, Conversion, Preaching, Travels, and Sufferings of Elias Smith* [Portsmouth, NH: Beck & Foster, 1816], 32–34)

A few years later, in May 1789, William Grow baptized Elias Smith in the Quechee River in Woodstock, Vermont. As Smith later recalled,

> "The brethren and others gathered round, and Elder Grow spake solemnly and intelligibly upon the subject, and then led me into the river, and baptized me in the name of the FATHER, SON, and HOLY GHOST; after which we both came up out of the water, following the example of our blessed Lord. When on the bank of the river, we sung a hymn which I had chosen for the occasion . . .The following are the first two verses:

"Blest be my God that I was born,
To hear the joyful sound;
That I was born to be baptis'd,
Where gospel truths abound.
I might have been a pagan born,
Or else a veiled Jew;
Or cheated with an Alcoran [Koran],
Among the Turkish crew."

(Ibid., 129–130)

106 McLoughlin, *Diary of Isaac Backus*, II:1122.

107 Hampton Baptist Church Records, vol. 1, pp. 48–49, 57–61, 101; McLoughlin, *Diary of Isaac Backus*, II:961; Davis, *John Grow of Ipswich*, 37.

108 Davis, *John Grow of Ipswich*, 37–39; McLoughlin, *Diary of Isaac Backus*, II:961; Henry Swan Dana, *History of Woodstock, Vermont* (Boston: Houghton Mifflin, 1889), 373–378; Kenny, *Perfect Law of Liberty*, 56–57; Gladys S. Adams, comp., *Bridgewater, Vermont, 1779–1976* (Bridgewater, VT: Bridgewater Cemetery Commission, 2005), 35, 168. Adams writes, "in Jan 1786" William "bought land in Bridgewater from Joseph Dunham and I. Churchill." (35)

109 David Stannard, *The Puritan Way of Death: A Study in Religion, Culture, and Social Change* (New York: Oxford University Press, 1977), 156–157; Allen I. Ludwig, *Graven Images: New England Stonecarving and its Symbols, 1650–1815*, 3rd ed. (Hanover and London: Wesleyan University Press, 1999), 124, 128, plate 57B. The stylistic features of Susanna Grow's gravestone are highly characteristic of the work of Abington stone-carver Lebbeus Kimball (1750/51–1839), whose family had established a hilltop farm on Kimball Hill a short distance south of Grow Hill. (James A. Slater, *The Colonial Burying Grounds of Eastern Connecticut and the Men Who Made Them*, rev. ed. [Hamden, CT: Archon Books for the Connecticut Academy of Arts & Sciences, 1996], 34–35, figure 25, 240–243)

110 "Thomas Grow and Martha Winter (both of Hampton) were married together November 10, 1786." (Hampton Town Records, Town Hall, Hampton, CT, Book A, p. 257) It is possible that Martha was the widow of Samuel Winter. Samuel Winter married a woman named Martha Ramont (or Raymond) in 1757 and she bore him five children between 1760 and 1767. (*Connecticut Vital Records to 1870 [The Barbour Collection]*, online database, AmericanAncestors.org, from original transcripts, Lucious Barbour, 1928, 1: 107) If Martha Winter's maiden name was in fact Ramont or Raymond, she might have been related to the James Raymond of Abington who hosted the January 1770 meeting at which Biel Ledoyt and seven Abington men, including Raymond, formed the local Baptist society that eventually led to the establishment of the Grow Hill Baptist Church. (Hampton Baptist Church Records, vol. 1, p. 1)

111 The transfer of the 100 acres and "appurtenances" from Thomas[3] to Thomas[4] is not recorded in the Pomfret land records. Nevertheless, on the Abington tax list for 1777, Thomas[4] Grow was for the first time assessed a significantly higher rate than his father (£123 to £81)—an indication that he had become the owner of substantial property on Grow Hill. The lower rate on Thomas[3'] 176 acres presumably reflects the fact that much of that acreage remained undeveloped. (List of the Poles and Ratable Estate of the Society of Abington . . . for the Year 1777, Town Hall, Pomfret, CT)

112 Pomfret Land Records, vol. 6, p. 188.

113 Ibid., vol. 7, pp. 128–129.

114 Nathaniel Grow married Susannah Dow of Pomfret on 16 January 1775. George W. Davis erroneously records Susannah's birth year as 1761, which would have made her 14 years of age at the time of her marriage. (*John Grow of Ipswich*, 39) According to her gravestone in Henderson, Jefferson County, NY, she died on 31 January 1814 at age 62, indicating that she was born in 1751 or 1752 and would have been about 23 at the time of her marriage to Nathaniel. (Find-A-Grave memorial #49511218, online at findagrave.com)

115 1790 Federal Census, Hampton, Windham County, CT, series M637, roll 1, page 272, online at heritagequestonline.com; Davis, *John Grow of Ipswich*, 40.

116 Bruce C. Daniels, *The Connecticut Town: Growth and Development, 1635–1790* (Middletown, CT: Wesleyan University Press, 1979), 46, 52–53; Daniels, "Economic Development and Colonial and Revolutionary Connecticut," 446–447; Buel, *Dear Liberty*, 7, 334; Lewis D. Stilwell, *Migration from Vermont* (Montpelier: Vermont Historical Society, 1948), 76–77.

117 Kenneth A. Lockridge, "Land, Population, and the Evolution of New England Society, 1630–1790," in Stanley N. Katz, ed., *Colonial America: Essays on Politics and Social Development* (Boston, Little, Brown, 1971), 476–482, 485; James A. Henretta, "Families and Farms: *Mentalité* in Pre-Industrial America," *William and Mary Quarterly*, 35:1 (January 1978): 21–22, 27; Toby L. Ditz, *Property and Kinship: Inheritance in Early Connecticut, 1750–1820* (Princeton, NJ: Princeton University Press, 1986), passim; Wood, *Radicalism of the American Revolution*, 47. According to the 8 April 1785 deed in which Thomas transferred half of his dwelling house and remaining land to Nathaniel, he did so in "consideration of the love and good will that I have and have unto my son Nathaniel Grow of Pomfret." (Pomfret Land Records, vol. 7, pp. 128–129)

118 Goen, *Revivalism and Separatism in New England*, 107, 251–252; McLoughlin, *New England Dissent*, 790; Randolph A. Roth, *The Democratic Dilemma: Religion, Reform, and the Social Order in the Connecticut River Valley of Vermont, 1791–1850* (New York: Cambridge University Press, 1987), 34–36, 41–42, 73; *Official History of Guilford, Vermont, 1678–1961: With Genealogies and Biographical Sketches* (Guilford: Town of Guilford and Broad Brook Grange No. 151, 1961), 247–248.

119 Hampton Baptist Church Records, vol. 1, p. 63; *Official History of Guilford, Vermont*, 248, 314.

120 *Official History of Guilford, Vermont*, 303, 314, and district map; Guilford Land Records, Town Offices, Guilford, VT, vol. 3, p. 222. The Grow farm appears to have been located in the immediate vicinity of present-day 563 and 615 Stage Road. Traces of an old farm road can be seen extending from Stage Road up a hillside between the two properties. In 1808, following his father's death and his relocation to Henderson, New York, Nathaniel sold the property to John Barney for $2,200.

121 1800 Federal Census, Guilford, Windham County, VT, series M32, roll 52, page 518, online at heritagequestonline.com.

122 "Vermont Death Records to 1871," in "Vermont Births, 1871–2008; Marriages, 1871–2008; Deaths to 2008," New England Historic Genealogical Society, 2013, online database, AmericanAncestors.org.

123 Deetz, *In Small Things Forgotten: An Archeology of Early American Life*, rev. ed. (New York: Anchor Books, 1996), 95, 97, 99–100; Ludwig, *Graven Images*, 63–64, 142, plates 192C, 192D, 193A, 193B; Stannard, *Puritan Way of Death*, 180–181.

124 Philip Greven, *The Protestant Temperament: Patterns of Child-Rearing, Religious Experience, and the Self in Early America* (New York: Knopf, 1977), chs. 2–3; McLoughlin, *New England Dissent*, 358, 434; J. M. Opal, *Beyond the Farm: National Ambitions in Rural New England* (Philadelphia: University of Pennsylvania Press, 2008), 86.

125 Ditz, *Property and Kinship*, 58, 117–126, 158–160; Allan Kulikoff, *From British Peasants to Colonial American Farmers* (Chapel Hill: University of North Carolina Press, 2000), 230–232.

GENERATION 4: THOMAS GROW (1743–1824)

1   George W. Davis, *John Grow of Ipswich/John (Groo) Grow of Oxford* (Washington, D.C.: privately printed by the Carnahan Press, 1913), 35. Davis provided an incorrect birth date for Experience Goodell; she was born on 23 April 1747. (*Connecticut Vital Records to 1870, [The Barbour Collection]*, online database, AmericanAncestors. org, citing Pomfret Vital Records, 1:51; also see George E. Williams, *A Genealogy of the Descendants of Robert Goodale/Goodell of Salem, Massachusetts* [West Hartford, CT: published by the author, 1984], 60)

2   See Generation Three.

3   Steven Mintz and Susan Kellogg, *Domestic Revolutions: A Social History of American Family Life* (New York: The Free Press, 1988), 51; Gloria L. Main, *Peoples of a Spacious Land: Families and Cultures in Colonial New England* (Cambridge, MA: Harvard University Press, 2001), 104.

4   Allan Kulikoff, *From British Peasants to Colonial American Farmers* (Chapel Hill: University of North Carolina Press, 2000), 263; Charles Neimeyer, *America Goes to War: A Social History of the Continental Army* (New York: New York University Press, 1996), 129; Robert A. Gross, *The Minutemen and Their World* (New York: Hill and Wang, 1976), 146–152.

5   Thomas Grow was a private in Captain Walter Hyde's Company of a Connecticut militia regiment commanded by Colonel Erastus Wolcott of Windsor. On 21 September 1776, the 45-man unit was encamped near Kings Bridge, a strategically important bridge across the Harlem River at the northern tip of Manhattan. Alfred Carlos Bates, ed., *Rolls and Lists of Connecticut Men in the Revolution, 1775–1783 (Collections of the Connecticut Historical Society, Vol. 8)* [Hartford: Connecticut Historical Society, 1901] 149; repr., Bowie, MD: Heritage Books, 2000) To defend Kings Bridge from capture by the British, an event that would have

cut off access to the mainland for American forces on Manhattan and Long Island, George Washington had deployed two brigades to the area surrounding the bridge two weeks earlier. (Barnet Schecter, *The Battle for New York: The City at the Heart of the American Revolution* [New York: Walker & Co., 2002], 72, 79–80, 116, 160, 171) Captain Hyde "died at Horseneck [Greenwich, CT] about Sept. 25." (Henry P. Johnston, ed., *Record of Service of Connecticut Men in the War of the Revolution* [Hartford: Case, Lockwood & Brainard Co., 1889], 629) For the military context of Connecticut militia deployments to New York in September 1776, see Richard Buel Jr., *Dear Liberty: Connecticut's Mobilization for the Revolutionary War* (Middletown, CT: Wesleyan University Press, 1980), 70–80.

6　Letter, Gen. George Clinton to the New York Committee of Correspondence, 18 September 1776, in Dennis P. Ryan, ed., *A Salute to Courage: The American Revolution as Seen Through Wartime Writings of Officers of the Continental Army and Navy* (New York: Columbia University Press, 1979), 44; letter, Lewis Morris Jr., to Lewis Morris, 6 September 1776, quoted in George F. Scheer and Hugh F. Rankin, *Rebels and Redcoats* (Cleveland and New York: World Publishing Co., 1957), 176. "As for the militia of Connecticut, Brigadier Wolcott and his whole brigade have got the cannon fever and very prudently skulked home. Such people are only a nuisance and had better be in the chimney corner than in the field of Mars." (Ibid.) Gen. Clinton added: "We are getting a new Supply of Connecticut militia in here. If they are not better than the last I wish they would keep them at home." (Ryan, ed., *Salute to Courage*, 45) The term "raw militiamen" is taken from Buel, *Dear Liberty*, 75. According to historian Joseph Ellis, "about 10,000 militia" deserted "during the first two weeks of September.[;] . . .whole regiments of Connecticut militia . . . toss[ed] aside their muskets and knapsacks when confronted by only token British opposition." (*Revolutionary Summer: The Birth of American Independence* [New York: Knopf, 2013], 135, 149. Also see Schecter, *Battle for New York*, 181–187.)

7　Jolene Roberts Mullen, *Connecticut Town Meeting Records during the American Revolution*, 2 vols. (Westminster, MD: Heritage Books, 2011), II:192.

8　Pomfret Town Meeting Records, 1719–1788, in "Copy of First Records," pp. 142, 147, 150, Town Hall, Pomfret, CT.

9　"Pomfret Soldiers in the War of the American Revolution in the Pomfret Selectmen's Account, 1781–1848" (Hartford: Connecticut State Library, 1928), p. 2 (copy in Pomfret Town Hall). It was not uncommon for private citizens to pay revolutionary war soldiers' wages out of their own pockets during periods when the public treasuries were empty; see Ellen Larned, *History of Windham County, Connecticut*, 2 vols. (Worcester, MA: published by the author, 1874, 1880), II:186.

10　Pomfret Town Meeting Records, 1719–1788, in "Copy of First Records," pp. 146–147; Mullen, *Connecticut Town Meeting Records during the American Revolution*, II:196. Historian Robert A. Gross writes: "Throughout the war local committees were responsible for furnishing men and materiel to the central authorities. Hometowns helped equip their troops, often paid their wages, and supported the needy families of men away at war." (*The Minutemen and Their World*, 133)

11　Pomfret Town Meeting Records, 1719–1788, in "Copy of First Records," pp. 156–158.

12　Hampton Town Records, Book A, pp. 7, 12, 40, Town Hall, Hampton, CT.

13　Ibid., pp. 5, 32.

14　Ibid., pp. 28, 36.

15　Ibid., p. 46.

16　Jackson Turner Main, *Society and Economy in Colonial Connecticut* (Princeton, NJ: Princeton University Press, 1985), 55; Edward M. Cook Jr., *The Fathers of the Towns: Leadership and Community Structure in Eighteenth-Century New England* (Baltimore: Johns Hopkins University Press, 1976), 1–2, 18, 26, 85, 191.

17　Hampton Town Records, Book A, pp. 59, 71, 75, 80.

18　Ibid., pp. 103, 108.

19　Ibid., pp. 66, 86; Bruce C. Daniels, *The Connecticut Town: Growth and Development, 1635–1790* (Middletown, CT: Wesleyan University Press, 1979), 87–88; Cook, *Fathers of the Towns*, 25.

20　"Pomfret Selectmen's Accounts, 1781–1848," ms. 974.62/P76se, Connecticut State Library, Hartford; Marilyn Labbe, *The Poor and Others to be Pitied: Eighteenth and Nineteenth Century Selectmen's Records of Town Welfare Cases—Windham County, Connecticut* (Westminster, MD: Heritage Books, 2005), 286.

21　Miscellaneous Town Records, 1789–1813, pp. 4, 5, 7, 9, 11, 13, 79; and Miscellaneous Town Records, 1812–1854, p. 62, Town Hall, Hampton, CT.

22 Hampton Baptist Church Records, 1770–1853, ms. 974.62/H182b, Connecticut State Library, Hartford, vol. 1 ("Meetings of the Church, 1770–1817"), pp. 53, 88, 103.

23 Hampton Baptist Church Records, vol. 3, part 1 ("Meeting House Subscriptions 1791").

24 Ibid., vol. 4 ("Subscriptions, 1796–1817").

25 Ibid, vol. 1, p. 103; Jackson Turner Main, *Connecticut Society in the Era of the American Revolution* (Hartford: American Revolution Bicentennial Commission, 1977), 46.

26 Larned, *History of Windham County,* II:246.

27 Davis, *John Grow of Ipswich,* 36.

28 Ibid.

29 Gordon S. Wood, *The Radicalism of the American Revolution* (New York: Vintage Books, 1991), 313–316, and *Empire of Liberty: A History of the Early Republic, 1789–1815* (New York: Oxford University Press, 2009), 2, 702–704, 706–707, 728–729; Christopher Clark, *The Roots of Rural Capitalism: Western Massachusetts, 1780–1860* (Ithaca, NY: Cornell University Press, 1990), 8, 10; Joyce Appleby, *Inheriting the Revolution: The First Generation of Americans* (Cambridge, MA: Harvard University Press, 2000), 5–7, 57–59, 84–85. Gordon Wood writes that "No event in the eighteenth century accelerated the capitalistic development of America more than did the Revolutionary War. It brought new producers and consumers into the market economy, it aroused latent acquisitive instincts everywhere, and it stimulated internal trade as never before." "The inexhaustible needs of three armies—the British and French as well as the American—for everything from blankets and wagons to meat and rum brought into being hosts of new manufacturing and entrepreneurial interests and made market farmers out of husbandmen who before had scarcely ever traded out of their neighborhoods." (*Radicalism of the American Revolution,* 248)

30 Bruce C. Daniels, "Economic Development in Colonial and Revolutionary Connecticut: An Overview," *William and Mary Quarterly,* 37:3 (July 1980): 434, 437–438; Larned, *History of Windham County,* II:214, 238, 262, 287, 388; *Historic and Architectural Survey of Abington in the Town of Pomfret, Connecticut* (Pomfret Historical Society and Connecticut Historical Commission, May 1998), 37–38, 40, 79, 82; Richard J. Purcell, *Connecticut in Transition: 1775–1818,* 2nd ed. (Middletown, CT: Wesleyan University Press, 1963), 74, 81–83, 90; John C. Pease and John M. Niles, *A Gazetteer of the States of Connecticut and Rhode-Island* (Hartford: William S. Marsh, 1819), 219.

31 Daniels, *Connecticut Town,* 46–47, 51–53, and "Economic Development in Colonial and Revolutionary Connecticut," 434, 446–447; Lewis D. Stilwell, *Migration from Vermont* (Montpelier: Vermont Historical Society, 1948), 75–77; Buel, *Dear Liberty,* 10; Larned, *History of Windham County,* II:388; Clark, *Roots of Rural Capitalism,* 60, 63–64.

32 Except where otherwise noted, the following description of Thomas[4'] farming operations is drawn from two valuable primary sources: Hampton List Book for the year 1809 (Hampton, CT's 1809 tax list), box 5, Hampton Antiquarian and Historical Society Collection, Dodd Research Center, University of Connecticut, Storrs; and Thomas Grow's estate inventory at the time of his death in 1824, in Thomas Grow Estate Papers (Hampton 1824), Windham Probate District file no. 1706, in Probate Estate Papers, Records of the Windham District Probate Court, Connecticut State Library, Hartford, available on microfilm in "Windham Probate District Packets, 1719–1880," reel 1554, Connecticut State Library, Hartford, and from the Family History Library of the Church of Jesus Christ of Latter Day Saints, Salt Lake City, Utah, reel 1032669.

33 One of the staples of the eighteenth-century Yankee farm family's diet was "a coarse brown bread made from home-grown rye and corn meal." (Gross, *Minutemen and Their World,* 85)

34 "Marks for Creatures," Pomfret Proprietors Records, 1713–1788, Town Hall, Pomfret, CT, entries for 6 March 1754, 11 April 1754, 19 February 1779; New Testament, "Book of Revelation," chs. 6, 8, 9, 11. For further discussion of the Grows and the second coming of Christ, see Generation Three.

35 Pease and Niles, *Gazetteer of the States of Connecticut and Rhode-Island,* 219; Percy Bidwell, "Rural Economy in New England at the Beginning of the Nineteenth Century," *Transactions of the Connecticut Academy of Arts and Sciences,* vol. 20 (April 1916): 322–325, 327n5, 337–339; Paul E. Waggoner, "Fertile Farms Among the Stones," in *Voices of the New Republic: Connecticut Towns, 1800–1832,* 2 vols. (New Haven: Connecticut Academy of Arts and Sciences, 2003), II:49.
     Among the items in Thomas' estate at the time of his death in 1824 was an extensive array of weaving equipment (including a "flax sieve," a "hetchel," "2 linen wheels," a "woolen wheel," and an unspecified "weaving apparatus") and dairying equipment (15 milk pans [11 made of tin, four of earthenware], churns,

a cheese tub, a cheese press, a cheese basket, and eight cheese hoops). (Distribution of Thomas Grow Estate, Thomas Grow Estate Papers [Hampton 1824], Windham Probate District file no. 1706, in Probate Estate Papers, Records of the Windham District Probate Court, Connecticut State Library, available on microfilm in "Windham Probate District Packets, 1719–1880," reel 1554, Connecticut State Library, Hartford. (See endnote 32.)

Candles made from bayberry tallow were valued for burning longer and cleaner than other candles. According to an old New England verse: "A bayberry candle burned to the socket brings food to the larder and gold to the pocket." (Personal communication, antiquarian Hollis Brodrick, Portsmouth, NH, to author, 2013) They were being exported from Connecticut to Europe from the early eighteenth century onward. (Howard S. Russell, *A Long, Deep Furrow: Three Centuries of Farming in New England* [Hanover, NH: University Press of New England, 1976], 116, 201)

It is estimated that Connecticut farm women generated "half the value of all exports [in the state] and at least half of every family's subsistence" during this period. (Ruth Barnes Moynihan, "With 'Unshaken Heroism and Fortitude:' Connecticut Women's Life and Work Two Hundred Years Ago," in *Voices of the New Republic,* II:94)

36   William B. Grow, *Eighty-Five Years of Life and Labor* (Carbondale, PA: published by the author, 1902), 3–4; broadside, "An Appeal to the Public" by Samuel Green and Thomas Grow, 19 November 1799, Broadsides 1799 G798a, Connecticut Historical Society, Hartford; Hampton Town Records, Town Hall, Hampton, CT, Book E, p. 92. At an 1885 family reunion in Waterford, Michigan, Thomas' descendants remembered him as "a large farmer" and "a keeper of a store for general merchandise." ("Wonderful Re-Union," *Bay City* [Michigan] *Tribune,* 30 August 1885) His son Joseph was identified as a "'merchant" in the 1809 Hampton tax list (see endnote 32).

37   Hampton Baptist Church Records, 1770–1853 (ms. 974.62/H182b), Connecticut State Library, Hartford, vol. 1: Meetings of the Church, 1770–1817, pp. 99–100.

38   Ebenezer Devotion account book, 1809–1813, p. 155. Ebenezer Devotion (1740–1829) was a prominent merchant and judge in Scotland, CT, 5 miles south of Hampton. In 1812 he and Thomas Grow collaborated in the sale of oxen in New London. Devotion's account book is privately owned by J. Bradley Vincent, the current owner of Devotion's house, at 4 Palmer Road (State Route 14), in Scotland. Vincent found the account book in a wall of the house.

39   Olive Pike Wetherbee, *The Old Fulling Mill of Pomfret, Connecticut* (Pomfret Center, CT: published by the author, 1971), 58, 109.

40   Wood, *Radicalism of the American Revolution,* 67–68, 139–140, 163; Christopher Clark, *Social Change in America: From the Revolution through the Civil War* (Chicago: Ivan R. Dee, 2006), 115–116, 119; Bruce H. Mann, *Neighbors and Strangers: Law and Community in Early Connecticut* (Chapel Hill: University of North Carolina Press, 1987), 13–14, 27–28, 30–34, 39, 41–42. For a path-breaking analysis of similar patterns of rural economic change, including increased reliance on promissory notes, in the Connecticut River Valley of Massachusetts during this same period, see Clark, *Roots of Rural Capitalism,* chs. 1–2. For a detailed description of the use of promissory notes in the commercial life of Hampton in the early nineteenth century, see James Oliver Robertson and Janet C. Robertson, *All Our Yesterdays: A Century of Family Life in an American Small Town* (New York: HarperCollins, 1993), 60–63.

41   Windham County Court Records, June 1726–March 1855, 35 vols., Record Group 3, Connecticut State Library, Hartford, vol. 18, p. 172; vol. 20, p. 122; vol. 23, p. 457; vol. 27, pp. 50, 161.

42   Thomas Grow estate inventory (see endnote 32).

43   Pomfret Land Records, Town Hall, Pomfret, CT, vol. 6, p. 187; vol. 7, pp. 180, 201, 271; vol. 8, pp. 11, 24, 36, 86; vol. 9, pp. 14, 229, 236, 313, 335; vol. 10, p. 168; vol. 11, pp. 402, 432; vol. 12, pp. 45, 57; Hampton Town Records, Town Hall, Hampton, CT, Book B, pp. 327, 368, 369; Book C, pp. 3–6, 8, 10, 12, 18, 19, 24, 41, 60, 109, 144, 148, 153, 183, 209, 224, 235, 300, 344, 366, 369, 375, 382, 399, 401, 432, 471, 559; Book D, pp. 67, 272, 563; Book E, pp. 91, 116, 279, 298.

44   Hampton Town Records, Book C, pp. 60, 109, 471.

45   *Official History of Guilford, Vermont, 1678–1961* (published by the Town of Guilford and Broad Brook Grange No. 151, 1961), 303, 307; Guilford Land Records, Town Offices, Guilford, VT, vol. 7, pp. 10, 188, 189; vol. 8, pp. 236, 257. Thomas purchased his father's former farm from John Barney in 1810 for $2,243 and sold it to William Bigelow Jr., a relative of his niece Rebeckah (Grow) Bigelow, for $1,900 in 1813. He

bought the 50-acre parcel from the aforementioned William Bigelow Jr. for $100 in May 1813 and sold it to David Dean of Guilford for $900 in October 1814.

46　Wood, *Empire of Liberty*, 323.

47　Pomfret Land Records, vol. 11, p. 402; vol. 12, pp. 45, 57; Larned, *History of Windham County*, II:445.

48　Thomas Grow estate inventory. The Norwich Bank was chartered by the state of Connecticut in 1797 with an initial capitalization of $75,000. In 1813, Connecticut bank stocks were paying 9.5 percent annual interest. (Purcell, *Connecticut in Transition*, 67, 68n16)

49　Thomas Grow estate inventory. The total value of the estate did not reflect the 105 acres of the Grow Hill farm and other parcels of land that Thomas had transferred to his son Thomas Jr.'s ownership thirteen years earlier. (Hampton Town Records, Book D, p. 387)

50　measuringworth.com/uscompare.

51　Davis, *John Grow of Ipswich*, 35, 51; Larned, *History of Windham County*, II:520–523, 563–564; "Wonderful Re-Union."

52　A basic checklist of the scholarly literature on this fundamental question in the historiography of the early republic would include: James A. Henretta, "Families and Farms: *Mentalité* in Pre-Industrial America," *William and Mary Quarterly*, 35:1 (January 1978); Toby L. Ditz, *Property and Kinship: Inheritance in Early Connecticut, 1750–1820* (Princeton, NJ: Princeton University Press, 1986); Clark, *Roots of Rural Capitalism;* Wood, *Radicalism of the American Revolution;* Richard L. Bushman, "Markets and Composite Farms in Early America," *William and Mary Quarterly*, 55:3 (July 1998); Naomi R. Lamoreaux, "Rethinking the Transition to Capitalism in the Early American Northeast," *Journal of American History*, 90:2 (September 2003); Appleby, *Inheriting the Revolution;* J. M. Opal, *Beyond the Farm: National Ambitions in Rural New England* (Philadelphia: University of Pennsylvania Press, 2008); and Wood, *Empire of Liberty.*

53　Jonathan Holt account ledger, p. 68, "Revolutionary War Pensions," footnote.com, accessed August 2009; Wood, *Empire of Liberty*, 324; Opal, *Beyond the Farm*, 53. As late as the 1960s, Grow Hill's fields were still divided by an intricate gridwork of stone walls, which owners of the property subsequently buried with backhoes or sold to landscapers from upscale towns in southern Connecticut and New York.

54　Thomas Grow estate inventory.

55　Jonathan Holt account ledger; Clark, *Roots of Rural Capitalism*, 8, 14.

56　Bushman, "Markets and Composite Farms," 364–366, 369; Clark, *Roots of Rural Capitalism*, 60, 84–85; Henretta, "Families and Farms," 16–19. The vast majority of nineteenth-century northern farmers who "sold on markets, sold in small lots, perhaps without using money, and as a minor part of their farming effort." (Walter Nugent, *Structures of American Social History* [Bloomington: Indiana University Press, 1981], 80)

57　Thomas Grow estate inventory; Clark, *Roots of Rural Capitalism*, 67.

58　Clark, *Roots of Rural Capitalism*, 88.

59　Distribution of Thomas Grow estate (see endnote 35).

60　Hampton List Book for the Year 1809 (see endnote 32).

61　Beverly J. Johnson, "The Material World of the Devotion Family," in Lance Mayer and Gay Myers, eds., *The Devotion Family: The Lives and Possessions of Three Generations in Eighteenth-Century Connecticut* (New London, CT: Lyman Allyn Art Museum, 1991), 45–57; David Jaffee, "The Ebenezers Devotion: Pre- and Post-Revolutionary Consumption in Rural Connecticut," *New England Quarterly*, 76:2 (June 2003): 241, 249–250, 260, 264; Wood, *Empire of Liberty*, 28, 324, 716–717; Main, *Peoples of a Spacious Land*, 220–226.

62　Distribution of Thomas Grow estate; William Gilmore, *Reading Becomes a Necessity of Life: Material and Cultural Life in Rural New England, 1780–1835* (Knoxville: University of Tennessee Press, 1989), 17, 53, 60–61, 83, 116, 251, 263–264, 266, 269, 282, 290–291, 300, 327, 461n7; Russell, *Long, Deep Furrow*, 245–246; Opal, *Beyond the Farm*, 134; Richard Bushman, *The Refinement of America: Persons, Houses, Cities* (New York: Knopf, 1992), ch. II; Alan Heimert, *Religion and the American Mind: From the Great Awakening to the Revolution* (Cambridge, MA: Harvard University Press, 1966), 174, 313–314. A Southerner traveling through New England in 1793 "observed that on Sundays many farmers could be found reading—mostly 'religious books, the public laws, and the newspapers.'" (Russell, *Long, Deep Furrow*, 269) A recent academic study found that "half the [New England] women born around 1730 were illiterate; [but that] virtually all the women born around 1810 were literate." (Joel Perlmann and Dennis Shirley, "When Did New England Women Acquire Literacy?" *William and Mary Quarterly*, 48:1 [January 1991]: 52)

63   Hampton List Book for the Year 1809. In September 1802 Thomas gave Elisha 110 acres of land valued at $2,000. (Pomfret Land Records, Town Hall, Pomfret, CT, vol. 9, p. 335). In November 1808, he sold 13 acres to Joseph for an unspecified price. (Hampton Town Records, Town Hall, Hampton, CT, Book D, p. 272)

64   1790 Federal Census, Hampton, Windham County, CT, series M637, roll 1, page 272, online at heritagequestonline.com. For James Grow, see Davis, *John Grow of Ipswich,* 45–48. The construction boom that accompanied economic growth in the Grow Hill area in the post-revolutionary-war period is discussed in *Historic and Architectural Survey of Abington in the Town of Pomfret, Connecticut* (Pomfret Historical Society and Connecticut Historical Commission, May 1998), 79–82.

65   Davis, *John Grow of Ipswich,* 35–36, 53, 54, 56.

66   Ebenezer Grow pension file (no. 36566), "Revolutionary War Pensions," online at footnote.com, accessed August 2009. The file includes several documents submitted by Ebenezer between 1818 and 1821, along with statements of support from Thomas Grow, Thomas Grosvenor, Amasa Copeland of Pomfret, and Reuben Sharp of Hampton.

67   Hampton Baptist Church Records, vol. 1, pp. 98, 100, 101, 103–104.

68   Ibid., vol. 1, pp. 102–106. "Capt. Nathan Paine married Hannah Edmonds" in Pomfret on 19 December 1799. (*Connecticut Vital Records to 1870 [The Barbour Collection]* online database, AmericanAncestors.org, citing Pomfret Vital Records, 2:79)

69   Hampton Baptist Church Records, vol. 2: Meetings of the Church, 1817–1853, pp. 1–10; Davis, *John Grow of Ipswich,* 36; Larned, *History of Windham County,* II:417–418.

70   Thomas Grow estate inventory.

71   Davis, *John Grow of Ipswich,* 36.

72   Thomas Grow-Experience Abbott Prenuptial Agreement (11 March 1820), Thomas Grow Estate Papers (Hampton 1824), Windham Probate District file no. 1706, in Probate Estate Papers, Records of the Windham District Probate Court, Connecticut State Library, Hartford (see endnote 32).

73   Main, *Peoples of a Spacious Land,* 174–176; Barbara McLean Ward, "Women's Property and Family Continuity in Eighteenth-Century Connecticut," in Peter Benes, ed., *Early American Probate Inventories* (Boston University, Dublin Seminar for New England Folklife Annual Proceedings, 1987), 81.

74   Hampton List Book for the Year 1809; Hampton Town Records, Book D, p. 387; Book G, p. 70; Thomas Grow estate inventory.

75   Grow, *Eighty-Five Years of Life and Labor,* 5.

76   Distribution of Thomas Grow Estate.

77   Hampton Town Records, Book F, pp. 85–86.

78   Hampton Town Records, Book H, pp. 351–352; Book I, pp. 179, 311–312, 551–552; Book J, pp. 27–28, 331, 571–573, 575–576, 578, 614–616; Book K, p. 33. In 1854, Thomas Jr.'s widow was forced to sell several parcels of her late husband's land "by virtue of an Order of [Hampton's] Court of Probate directing [her] to sell at public or private sale the personal and so much of the real estate of said Grow's estate as shall be sufficient to pay the indebtedness of the estate." (Ibid., Book J, pp. 568–569, 573–575)

79   James Slater, *The Colonial Burying Grounds of Eastern Connecticut and the Men Who Made Them,* rev. ed. (New Haven: Connecticut Academy of Arts & Sciences, 1996), 192. In 1833, Thomas' son Thomas Jr. sold the burying ground "for the sum of Five Dollars" to "The Inhabitants of the school society of Abington in the towns of Pomfret and Hampton." (Copies of the deed of sale can be found in the "Cemetery File" of the Pomfret Town Hall, Pomfret, CT and in the files of the Hampton Cemetery Association, Hampton, CT.) The graveyard is presently maintained by the Hampton Cemetery Association.

80   James Deetz, *In Small Things Forgotten: An Archeology of Early American Life,* rev. ed. (New York: Anchor Books, 1996), 99–100; Allan I. Ludwig, *Graven Images: New England Stonecarving and its Symbols,* 3rd ed. (Hanover, NH: Wesleyan University Press, 1999), 64; Lance Mayer and Gay Myers, "Bringing Together a Family's Past," in Mayer and Myers, eds., *The Devotion Family,* 22–23.

81   Holly V. Izard, "The State of Connecticut Agriculture in 1800," *Voices of the New Republic,* II:60; Purcell, *Connecticut in Transition,* 92, 97–98.

82   Davis, *John Grow of Ipswich,* 36, 53–56.

GENERATION 5: ELISHA GROW (1779–1850)

1   George W. Davis, *John Grow of Ipswich/John (Groo) Grow of Oxford* (Washington, D.C.: privately printed by the Carnahan Press, 1913), 53; Ellen Larned, *History of Windham County, Connecticut,* 2 vols. (Worcester, MA: published by the author, 1874, 1880), II:246; Hampton Town Records, Book C, p. 209, Town Hall, Hampton, CT.

2   Pomfret Land Records, vol. 9, p. 335, Pomfret Town Hall, Pomfret, CT; Davis, *John Grow of Ipswich,* 54; "Wonderful Re-Union," *Bay City* [Michigan] *Tribune,* 30 August 1885.

3   No Pomfret tax lists for the early nineteenth century have been located, but Elisha's 110 acres of land would have ranked him among approximately the top fifth of all landowners (53rd out of 254) in neighboring Hampton in 1809. (Hampton List Book for the year 1809, box 5, Hampton Antiquarian and Historical Society Collection, Dodd Research Center, University of Connecticut, Storrs)

4   Olive Pike Wetherbee, *The Old Fulling Mill of Pomfret, Connecticut* (Pomfret Center, CT: published by the author, 1971), 73, 109.

5   Jonathan Clark Journal, 1789–1831 (ms. 82323), Connecticut Historical Society, Hartford, entry for 2 May 1803; Larned, *History of Windham County,* II:244–245; James Oliver Robertson and Janet C. Robertson, *All Our Yesterdays: A Century of Family Life in an American Small Town* (New York: HarperCollins, 1993), 41; Susan Jewett Griggs, *Folklore and Firesides of Pomfret, Hampton and Vicinity* (Abington, CT: privately printed, 1950), Hampton: 76. Militia musters and training days were frequently occasions for heavy drinking and public disorder. (Jack Larkin, *The Reshaping of Everyday Life, 1790–1840* [New York: Harper & Row, 1988], 274–275)

That Elisha was serving in a Hampton militia unit in 1803 at a time when he was a resident of Pomfret can probably be explained by the likelihood that, like most able-bodied young men in early nineteenth-century New England, he joined his local militia at age 16, at a time when he was still living with his parents on Grow Hill in Hampton; he then remained a member of the Hampton unit after he established residence in Pomfret in 1802.

6   Lois Kimball Mathews, *The Expansion of New England: The Spread of New England Settlement and Institutions to the Mississippi River, 1620–1865* (New York: Russell & Russell, 1962), 153, 156–157, 169; Walter Nugent, *Structures of American Social History* (Bloomington: Indiana University Press, 1981), 70–71, 79; Kenneth Lockridge, "Land, Population, and the Evolution of New England Society, 1630–1790," in Stanley N. Katz, ed., *Colonial America: Essays in Politics and Social Development* (Boston: Little, Brown, 1971), 474, 482n44; Christopher Clark, *Social Change in America: From the Revolution Through the Civil War* (Chicago: Ivan R. Dee, 2006), 89–90; James A. Henretta, *The Evolution of American Society, 1700–1815: An Interdisciplinary Analysis* (Lexington, MA: D. C. Heath, 1973), 202; Gordon S. Wood, *Empire of Liberty: A History of The Early Republic, 1789–1815* (New York: Oxford University Press, 2009), 2, 119; Lewis D. Stilwell, *Migration From Vermont* (Montpelier: Vermont Historical Society, 1948), 120–121. A resident of Albany, NY counted 500 sleighs passing westward through the city on a single winter day in 1795. (Stilwell, *Migration Through Vermont,* 120)

In February 1808, at age 54, Nathaniel Grow sold the Guilford, Vermont farm that he and his late father had purchased in 1794 and migrated west to Henderson (Jefferson County), New York, a few miles south of Watertown. He died there in 1838 at age 85. (Davis, *John Grow of Ipswich,* 39; Guilford Land Records, Town Offices, Guilford Center, VT, vol. 6, pp. 122-123; online at findagrave .com memorial 49511218)

7   Larned, *History of Windham County,* II:229, 245, 265, 294, 388; Lockridge, "Land, Population, and the Evolution of New England Society," 474; Richard J. Purcell, *Connecticut in Transition: 1775–1818,* 2nd ed. (Middletown, CT: Wesleyan University Press, 1963), 92–94, 98 and notes 33, 34; Clark, *Social Change in America,* 85, 164.

8   Larned, *History of Windham County,* II:388–389, 397.

9   William B. Grow, *Eighty-Five Years of Life and Labor* (Carbondale, PA: published by the author, 1902), 13.

10   Pomfret Land Records, vol. 11, pp. 321, 325, 326, 352.

11   Grow, *Eighty-Five Years of Life and Labor,* 13; "Early Roads, Bridges and Tavern Tales," *Cortland County Chronicles: Papers from the Collections of the Cortland County Historical Society,* 5 vols. (Cortland, NY: Cortland County Historical Society, 1957–1988), 2:211. Migration from Connecticut to New York usually took place in the winter, when ice and snow filled some of the ruts in the wretched road surfaces and "sleds drawn by plodding oxen could avoid the stumps and rocks that so often wrecked wheeled vehicles." (Herbert Barber Howe, *Jedediah Barber, 1787–1876: A Footnote to the History of the Military Tract of Central New York* [New York:

Columbia University Press, 1939], 30–31) If the Grows were typical Connecticut migrants, they probably crossed the Connecticut River over the "great covered bridge" at Hartford, then followed "the Greenwood turnpike" through northwestern Connecticut, and on through Sheffield, Massachusetts to the Hudson River. After crossing the Hudson on "the Greenbush ferry," they would have continued on the Cooperstown turnpike from Albany "westward into the central portion of the state," where they would have followed a branch of the Great Western Turnpike (also known as the Albany Post Road or Cherry Valley Turnpike) to Homer. (Ibid.; Harry P. Smith, *History of Cortland County, with Illustrations and Biographical Sketches of Some of its Prominent Men* [Syracuse, NY: D. Mason & Co., 1885], 204; "Early Roads, Bridges and Tavern Tales," 2: 205, 212)

12   Cortland County Deeds, Grantee Book, vol. B, pp. 449–500, 570–571, Office of the County Clerk, Cortland, NY (accessible online through the county clerk's website link to searchiqs.com, accessed September 2015).

13   Dollar figures calculated from the land-transfer records cited in endnotes 10 and 12.

14   Thomas F. Gordon, *Gazetteer of the State of New York* (New York: privately published by the author, 1836), 415; Hermon Camp Goodwin, *Pioneer History; or, Cortland County and the Border Wars of New York* (New York: A. B. Burdick, 1859), 166; Harry R. Melone, *History of Central New York*, 3 vols. (Indianapolis, IN: Historical Publishing Co., 1932), 1:415.

15   Davis, *John Grow of Ipswich*, 36, 51–53, 55.

16   Find-A-Grave memorial 96901428, online at findagrave.com.

17   Hezekiah Harvey, *Memoir of Alfred Bennett, First Pastor of the Baptist Church, Homer, N.Y., and Senior Agent of the Baptist Missionary Union*, 3rd ed. (New York: Edward H. Fletcher, 1852), 54; Smith, *History of Cortland County*, 62n2, 64, 197; Howe, *Jedediah Barber*, 41; Larkin, *Reshaping of Everyday Life*, 111.

18   Smith, *History of Cortland County*, 65; Goodwin, *Pioneer History*, 169–170.

19   Harvey, *Memoir of Alfred Bennett*, 54–55.

20   Smith, *History of Cortland County*, 62–63, 66, 207–208, 222, 225; Goodwin, *Pioneer History*, 175, 266.

21   Smith, *History of Cortland County*, 204–206; Melone, *History of Central New York*, 1:423; Whitney R. Cross, *The Burned-over District: The Social and Intellectual History of Enthusiastic Religion in Western New York, 1800–1850* (Ithaca, NY: Cornell University Press, 1950), 79–80.

22   Howe, *Jedediah Barber*, 62.

23   Martin P. Sweeney, "Little York: A Hamlet Not to be Overlooked," *The Homer News*, part 1 (17 October 2013) and part 2 (7 November 2013); email communication, Martin P. Sweeney, Homer town historian, to author, 1 December 2015. According to Sweeney, another former Pomfret resident, Noah Carpenter, settled on Homer's northern border at "about the same time" as Cushing, while two other Pomfret migrants, John Frazier and Samuel Griggs, took up residence in the township in 1803—suggesting that Elisha's kinship-based chain migration might have had aspects of a neighborhood- or community-based chain migration as well. (Sweeney, "Little York," part 1; Smith, *History of Cortland County*, 194–195)

24   Allan Kulikoff, *From British Peasants to Colonial American Farmers* (Chapel Hill: University of North Carolina Press, 2000), 145.

25   Howe, *Jedediah Barber*, 41.

26   Grow, *Eighty-Five Years of Life and Labor*, 13–14.

27   Curtis D. Johnson, *Islands of Holiness: Rural Religion in Upstate New York, 1790–1860* (Ithaca, NY: Cornell University Press, 1989), 4, 27, 33, 36; Howe, *Jedediah Barber*, 55, 57–59, 68; Smith, *History of Cortland County*, 65, 204.

28   Grow, *Eighty-Five Years of Life and Labor*, 15. Depending on the quality on the soil, farmers during this period harvested between twenty-five and fifty bushels of corn per acre. The average farm family consumed approximately twenty-five to thirty bushels per year. (Howard S. Russell, *A Long, Deep Furrow: Three Centuries of Farming in New England* [Hanover, NH: University Press of New England, 1976], 135, 278)

29   Sweeney, "Little York," parts 1–2; Clara A. Elder, "Little York Lake," *Cortland County Chronicles*, 2:234; Smith, *History of Cortland County*, 231. The Homer Woolen Manufacturing Company was "about the size of a one-car garage." (Sweeney, "Little York," part 2)

30   Sweeney, "Little York," part 2.

31   Davis, *John Grow of Ipswich,* 55, 91–97.

32   Nugent, *Structures of American Social History,* 25–28, 55, 68–69; Wood, *Empire of Liberty,* 2, 14, 315–318; Allan Kulikoff, *The Agrarian Origins of American Capitalism* (Charlottesville: University of Virginia Press, 1992), 47–48, 150, 208–213.

33   Larkin, *Reshaping of Everyday Life,* 17–30.

34   Grow, *Eighty-Five Years of Life and Labor,* 14; Sweeney, "Little York," part 2.

35   Davis, *John Grow of Ipswich,* 93.

36   Grow, *Eighty-Five Years of Life and Labor,* 14–18; Davis, *John Grow of Ipswich,* 90.

37   Larkin, *Reshaping of Everyday Life,* 24–27, 50–52, 184–185, 187–190, 299; Howe, *Jedediah Barber,* 79–80; Mary Ryan, *Cradle of the Middle Class: The Family in Oneida County, New York, 1790–1865* (Cambridge, U.K. and New York: Cambridge University Press, 1981), 64; Cross, *Burned-Over District,* 84; Johnson, *Islands of Holiness,* 35.

38   Davis, *John Grow of Ipswich,* 91–92.

39   Stephanie Coontz, *The Social Origins of Private Life: A History of American Families, 1600–1900* (London and New York: Verso, 1988), 168, 174–175.

40   Grow, *Eighty-Five Years of Life and Labor,* 17–18.

41   Ibid.

42   Davis, *John Grow of Ipswich,* 85–92.

43   Ibid., 88; Howe, *Jedediah Barber,* 100–101, 103. Founded in 1819, the Cortland Academy recruited its faculty from some of the leading colleges of the Northeast, including Dartmouth, Amherst, Williams, and Hamilton. In 1824, it had 163 students, 80 males and 83 females. Those enrolled in the school's "higher curricula" paid $4 per term. In 1836, the Academy had a 600-volume library. Among its trustees was Stillman Grow's uncle, Rev. Alfred Bennett, the pastor of the Homer Baptist Church. (Howe, *Jedediah Barber,* 110; Goodwin, *Pioneer History,* 320, 398, 413; Seymour B. Dunn, "The Early Academies of Cortland County," *Cortland County Chronicles,* 1:60–61)

44   Davis, *John Grow of Ipswich,* 55; Sweeney, "Little York," part 2. A hand-rubbed image of Olive Grow's elaborately decorated gravestone can be viewed online at findagrave.com, memorial 118914231.

45   Davis, *John Grow of Ipswich,* 87, 91, 94; Grow, *Eighty-Five Years of Life and Labor,* 16.

46   Homer Town Meeting Records, 1794–1824, Cortland County Historical Society, Cortland, NY; "Early Roads, Bridges and Tavern Tales," *Cortland County Chronicles,* 2:207.

47   William G. McLoughlin, *New England Dissent, 1630–1833: The Baptists and the Separation of Church and State* (Cambridge, MA: Harvard University Press, 1971), 743, 952–961.

48   Grow, *Eighty-Five Years of Life and Labor,* 23.

49   Harvey, *Memoir of Alfred Bennett,* 9–68, 75–76, 82–83, 101–103, 115–117; Davis, *John Grow of Ipswich,* 52, 55; Grow, *Eighty-Five Years of Life and Labor,* 21–22; Smith, *History of Cortland County,* 223.

50   Clark, *Social Change in America,* 120; Wood, *Empire of Liberty,* 608–609; Johnson, *Islands of Holiness,* 42, 44, 47–48, 50, 108.

51   Harvey, *Memoir of Alfred Bennett,* 13–14, 15–18, 36, 80, 92, 97, 98; Johnson, *Islands of Holiness,* 41–42, 44, 47, 96.

52   In his memoir, Elisha's son William praised the Bennetts and other pioneer pastors for "cherish[ing] the faith of their fathers"—an indication, perhaps, that the family's religious views were grounded in old-style Calvinism. (*Eighty-Five Years of Life and Labor,* 21)

53   Harvey, *Memoir of Alfred Bennett,* 53; Smith, *History of Cortland County,* 204–205, 216, 218; Johnson, *Islands of Holiness,* 94–95, 115–116, 117n12. Not even Baptist ministers were immune from alcohol abuse. "Elder Powers" of the neighboring Virgil Baptist Church "was led away by his appetite for Alcoholic drink," while in 1814 the Scott Baptist Church a few miles north of Homer found their preacher Aaron Town "repeatedly Guilty of the excesive [*sic*] use of Ardent Spirits" and excluded him from the church. (Johnson, *Islands of Holiness,* 27) According to historian Whitney Cross, "Most people bred in the New England

tradition still considered dancing, cards, and novels immoral, and outlawed the stage, the circus, and most other public amusements, at least for females." (*Burned-Over District,* 87)

54   Joyce Appleby, *Inheriting the Revolution: The First Generation of Americans* (Cambridge, MA: Harvard University Press, 2000), 250–252; Harvey, *Memoir of Alfred Bennett,* 59, 111; Johnson, *Islands of Holiness,* 56.

55   Harvey, *Memoir of Alfred Bennett,* 112.

56   Seymour Cook, "Early Days in Homer," *Cortland County Chronicles,* 2:193.

57   Grow, *Eighty-Five Years of Life and Labor,* 15–16.

58   Sweeney, "Little York," part 2.

59   Johnson, *Islands of Holiness,* 4; Goodwin, *Pioneer History,* 175; Gordon, *Gazetteer of the State of New York,* 416. In 1829, Homer was divided into two separate townships, Homer and Cortlandville. The population figure for 1830 combines the populations of the two newly divided townships in that year.

60   Horatio Gates Spafford, *A Gazetteer of the State of New-York* (Albany, NY: B. D. Packard, 1824), 235; Goodwin, *Pioneer History,* 266–267; Howe, *Jedediah Barber,* 55–59, 69, 137; Johnson, *Islands of Holiness,* 16, 34; Smith, *History of Cortland County,* 197.

61   Johnson, *Islands of Holiness,* 16, 34; Cross, *Burned-Over District,* 66.

62   Johnson, *Islands of Holiness,* 16, 34–35, 37, 65, 107; Smith, *History of Cortland County,* 75.

63   The figure of 252 acres was calculated on the basis of the 173 acres of "Lot 7" that Elisha sold in 1837 to Russell Daily for $6,139.70 together with parcels of 28 acres and 51 acres in Lot 7 that he appears to have mortgaged or rented to Peter Walrod and Charles Goodale, respectively, that same year, and which were not officially sold until 1845. (Cortland County Deeds, Grantor Book, vol. Y, pp. 304–305; vol. 9, p. 575; vol. 10, p. 32) The 252-acre total is 19 acres less than the 271 acres that Elisha purchased upon arrival in Homer in 1812, but he subsequently sold two 4-acre parcels (in 1814 and 1823) and gave two additional parcels of undetermined size to the town of Homer for a school-building lot and a cemetery. (Cortland County Deeds, Grantor Book, vol. D, pp. 250–251; vol. K, p. 360; vol. O, pp. 474–475)

64   The earliest Homer tax list known to have survived is the town's Assessment Roll for 1838, compiled a year after the Grows left Homer for Michigan. The 252 acres that Elisha owned at the time of the family's departure in 1837 would have made him the tenth largest landowner in Homer (out of 453 taxpayers) in 1838 and would have ranked him in the top 2.2 percent of local landowners for that year. (Homer, New York, Assessment Roll for 1838, Cortland County Historical Society, Cortland, NY) In 1835, farmers who owned more than 150 acres of "improved land" "were among the wealthiest one percent of Cortland County household heads," according to Curtis Johnson. (*Islands of Holiness,* 107)

65   Cortland County Deeds, Grantor Book, vol. 3, pp. 432–433.

66   Davis, *John Grow of Ipswich,* 90.

67   Willis F. Dunbar and George S. May, *Michigan: A History of the Wolverine State,* rev. ed. (Grand Rapids, MI: William B. Eerdmans Publishing Co., 1980), 195.

68   Thomas J. Drake, "History of Oakland County," *Michigan Pioneer and Historical Collections,* 40 vols. (Lansing, MI: Michigan Historical Commission [etc.], 1874–1929), 22 (1893): 419; Thaddeus D. Seeley, *History of Oakland County, Michigan: A Narrative of its Historical Progress, its People, and its Principal Interests,* 2 vols. (Chicago: Lewis Publishing Company, 1912), 1:31–32. Although the United States had established its own decimal currency in 1793, many rural Americans well into the nineteenth century "continued to think in terms of the disused English pounds, shillings and pence when they figured prices and wages. They then translated from the traditional 'currency of reckoning' into American dollars and cents when it was time to total up and pay." (Larkin, *The Reshaping of Everyday Life,* 38) In 1820s–1830s Michigan, 37 cents was the equivalent of 3 English shillings, making $1.25 approximately equal to 10 shillings—hence the "Ten Shilling Act." (Kenneth E. Lewis, *West to Far Michigan: Settling the Lower Peninsula, 1815–1860* [East Lansing, Michigan State University Press, 2002], 175)

69   Carol Sheriff, *The Artificial River: The Erie Canal and the Paradox of Progress, 1817–1862* (New York: Hill & Wang, 1996), 8, 26, 32; Eric Freedman, *Pioneering Michigan* (Franklin, MI: Altwerger and Mandel, 1992), 42.

70   Freedman, *Pioneering Michigan,* 65; Stewart H. Holbrook, *The Yankee Exodus: An Account of Migration from New England* (New York: Macmillan, 1950), 33, 87, 89, 94.

71   Dunbar and May, *Michigan,* 193; Holbrook, *Yankee Exodus,* 86; Henry Oral Severance, *Michigan Trailmakers* (Ann Arbor, MI: George Wahr, 1930), 15. Another "tune of the day," the "Emigrant Song," also captures the promotional spirit of the period:

> *Here is the place to live at ease,*
> *To work or play, just as you please;*
> *With any prudence any man*
> *Can soon get rich in Michigan.*
> *We here have soils of various kinds*
> *To suit men who have different minds,*
> *Prairies, openings, timbered land,*
> *And burr oak plains, in Michigan.*

(Freedman, *Pioneering Michigan,* 67)

72   Dunbar and May, *Michigan,* 195; Freedman, *Pioneering Michigan,* 121; Susan E. Gray, *The Yankee West: Community Life on the Michigan Frontier* (Chapel Hill: University of North Caroline Press, 1996), 47; Holbrook, *Yankee Exodus,* 83.

73   Lewis, *West to Far Michigan,* 223; Freedman, *Pioneering Michigan,* 61.

74   Dunbar and May, *Michigan,* 194; Severance, *Michigan Trailmakers,* 52.

75   Bill Loomis, "How One Bad Review Delayed the Settlement of Michigan," *Detroit News* [online edition], 3 June 2012.

76   Johnson, *Islands of Holiness,* 36–37; Sheriff, *Artificial River,* 17, 20, 52, 54, 95, 121; Nora Faires, "Leaving the 'Land of the Second Chance': Migration from Ontario to the Upper Midwest in the Nineteenth and Early Twentieth Centuries," in John J. Bukowczyk, ed., *Permeable Border: The Great Lakes Basin as Transnational Region, 1650–1990* (Pittsburgh, PA: University of Pittsburgh Press, 2005), 32; John J. Bukowczyk, "Migration, Transportation, Capital, and the State in the Great Lakes Basin, 1815–1890," in Bukowczyk, *Permeable Border,* 195nn13, 15; Dunbar and May, *Michigan,* 189.

77   Dunbar and May, *Michigan,* 189; Sheriff, *Artificial River,* 52.

78   Davis, *John Grow of Ipswich,* 54, 88, 90.

79   "Wonderful Re-Union." For land speculation in the "Grand River district," see John M. Gordon, "A Speculator's Diary," in Justin L. Kestenbaum, ed., *The Making of Michigan, 1820–1860: A Pioneer Anthology* (Detroit: Wayne State University Press, 1990), 222–225.

80   Davis, *John Grow of Ipswich,* 54, 88, 90.

81   Grow, *Eighty-Five Years of Life and Labor,* 28, 30.

82   "Wonderful Re-Union"; Davis, *John Grow of Ipswich,* 54, 85–96. The sequence of steps that led the Grow family to Michigan was similar to that of most New Yorkers and New Englanders who moved there as pioneers. See Brian C. Wilson, *Yankees in Michigan* (East Lasing: Michigan State University Press, 2008), 29–30; and Lewis, *West to Far Michigan,* 131.

83   Davis, *John Grow of Ipswich,* 85–97. Elisha and Lois' 31-year-old daughter Dilla (Grow) Phillips and her husband and two daughters elected to remain behind in Homer. (Ibid., 87)

84   Severance, *Michigan Trailmakers,* 9–10; Loomis, "How One Bad Review Delayed the Settlement of Michigan"; Edward W. Barber, "A Zion in the Wilderness," in Kestenbaum, ed., *The Making of Michigan, 1820–1860,* 161; Ronald E. Shaw, *Erie Water West: A History of the Erie Canal, 1792–1854* (Lexington: University of Kentucky Press, 1990), 210, 221–225; Sheriff, *Artificial River,* 54, 119, 142–148, 158, 167, 226. In 1831, one canal town newspaper, the Rochester *Observer,* suggested that in view of the "prostitution, gambling, and all species of vice practiced on our canals," the "Big Ditch" should be called the "Big Ditch of Iniquity." (Shaw, *Erie Water West,* 221)
     Among the household possessions that Elisha and Lois transported with them to Michigan was "the old family bible." ("Wonderful Re-Union")

85   Davis, *John Grow of Ipswich,* 92; Samuel W. Durant, *History of Oakland County, Michigan* (Philadelphia: L. H. Everts, 1877), 150, 166, 231, 308; Edwin C. Guillet, *Pioneer Travel in Upper Canada* (University of Toronto Press, 1966), 126–127, 156–158, 169–170; John Gilbert pioneer reminiscences, *Michigan Pioneer and Historical Collections,* 26 (1894–1895): 488.

86 Bill Loomis, "Wild Times at the Farmers Market," *Detroit News* [online edition], 31 July 2011, quoting Anna Brownell Jameson, *Winter Studies and Summer Rambles in Canada* (London: Saunders and Olney, 1838).

87 Severance, *Michigan Trailmakers,* 18; Loomis, "How One Bad Review Delayed the Settlement of Michigan."

88 Bruce Catton, *Michigan: A Bicentennial History* (New York: W. W. Norton, 1976), 79.

89 Supply Chase, "A Pioneer Minister," *Michigan Pioneer and Historical Collections,* 5 (1882): 53; John M. Norton, "A Picture of Memory—Settlement of Oakland County," *Michigan Pioneer and Historical Collections,* 22 (1893): 407; Loomis, "How One Bad Review Delayed the Settlement of Michigan." A local newspaperman, George C. Bates, wrote that "Except for the Black Swamp . . . there were no more fearful and horrid roads to be found than all those leading out of Detroit in 1833 to 1837." (Quoted in Lewis, *West to Far Michigan,* 170) According to a humorous "tall tale" popular at the time, "Several strangers looking for land started out on this Pontiac road and were winding their way over bogs and around stumps, sometimes on this side of the road and sometimes on that, and in constant danger of being swallowed up in the mire. One of these men, a little in advance of the rest of them discovered as he thought a good beaver hat, lying on the center of the road. He called to his companions to halt while he ventured to secure it at the risk of his life. He waded out, more than knee deep to the spot, and seizing the hat to his surprise he found a live man's head under it, but on lustily raising a cry for help, the stranger in the mire declined all assistance saying, 'Just leave me alone, I have a good horse under me, and have just found bottom.'" (Severance, *Michigan Trailmakers,* 22)

90 Grow, *Eighty-Five Years of Life and Labor,* 18–19. The "lake-boat" that William referred to was one of the many steamships transporting settlers and their possessions across Lake Erie in the 1830s. In 1837, an average of three steamships arrived in Detroit every day, each of them carrying approximately 500 passengers. In May 1837, Mrs. Richard Dye of Ionia, NY, described her experience aboard the steamer *Daniel Webster:* "we boarded" and were immediately "surprised to behold the most obnoxious place I had ever witnessed. It was filled with foreigners of every description, and fairly alive with the 'dregs of humanity,' whose indulgence in tobacco and liquors fraught the air with an odor too vile to be described by human language." (Mrs. Richard Dye, "Coming to Michigan," *Michigan Pioneer and Historical Collections,* 8 [1885]: 261)

91 Durant, *History of Oakland County,* 299; Freedman, *Pioneering Michigan,* 174; "Journal of Cyrus P. Bradley," *Ohio Archeological and Historical Collections,* 15 (1906): 259; B. D. Williams pioneer reminiscences, *Michigan Pioneer and Historical Collections,* 7 (1884): 576; Gordon, "Speculator's Diary," 123–124; Lewis, *West to Far Michigan,* 72; Wilson, *Yankees in Michigan,* 24, 30; Dunbar and May, *Michigan,* 196–197.

92 Lewis, *West to Far Michigan,* 111; Gordon, "Speculator's Diary," 122–125; Clark, *Social Change in America,* 149.

93 Oakland County Title Abstracts, Maceday Gardens Subdivision on the northeast quarter of Section 8, Town 3 north, range 9 east in the Township of Waterford, Conveyances, Liber 48 of Plat, page 30, Oakland County Register of Deeds, Pontiac, MI. In the Grand River district of southern Michigan during this period, "speculative fever" had pushed the price of land from $1.25 an acre to more than $60 an acre in a period of five or six years. (Gordon, "Speculator's Diary," 122–125)

94 Cortland County Deeds, Grantor Book, vol. Y, pp. 304–305.

95 Oakland County Title Abstracts, Maceday Gardens Subdivision . . . Township of Waterford, Encumbrances [see endnote 92]; Lewis, *West to Far Michigan,* 105–106; David M. Richards, "Reminiscences of Early Days," *Michigan Pioneer and Historical Collections,* 38 (1912): 364.

96 Oakland County Title Abstracts, Maceday Gardens Subdivision . . . Township of Waterford, Encumbrances.

97 "Wonderful Re-Union."

98 Oakland County Title Abstracts, Maceday Gardens Subdivision . . . Township of Waterford, Conveyances. The Maceday subdivision was named for early Waterford settler Mason ("Mase") Day. (Durant, *History of Oakland County,* 299)

99 *Portrait and Biographical Album of Oakland County, Michigan* (Chicago: Chapman Bros., 1891), 320.

100 Julia Taft Beach and Stewart Taft Beach, "A Century of Living: Julia Bishop Taft," in Lillian Drake Avery, comp., *Old Oakland County Families,* 2 vols. (Pontiac, MI: Daughters of the American Revolution—General Richardson Chapter, 1934–1945), II:80–81. Nineteenth-century Oakland County atlases locate the family's farmhouse in the immediate vicinity of present-day 6175 Williams Lake Road.

101 Mary E. Shout, "Reminiscences of the First Settlement at Owosso," *Michigan Pioneer and Historical Collections,* 30 (1912): 350; Severance, *Michigan Trailmakers,* 36; "Journal of Cyrus P. Bradley," 257; William

Nowlin, *The Bark Covered House, or back in the woods again: being a graphic and thrilling description of real pioneer life in the wilderness of Michigan* (Detroit: published by the author, 1876), 32–35, 48–49, 62–63, 76–77, 166–174.

102 Andrew McClary, "Don't Go to Michigan, That Land of Ills," *Michigan History,* 67:1 (January-February 1983): 46–47; Severance, *Michigan Trailmakers,* 54–55; "Journal of Cyrus P. Bradley," 258.

103 Mrs. William Warren pioneer reminiscences, *Michigan Pioneer and Historical Collections,* 8 (1885): 92; Lewis, *West to Far Michigan,* 160–161, 171–172; Gray, *The Yankee West,* 58; Nowlin, *Bark Covered House,* 45, 124–128, 155–165, 188–191; Shout, "Reminiscences of the First Settlement at Owosso," 350.

104 Dunbar and May, *Michigan,* 261–281; Gray, *The Yankee West,* 43–47, 54–55, 58, 89; Lewis, *West to Far Michigan,* 65, 113–114, 175–178; Wilson, *Yankees in Michigan,* 43; Martin J. Hershock, *The Paradox of Progress: Economic Change, Individual Enterprise, and the Political Culture in Michigan, 1837–1878* (Athens: Ohio University Press, 2003), 1–3, 10, 41, 54; Steven C. Wilkshire, "Markets and Market Culture in the Early Settlement of Ionia County, Michigan," *Michigan Historical Review,* 24:1 (Spring 1998): 8–9; Goodenough Townsend, "Early History of the Township of Davison, "*Michigan Pioneer and Historical Collections,* 22 (1893): 547.

105 Davis, *John Grow of Ipswich,* 54, 85–94; Grow, *Eighty-Five Years of Life and Labor,* 27–31.

106 Lewis, *West to Far Michigan,* 114; Wilkshire, "Markets and Market Culture," 4; Durant, *History of Oakland County,* 74.

107 Assessment Roll of Real and Personal Property in the Township of Waterford, State of Michigan, for the Year 1840, "Tax Rolls of Oakland County, Michigan, 1834–1840," (Pontiac, MI: General Richardson Chapter—Daughters of the American Revolution, 1952), copy in Oakland County Pioneer and Historical Society library, Pontiac; Assessment Roll of Real and Personal Property, Waterford Township, Michigan, 1841, Record Group 37: "Records of Oakland County, Office of the Treasurer," microfilm roll 9151, Archive of Michigan, Lansing; Assessment Roll for the Township of Waterford in the County of Oakland, for the Year 1845, Record Group 37: "Records of Oakland County, Office of the Treasurer," microfilm roll 9153, Archive of Michigan, Lansing.

108 Oakland County Title Abstracts, Maceday Gardens Subdivision . . . Township of Waterford, Conveyances.

109 Davis, *John Grow of Ipswich,* 54, 95–96; Elisha Grow death notice, *The Oakland Gazette* [Pontiac, MI], 24 August 1850, "Digital Michigan Newspapers," online at digmichnews.cmich.edu.

110 Appleby, *Inheriting the Revolution,* 5–7, 15, 63–64, 264; Wood, *Empire of Liberty,* 2, 317.

111 "Wonderful Re-Union."

112 See, for example, David M. Potter, *People of Plenty: Economic Abundance and the American Character* (Chicago, IL: University of Chicago Press, 1954), 150, 154.

113 Alexis de Toqueville, "A Fortnight in the Wilderness," in Kestenbaum, ed., *The Making of Michigan, 1820–1860,* 18. In an analysis of New England-born farmers in the Northwest Territory from the 1830s to the 1860s, economists Jeremy Atack and Fred Bateman concluded that it probably took "at least one and possibly two decades for a Yankee farm family to recoup the costs of migration to the Old Northwest" and that "Such a long repayment period lends credence to the argument that Yankee farmers migrated westward so that they might pass on working farms (or the capital to buy one) to their sons." (Atack and Bateman, "Yankee Farming and Settlement in the Old Northwest: A Comparative Analysis," in David C. Klingaman and Richard K. Vedder, eds., *Essays on the Economy of the Old Northwest* (Athens: Ohio University Press, 1987), 81, 85)

114 See endnote 9.

115 Quoted in Clark, *Social Change in America,* 145–146 (emphasis in original).

116 Davis, *John Grow of Ipswich,* 85–96; *Portrait and Biographical Album of Oakland County,* 320 (Thomas), 332 (Edward), 351 (Abel); Durant, *History of Oakland County,* 155–156 (Stillman); Grow, *Eighty-Five Years of Life and Labor,* passim (William); Beach and Beach, "A Century of Living: Julia Bishop Taft," 78–81 (Anne).

117 Based on the assumption that John Grow was an Englishman who migrated to the seaboard frontier of seventeenth-century Massachusetts Bay in search of a better life in the New World.

118 Nugent, *Structures of American Social History,* chs. II–IV.

GENERATION SIX: THOMAS GROW (1818–1902)

1   George W. Davis, *John Grow of Ipswich/John (Groo) Grow of Oxford* (Washington, D.C.: privately printed by the Carnahan Press, 1913), 93.

2   Ibid.; *Portrait and Biographical Album of Oakland County, Michigan* (Chicago: Chapman Bros., 1891), 320.

3   Dominic A. Pacyga, *Chicago: A Biography* (Chicago: University of Chicago Press, 2009), 10–11, 18–24, 407; Donald L. Miller, *City of the Century: The Epic of Chicago and the Making of America* (New York: Simon & Schuster, 1996), 67, 74–76, 87, 93; Davis, *John Grow of Ipswich*, 93; Ronald E. Shaw, *Canals for a Nation: The Canal Era in the United States, 1790–1860* (Lexington: University of Kentucky Press, 1990), 144.

4   Shaw, *Canals for a Nation*, 144, 170–171; Miller, *City of the Century*, 52–53, 77, 441; Peter Way, *Common Labour: Workers and the Digging of North American Canals, 1780–1860* (Cambridge, U.K.: Cambridge University Press, 1993), 165.

5   Shaw, *Canals for a Nation*, 171; Way, *Common Labour*, 154.

6   Way, *Common Labour*, 210, 290, Table 17.

7   Davis, *John Grow of Ipswich*, 93; *Portrait and Biographical Album of Oakland County*, 320; Shaw, *Canals for a Nation*, 170–171; Carol Sheriff, *The Artificial River: The Erie Canal and the Paradox of Progress, 1817–1862* (New York: Hill and Wang, 1996), 44.

8   Davis, *John Grow of Ipswich*, 93; *Portrait and Biographical Album of Oakland County*, 320. Margaret was the daughter of Lewis L. and Eve Morris, pioneers from Wayne County, New York, who had migrated to Oakland County in 1839. (*Portrait and Biographical Album of Oakland County*, 320) Margaret's age at marriage was calculated from the inscription on her gravestone in Pontiac's Oak Hill Cemetery, which states that she was born in 1821. (Online at findagrave.com memorial 47646373) One of her obituaries, however, indicates that she was born in 1822. (Margaret Grow obituary, 30 July 1899, in unidentified Pontiac, MI newspaper, obituary clipping file, Oakland County Pioneer and Historical Society library, Pontiac, MI)

9   *Portrait and Biographical Album of Oakland County*, 320. Thomas and Margaret's first child was born in White Lake on 13 January 1843. (Davis, *John Grow of Ipswich*, 94, 130) Margaret's father, Lewis L. Morris, died prematurely at age 47 on 28 August 1841, less than two months before Thomas and Margaret's wedding. (Online at findagrave.com memorial 42105688)

10   *Portrait and Biographical Album of Oakland County*, 320. On 21 November 1846, Eve Morris transferred the deed to 160 acres in the southeast quarter of Section 14 in White Lake Township to Thomas Grow "for considerations of $200." (Oakland County Deeds, Liber 44, pp. 390–391, Oakland County Register of Deeds, Pontiac, MI)

11   Paul Trap, "The Detroit and Pontiac Railroad," *Railroad History*, 168 (1993): 25, 36–37.

12   Kenneth E. Lewis, *West to Far Michigan: Settling the Lower Peninsula, 1815–1860* (East Lansing, MI: Michigan State University Press, 2002), 183, 217, 232; Clarence H. Danhof, *Change in Agriculture: The Northern United States, 1820–1870* (Cambridge, MA: Harvard University Press, 1969), 12; Ronald E. Shaw, *Erie Water West: A History of the Erie Canal, 1792–1854* (Lexington: University Press of Kentucky, 1990), 275–276, 284, 296–298. Prior to the completion of the Detroit & Pontiac Railroad, "it cost as much to ship grain from Pontiac to Detroit as it did to ship it from Detroit to New York," and as a result, "The price of grain in Pontiac remained low and much of it was made into whiskey." (Trap, "The Detroit and Pontiac Railroad," 18) With the opening of the railroad, "the price of transporting a barrel of flour from Pontiac to Detroit was reduced from a dollar and a quarter [per] barrel to 18.75 cents, which . . . was sufficient to double the value of all wheat land in the country." (Sherman Stevens, "Continuation of 'Early Days in Genessee County,'" *Michigan Pioneer and Historical Collections*, 40 vols. [Lansing, MI: Michigan Historical Commission, etc., 1874–1929], 7 [1884], 397–398) Local farmers were quick to recognize that, as one of them put it, "This railroad gives us eastern markets by way of Detroit and the Great Lakes." (Henry Severance, *Michigan Trailmakers* [Ann Arbor, MI: George Wahr, 1930], 93)

13   Martin J. Hershock, *The Paradox of Progress: Economic Change, Individual Enterprise, and Political Culture in Michigan, 1837–1878* (Athens: Ohio University Press, 2003), 53–55, 62–63; Lewis, *West to Far Michigan*, 243, 247.

14   "Reminiscences of Mortimer A. Leggett," *Michigan Pioneer and Historical Collections*, 35 (1907): 688–689; Lewis, *West to Far Michigan*, 244, 275.

15   Trap, "Detroit and Pontiac Railroad," 41. By the 1850s, "Shipments from Detroit [had] helped to make

Michigan the second largest exporter of western wheat after Ohio until the Civil War." (Susan E. Gray, *The Yankee West: Community Life on the Michigan Frontier* [Chapel Hill: University of North Carolina Press, 1996], 59)

16 Severance, *Michigan Trailmakers*, 95.

17 United States 1850 Federal Census: White Lake, Michigan, online database, AmericanAncestors.org, New England Historic Genealogical Society.

18 Products of Agriculture: White Lake Township, Oakland County, Michigan, pp. 32–35, Federal Non-Population Census Schedule, 1850, Oakland County Pioneer and Historical Society library, Pontiac, MI. Thomas' livestock in 1850 were valued at $389, the sixth highest total among White Lake's 137 farmers, ranking him in the top 4 percent of the township in that census category. (Ibid.) By comparison, the mean value of Michigan farmers' livestock herds statewide in 1850 was $225. (Hershock, *Paradox of Progress*, 50)

19 Hershock, *Paradox of Progress*, 49.

20 Assessment Roll for the Township of White Lake in the County of Oakland, for the Year 1850, Record Group 37: Records of Oakland County, Office of the Treasurer, microfilm roll 9159, Archive of Michigan, Lansing.

21 David Blanke, *Sowing the American Dream: How Consumer Culture Took Root in the Rural Midwest* (Athens: Ohio University Press, 2000), 8, 10, 22; Danhof, *Change in Agriculture*, 4, 14–15, 18, 21, 32–33.

22 Oakland County Deeds, White Lake Township, Liber 42, pp. 157–158 and Liber 44, pp. 390-391; Pontiac Township, Liber 44, pp. 564–566, Liber 47, pp. 104–105. Thomas purchased his 16-acre White Lake farm, located in the southeast quarter of section 14 of that township, from his mother-in-law, Eve Morris, for $200 on 21 November 1846, and sold it to Asa L. Kelly on 26 March 1851 for $2,000. He then finalized the purchase of 110.3 acres in the western half of the northwest quarter of section 15, Pontiac Township, from Levi and Amanda Dewey on 28 April 1852 for $1,000, and purchased an adjoining 20-acre parcel from Joseph and Sarah Morrison on 4 February 1853 for $500.

23 Blanke, *Sowing the American Dream*, 32–33; Arthur A. Hagman, ed., *Oakland County Book of History* (Pontiac: Oakland County Board of Commissioners, Sesquicentennial Executive Committee, 1970), 28.

24 Lewis, *West to Far Michigan*, 279, 286; Hershock, *Paradox of Progress*, 58.

25 Hershock, *Paradox of Progress*, 58; Lewis, *West to Far Michigan*, 274–275, 280.

26 Lewis, *West to Far Michigan*, 280; Hagman, *Oakland County Book of History*, 28.

27 Lewis, *West to Far Michigan*, 258–261, 282; Danhof, *Change in Agriculture*, 181, 183, 196n50, 209–211, 217–218, 225, 243, 247, 279; Blanke, *Sowing the American Dream*, 26, 32–33; Brian C. Wilson, *Yankees in Michigan* (East Lansing: Michigan State University Press, 2008), 46; Robert J. Heilbroner, *The Economic Transformation of America* (New York: Harcourt Brace Jovanovich, 1977), 47.

28 Lewis, *West to Far Michigan*, 245, figure 11.4, 246, figure 11.5; Hershock, *Paradox of Progress*, 61–62; Blanke, *Sowing the American Dream*, 27.

29 Richard H. Sewell, "Michigan Farmers and the Civil War," *Michigan History*, 44 (1960): 354–356, 360–365; Lewis, *West to Far Michigan*, 260; Danhof, *Change in Agriculture*, 279–280; Lewis Beeson, review of Joseph J. Marks, ed., *Effects of the Civil War on Farming in Michigan*, in *Michigan History Magazine*, 49:4 (December 1965): 377–378.

30 Assessment Roll for the Township of Pontiac in the County of Oakland, for the Year 1867, Record Group 37: Records of Oakland County, Office of the Treasurer, microfilm roll 9178, Archive of Michigan, Lansing.

31 Walter Nugent, *Structures of American Social History* (Bloomington: Indiana University Press, 1981), 84–85; Steven Mintz and Susan Kellogg, *Domestic Revolutions: A Social History of American Family Life* (New York: Free Press, 1988), 100; John D'Emilio and Estelle B. Freedman, *Intimate Matters: A History of Sexuality in America* (New York: Harper & Row, 1988), 58.

32 D'Emilio and Freedman, *Intimate Matters*, 59–60, 161; Robert V. Wells, *Revolutions in Americans' Lives: A Demographic Perspective on the History of Americans, Their Families, and Their Society* (Westport, CT: Greenwood, 1982), 96–99; Daniel E. Sutherland, *The Expansion of Everyday Life, 1860–1876* (New York: Harper & Row, 1989), 123; Linda Gordon, *Woman's Body, Woman's Right: A Social History of Birth Control in America* (New York: Grossman, 1976), chs. 2–3. For a useful overview of birth control in the United States during the

nineteenth century, see Carl N. Degler, *At Odds: Women and the Family in America from the Revolution to the Present* (New York: Oxford University Press, 1980), ch. IX.

33   "Wonderful Re-Union," *Bay City* [Michigan] *Tribune,* August 30, 1885.

34   *Portrait and Biographical Album of Oakland County,* 320.

35   Products of Agriculture: Pontiac Township, Oakland County, Michigan, pp. 55–58, Federal Non-Population Census Schedule, 1870, Oakland County Pioneer and Historical Society library, Pontiac, MI.

36   *Portrait and Biographical Album of Oakland County,* 320, 332; Davis, *John Grow of Ipswich,* 93; Robert J. Gordon, *The Rise and Fall of American Growth: The U.S. Standard of Living since the Civil War* (Princeton, NJ: Princeton University Press, 2016), 252–253; Carl Degler, *The Age of the Economic Revolution, 1876–1900* (Glenview, IL: Scott, Foresman, 1967), 22, 36, 39; Pontiac city directories, 1880s-1890s. The couple's new city residence was located on the southwest corner of the intersection of School and Perry streets. (*Pontiac City and Oakland County Directory 1886* [Detroit: T. W. Aston & Co., 1886], 82)
   During the latter decades of the nineteenth century, the rising value of farmland and the general profitability of agriculture enabled growing numbers of affluent midwestern farmers to leave the labor force and retire to neighboring towns or villages. They secured the funds needed for retirement "by renting, leasing, or selling" their farms. (Carol Haber and Brian Gratton, *Old Age and the Search for Security: An American Social History* [Bloomington: Indiana University Press, 1994], 93–95, 104, 181)

37   Nugent, *Structures of American Social History,* ch. IV; Degler, *Age of the Economic Revolution,* 43, 73; Alan Trachtenberg, *The Incorporation of America: Culture and Society in the Gilded Age,* rev. ed. (New York: Hill and Wang, 2007), 114; Allan Kulikoff, *The Agrarian Origins of American Capitalism* (Charlottesville: University Press of Virginia, 1992), 266. "Between 1870 and 1900," as a combined result of rural-urban migration, natural increase, and large-scale foreign immigration, "the number of [US] cities of 25,000 or more jumped from 52 to 160, and their number of residents by 338 percent." (Nugent, *Structures of American Social History,* 105)

38   Samuel W. Durant, *History of Oakland County, Michigan* (Philadelphia: L. H. Everts, 1877), 81, 85; Thaddeus D. Seeley, *History of Oakland County, Michigan: A Narrative Account of its Historical Progress, its People, and its Principal Interests,* 2 vols. (Chicago: Lewis Publishing Co., 1912), 1:302, 304, 307. Pontiac population figures for 1870 and 1900 were drawn from Wikipedia, the Free Encyclopedia: "Pontiac, Michigan" (Online at en.wikipedia.org/wiki/Pontiac,Michigan).

39   Nugent, *Structures of American Social History,* 115, 124; Stuart M. Blumin, *The Emergence of the Middle Class: Social Experience in the American City, 1760–1900* (Cambridge, U.K.: Cambridge University Press, 1989), 288–290; Thomas J. Schlereth, *Victorian America: Transformations in Everyday Life, 1876–1915* (New York: HarperCollins, 1991), xiii, 29. The first American dictionary definition of the term "middle class" appeared in *The Century Dictionary* in 1889. (Burton J. Bledstein, *The Culture of Professionalism: The Middle Class and the Development of Higher Education in America* [New York: W. W. Norton, 1976], 13)

40   Schlereth, *Victorian America,* xiv, 141–142, 296, and Schlereth, "Country Stores and Mail-Order Catalogues: Consumption in Rural America," in Simon J. Bronner, ed., *Consuming Visions: Accumulation and Display of Goods in America, 1880–1920* (New York: W. W. Norton, 1989), 373–375; Michael Burton, "The Victorian Jeremiad: Critics of Accumulation and Display," in Bronner, ed., *Consuming Visions,* 57, 68, 70; Daniel Horowitz, *The Morality of Spending: Attitudes toward the Consumer Society in America, 1875–1940* (Baltimore: Johns Hopkins University Press, 1985), xxvii, 68–69, 85, 107; Wells, *Revolutions in Americans' Lives,* 204; Blanke, *Sowing the American Dream,* 159.

41   *Portrait and Biographical Album of Oakland County,* 320–321; *Pontiac City Directory, 1895* (Pontiac, MI: J. H. Harger and Co., 1895), 150; Karen Zukowski, *Creating the Artful Home: The Aesthetic Movement* (Layton, UT: Gibbs Smith, 2006), 80–104, 137–143; Daniel J. Boorstin, *The Americans: The Democratic Experience* (New York: Random House, 1973), 355; Gordon, *Rise and Fall of American Growth,* 126. Thorstein Veblen, a prominent critic of capitalism and conspicuous consumption at the time, wrote that many Queen Anne houses were designed purely to proclaim status. (Zukowski, *Creating the Artful Home,* 103)

42   *Portrait and Biographical Album of Oakland County,* 320–321; George S. May, *Pictorial History of Michigan: The Early Years* (Grand Rapids, MI: William R. Eerdmans Publishing Co., 1967), 159–160; Rhonda Frevert, "Tales from the Vault: Mug Books," *Common-Place,* 3:1 (October 2002), online at common -place.org, accessed 24 November 2016.

43   Hershock, *Paradox of Progress,* xv–xvi, 193-218; Wilson, *Yankees in Michigan,* 71–73; Kulikoff, *Agrarian Origins of American Capitalism,* 220.

44 "Wonderful Re-Union."

45 Galusha Grow was born in Ashford, Windham County, CT, in 1823, the fifth son of Elisha Grow's "improvident" younger brother Joseph Grow (1787–1827). A few years after his father's premature death, Galusha's mother, Elizabeth (Robbins) Grow (1787–1863) relocated the family to northern Pennsylvania, where she became a successful businesswoman. Galusha was educated at Franklin Academy and Amherst College, after which he joined the law firm of David Wilmot, a Pennsylvania politician in the "free-soil" wing of the Democratic Party and author of the famous Wilmot Proviso of 1846, which sought to ban slavery from any territory acquired from Mexico in the Mexican War of 1846–1848. In 1850, as Wilmot's political protegé, Grow was elected to the US House of Representatives and went on to serve six consecutive terms as a Pennsylvania congressman.

When he arrived in Washington, DC, the national conflict over slavery was inexorably pushing the United States toward civil war. An outspoken opponent of slavery and its expansion into any future states of the Union, Galusha—like many of his Pennsylvania colleagues—left the Democratic Party in the mid-1850s to join the new Republican Party. A skillful debater with a sharp tongue, a sarcastic oratorical style, and an uncompromising demeanor, he soon emerged as an influential voice among the "radical" faction of the Republicans, making many political enemies among Southern Democrats on Capitol Hill during a period when congressional politics was growing increasingly confrontational and violent. In 1856, a hotheaded South Carolina congressman, Preston Brooks, had physically assaulted Massachusetts' abolitionist senator Charles Sumner on the floor of the Senate, severely injuring him. Then, in May 1858, during a late-night House filibuster on Kansas, Galusha Grow crossed the aisle separating Republican and Democratic representatives on the floor of the House to confer with a Northern Democratic colleague when Rep. Laurence M. Keitt, a South Carolina Democrat, warned him to stay on the Republican side of the aisle, calling him a "Black Republican puppy." When Galusha replied that "I shall occupy such place in this hall as I please, and no nigger driver shall crack his whip over me," Keith lunged for his throat in an attempt to strangle him and Grow knocked him down with a punch below the right ear, precipitating an ugly brawl on the House floor involving some fifty congressmen. (The following day, both Keitt and Grow formally apologized for violating the decorum of the House of Representatives.) Twenty months later, when Galusha accused North Carolina congressman Lawrence Branch of unparliamentary and ungentlemanly behavior, Branch challenged him to a duel. Grow refused, and his friends in Congress feared that he would be physically attacked by Branch and his supporters. The following morning, Grow and his close friend Rep. John Potter of Wisconsin walked from Grow's 7th Street residence to the Capitol, "both armed with revolvers and Potter with a bowie knife," without further incident. (Both Keitt and Branch subsequently died fighting for the Confederacy during the Civil War—Keitt at the Battle of Cold Harbor in 1864, Branch at Antietam in 1862.)

The pinnacle of Grow's political career came in July 1861 when he was elected Speaker of the House of Representatives during the momentous first congressional term of the Civil War. His Speakership commenced a few weeks after the fall of Fort Sumter and seventeen days before the disastrous Union military defeat by Confederate forces at the Battle of Bull Run. As Speaker, he worked closely, and by all accounts competently, with President Abraham Lincoln to steer war legislation through the House. Initially, many Republican congressmen were frustrated with Lincoln's leadership, believing that he was too moderate and conciliatory in his prosecution of the war, and instead valuing him primarily as dispenser-in-chief of political patronage. Grow seems to have subscribed at least partially to that point of view. One of Lincoln's Illinois acquaintances later recalled: "'I was with the President one day [in the White House] when Mr. Grow . . . came in, and in an excited manner' demanded that his brother-in-law be appointed as a territorial judge. President Lincoln apologized for the oversight and said an appointment would soon be made. 'Mr. Grow was very angry, and talked, as it looked to me, impertinently. Mr. Seward came in and took part [in] defending Mr. Lincoln. Mr. Grow used threats that surprised me. After Mr. Grow and Mr. Seward had retired, and we were alone, he was troubled. Said he had been President five months, and was surprised anybody would want the office.'" Lincoln later told his Illinois acquaintance that "he was so badgered with applications for appointments" he sometimes thought "that the only way . . . he could escape from them would be to take a rope and hang himself" from one of the trees on the White House lawn.

Grow's most significant accomplishment as Speaker of the House was passage of the 1862 Homestead Act, legislation that spurred the agricultural development of the American West by enabling individual settlers to obtain up to 160 acres of free land from the public domain west of the Mississippi River. His most costly mistake as Speaker was to make a political enemy of Pennsylvania Republican Simon Cameron by criticizing Cameron's performance as Lincoln's first secretary of war. In 1862, Grow was defeated in his bid for a seventh term in Congress when gerrymandering by his political opponents shifted his Pennsylvania home district into the Democratic camp. Thereafter, Cameron—as the boss of Pennsylvania's Republican political machine—saw to it that Grow's subsequent campaigns for the House, the Senate, and the Pennsylvania governorship were also unsuccessful. During the 1870s and 1880s, Galusha made his living as a successful private businessman, amassing considerable wealth in the railroad and coal industries. Late in life, he returned to the House of Representatives as a Pennsylvania congressman-at-large, serving four consecutive terms between 1894 and 1900. He died in 1907 at age 84, a lifelong bachelor.

(Sources: James T. Dubois and Gertrude S. Mathews, *Galusha Grow: Father of the Homestead Law* [Boston: Houghton Mifflin, 1917]; Robert D. Ilisevich, *Galusha A. Grow: The People's Candidate* [Pittsburgh, PA: University of Pittsburgh Press, 1988]; Allan G. Bogue, *The Congressman's Civil War* [New York: Cambridge University Press, 1989]; Joanne Freeman, *The Field of Blood: Violence in Congress and the Road to Civil War* [New York: Farrar, Straus and Giroux, 2018], 236–243, 248–254; *New York Times*, 6 February 1858; Douglas L. Wilson and Rodney O. Davis, eds., *Herndon's Informants: Letters, Interviews, and Statements about Abraham Lincoln* [Urbana: University of Illinois Press, 1998])

(Note: in his Grow family genealogy *John Grow of Ipswich/John (Groo) Grow of Oxford*, George W. Davis made the unfounded claim that at the 1864 Republican national convention Galusha Grow lost to Andrew Johnson by a single vote in a party referendum to choose Lincoln's vice presidential running mate for that year's presidential election, and that Grow would consequently have become president following Lincoln's assassination had he won. Davis was mistaken. Grow was not a candidate for the Republican vice presidential nomination in 1864.)

46   "Sixty Five Years" (Thomas Grow obituary), *The Daily Press* [Pontiac, MI], 25 October 1902, p. 1; Davis, *John Grow of Ipswich*, 94.

47   Edwin S. Gaustad, *The Great Awakening in New England* (New York: Harper, 1957), 273; William G. McLoughlin, *New England Dissent, 1630–1833: The Baptists and the Separation of Church and State* (Cambridge, MA: Harvard University Press, 1972), 756. "The temperance movement did not begin among the Baptists until the late 1820s." (McLoughlin, *New England Dissent*, 829n43)

48   Mark Edward Lender and James Kirby Martin, *Drinking in America: A History* (New York: Free Press, 1982), 9, 14, 51; Barbara Epstein, *The Politics of Domesticity: Women, Evangelism, and Temperance in Nineteenth-Century America* (Middletown, CT: Wesleyan University Press, 1981), 91; Lewis, *West to Far Michigan*, 239; Wilson, *Yankees in Michigan*, 67.

49   Thomas Pegram, *Battling Demon Rum: The Struggle for a Dry America, 1800–1933* (Chicago: Ivan Dee, 1999), xii, 6–7; Lender and Martin, *Drinking in America*, 46–47, 95; Epstein, *Politics of Domesticity*, 91.

50   Hershock, *Paradox of Progress*, 106; Epstein, *Politics of Domesticity*, 102; Pegram, *Battling Demon Rum*, xi, 7.

51   Lender and Martin, *Drinking in America*, chs. 2–3; Wilson, *Yankees in Michigan*, 67-68; Hershock, *Paradox of Progress*, 107–110.

52   Davis, *John Grow of Ipswich*, 90.

53   William B. Grow, *Eighty-Five Years of Life and Labor* (Carbondale, PA: published by the author, 1902), 187.

54   J. C. Furnas, *The Life and Times of the Late Demon Rum: An Irreverent History of the Temperance Movement in the United States* (New York: Capricorn Books, 1965), 99; Lender and Martin, *Drinking in America*, 58–60.

55   Durant, *History of Oakland County*, 184–187, 189.

56   Furnas, *Life and Times of the Late Demon Rum*, 267; Wilson, *Yankees in Michigan*, 67.

57   Furnas, *Life and Times of the Late Demon Rum*, 176, 178; Jacob Samuel Vandersloot, *The True Path, or Gospel Temperance; Being the Life, Work, and Speeches of Francis Murphy, Dr. Henry A. Reynolds, and Their Co-Laborers* (New York: H. S. Goodspeed, 1878), 443–464; William Haven Daniels, *The Temperance Reform and its Great Reformers* (New York: Nelson & Phillips, 1878), 408–430; Durant, *History of Oakland County*, 110; Lender and Martin, *Drinking in America*, 116–117. The Red Ribbon movement's motto was "Dare to do Right." (Vandersloot, *The True Path*, 459)

58   Vandersloot, *The True Path*, 446.

59   Blumin, *Emergence of the Middle Class*, 193, 195–196.

60   Margaret Grow obituary, 30 July 1899 (see endnote 8); Thomas Grow obituary (see endnote 46); Sutherland, *Expansion of Everyday Life*, 80–81; Gary Laderman, *The Sacred Remains: American Attitudes Toward Death, 1799–1883* (New Haven, CT: Yale University Press, 1996), 170; Paul A. Carter, *The Spiritual Crisis of the Gilded Age* (DeKalb: Northern Illinois University Press, 191), 99.

61   Grow, *Eighty-Five Years of Life and Labor*, 41, 109; Davis, *John Grow of Ipswich*, 90–91.

62   Sutherland, *Expansion of Everyday Life,* 82; Carter, *Spiritual Crisis of the Gilded Age,* 45–47, 50; Epstein, *Politics of Domesticity,* 47–50, 83; William Leach, *Land of Desire: Merchants, Power, and the Rise of a New American Culture* (New York: Pantheon, 1993), 195.

63   Carter, *Spiritual Crisis of the Gilded Age,* 10, 14, 32–33, 49–50, 89, 99, 137; Zukowski, *Creating the Artful Home,* 20–21; Degler, *Age of the Economic Revolution,* 163, 174, 178.

64   Leach, *Land of Desire,* 149, 195; Wilson, *Yankees in Michigan,* 88; Schlereth, *Victorian America,* 172.

65   Sutherland, *Expansion of Everyday Life,* 80, 86; Degler, *Age of the Economic Revolution,* 157; Lewis O. Saum, *The Popular Mood in America, 1860–1890* (Lincoln: University of Nebraska Press, 1990), 39, 68–69, 71, 85–86, 203. By the end of the nineteenth century, Thomas C. Cochran writes, "Protestant churches in the larger cities" were trying "to minimize strict doctrine and move in the direction of rendering social service by means of Sunday schools, parish houses, social clubs, and missionary work aimed more at social than religious values. . . .The successful preacher in a prosperous urban or suburban parish sought to achieve a good adjustment by being a good businessperson and a good social leader rather than a proclaimer of eternal laws. In urban congregations, educated Protestants . . . came to apply some of the questioning attitudes of science to their religion. Faith survived, but it was in the background. It was not the active, implicit faith of the mid-nineteenth century. Parishioners valued their church as a social institution, doctrine was approved more pragmatically on the basis of its credibility and utility, and church attendance was seen as a social as well as a religious ritual." (*Challenges to American Values: Society, Business and Religion* [New York: Oxford University Press, 1985], 86–87)

66   Sheila M. Rothman, *Woman's Proper Place: A History of Changing Ideals and Practices, 1870 to the Present* (New York: Basic Books, 1978), 13–14, 17–18; Epstein, *Politics of Domesticity,* 2, 81; Zukowski, *Creating the Artful Home,* 20; Sutherland, *Expansion of Everyday Life,* 55, 64, 70; Gordon, *Rise and Fall of American Growth,* 72–72; Schlereth, *Victorian America,* 161–164, 174; Boorstin, *Americans: The Democratic Experience,* 313, 315–316. "The first chain grocery store—the New York-based Atlantic and Pacific Tea Company [or "A & P"]—won almost instant approval when it opened its doors in 1864. By 1880, the company had over one hundred stores scattered throughout the country." (Sutherland, *Expansion of Everyday Life,* 70, 151–152)

67   Blumen, *Emergence of the Middle Class,* 184–187; Rothman, *Woman's Proper Place,* 13–14, 21; Schlereth, *Victorian America,* 141; Charles C. Calhoun, "Introduction," in Charles C. Calhoun, ed., *The Gilded Age: Perspectives on the Origins of Modern America,* 2nd ed. (Lanham, MD: Rowman & Littlefield, 2007), 4; Zukowski, *Creating the Artful Home,* 7–8, 20–22.

68   *Portrait and Biographical Album,* 321; Epstein, *Politics of Domesticity,* 36.

69   Margaret Grow obituary (see endnote 8).

70   Ibid.

71   James J. Farrell, *Inventing the American Way of Death, 1830–1920* (Philadelphia: Temple University Press, 1980), ch. 5; Laderman, *Sacred Remains,* 9, 166–168, 175. According to Farrell, "Funeral costs increased as much as 250 percent between 1880 and 1920, but funeral directors were not wholly to blame. [Casket m]anufacturers, cemeteries, florists, livery stables, mausoleum companies, and industrial insurance companies all contributed to the quality and increased cost of the funeral." (*Inventing the American Way of Death,* 181)

72   Thomas Grow obituary (see endnote 46). Details of Elisha Palmer Grow's death in the *Bay City Times,* 2 December 1901, and online at findagrave.com, memorial 47646131.

GENERATION SEVEN: DEWITT GROW (1850–1921)

1   George W. Davis, *John Grow of Ipswich/John (Groo) Grow of Oxford* (Washington, D.C.: privately printed by the Carnahan Press, 1913), 94, 130.

2   Robert L. Heilbroner, *The Economic Transformation of America* (New York: Harcourt Brace Jovanovich, 1977), 74, 146–147; Thomas J. Schlereth, *Victorian America: Transformations in Everyday Life, 1876–1915* (New York: HarperCollins, 1991), 29; Walter Nugent, *Structures of American Social History* (Bloomington: Indiana University Press, 1981), 118; Stuart M. Blumin, *The Emergence of the Middle Class: Social Experience in the American City, 1760–1900* (Cambridge, U.K.: Cambridge University Press, 1989), 267–268, 291.

3   Burton J. Bledstein, *The Culture of Professionalism: The Middle Class and the Development of Higher Education in America* (New York: W. W. Norton, 1976), 43.

4   Blumin, *Emergence of the Middle Class,* 289, 309–310.

5   David B. Danbom, *Born in the Country: A History of Rural America* (Baltimore: Johns Hopkins University Press, 1995), 90; Robert L. Griswold, *Fatherhood in American: A History* (New York: Basic Books, 1993), 28–29; Daniel E. Sutherland, *The Expansion of Everyday Life, 1860–1876* (New York: HarperCollins, 1989), 54, 134–135, 140.

6   Sutherland, *Expansion of Everyday Life,* 190; Olivier Zunz, *Making America Corporate, 1870–1920* (Chicago, IL: University of Chicago Press, 1990), 150–151.

7   Schlereth, *Victorian America,* 7–8; Heilbroner, *Economic Transformation of America,* 150; Sutherland, *Expansion of Everyday Life,* 132, 158.

8   "Reminiscences of Mortimer A. Leggett," *Michigan Pioneer and Historical Collections,* 40 vols. (Lansing, MI: Michigan Historical Commission, etc., 1874–1929), 35 (1907), 688-690. According to Leggett, during "the first part of the [New Year's] dance the girls would wear calico dresses, at midnight they would all bloom out in white, and towards morning change to silks of different colors; it was hard work to keep track of your girl."

9   Mark C. Carnes, *Secret Ritual and Manhood in Victorian America* (New Haven, CT: Yale University Press, 1989), 116; Zunz, *Making America Corporate,* 128, 145; Maury Klein, *The Flowering of the Third America: The Making of an Organizational Society, 1850–1920* (Chicago. IL: Ivan R. Dee, 1993), 111; A. J. Angulo, *Diploma Mills: How For-Profit Colleges Stiffed Students, Taxpayers, and the American Dream* (Baltimore: Johns Hopkins University Press, 2016), ch. 1. For a useful overview of the early history of private vocational and commercial colleges in the United States, see Caitlin Rosenthal, "The Long and Controversial History of For-Profit Colleges," online at bloomberg.com (25 October 2012).

10   *History of Bay County, Michigan, With Illustrations and Biographical Sketches of Some of its Prominent Men and Pioneers* (Chicago, IL: H. R. Page, 1883), 124; John Cumming, *Little Jake of Saginaw* (Mount Pleasant, MI: Rivercrest House, 1978), 18. Founded in 1859, the Eastman Business College of Poughkeepsie was "for a time one of the largest commercial schools in the United States." (Online at lostcolleges.com/eastman-business-college, accessed 22 May 2017) Several private business colleges were operating in Detroit in the 1860s, including Goldsmith's Commercial College and Cochran's Business College. (Silas Farmer, *The History of Detroit and Michigan,* 2 vols. [Detroit: Silas Farmer, 1889], 2:1146)

11   Daniel J. Boorstin, *The Americans: The Democratic Experience* (New York: Random House, 1973), 97–100, 188–189; Claudia B. Kidwell and Margaret C. Christman, *Suiting Everyone: The Democratization of Clothing in America* (Washington, D.C.: Smithsonian Institution Press for the National Museum of History and Technology, 1974), 15, 91–101, 111, 113, 115, 145, 159, 165, 167; Heilbroner, *Economic Transformation of America,* 59; David Blanke, *Sowing the American Dream: How Consumer Culture Took Root in the Rural Midwest* (Athens: Ohio University Press, 2000), 152; Blumin, *Emergence of the Middle Class,* 139–141, 144; Klein, *Flowering of the Third America,* 139.

12   Cumming, *Little Jake,* 1–10, 16, 18, 37–41, 45, 47–48, 59, 73–75, 82–83, 89, 92–96, 99, 105–115, 141.

13   Zunz, *Making America Corporate,* 127; Blumin, *Emergence of the Middle Class,* 291–292.

14   Cumming, *Little Jake,* 39, 90; *History of Bay County, Michigan, With Illustrations and Biographical Sketches of Some of its Prominent Men and Pioneers,* 124.

15   Augustus H. Gansser, *History of Bay County, Michigan and Representative Citizens* (Chicago, IL: Richmond & Arnold, 1905), 199; Jeremy W. Kilar, *Michigan's Lumbertowns: Lumbermen and Laborers in Saginaw, Bay City, and Muskegon, 1870–1905* (Detroit, MI: Wayne State University Press, 1990), 15, 21–26, 34–42, 67; "The Heyday of Michigan's Lumber Industry," *Detroit News* online edition, 12 February 2017; Cumming, *Little Jake,* 2, 23; "Shanty Boys, River Hogs, and the Forests of Michigan," *Detroit News* online edition, 8 April 2012.

16   Kilar, *Michigan's Lumbertowns,* 15, 20, 54, 86; *The Encyclopedia of Michigan* (St. Clair Shores, MI: Somerset Publishers, 1999), 1:166; "The Heyday of Michigan's Lumber Industry"; Gansser, *History of Bay County, Michigan,* 179. In 1877, the Bay City sawmill of John McGraw and Company was "believed to be the largest in the world," with 350 workers. (Kilar, *Michigan's Lumbertowns,* 55) According to one descriptive account of Bay City's sawmill operations, stacks of drying boards lined the banks of the Saginaw "so solidly" that the river "appeared to flow between wooden walls." (*Encyclopedia of Michigan,* 1:166)

17   Kilar, *Michigan's Lumbertowns,* 39, 56, 173.

18   Kenneth E. Lewis, *West to Far Michigan: Settling the Lower Peninsula, 1815–1860* (East Lansing: Michigan State University Press, 2002), 309–310; D. Lawrence Rogers, "Founded by Risktakers," *Michigan History* (March-April 2009): 55–56; Kilar, *Michigan's Lumbertowns,* 50, 55, 61, 64, 67–68, 71–72; Cumming, *Little Jake,*

96; *History of Bay County, Michigan, With Illustrations and Biographical Sketches of Some of its Prominent Men and Pioneers,* 124. For the location of Seligman's clothing store, see endnote 20 below.

19 "Bay City," *Encyclopedia of Michigan,* 1:166; Rogers, "Founded by Risktakers," 55–56; Kilar, *Michigan's Lumbertowns,* 13, 50, 68, 71–75, 92, 104, 112, 116–117, 121, 125–127, 302.

20 Little Jake's Bay City clothing store was "in the Birney block on Water Street. Later [the Grow brothers] moved across the street, five doors south of the Campbell house." ("Fatal Accident" [a published report of E. Palmer Grow's death], *Bay City Times-Press,* 2 December 1901) The Birney Block and Campbell House were both located on Water Street immediately south of the intersection with Third Street, the southern boundary of Water Street's "Hell's Half Mile" saloon district. ("Public Buildings & Places of Bay City, MI [1875]," online at bay-journal.com/bay/1he/writings/bc-public-buildings-places-1875.html [accessed 21 June 2017]; Kilar, *Michigan's Lumbertowns,* 72) According to Jamie Kramer of the Bay County [MI] Historical Society, "Water Street as a whole was the 'rough' section of town. . . .The intersection of 3rd [Street] and Water . . . would have been the approximate location of the Campbell House [and] the Birney Block was between 4th and 5th streets. When the Grow Bros. were in this block they would have been in the heart of th[e] saloon district. However, in 1877 and 1878 the [city] directories indicate their location to be 304 N. Water. This would put them out quite a ways from both the Birney Block and Campbell House." (Email communication to author, 11 July 2017)

21 *History of Bay County, Michigan, With Illustrations and Biographical Sketches of Some of its Prominent Men and Pioneers,* 124.

22 Davis, *John Grow of Ipswich,* 131; *Portrait and Biographical Album of Oakland County, Michigan* (Chicago: Chapman Bros., 1891), 617–618.

23 John D'Emilio and Estelle B. Freedman, *Intimate Matters: A History of Sexuality in America* (New York: Harper & Row, 1988), 58, 174; Steven Mintz and Susan Kellogg, *Domestic Revolutions: A Social History of American Family Life* (New York: Free Press, 1988), 51–52; Blumin, *Emergence of the Middle Class,* 187; Robert V. Wells, *Revolutions in Americans' Lives: A Demographic Perspective on the History of Americans, Their Families, and Their Society* (Westport, CT: Greenwood Press, 1982), 99; Christopher Lasch, *Haven in a Heartless World: The Family Besieged* (New York: Basic Books, 1977), 8–9.

24 Mintz and Kellogg, *Domestic Revolutions,* 120; Robert J. Gordon, *The Rise and Fall of American Growth: The U.S. Standard of Living since the Civil War* (Princeton, NJ: Princeton University Press, 2016), 229; Jack Larkin, *The Reshaping of Everyday Life, 1790–1840* (New York: Harper & Row, 1988), 97–98. As late as 1900, according to Robert J. Gordon, "only 5 percent of American women delivered their babies in hospitals." (*Rise and Fall of American Growth,* 229) For the history of Bay City's first hospital, see Kilar, *Michigan's Lumbertowns,* 94.

25 Carl N. Degler, *At Odds: Women and the Family in America from the Revolution to the Present* (New York: Oxford University Press, 1980), 222, 262–263, 295; D'Emilio and Freedman, *Intimate Matters,* 55, 175–176. The survey made no mention of abortion as a birth control method. Nevertheless, an 1878 report by Michigan's state board of health estimated that a third of all pregnancies in the state were terminated by abortions and that 70 to 80 percent of the abortions were secured by "prosperous and otherwise respectable married women." (D'Emilio and Freedman, *Intimate Matters,* 65)

26 Mintz and Kellogg, *Domestic Revolutions,* 50–53; Robert L. Griswold, *Fatherhood in America: A History* (New York: Basic Books, 1993), 13–16, 23–24; John Demos, *Past, Present, and Personal: The Family and the Life Course in American History* (New York: Oxford University Press, 1986), 31–32, 47, 51–52; Degler, *At Odds,* 77.

27 Mintz and Kellogg, *Domestic Revolutions,* 50–51; Barbara Epstein, *The Politics of Domesticity: Women, Evangelism, and Temperance in Nineteenth-Century America* (Middletown, CT: Wesleyan University Press, 1981), 2; Karen Zukowski, *Creating the Artful Home: The Aesthetic Movement* (Layton, UT: Gibbs Smith, 2006), 21–22. The wife's domestic role as homemaker was reinforced by new women's magazines that were flooding the publishing market in the 1870s and 1880s, including *Women's Home Companion* (1873), *Women's Home Journal* (1878), *Ladies Home Journal* (1883), and *Good Housekeeping* (1885)—publications that offered the housewife advice on "the proper management of her . . . household," and through their seductive advertisements introduced her to the latest, most desirable new consumer goods that no fashionable middle-class home should be without. (Bledstein, *Culture of Professionalism,* 62–63)

28 Mintz and Kellogg, *Domestic Revolutions,* 53; Demos, *Past, Present, and Personal,* 31–33, 35; Stephen M. Frank, *Life with Father: Parenthood and Masculinity in the Nineteenth-Century American North* (Baltimore: Johns Hopkins University Press, 1998), 72, 80–81; Arlene Skolnick, *Embattled Paradise: The American Family in an Age of Uncertainty* (New York: Basic Books, 1991), 31, 37–38; Lasch, *Haven in a Heartless World.*

29 Gordon, *Rise and Fall of American Growth*, 46, 255.

30 Kilar, *Michigan's Lumbertowns*, 106. From at least 1883 through 1896, the couple resided at 1115 Fifth Street. In 1897 they were living at 1109 Fifth Street. From 1907 (or before) until their deaths, they resided at 909 North Farragut Street. (Bay City directories)

31 *History of Bay County, Michigan, With Illustrations and Biographical Sketches of Some of its Prominent Men and Pioneers*, 124–125, 151; "Do You Remember . . .Your Five Dollar Overcoat?" undated *Bay City Times* article, probably from the 1940s, in newspaper clipping file, Butterfield Memorial Research Library, Bay County Historical Society, Bay City, MI; "Fatal Accident" [E. Palmer Grow obituary], *Bay City Times-Press*, 2 December 1901; DeWitt Grow obituary, *Bay City Times Tribune*, Bay City, MI, 25 May 1921.

32 Cumming, *Little Jake*, 89–93.

33 Kilar, *Michigan's Lumbertowns*, 208, 229–242, 288–289; Victor J. Mobley, "Ten Hours or No Sawdust," *Michigan History* (March-April 2012): 22–27.

34 Kilar, *Michigan's Lumbertowns*, 16, 162, 187, 249, 260–265; "Shanty Boys, River Hogs, and the Forests of Michigan"; Mobley, "Ten Hours or No Sawdust," 26; Gansser, *History of Bay County, Michigan and Representative Citizens*, 179; "Bay City," *Encyclopedia of Michigan*, 1:166.

35 *West Bay City Sunday Times*, 26 May 1895, newspaper clipping file, Butterfield Memorial Research Library, Bay County Historical Society, Bay City, MI.

36 DeWitt Grow obituary (see note 31 above); Bay City directories, 1905–1918; United States 1910 Federal Census: Bay City, MI, online at HeritageQuest.org.

37 "Michigan Coal Mining and the Saginaw Valley," online at bay-journal.com; Charles Moore, *History of Michigan*, 4 vols. (Chicago: Lewis Publishing Co., 1915), 2:712–713; "Gene Gillette Digs into Bay County Coal Mines," online at mybaycity.com.

38 Alan Trachtenberg, *The Incorporation of America: Culture and Society in the Gilded Age* (New York: Hill and Wang, 2007), xiv, 5; Schlereth, *Victorian America*, 300; Lynn Dumenil, *Freemasonry and American Culture, 1880–1930* (Princeton, NJ, Princeton University Press, 1984), 88–91.

39 Robert H. Wiebe, *The Search for Order, 1877–1920* (New York: Hill and Wang, 1967), vii, 40–41; Demos, *Past, Present, and Personal*, 54–55; William Leach, *Land of Desire: Merchants, Power, and the Rise of a New American Culture* (New York: Pantheon, 1993), 8; Michael Kimmel, *Manhood in America: A Cultural History* (New York: Free Press, 1996), 103–104.

40 Schlereth, *Victorian America*, 301; Danbom, *Born in the Country*, 96.

41 Griswold, *Fatherhood in America*, 13–14, 25; Demos, *Past, Present, and Personal*, 51–52; Mintz and Kellogg, *Domestic Revolutions*, 116–117. By 1900, according to one commentator, fatherhood in the United States had become "almost entirely a Sunday institution." (Demos, *Past, Present, and Personal*, 61)

42 Griswold, *Fatherhood in America*, 33, 89; Daniel Horowitz, *The Morality of Spending: Attitudes toward the Consumer Society in America, 1875–1940* (Baltimore: Johns Hopkins University Press, 1985), 85, 118; Demos, *Past, Present, and Personal*, 52; Robert V. Wells, *Revolutions in Americans' Lives*, 204.

43 Dumenil, *Freemasonry and American Culture*, 89–90; Danbom, *Born in the Country*, 85; Thomas C. Cochran, *Challenges to American Values: Society, Business and Religion* (New York: Oxford University Press, 1985), 64; Leach, *Land of Desire*, 5, 7.

44 Trachtenberg, *Incorporation of America*, 39–40; Heilbroner, *Economic Transformation of America*, 106–107.

45 Horowitz, *Morality of Spending*, 69; Leach, *Land of Desire*, 7.

46 Charles C. Calhoun, "Introduction," in Charles C. Calhoun, ed., *The Gilded Age: Perspectives on the Origins of Modern America*, 2nd ed. (Lanham, MD: Roman & Littlefield, 2007), 4; Trachtenberg, *Incorporation of America*, 130.

47 Dumenil, *Freemasonry and American Culture*, 89.

48 Joppa Lodge No. 315 membership records provided by lodge Past Master Christopher Sova, email communication to author, 25 July 2017. DeWitt was initiated as an "Entered Apprentice" on 9 December 1873, "passed" to the degree of "Fellowcraft" one week later, and "raised" to the degree of "Master Mason" the following year. He became a "Life Member" in 1916. He was again following in the footsteps of his older brother Palmer, who had become a Mason in Pontiac in 1870 before transferring his membership to Bay City's Joppa Lodge in 1875. (Ibid.) Joppa Lodge was formed in 1873 with 27 charter members. By the end of

1873 it had 32 members, and by 1896, 298 members. (Jefferson S. Conover, comp., *Freemasonry in Michigan: A Comprehensive History of Michigan Masonry from its Earliest Introduction in 1764*, 2 vols. [Coldwater, MI: Conover Engraving and Printing Co., 1897–1898], 2:558)

49   Dumenil, *Freemasonry and American Culture*, xi–xii, 7–8, 14, 19, 21–23, 30; Carnes, *Secret Ritual and Manhood in Victorian America*, 2, 14, 18.

50   Dumenil, *Freemasonry and American Culture*, xii–xiii, 9, 12–14, 25, 30, 88, 90–91, 93, 97, 108–111; Carnes, *Secret Ritual and Manhood in Victorian America*, 2–4, 31; Kimmel, *Manhood in America,* 172–173; Cochran, *Challenges to American Values*, 47–48.

51   Dumenil, *Freemasonry and American Culture*, 30, 72–75, 83, 88, 90–91, 94–98, 106–109.

52   Paul A. Carter, *The Spiritual Crisis of the Gilded Age* (DeKalb: Northern Illinois University Press, 1971), 10, 12, 14, 49–50; Carnes, *Secret Ritual and Manhood in Victorian America*, 56; Dumenil, *Freemasonry and American Culture*, 43–47.

53   Carnes, *Secret Ritual and Manhood in Victorian America*, 39–49, 52, 54–65, 75–76, 149; Dumenil, *Freemasonry and American Culture*, xii–xiii, 9, 24, 34–37, 39, 42–43, 48–50, 61–64, 66–71, 108–109.

54   *Holy Bible, Containing the Old and New Testaments, Translated Out of the Original Tongues, and With the Former Translations Diligently Compared and Revised; Together With Marginal References, Apocrypha, Concordance and Psalms* (Philadelphia: William W. Harding, 1873), personally inscribed in gilt on cover: to "Alice, From Grandma Smith," from the author's family history collection. Emphasis added.

55   DeWitt Grow obituary (see endnote 31).

56   Alice Grow obituary, *Bay City Daily Times*, Bay City, MI, 20 December 1915.

57   A detailed biographical sketch of Dr. Van H. Dumond (1887–1951) can be found in George E. Butterfield, ed., *Historic Michigan*, vol. 3: *Bay County* (Dayton, OH: National Historical Association, n.d.), 189. At one point in his career, Dumond was credited with a medical miracle. In an undated clipping from an unidentified Bay City newspaper (copy in the author's family history collection), it was reported:

> A baby boy purported to have been born dead was given life Friday afternoon through the heroic work of Dr. V. Dumond, aided by two pulmotors and three operators from the Michigan Light and Gas Company. The infant, born to Mr. and Mrs. George Schiedler, 103 Stanton Avenue . . . was born apparently dead at 12:15 o'clock. Dr. Dumond worked over the child 45 minutes. By the tireless breathing into the child's mouth he was able to restore a slight heart action which resulted in respiration of not more than two gasps a minute. Realizing that he was exhausted as the result of his strenuous efforts and that the child would die unless a pulmotor was secured, he ordered the nurse to telephone the Michigan Light and Gas Company for one of their machines.
>
> The situation was outlined in a few hurried words to Manager Samuel Ball, who sent both of the pulmotors owned by the company with three operators and enough oxygen cartridges to last eight hours. They arrived in exactly seven minutes during which time the doctor continued his work over the baby.
>
> The machines arrived at one o'clock, one of which was attached and in operation in little more than a minute. At that time a slight pulse was faintly distinguishable. Dr. Dumond and his three assistants worked until five o'clock at which time the heart action was strong and the infant was breathing regularly. Dr. Dumond declared that the baby was practically out of danger.
>
> Saturday morning a call revealed the little fellow awake and full of life.

58   DeWitt Grow obituary (see endnote 31).

GENERATION EIGHT: MARTIN SMITH GROW (1880–1942)

1   Olivier Zunz, *Making America Corporate, 1870–1920* (Chicago, IL: University of Chicago Press, 1990), ch. 7; Alan Trachtenberg, *The Incorporation of America: Culture and Society in the Gilded Age* (New York: Hill and Wang, 2007), 135–138; Harvey Green, *The Uncertainty of Everyday Life, 1915–1945* (New York: HarperCollins, 1992), 19; Thomas J. Schlereth, *Victorian America: Transformations in Everyday Life, 1876–1915* (New York: HarperCollins, 1991), xiii, ch. 4, and "Country Stores, County Fairs, and Mail-Order Catalogues: Consumption in Rural America," in Simon J. Bonner, ed., *Consuming Visions: Accumulation and Display of Goods in America, 1880–1920* (New York: W. W. Norton, 1989), 342–344, 354, 361; Robert J. Gordon, *The Rise and Fall of American Growth: The U.S. Standard of Living since the Civil War* (Princeton, NJ: Princeton

University Press, 2016), 74; Maury Klein, *The Flowering of the Third America: The Making of an Organizational Society, 1850–1920* (Chicago: Ivan R. Dee, 1993), 152–153; Michael Kimmel, *Manhood in America: A Cultural History* (New York: Free Press, 1996), 103. During the period when Martin Grow entered the labor market, "mass-production and mass-distribution" were combining to "transform the American economy." (Louis Galambos, *The Creative Society—And the Price Americans Paid for It* [New York: Cambridge University Press, 2012], 22n2)

2   Bay City and Saginaw city directories, 1899–1911, online at HeritageQuest.org.

3   Saginaw City Directory 1909, online at HeritageQuest.org; George W. Davis, *John Grow of Ipswich/John (Groo) Grow of Oxford* (Washington, D.C.: privately printed by the Carnahan Press, 1913), 130, 162; 1910 US Federal Census and 1920 US Federal Census, online at AmericanAncestors.org.

4   Steven Mintz and Susan Kellogg, *Domestic Revolutions: A Social History of American Family Life* (New York: Free Press, 1988), 108; William J. O'Neill, "Divorce in the Progressive Era," in Michael Gordon, ed., *The American Family in Socio-Historical Perspective,* 2nd ed. (New York: St. Martin's, 1978), 146. According to Mintz and Kellogg, "In the half century between 1870 and 1920, the number of divorces granted nationwide increased fifteen fold." (*Domestic Revolutions,* 109) In 1880, one out of every twenty-one marriages ended in divorce (Joe Dubbert, *A Man's Place: Masculinity in Transition* [Englewood Cliffs, NJ: Prentice-Hall, 1979], 104); in 1915, one out of every seven. "By 1915, the United States had the highest divorce rate in the world." (Schlereth, *Victorian America,* 280–281)

5   Mintz and Kellogg, *Domestic Revolutions,* 120. As late as 1935, only 37 percent of American women delivered their babies in hospitals. By 1945, the figure had reached 79 percent. (Ibid.)

6   John D'Emilio and Estelle B. Freedman, *Intimate Matters: A History of Sexuality in America* (New York: Harper & Row, 1988), 174, 246; Mintz and Kellogg, *Domestic Revolutions,* 116. According to D'Emilio and Freedman, in 1910 "almost two-thirds" of middle-class couples "had two children or less." (*Intimate Matters,* 174)

7   Tana Mosier Porter, *Toledo Profile: A Sesquicentennial History* (Toledo, OH: Toledo Sesquicentennial Commission, 1987), 50–57, 62, 72; James C. Marshall, *A Promise Kept: A History of the Village of Ottawa Hills* (Maumee, OH: Woodland Publishing, 2003), 3, 5, 7, 59.

8   Porter, *Toledo Profile,* 50; Harvey Scribner, *Memoirs of Lucas County and the City of Toledo: From the Earliest Historical Times Down to the Present,* 2 vols. (Madison, WI: Western Historical Association, 1910), 1:559; "The Lion Coffee Saga," online at thefreelibrary.com/The+Lion+Coffee+Saga.-a08943605.

9   "Modernity in Coffee Roasting Factories: The New Plant of the Woolson Spice Co., Toledo, O," *The Spice Mill: Devoted to the Interests of the Tea, Coffee and Spice Trade,* vol. XXXV, no. 1 (January 1912): 28; "Four Woolson Salesmen Open Up 700 New Accounts: How the Woolson Spice People Put Over Golden Sun Coffee in the Indianapolis Market in Jig Time," *Sales Management,* vol. 3 (September 1921): 544; Zunz, *Making America Corporate,* 176.

10   Thomas C. Cochran, *Challenges to American Values: Society, Business and Religion* (New York: Oxford University Press, 1985), 64, 74–75; Green, *Uncertainty of Everyday Life,* 10, 21; C. Wright Mills, *White Collar* (New York: Oxford University Press, 1951), xvi–xvii, 263–264; Zunz, *Making America Corporate,* 12–13, 188; Karen Halttunen, *Confidence Men and Painted Women: A Study of Middle-Class Culture in America, 1830–1870* (New Haven, CT: Yale University Press, 1982), 203–204, 207–208; David M. Potter, *People of Plenty: Economic Abundance and the American Character* (Chicago, IL: University of Chicago Press, 1954), 52.

11   Robert L. Heilbruner, *The Economic Transformation of America* (New York: Harcourt Brace Jovanovich, 1977), 135; Kimmel, *Manhood in America,* 87; Green, *Uncertainty of Everyday Life,* 19; Trachtenberg, *Incorporation of America,* 135; Schlereth, *Victorian America,* 67–68; D'Emilio and Freedman, *Intimate Matters,* 189; Sheila M. Rothman, *Woman's Proper Place: A History of Changing Ideals and Practices, 1870 to the Present* (New York: Basic Books, 1978), 47–51. Also see Mills, *White Collar,* 198–204.

12   D'Emilio and Freedman, *Intimate Matters,* 172, 195–196, 201, 224, 231, 233–235; Daniel Horowitz, *The Morality of Spending: Attitudes toward the Consumer Society in America, 1875–1940* (Baltimore, MD: Johns Hopkins University Press, 1985), xxvii; Mintz and Kellogg, *Domestic Revolutions,* 108, 110–112, 125; Christopher Lasch, *Haven in a Heartless World: The Family Besieged* (New York: Basic Books, 1977), 10–11; Schlereth, *Victorian America,* 193, 200–206; Mark C. Carnes, *Secret Ritual and Manhood in Victorian America* (New Haven, CT: Yale University Press, 1989), 153–154. A 1913 US magazine declared that the clock had struck "sex o'clock" in America. (Mintz and Kellogg, *Domestic Revolutions,* 111) In 1910 there were "ten thousand movie theaters" in the United States "playing to a nationwide audience of over 10 million." (Schlereth, *Victorian*

America, 200) By 1919, residents of Toledo, Ohio, were attending 1.3 movies per week on average. A study of the city's movie attendance for that year "tallied a weekly attendance of 316,000 in a population of 243,000." (Gordon, *Rise and Fall of American Growth,* 200)

13   Porter, *Toledo Profile,* 62–63, 72, 74, 78–80; Marshall, *Promise Kept,* 3; "Biography—Cyclomobile: Earl M. Morley," online at sites.google.com/a/emageusa.com/cyclomobile/biography (accessed 21 January 2018); *The American Architect,* 20 June 1928, p. 37; James J. Flink, *The Automobile Age* (Cambridge, MA: MIT Press, 1988), 51. By 1927, 56 percent of US families owned automobiles. (Ibid., 131)

14   Porter, *Toledo Profile,* 75–80; Heilbruner, *Economic Transformation of America,* 162; Green, *Uncertainty of Everyday Life,* 42, 60, 62–63, 109; Gordon, *Rise and Fall of American Growth,* 61, 114, 121, 129–130, 170, 190, 285.

15   In August 1924, three years after the death of DeWitt Grow in Bay City, Martin and Delia purchased a residential lot (number 249) in recently opened Plat number two in Ottawa Hills. The deed transfer records unfortunately failed to include the purchase price. In July 1926, soon after Martin became Air-Scale's sales manager, he and Delia began construction of a residence on that lot, aided by a $12,000 mortgage loan from the Prudential Insurance Company of America. (Deed no. 646-198 [29 August 1924] and mortgage no. 818-96 [26 July 1926], Title Transfer Records, Lucas County Auditor's Office, Suite 600, One Government Center, Toledo, OH. Information provided by Teresa M. Roehrig, president and chief examiner, Aggressive Title Agency, Sylvania, OH)

16   Marshall, *Promise Kept,* 3–19, 45, 79; Porter, *Toledo Profile,* 63, 75; Robert C. Barrows, "Urbanizing America," in Charles C. Calhoun, ed., *The Gilded Age: Perspectives on the Origins of Modern America,* 2nd ed. (Lanham, MD: Rowman and Littlefield, 2007), 110; "Ottawa Hills is born," online at toledohistorybox. com/2011/02/09/ottawa-hills-is-born/ (accessed 28 March 2017); Ottawa Hills prospectus, *Toledo News-Bee,* 7 August 1915, in ibid.; "The Village of Ottawa Hills: History and Tradition," online at ottawahills.org/villagelife (accessed 28 March 2017); Green, *Uncertainty of Everyday Life,* 106; Ian Frazier, *Family* (New York: HarperCollins, 1995), 203–204. In 1948, the US Supreme Court ruled that restrictive ownership covenants such as those in use in Ottawa Hills were unconstitutional. ("Ottawa Hills is born")

17   Green, *Uncertainty of Everyday Life,* 217; Flink, *Automobile Age,* 158; Gordon, *Rise and Fall of American Growth,* 164.

18   Lynn Dumenil, *Freemasonry and American Culture, 1880–1930* (Princeton, NJ: Princeton University Press, 1984), 157, 159, 181, 183.

19   Cheryl Natzmer Valentine, "Walker Tavern," *Michigan History* (May-June 2008): 55.

20   Elizabeth Stillinger, *The Antiquers: The Lives and Careers, the Deals, the Finds, the Collections of the Men and Women Who Were Responsible for the Changing Taste in America Antiques, 1850–1930* (New York: Knopf, 1980), xi–xii, 45, 50–51, 124, 189, 196.

21   Green, *Uncertainty of Everyday Life,* 217-218; Heilbruner, *Economic Transformation of America,* 158; Schlereth, *Victorian America,* 214; Flink, *Automobile Age,* ch. 10.

22   Heilbruner, *Economic Transformation of America,* 171–180, 184; Green, *Uncertainty of Everyday Life,* 71–78, 82; Mintz and Kellogg, *Domestic Revolutions,* 133–136.

23   Flink, *Automobile Age,* 221, 231-232; Porter, *Toledo Profile,* 81, 84-90. According to some estimates, unemployment in Toledo reached a high of 80 percent at one point in the Great Depression. See, for example, Mintz and Kellogg, *Domestic Revolutions,* 132.

24   Toledo city directories, 1929–1935, online at HeritageQuest.org; Toledo city directories, 1936–1939, information provided by the Local History and Genealogy Department of the Toledo-Lucas County Public Library, Toledo, OH.

25   1940 US Federal Census, online at HeritageQuest.org.

26   Martin Grow obituary, *Toledo Blade,* 28 December 1942, "The [Toledo] Blade Obituary Index" database, Toledo-Lucas County Public Library, Toledo, OH, online at toledolibrary.org/obits (accessed 4 November 2015).

27   Deed no. 793-239 (24 October 1930) and mortgage deed no. 996-272 (27 July 1931), Title Transfer Records, Lucas County Auditor's Office, Toledo, OH (see endnote 15); Toledo city directories, 1929–1935, online at HeritageQuest.org. Their new street address in West Toledo was 1954 Milburn Avenue.

28   1940 US Federal Census, online at HeritageQuest.org; 1930 US Federal Census, online at AmericanAncestors.org.

29   Street address: 3381 Detroit Avenue. (Martin Grow obituary, *Toledo Blade,* 28 December 1942)

30   Martin Grow obituary, *Toledo Blade,* 28 December 1942.

31   California Department of Public Health death certificate no. 69-130884, date of death: 5 October 1969, Sacramento County Clerk-Recorder, 600 8th Street, Sacramento, CA; email communication, Cory S. Shuster, East Lawn Memorial Parks, Mortuaries & Crematory, Sacramento, CA, to author, 28 February 2018; email communication, Margaret Monroe, Russ Monroe's Cremation & Funeral Services, Fair Oaks, CA, to author, 21 April 2018. By the 1920s, cremation was an option offered by increasing numbers of US funeral homes, but traditional religious prejudice against the practice—based on "a traditional belief in the resurrection of the body"—kept it from gaining widespread acceptance for several more decades. (James J. Farrell, *Inventing the American Way of Death, 1830–1920* [Philadelphia, PA: Temple University Press, 1980], 166) By the late 1960s, however, "the weakening hold of religion on American life," along with economic considerations—cremation being considerably less expensive than traditional forms of burial—had brought the practice more fully into the US cultural mainstream. In 2016, the US cremation rate finally surpassed that of traditional burials for the first time in history. ("In a Move Away From Tradition, Cremations Increase," *New York Times* online edition, 10 August 2017)

GENERATION NINE: MARTIN DEWITT GROW (1910–1991)

1   Thomas J. Schlereth, *Victorian America: Transformations in Everyday Life* (New York: HarperCollins, 1991), 29; Walter Nugent, *Structures of American Social History* (Bloomington: Indiana University Press, 1981), 115–118, 124–125; C. Wright Mills, *White Collar* (New York: Oxford University Press, 1951), ix–x, 13, 34, 46, 64; Stuart M. Blumin, *The Emergence of the Middle Class: Social Experience in the American City, 1760–1900* (Cambridge, U.K.: Cambridge University Press, 1989), 2.

2   Nugent, *Structures of American Social History,* 125; Mills, *White Collar,* 245–246, 266–267, 269.

3   Jeffrey Mirel, "The Traditional High School: Historical Debates Over its Nature and Function," *Education Next,* 6:1 (Winter 2006), online at educationnext.org/the-traditional-high-school; Arlene Skolnick, *Embattled Paradise: The American Family in an Age of Uncertainty* (New York: Basic Books, 1991), 56.

4   Ethyl Marie Zimmerman was born 12 September 1908 in Swanton, Ohio, a rural town 20 miles southwest of Toledo. Her father, Samuel Zimmerman (1883–1927), was a purchasing agent for the A. D. Baker Company of Swanton, a manufacturer of tractors, grain threshers, and engines for farm machinery and locomotives. (LeRoy W. Blake, "Remembering the A. D. Baker Company," *Farm Collector* [May-June 1979], online at farmcollector.com/steam-traction/ad-baker-company-incidents) Her mother was Maude Florine (Deck) Zimmerman (1886–1966), a housewife. When her father died prematurely of a heart attack in 1927 at age 44, Ethyl was forced to go to work to help support her mother and three younger siblings. She had recently graduated from the Davis Business College of Toledo and was employed as a stenographer when she met De at Devil's Lake in 1929.

5   "Application for Membership," 12 March 1943, M. DeWitt Grow membership file, American Institute of Architects, Washington, DC, online at public.aia.org/sites/hdoaa/wiki/Wiki%20Pages/ahd1017316.aspx; "Questionnaire for Architects' Roster and/or Architects Qualified for Federal Public Works," M. DeWitt Grow, 20 May 1946, American Institute of Architects, Washington, DC, document in author's family history collection; "History of the Firm of Britsch & Munger, Architects" (1950), unpublished document in author's family history collection; Carl C. Britsch obituary, *Toledo Blade,* 28 December 1974; Harold H. Munger obituary, *New York Times,* 18 November 1970.

6   "Questionnaire for Architects' Roster . . ." (see endnote 5); "Application for Membership," (see endnote 5); Tana Mosier Porter, *Toledo Profile: A Sesquicentennial History* (Toledo, OH: Toledo Sesquicentennial Commission, 1987), 87–89; 1940 US Federal Census, online at HeritageQuest.org.

7   Robert L. Heilbruner, *The Economic Transformation of America* (New York: Harcourt Brace Jovanovich, 1977), 205–207; Robert J. Gordon, *The Rise and Fall of American Growth: The U.S. Standard of Living since the Civil War* (Princeton, NJ: Princeton University Press, 2016), 536–537, 548–553. The US gross domestic product (GDP) grew from $86 billion in 1938 to $223 billion in 1945. (Louis Galambos, *The Creative Society— and the Price Americans Paid for It* [New York: Cambridge University Press, 2012], 125–126)

8   Porter, *Toledo Profile,* 98; "History of the Firm of Britsch & Munger, Architects" (see endnote 5); "Questionnaire for Architects' Roster . . ."

9   Ethyl had previously lost a female fetus during a miscarriage in the late 1930s.

10   Steven Mintz and Susan Kellogg, *Domestic Revolutions: A Social History of American Family Life* (New York: Free Press, 1988), 137.

11   John D'Emilio and Estelle B. Freedman, *Intimate Matters: A History of Sexuality in America* (New York: Harper & Row, 1988), 246; Sheila M. Rothman, *Woman's Proper Place: A History of Changing Ideals and Practices, 1870 to the Present* (New York: Basic Books, 1978), 199.

12   Mintz and Kellogg, *Domestic Revolutions,* 120; Harvey Green, *The Uncertainty of Everyday Life, 1915–1945* (New York: HarperCollins, 1992), 121, 179–180; Gordon, *Rise and Fall of American Growth,* 228–231.

13   Gordon, *Rise and Fall of American Growth,* 303, 353, 363, 371; William L. O'Neill, *American High: The Years of Confidence, 1945–1960* (New York: Free Press, 1986), 1, 12–13; Elaine Tyler May, *Homeward Bound: American Families in the Cold War Era* (New York: Basic Books, 1988), 168.

14   Green, *Uncertainty of Everyday Life,* 153; O'Neill, *American High,* 16–17, 19; Gordon, *Rise and Fall of American Growth,* 364–365; May, *Homeward Bound,* 169; Mintz and Kellogg, *Domestic Revolutions,* 174, 183–184.

15   "History of the Firm of Britsch & Munger, Architects."

16   "Questionnaire for Architects' Roster . . ."

17   "The House at 3921 Brookside Rd: Still Different," *Toledo Blade,* 20 July 1986, C-1; Jules Jay Roskin obituary, *Albuquerque Journal,* 11 March 2004; James C. Marshall, *A Promise Kept: A History of the Village of Ottawa Hills* (Maumee, OH: Woodland Publishing, 2003), 87–88.

18   American Institute of Architects Toledo chapter, "Past Presidents, 1914–2013," online at aiatoledo.org/index.php.community/77-presidents.

19   Marshall, *A Promise Kept,* 20.

20   In 1950, 9 percent of US households owned a television set, a figure "that had increased to 64.5 percent only five years later" and to "more than 90 percent . . . by the early 1960s." (Gordon, *Rise and Fall of American Growth,* 415)

21   Deep Lake, a 65-acre body of water in Lenawee County.

22   John Demos, *Past, Present, and Personal: The Family and the Life Course in American History* (New York: Oxford University Press, 1986), 114–123; Michael Kimmel, *Manhood in America: A Cultural History* (New York: Free Press, 1996), 104, 238, 242–243, 254, 257–258; Jonathan Rauch, "The Real Roots of Midlife Crisis," *The Atlantic* (December 2014); Barbara Ehrenreich, *The Hearts of Men: American Dreams and the Flight from Commitment* (Garden City, NY: Anchor Press, 1983), 30–32, 51, 55. Also see Skolnick, *Embattled Paradise,* 161–162. For some men, Jonathan Rauch writes, success is accompanied in middle age by the feeling of being trapped, by the feeling that life is passing them by. With their mortality now visible on the time horizon come impulses to live in the moment, to escape the "rut" and the "rat-race" in which they find themselves by having exciting new experiences. ("The Real Roots of Midlife Crisis")

According to writer Donald Richie, "Midlife crisis begins sometime in your 40s, when you look at your life and think, *Is this all?*" In her best-selling 1977 book *Passages: Predictable Crises of Adult Life,* author Gail Sheehy depicted the midlife crisis with the example of a 40-year-old man who "has reached his professional goal but feels depressed and unappreciated. He blames his job or his wife or his physical surroundings for imprisoning him in this rut. Fantasies of breaking out begin to dominate his thoughts. An interesting woman he has met, another field of work, an Elysian part of the country—any or all of these become magnets for his wishes of deliverance." (Quoted in Rauch, "The Real Roots of Midlife Crisis")

There is little historical evidence to suggest that the midlife crisis had pre-twentieth-century antecedents. The term "midlife crisis" itself, in fact, first appears in the literature only in 1965. Historian John Demos believes that the explanation centers on the abundance of choices available to men in the modern world. Although "a very sensitive review of religious literature in colonial America . . . might reveal at least glimmerings of middle-aged reappraisal," he writes, "it would not add up to a great deal [due to] the relative absence of something that bulks very large in our own time," namely "the whole dimension of *choice* in our lives—as contrasted to theirs. . . . [T]he problem [in mid-life today] is . . . how to live with the choices already made. The situation is necessarily compounded when there appear to be so many choices not made, so many alternatives missed or simply ignored. For our colonial ancestors, the middle years must have been easier—because their alternatives were fewer, their verities less open to challenge or change." (*Past, Present, and Personal,* 122–123)

23   Personal communication, Marilyn Grow (De's third wife) to author, 20 April 1993.

24   Alan Trachtenberg, *The Incorporation of America: Culture and Society in the Gilded Age* (New York: Hill and Wang, 2007), 24.

25   Mailer, "The White Negro" (1957), quoted in Kimmel, *Manhood in America*, 242.

26   Daniel J. Boorstin, *The Americans: The Democratic Experience* (New York: Random House, 1973), 70–72; "Betty Goes to Reno" (21 July 2010), online at slate.com/articles/arts/culturebox/2010/07/betty-goes-reno. html; "Remembering When Reno Was the Divorce Capital of America" (12 February 2014), online at bitchmedia.org/post/remembering-when-reno-was-the-divorce-capital-of-america.

27   Application for Marriage License, M. DeWitt Grow and Eva Modar, 17 November 1953, and Certificate of Marriage #57549, Book 39: "Marriages" (page 507), Office of the Carson City Clerk-Recorder, 885 Musser Street, Suite 1025, Carson City, NV 89701. The author is grateful to Deputy Clerk Elizabeth Phelps for her assistance in providing copies of De and Eva's marriage records. Also see "Carson City, Nevada, Marriage Index, 1855–1985," record #39687101, online at ancestry.com. The couple's wedding ceremony was performed by the pastor of the Lutheran Church of the Good Shepherd in Reno on 17 November 1953, the same day they applied for their marriage license.

28   Ohio Department of Health certificate of death, 28 December 1987, Bureau of Vital Statistics, Toledo Department of Health, Toledo, OH.

29   Swanton Cemetery, County Road 1, Swanton, OH.

30   Most middle-class women of the 1940s and 1950s embraced the "traditional gender role" of homemaker and "gracious wife." According to middle-class cultural values at the time, for a married woman to work implied "lower-class status or a husband in dire financial straits," (Skolnick, *Embattled Paradise*, 53; May, *Homeward Bound*, 53, 56) and a married middle-class man "took pride in the fact that his wife didn't 'have' to work." (Ehrenreich, *Hearts of Men*, 7)

31   Undated letter, M. DeWitt Grow to American Institute of Architects, M. DeWitt Grow membership file, American Institute of Architects (see endnote 5).

32   *Reno Evening Gazette*, 15 December 1954, p. 3.

33   Personal communications, Marilyn Grow and Jana Cortez (Marilyn Grow's daughter by a previous marriage) to author.

34   Letter, M. DeWitt Grow to author, 20 January 1964.

35   Personal communications, Marilyn Grow to author, 1991–1993.

36   Ibid.; California Divorce Index, 1966–1984, online at familysearch.org/search/collection/2015584.

37   Personal communications, Marilyn Grow to author, 1991–1993; California Marriage Index, 1960–1985, online at familysearch.org/search/collections/1949339. Marilyn A. Russell was born in Sacramento on 16 June 1923, divorced a husband named Reynolds prior to her marriage to M. DeWitt Grow, and died in Sacramento on 28 August 2017.

38   Personal communications, Marilyn Grow to author, 1991–1993; California Death Index, 1940–1997, online at familysearch.org/search/collection/2015582.

39   Email communication, Patricia Kerley, Mortuary Manager, Sacramento Memorial Lawn, to author, 6 March 2018.

40   Personal communications, Marilyn Grow to author, 1991–1993; personal communication, Dale B. Henly to author.

41   Personal communications, Marilyn Grow to author, 1991–1993.

42   Letter, M. DeWitt Grow to author, 13 January 1988.

43   David Riesman, *The Lonely Crowd* (New Haven, CT: Yale University Press, 1961), 145, 150, 158; Christopher Lasch, *Haven in a Heartless World: The Family Besieged* (New York: Harper Colophon, 1977), xxiv; Michael Hunt, *The American Ascendancy: How the United States Gained and Wielded Global Dominance* (Chapel Hill: University of North Carolina Press, 2009), 84–85.

44   "Frank Lloyd Wright," documentary film by Ken Burns and Lynn Novick, Public Broadcasting System (PBS), 1998.

45   (New York: Bobbs-Merrill)

46   Personal communication, Marilyn Grow to author, 20 September 1991.

GENERATION TEN: MICHAEL ROBERT GROW (1944–   )

1   James C. Marshall, *A Promise Kept: A History of the Village of Ottawa Hills* (Maumee, OH: Woodland Publishing, 2003), 113, 123, 125.

2   Christopher J. Lucas, *American Higher Education: A History* (New York: St. Martin's Press, 1994), 233.

3   "The War at Home," a documentary film by Glenn Silber and Barry Alexander Brown (First Run Features, 1979), effectively captures the atmosphere of this period on the University of Wisconsin campus.

4   US Department of Commerce, "Current Population Reports: Consumer Income," Series P-60, No. 65, 31 October 1969.

5   "'Murder Capital' Label Has Long Stalked D.C.," *Washington Post*, 4 April 1989; "District of Columbia Crime Rates 1960–2016," online at disastercenter.com/crime/dccrime.htm.

6   John R. Thelin, *A History of American Higher Education* (Baltimore: Johns Hopkins University Press, 2004), 260–261, 280–282, 298, 311, 331–332; Lucas, *American Higher Education*, 228; Clark Kerr, *The Great Transformation in Higher Education, 1960–1980* (Albany: State University of New York Press, 1991), 145–146.

7   Thelin, *History of American Higher Education*, 316, 317, 319, 321, 331–332, 336; Kerr, *Great Transformation in Higher Education*, 150; Robert B. Townsend, "Precedents: The Job Crisis of the 1970s," American Historical Association *Perspectives*, April 1997.

8   Robert J. Gordon, *The Rise and Fall of American Growth: The U.S. Standard of Living since the Civil War* (Princeton, NJ: Princeton University Press, 2016), 503, 605; Arlene Skolnick, *Embattled Paradise: The American Family in an Age of Uncertainty* (New York: Basic Books, 1991), 96, 122, 135–136, 138, 140, 213; "Historic Inflation United States—CPI Inflation," online at inflation.eu/inflation-rates/united-states/historic-inflation/cpi-inflation-united-states.aspx.

9   Median gross rents—unadjusted, Washington, D.C., online at www2.census.gov/programs-surveys/decennial/tables/time-series/coh-grossrents/grossrents-unadj.txt.

10   In addition, she bequeathed him two pieces of furniture—a cherry sewing table made in New York State in the 1830s, and a three-drawer oak "bachelor's chest," c. 1870s—that had descended in the family, along with an elaborate platinum-and-diamond dinner ring featuring a large one-carat diamond given to her as an engagement present by her parents DeWitt and Alice Grow and valued at $15,000. The bulk of her estate, worth an estimated $550,000, was divided up among seven principal beneficiaries (Michael and six of her late husband Dr. Van H. Dumond's relatives), the Bay Medical Center of Bay City, MI, and various charitable organizations.

11   Gordon, *Rise and Fall of American Growth*, 486; Skolnick, *Embattled Paradise*, 88–89. "By the end of the 1970s, as a national average, women [in the United States] were having 1.8 children in their lifetimes." (Walter Nugent, *Structures of American Social History* [Bloomington: Indiana University Press, 1981], 140)

12   He had dinner with Fernando Henrique Cardoso, future president of Brazil (1995–2003), and Nicolás Ardito Barletta, future president of Panama (1984–1985), at Latin American Program events, and met Edward Seaga, prime minister of Jamaica (1980–1989), at another dinner hosted by the Latin American Program. He had earlier been assigned as a research assistant to Wilson Center visiting fellow Victor Paz Estenssoro, who in 1952 had led one of Latin America's major twentieth-century social revolutions and subsequently served three terms as president of Bolivia. (Paz Estenssoro graciously agreed to be a member of Michael's doctoral-dissertation examining committee at George Washington University in 1976.) While teaching summer school at George Washington in the late 1970s, Michael also had several conversations with Fernando Belaúnde Terry, a two-term president of Peru (1963–1968 and 1980–1985), who held an adjunct professorship at GWU while in exile. On one occasion in 1976, Belaúnde Terry and Paz Estenssoro discussed Michael's dissertation while relaxing beside the pool of the northwest DC apartment building where they were both living.

13   The *International History Review* described the book as "possibly the best study of U.S. foreign policy in Latin America that has ever been written." (November 1982: 614) The *American Historical Review*, the history profession's preeminent US journal, characterized it as "a major contribution to [the] revisionist literature,"

and concluded that Grow's "contributions mark a major advance in the serious historiography of power relations in the hemisphere, for which he deserves our gratitude and applause." (April 1982: 571–572)

14   For a number of years, the chairman of the GWU Microbiology Department, Lewis Affronti, had generously given her time off from her work responsibilities as his laboratory assistant to take a biology course or two every semester. After passing doctoral field examinations in aquatic ecology, invertebrate zoology, ethology, and animal ecology, she successfully completed a dissertation on the "Behavioral Ecology of the Burrowing Crayfish *Cambarus diogenes diogenes* Girard" in 1979, and taught a few introductory biology courses part-time at George Washington and Montgomery College in Takoma Park, MD, before departing for Ohio. In 1978 and 1979, she gave several research presentations, including two at conferences of the Graduate Women in Science organization and one at the Smithsonian's Natural History Museum. Between 1980 and 1982, she published articles in the journals *Crustaceana, Animal Behavior, American Midland Naturalist,* and "The Islands" (a publication of the Nature Conservancy).

15   Catherine Anne Carbone was born in Syracuse, New York, on 7 January 1949, the daughter of an International Business Machines Corporation financial manager, Joseph Carbone, and his wife Ruth. At age 2, she relocated with her family to San Jose, California, where at age 20 she married Jesse Russell (1910–1979).

16   To list only a few: the distinguished American historians Gordon Wood and Joyce Appleby; Timothy Naftali, the director of the Richard M. Nixon Library; Ron Nessen, White House press secretary during the Gerald Ford administration; Ambassador Oleg Grinevsky, a high-ranking former Soviet national security official and Middle East diplomat; the eminent British historian Jeremy Black; the distinguished University of California–Berkeley economist Barry Eichengreen; and prominent Dartmouth political scientist Richard Ned Lebow.

17   Gordon, *Rise and Fall of American Growth,* 605, 615–616, 620; Skolnick, *Embattled Paradise,* 135–136, 196, 214; Robert L. Griswold, *Fatherhood in America: A History* (New York: Basic Books, 1993), 222–223, 252–253. "In 1950, 25 percent of married women living with their husbands worked outside the home; in the late 1980s the figure [was] nearly 60 percent." (Steven Mintz and Susan Kellogg, *Domestic Revolutions: A Social History of American Family Life* [New York: Free Press, 1988], 204)

18   "Household Income in the United States," online at cs.mcgill.ca. As part of its employee benefits package, Ohio University also provided free tuition to the children of faculty and staff—a benefit of major value during a period (1972–2015) when "the cost of a university education" in the United States rose "at more than triple the overall rate of inflation." (Gordon, *Rise and Fall of American Growth,* 626)

19   In 2005, the median annual income for full-time male workers in the US labor force was $41,383. (*Christian Science Monitor,* 5 September 2006, p. 20, citing US Census Bureau statistics)

20   National Association of Realtors, as reported by CNNMoney.com, 15 February 2006.

21   In 2006, according to US Department of Labor statistics, "professionals and related occupations," including "management, business, and financial occupations," constituted the upper 30 percent of the US labor force. (Louis Galambos, *The Creative Society—And the Price Americans Paid for It* [New York: Cambridge University Press, 2012], xivn8)

22   David Hackett Fischer, *Growing Old in America* (New York: Oxford University Press, 1978), ch. IV; Carole Haber and Brian Gratton, *Old Age and the Search for Security: An American Social History* (Bloomington: Indiana University Press, 1994), 84, 105–106, 112, 114–115, 170, 181–182; Gordon, *Rise and Fall of American Growth,* 500, 515–516, 518. "After the enactment of Social Security," Haber and Gratton write, "retirement became an expected part of the life cycle" for Americans. (*Old Age and the Search for Security,* 64) By 1983, some 30 percent of US workers had access to defined-benefit pension plans. (Gordon, *Rise and Fall of American Growth,* 518)

23   Andrew Delbanco, *The Real American Dream: A Meditation on Hope* (Cambridge, MA: Harvard University Press, 1999), 5; Skolnick, *Embattled Paradise,* 143, 151–153; Barbara Ehrenreich, *The Hearts of Men: American Dreams and the Flight from Commitment* (Garden City, NY: Anchor Press, 1983), ch. 7.

24   "New England: A Peaceful Pause in the Megalopolis," *New York Times,* 22 June 2003.

25   *The History and Architecture of Scotland, Connecticut: From an Architectural Survey, 1988–1989* (Town of Scotland Historic District Study Committee, 1989), numbers 16, 18, 23, 24.

26   The concluding sentence borrows shamelessly from Robert Tarule's excellent *The Artisan of Ipswich: Craftsmanship and Community in Colonial New England* (Baltimore: Johns Hopkins University Press, 2004), 131.

CONCLUSION

1   A notable exception to this statement was Galusha A. Grow (1823–1907), a Pennsylvania Republican congressman who served a term as Speaker of the US House of Representatives during the Civil War. Galusha Grow, however, was a nephew of Elisha Grow and from a different line of the family than the one under discussion here.

2   Walter Nugent, *Structures of American Social History* (Bloomington: Indiana University Press, 1981), 63, 87. As late as 1870, 75 percent of Americans still resided in rural areas. (Ibid., 26, table 1)

3   David Grayson Allen, *In English Ways: The Movement of Societies and the Transferral of English Local Law and Customs to Massachusetts Bay in the Seventeenth Century* (Chapel Hill: University of North Carolina Press, 1981), passim; Robert Terule, *The Artisan of Ipswich: Craftsmanship and Community in Colonial New England* (Baltimore: Johns Hopkins University Press, 2004), 13–14, 86–87.

4   Allen Kulikoff, *From British Peasants to Colonial American Farmers* (Chapel Hill: University of North Carolina Press, 2000), 110–113; Kenneth A. Lockridge, *A New England Town: The First Hundred Years* (New York: W. W. Norton, 1970), 82, 94; Alison I. Vannah, "'Crochets of Division': Ipswich in New England, 1633–1679" (PhD dissertation, Brandeis University, 1999), part IV.

5   Nugent, *Structures of American Social History*, ch. III.

6   Ibid., 117.

7   Ibid., 115.

8   David M. Potter, *People of Plenty: Economic Abundance and the American Character* (Chicago: University of Chicago Press, 1954), 93–96.

9   Gregory Clark, *The Son Also Rises: Surnames and the History of Social Mobility* (Princeton, NJ: Princeton University Press, 2014), 9, 10, 15, 16, 118, 274, 306.

INDEX